MODERNISM, THE VISUAL, AND CARIBBEAN LITERATURE

Vision is a recurring obsession in the work of twentieth-century Caribbean writers. This ambitious study offers a comprehensive analysis of the visual in authors from the Anglophone Caribbean as they intersect with mainstream modernism. While sound cultures have received more attention in studies of the black Atlantic, this is the first to analyze acts of seeing, inner vision, and reflections on visual art. Mary Lou Emery analyzes Caribbean art, theatre, and literature of the early twentieth century, including works by Edna Manley and Una Marson, then turns to George Lamming, C. L. R. James, Derek Walcott, Wilson Harris, and a younger generation including Jamaica Kincaid and David Dabydeen. She argues that their preoccupation with vision directly addresses philosophies of sensory perception developed at the height of the slave trade and emerges in conditions of diaspora continuing into the present. This study is an original and important contribution to transatlantic and postcolonial studies.

MARY LOU EMERY is Associate Professor of English at the University of Iowa where she teaches courses in Modernist, Caribbean, and Postcolonial Studies. She is the author of *Jean Rhys at "World's End": Novels of Colonial and Sexual Exile* (1990) as well as articles on other Caribbean writers and British modernists.

MODERNISM, THE VISUAL, AND CARIBBEAN LITERATURE

MARY LOU EMERY

CAMBRIDGE
UNIVERSITY PRESS

CAMBRIDGE UNIVERSITY PRESS
Cambridge, New York, Melbourne, Madrid, Cape Town, Singapore, São Paulo

Cambridge University Press
The Edinburgh Building, Cambridge CB2 2RU, UK

Published in the United States of America by Cambridge University Press, New York

www.cambridge.org
Information on this title: www.cambridge.org/9780521872133

First published 2007

Printed in the United Kingdom at the University Press, Cambridge

A catalogue record for this publication is available from the British Library

ISBN-13 978-0-521-87213-3 hardback

For Stephen and Claire

Contents

Illustrations

Acknowledgments

To Wilson Harris's remarkable writing, I owe the inspiration for this project, and I thank him for his welcoming response to my work and always generous replies to my questions. I am grateful to Hena Maes-Jelinek for introducing me to Wilson Harris and a community of Harris critics. Her encouragement has sustained this project at important stages. For lively conversations on the topic of the visual and insightful readings of chapter drafts, I thank my colleague Huston Diehl, whose friendship throughout the writing of this book has made it all the more a pleasure. I would also like to express my appreciation to Michaeline Crichlow for her interest in the project and help with my research in Kingston, Jamaica; Veerle Poupeye for kindly granting me an interview and facilitating the inclusion of Edna Manley's work; Annie Paul for engaging my questions about Jamaican art; Leah Rosenberg for exchanging drafts and sharing research materials related to Caribbean modernism; Elaine Savory, Teresa Mangum, Anne Donadey, Harilaos Stecopoulos, Kathleen Renk, Janet Winston, Kerry Johnson, Judith Misrahi-Barak, Priya Kumar, and Eric Gidal for thoughtful comments on portions of the manuscript; Mary Hanna and Rebecca Faery for help with archival materials; Brooks Landon for supporting my work during his tenure as Chair of the Department of English; Ania Spyra for expert research and proofreading assistance; Garrett Stewart for sage advice; Dee Morris for a generative gift; and Jon Wilcox, current Chair of English, and Linda Maxson, Dean of the College of Liberal Arts and Sciences at the University of Iowa, for support in bringing the project to publication. I thank the anonymous reviewers consulted by Cambridge University Press for their judicious readings of the manuscript. Maartje Scheltens, Jackie Warren, and Jacqueline French at Cambridge have been most helpful in guiding my preparation of the manuscript through the production process.

Working at the intersections of modernist, Caribbean, and postcolonial studies, I have benefited tremendously from exchanges with colleagues at conferences in these fields, including those of the Association for the Study of New Literatures in English, the Commonwealth and Postcolonial Studies Conferences, the Conference in Honor of Wilson Harris, those of the Caribbean Women Writers and Scholars, the Modernist Studies Association, the International Virginia Woolf Society and, at the University of Iowa, colloquia sponsored by the Caribbean, Diaspora, and Atlantic Studies Group. I thank also the students in my courses on Caribbean and postcolonial literatures at the University of Iowa and would like especially to mention Jonathan Highfield, Wallis Tinnie, Loretta Collins, Julie Minkler, Dean Makuluni, Michelle De Rose, Jodi Byrd, Heidi LaVine, Steve Almquist, and Mike Anderson for their enthusiasm, questions, and insights.

I am grateful for the assistance I received from the following librarians and archivists: the staff at the Tate Library, Tate Gallery Archive, British Library, British Newspaper Library, and the University of Sussex Special Collections Library; Nigel Rigby at the National Maritime Museum in Greenwich, England; David Boxer and Veerle Poupeye at the National Gallery of Jamaica; Eppie Edwards at the National Library of Jamaica; the staff at the West Indies Special Collections Libraries at the University of the West Indies, St. Augustine, Trinidad and Mona, Jamaica; the staff at the Schomburg Center for Research in Black Culture Library, New York City; and the late Jim Murray, Director of the C. L. R. James Institute, New York City.

Additionally, I would like to thank the Provost's Office, College of Liberal Arts and Sciences, International Programs, and the Department of English at the University of Iowa for funding my travels to these research sites. I am grateful to the Office of the Vice-President for Research for supporting this project in its final stages.

Portions of the manuscript in different form have appeared previously in the following journals: *Callaloo, Journal of Caribbean Literatures, Tulsa Studies in Women's Literature, Virginia Woolf: Across the Generations/Selected Papers from the Twelfth Annual Conference on Virginia Woolf* (Center for Virginia Woolf Studies at California State University, Bakersfield), *Journal of Commonwealth and Postcolonial Studies* (Georgia Southern University), and *Review of Contemporary Fiction*. Thanks to the editors for permission to reproduce this material.

For coping with my absences and my sometimes distracted presence, but most of all for the innumerable ways in which our everyday lives together have made the writing of this book even possible, my love and gratitude go to Stephen Wootton and Claire Emery-Wootton.

Transfigurations

The story told by Stuart Hall of how C. L. R. James, émigré writer from Trinidad, cast his eyes back and forth between the play on the cricket field before him to the postcard reproduction of Picasso's *Guernica* held in his hand suggests an individual's unique way of thinking and seeing.[1] But it also speaks for a transatlantic dynamic of vision, developed in the migrations of the Caribbean diaspora, which reshaped cultural identity and the arts in the twentieth century. James wrote about what he saw in the movement of his eyes between cricket match and painting from the perspective of a man steeped in the colonial cultures of Trinidad and England, inspired by the mass movements against fascism evoked by Picasso's painting, and convinced of the historically creative forces embodied in the players and the painting. His transatlantic vision, capable of linking such seemingly disparate visual events, characterizes a recurring obsession with seeing in the work of writers from the Caribbean throughout the twentieth century.

In this book, I analyze the work of twentieth-century writers and artists who have crossed from the Caribbean to Britain and, in some cases, Europe and the United States. Their work – in the form of sculpture, fiction, poetry, essays, and drama – centers, often obsessively, on acts of vision. These may be social acts of seeing, inner vision, or reflections on visual art. However, they all emerge from the migration of people and their cultures generated by British, European, and US colonization in the Caribbean. Most importantly, they illuminate the significance of vision to one of the major intellectual shifts of the twentieth century – the refiguring of identities across national, racial, and cultural boundaries.

The condition of exile and diaspora experienced by Caribbean émigrés, from the early 1900s to the present, has generated a radical transformation in the subjectivity of the writer; in many ways, it has recreated the Caribbean writer's identity as one who has gained the power to see and, thus, to create.[2] In 1960, the Barbadian writer George Lamming portrayed the social relationship involved in vision by referring to Shakespeare's Caliban. Describing Caliban as an emblem of the colonized person, Lamming writes: "Caliban is never accorded the power to see. He is always the measure of the condition which his physical presence has defined."[3] For Lamming, the "power to see" grants the Caribbean writer a claim to language and artistic agency. Derek Walcott, poet from St. Lucia and winner of the Nobel Prize for Literature, has also stressed the importance of vision to Caribbean writers, declaring that "only our own painful, strenuous looking, the learning of looking, could find meaning in the life around us."[4] James, Lamming, Walcott, and others such as Wilson Harris, and more recently, Jamaica Kincaid, Michelle Cliff, David Dabydeen, and Fred D'Aguiar repeatedly address the conditions of enslaved or indentured ancestors who were denied the power to see and used – as commodified objects of a market gaze, picturesque figures in a tropical paradise, or visual markers of nineteenth-century racialist categories – to constitute that power in others. In their writings, they reconstruct visionary subjectivity for these ancestors and their descendants. They also address, sometimes as a literal impairment of the eyes, the blindness of the imperial project. Caribbean writers thus engage the dynamic of vision as a transforming element in the process of cultural decolonization and, through it, claim the authority of their own perceptions. This authority became increasingly possible during the colonial movements for political independence of the early and mid-twentieth century. In the post-independence era, Caribbean writers and artists have continued to produce their own traditions of what Walcott has recently termed "the art of seeing"[5] in sometimes conflicted interaction with the international cultures of modernist, postmodern, and postcolonial literatures.

The topic of vision may seem to contradict the usual emphasis in Caribbean cultural studies on sound, orality, and music, as exemplified in studies by Kamau Brathwaite, Carolyn Cooper, Paul Gilroy, and Dick Hebdidge – but it does so by questioning the categories of sensory perception that implicitly guide them.[6] They have shaped in crucial ways the development of cultural studies and, more specifically, our understanding of Caribbean diasporic cultures, and they provide points of departure for my project. However, they risk replicating colonialist philosophies of discrete, hierarchically organized sensory development. Especially in the eighteenth century, at the height of the slave trade, these philosophies constructed the European man as the universal modern Subject, imbued with reason and, most significantly, the capacity for sight. Rather than celebrating, in opposition to this construction of modernity, the sound cultures of the black Atlantic, I begin, instead, with the creation in Caribbean literature and visual art of modernist countervisions. In my readings, early twentieth-century Caribbean sculptors and writers confront vision directly: they reflect on its role in determining the European man as the universal Subject; they create alternate, creolized figures of Caribbean visionaries; and they *see through* the double-bind of colonial imitation to which eighteenth-century aesthetic philosophy condemned them, achieving in the process visual subjecthood and creative agency. I then analyze the moves made by postcolonial Caribbean writers to work through and beyond the valorization of sight to an indiscrete sensory language, one in which poetic devices such as *synaesthesia*, *ekphrasis*, and *apophasis* create alternate ways of being and knowing, while re-imagining history and narrative temporality outside the "posts" of current (including my own) critical chronologies.

Throughout the twentieth century, Caribbean artists and writers have thus contributed to a reformulation of vision that often anticipates, re-contextualizes, and frequently contests mainstream philosophical and theoretical investigations into visuality. From the beginning of the century their arts of seeing have helped to shape what we have called modernism, extending it into a transatlantic politics of vision and an extraordinary postcolonial literature. Emerging from this literature, an aesthetic of trans-figuration re-imagines the sensory body and discovers in the footnotes – literally, as we shall see – of the dominant philosophical tradition the half-present, vanishing and reappearing "ghosts" of modernity. The artists and writers I discuss in this book gain the "power to see," but more than that, they transform vision itself as the basis for being and knowing, "extending the senses," in Wilson Harris's words, to trans-figure lost bodies of civilizations and humanity.

Modernism, the Visual, and Caribbean Literature thus opens a larger perspective in which to understand the ongoing literary creation of an alternate sensory body that counters the visual practices associated with European colonialism. It also makes evident the impact of an extended creolization within literature and the arts in which the indigenous and inter-African diasporic arts of the Caribbean help to shape European and, in the case of this study, twentieth-century British culture. More precisely, creolized Caribbean arts have made what has been called "British" culture part of a more extensive circum-Atlantic cultural network that did not begin, but certainly intensified, with the slave trade and its twin, modernity.[7]

MODERNITY, SLAVERY, AND SIGHT

As an example of one of these vision-obsessed works by a writer from the Caribbean, we can turn to a recent novel by David Dabydeen, *A Harlot's*

Progress, and in particular, to a scene which reflects in fictional terms on the historical reasons for the importance of visual cultures to writers from the Caribbean: In a room reserved for gentlemen at Johnson's Coffee House, amid the stink of eighteenth-century London streets, two sales take place, both advertised in the newspaper and attracting numerous bidders. One is the sale of a young African boy, the other a Renaissance painting. The same gentleman, Lord Montague, purchases both boy and painting, and they ride home together in his coach. Dabydeen portrays this scene as narrated by the African boy many years later when he is an old man, the oldest living African in London. Named, at different times in his life, Mungo, Noah, and Perseus, the old man now reluctantly breaks his silence in return for a few coins from the abolitionist Mr. Pringle who needs the story to "swell the coffers" of the Abolitionist Society.

As the title of the novel indicates, the scene and the entire narrative in which it takes place allude to the series of prints made by Hogarth titled *A Harlot's Progress*. The novel, in fact, spins its many, often conflicting stories from the figure in one of these prints of a small black boy who, in Dabydeen's novel, wears "a feathered turban, an English suit, slippers that might come from China" and a "small Arabian scimitar strapped to his side."[8] He enters the actual engraving at the lower right-hand corner, wearing turban and suit, and carrying a teapot. The tea table, however, has been upset by the harlot, Moll, in her dealings with "the Jew," and in the lower left-hand corner a small monkey, dressed up in a lady's hat anxiously strains away from the upset table and broken china. On the wall above their heads hang two large framed paintings and two smaller portraits.[9] Resonating from Hogarth's print through Dabydeen's imaginatively extended ekphrastic narrative is the intimate eighteenth-century relationship between art and commerce, especially the commerce in human bodies.

Recently, postcolonial critics have turned to the eighteenth century as a period crucial to understanding the cultural legacies of the slave trade. Simon Gikandi, David Lloyd, Ian Baucom, and Sander Gilman have all examined the confluence of a slave trade that reached its height in this century and the development in Britain and Europe of philosophies of the aesthetic. Dabydeen's fiction and his critical writing on Hogarth participate in this project of examining the eighteenth century from a postcolonial perspective. Throughout Mungo's often wildly varying tales, *A Harlot's Progress* portrays, among other things, the contradictions and moral ambiguities facing the English upper class and, in some cases, destroying them. These anxieties often center on the work of art, and in his critical study, *Hogarth's Blacks*, Dabydeen analyzes the representation of black people in both paintings and

1. William Hogarth, *A Harlot's Progress: Plate II* (1733), etching, 13⁵⁄₁₆ in. × 15¹⁄₁₆ in., University of California, Berkeley, Art Museum. Purchase made possible through a gift from Phoebe Apperson Hearst. 1998.2.2, photographed for the UC Berkeley Art Museum by Benjamin Blackwell.

prints of the period. Though cast as an autonomous or transcendent realm, art, along with every other kind of commodity, including slaves, was advertised, displayed, auctioned, and sold, leading Lord Montague to wonder in Dabydeen's novel about his motives in purchasing the painting as much as his motives in purchasing the boy. It is not just that the accoutrements of civilization, including works of art, which fill the homes of the aristocracy as well as the newly rich, depend on fortunes made through the slave trade. That is partly the cause of Lord Montague's anxiety; but it is also the leveling of all cultural acts, sacred and profane, to the single plane of commerce that troubles him. This leveling threatens his sense of his status as a subject capable of a *disinterested* aesthetic judgment and, therefore, imbued with the reason common to civilized and free men.

Inhabiting the realm of aesthetics, indeed making it possible, the painting Lord Montague purchases appears sullied, after all, by association with commerce and especially the commerce in human beings. By extension, the man of taste may feel troubled as to his capacity, and even that of his class, for the distanced, contemplative stance of aesthetic judgment supposedly exercised by men of reason. Doubts regarding this capacity would threaten also his status as a free man, for as eighteenth-century philosophers, such as Kant and Schiller, stressed, men constituted their freedom through disinterested aesthetic judgment.[10] This freedom, exercised in the act of seeing, becomes further troubled by its association with the figure of the not-free black person, as represented within images of art and as commodified in the same space that commercializes art.

In its reading of Hogarth's prints, Dabydeen's novel argues that the leveling of all cultural acts and relationships to that of commerce and the resulting anxieties experienced by men of property become matters of representation, and representation depends on how one sees. As Dabydeen puts it in *Hogarth's Blacks*, "Hogarth sees differently." Hogarth exposes in grotesque detail the whole fabric of daily life *and* what might be supposed transcendent of it as a matter of commercial exchange, permeated with avarice and cruelty. His prints counter the many paintings of the period in which typically adoring black servants appear as indicators of family wealth, power, and benevolence.[11] The countervision of Hogarth's prints provides a critical note to the signboards creaking loudly throughout eighteenth-century London streets on which commodities such as tobacco, bread, and horses were advertised through their visual association with the figure, usually caricatured, of a black person. Dabydeen states that these images were so prevalent that "London in the eighteenth century was *visually* black in this respect" (18).[12]

At the end of *Hogarth's Blacks*, Dabydeen remarks that, in spite of eighteenth-century misreadings of Hogarth's black figures in accordance with racist myths, Hogarth's "compassionate identification with the black is overwhelming" (131). He cites Hogarth's own impoverished background and his anti-colonial sentiments as responsible for this empathy with black slaves and servants and for his ability to "see differently."[13] I would argue, however, for an equally important point: that, through his prints, Hogarth establishes himself as one who *sees* – everything, and in minute detail. As a subject-who-sees, Hogarth clearly marks his difference from the black figures in his prints even while he expresses his compassion for them. He takes his place as a sovereign individual of civil society, who participates fully and actively in the public sphere. His prints are indeed everywhere, discussed, debated, bought, and sold by slaveowners and opponents of slavery alike.

Investigating the philosophical and historical conjunction of slavery and aesthetics in the eighteenth century, Simon Gikandi has argued for the centrality of this conjunction in the constitution of modernity. Gikandi explicates a footnote in David Hume's essay "Of National Characters" in which Hume states that "Negroes ... and other species of men" are "naturally inferior to the whites."[14] This footnote explains, according to Gikandi, the general principles of taste which Hume espouses in a later essay, "Of the Standard of Taste." In Gikandi's reading, the universality ascribed by Hume to principles of taste already, by virtue of the earlier essay's footnote, excludes "Negroes" and actually reinforces their difference from European men. This difference was constituted through and evidenced by the absence of arts, sciences, and ingenuity in people of "that complexion."[15] Gikandi points out that Hume did not categorize "Negroes" as inhuman, but as inferior due to an "original distinction," a difference that "manifested itself in aesthetic terms – in matters of ingenuity and taste."[16] I would argue, further, that this distinction and Hume's judgment of black people as inferior are crucial to an empiricist philosophy in which sight is privileged as a sensory basis for knowledge of reality.

Gikandi does not comment further on Hume's principles; however, it is clear that they depend on the repeated practice of seeing. For Hume, there exists a universal standard of taste, exemplified in great works of literature and art which remain truly great throughout the ages; however, only a few, rare men are capable of discerning their beauty. By imparting their sound judgments, they make others aware of the universal qualities of genius in, to cite Hume's major example, Homer. These men have "that *delicacy* of imagination," a rare quality, but one which can be practiced and thus developed.[17] Moreover such practice consists, in Hume's exposition, of "frequent survey or contemplation of a particular species of beauty," and he describes the development, through practice, from a state of optical confusion to one of clarity in which the eye as an organ is perfected.[18]

Returning to Hume's footnote to examine it and its context in the essay "On National Characters" more closely, it becomes apparent that Hume's empiricist values, privileging the sense of sight, also undergird his arguments concerning national character. He argues against geography, climate, or "air" as physical causes of national character, and contends, instead, that in addition to the effects of what he calls "moral causes" such as forms of government, national character results from the quality of the human mind which "is of a very imitative nature."[19] This imitative nature inclines men toward company with one another and a mutual education in manners and sensibilities which then results in a national character. Hume dismisses climate or "air" because, as he states emphatically: "It is a maxim in all philosophy, that causes which do not appear are to be considered as not existing."[20] The evidence gained from *seeing* that which *appears* thus determines the reality of existence.

If Hume did not append to his argument the footnote concerning the inferiority of black people, he would have to include them among the many nations and cultures that make up his extensive examples, and they would be deemed capable of change, development, education, and even, by extension, the development of a standard of taste, through the association and company of other men. Instead, he judges them incapable of "forming a civilized nation," and as having "no arts, no sciences."[21] As the remainder of his footnote makes clear, these are not accomplishments that might be developed among "Negroes" on either a collective or an individual basis. Even when it "appears" before our eyes, such development is not to be trusted: "In Jamaica, indeed, they talk of one Negro as a man of parts and learning; but it is likely he is admired for slender accomplishments, like a parrot who speaks a few words plainly."[22] This man (whom Gikandi identifies as the poet Francis Williams) might have provided Hume with his best example in support of his argument concerning the imitative quality of the human mind. The abilities of an enslaved African to realize this quality of mind to the extent that he becomes a poet in the English language gives rise, however, to another category of imitation, that of a superficial kind as exercised by a parrot. If "naturally inferior," Africans or people of African descent cannot participate in the development of the senses and the practice of viewing objects of beauty that create men of taste and form a national character and civilization. They remain objects of the civilized man's judgment, assessed as incapable of the arts and sciences. They are, thus, assessed inferior due to their inability to see with the practiced and perfected eye that characterizes the man of taste who retains the power to judge them as so lacking.

This judgment extends at times to other people whom Hume deems incapable of aesthetic taste and, again, the second category of imitation emerges: "The coarsest daubing contains a certain luster of colors and exactness of imitation, which are so far beauties, and would affect the mind of a peasant or Indian with the highest admiration."[23] Hume's simile of the parrot in his footnote referring to Francis Williams and his description of the coarseness appreciated by peasants and colonized people as "imitation" present a problem faced by colonial artists of color – the requirement that they enter the realm of art in order to develop as a modern subject-who-sees, and the immediate risk of imitation, that is, of *being seen* as only parroting, rather than truly creating, within the realm of aesthetics.

The ontological economy of the modern subject in fact requires and develops from this response to the colonized artist. The status of the universalized subject-who-sees depends upon a notion of the development of the senses which casts the "Negro" as incapable of artistic judgment or agency. Such incapacity coincides with a lack of freedom – in the processes of the mind and, frequently, in social and legal status. Following Hume, both Kant and Schiller conceptualized the free man of reason through their philosophies of an aesthetic realm in which freedom was developed and exercised. In the practice of aesthetic judgment, defined as both disinterested and universal, the individual constituted himself as free personally and also socially within an emergent public sphere. Though Kant wrote in opposition to Hume's skepticism,[24] he nevertheless formulated a universal "Subject without properties" (that is, unmarked as different) as one who has developed through an organization of the senses in which seeing predominates.[25] Schiller contested Kant's emphasis on the subject in the aesthetic relation but, nevertheless, reinforced the significance of sight for the development of taste. Describing the entry of "the savage" into the aesthetic realm, Schiller emphasizes the eye and the ear as affording more distance than the "more animal senses" such as touch. However, in elaborating further, he writes only of the eye: "What we actually see with the eye is something different from the sensation we receive; for the mind leaps out across light to objects."[26] It is this leap of the eye across a distance that enables the free play of aesthetic pleasure, free that is of "all claims to reality" or of personal interest. Through the eye, the subject constitutes himself as free: "Once he does begin to enjoy through the eye, and seeing acquires for him a value of its own, he is already aesthetically free and the play-drive has started to develop."[27]

In this parallel development of the senses in a hierarchy dominated by vision and in accord with the development of the human race, Kant and Schiller distinguished those incapable, at least as yet, of this "higher sense" of distanced, contemplative sight. In doing so, they remained under the influence of Hume's footnote concerning the inferiority of "Negroes . . . and other species of men." The other species of men included indigenous peoples of the Americas whom eighteenth-century writers sometimes confused with people from Africa and whom Kant names specifically as occupying the lower stages of development. Though promoting a more developmental model, Kant and Schiller nevertheless reinforced a distinction in ways of seeing that, as I will argue later in this chapter, continued to

shape aesthetic theory into the twentieth century. The subject marked as
different is the one Kant describes as exemplified by the Caribs or Iroquois
for whom pleasure in color or form amounts to a private charm, rather than
an aesthetic value that is universally communicable.[28] It is not a general
inferiority, but the absence of freedom, in the imaginative and the cogni-
tive faculties, that then distinguishes the unmodern or pre-modern subject.
Such freedom cannot be exercised in simple imitation of existing aesthetic
models; it demands an apparent originality in both the judgment and
production of art.

When George Lamming states in *The Pleasures of Exile* that "Caliban is
never accorded the power to see," he describes precisely the effect on the
colonized person of the advent of the modern, universalized Subject as one
who sees and whose power to see hinges on the denial of that power to
those who bear marks of difference or, as Lamming puts it, are known by
"the measure of the condition which [their] physical presence has defined."
Lamming's phrasing suggests a point on which David Lloyd has more
recently insisted – that the visual structure of racism is not based on an
antagonistic recognition of visual difference, but on establishment of a
subject-who-sees as the universal human Subject.[29]

Hume's footnote, thus, confirms Hume as the subject-who-sees and
judges, a position then sustained by exempting black people from the
potential of sensory development. However, it also reveals an anxiety
that comes from what Gikandi refers to as being "haunted by that which
it excludes which needs to be smuggled in through the footnote or paren-
thesis."[30] Such hauntings appear also in visual forms – in the art collections
of anxious white creoles, images on playing cards, and the commercial signs
of commodity culture – as well as in additional footnotes scattered across
the pages of eighteenth-century philosophy.

The moral unease felt by Lord Montague on his simultaneous purchase
of a black child and a painting intensified even further for men such as
William Beckford, the white creole who inherited a fortune made by his
grandfather on plantations in Jamaica. Insisting that the categories of the
aesthetic and of slavery "operated within the same economy of discourse,"
Gikandi argues that Beckford, perceived as "not quite white," became an
aesthete for two reasons: as the only way to enter English high society and
also "as an instrument of reconciling two of the great antinomies of 18th-
century culture – commerce and taste."[31] This is the split that also haunts
the character of Lord Montague in Dabydeen's novel, giving him a con-
science that makes him question the commerce in a Renaissance masterpiece along with that in human bodies. Beckford experienced this split a

little differently and perhaps more urgently, as a "ghost of colonialism past," in the knowledge that his life as a man of the arts was made directly possible by slave labor. Beckford turned to architecture and art collecting, erecting an English Gothic palace, Fonthill Abbey, in which he mounted an enormous art collection, including, as Dabydeen notes, Hogarth's *A Rake's Progress* and *A Harlot's Progress*. Gikandi analyzes Beckford's art collecting as representative of another subjective dimension, experienced by the white Creole, of colonial anxiety: "Beckford's Abbey marked the 'not quite white' subject's attempt to literally possess and contain the high culture which had marked [him] as different."[32] The possession of art thus mirrors the possession of human beings; at the same time it promises admittance to a sensibility and marker of social status that appears free of such economic and moral constraints. This fracturing of art's status as object negotiates but also fuels the racial and class anxieties that drive the purchaser and collector of art.

Other forms of visual representation also depended on the figure of the black person. As early as the late seventeenth century and continuing into the nineteenth century, decks of playing cards portrayed numerous images of Africans. Meant to be educational, they used one of the two "black" suits, and usually the spades, to represent different regions of Africa, portraying individual African figures along with textual "facts" concerning the region and its people. Eighteenth-century versions of these cards, according to Mario Relich, conveyed a racialized and ambivalent notion of the "noble savage" with sometimes heroically idealized images along with disparaging comments in the brief textual portions of the cards. Relich comments on the popularity of these playing cards and suggests that they may have influenced writers such as Alexander Pope and Aphra Behn in their depictions of African warriors and princes. However, none of these cards raised questions concerning slavery or the slave trade. Relich comments that such questions might have appeared on the more politically oriented cards such as the "South Sea Bubble" cards published in 1720 and meant to satirize the financial scandal of the South Sea Company's bankruptcy. However, though they portrayed black servants in some of the images and satirized "all sorts of follies," the slave trade itself was not one of their targets.[33]

Beyond the art collecting and amusements of the upper classes, visual images of black people pervaded London and other cities and towns of Britain. In Dabydeen's description of eighteenth-century London as "*visually* black," he points to advertisements for the sale of black bodies and to signboards deploying black bodies in order to sell other commodities.

In this more popular realm of images, visual representation fuses with, rather than splits from, the buying and selling of commerce. The point of fusion is the figure of the black person. While from 10,000 to 15,000 people of color actually populated Britain by the eighteenth century,[34] a visual discourse of the South Asian, African, or Afro-Caribbean person came to the public through commercial images and display; conversely, the images of commodity culture were experienced *through* the visual figure of the black person. Peter Fryer documents the numerous innkeepers and tobacconists who used portraits or caricatures of black people to advertise their goods. He states that "[b]etween 1541 and the middle of the nineteenth century 61 taverns called 'Black Boy' are recorded in the capital and many more in the provinces; and in the same period London had 51 establishments known as 'The Blackamoor's Head.'"[35] Gretchen Gerzina lists seventeen streets, lanes, alleys, courts and yards, all cited in a 1761 guidebook to London, that were named after black people. These included eight Black Boy Alleys, four Blackmoor Alleys, and various Black Boy Courts and Blackmoor Streets. She points out that these street names derived from the signs hung to advertise local businesses. "Where signboards helped identify the unnamed and unnumbered addresses of London they also came to identify the entire street."[36] That so many locations in the rapidly expanding commercial center of London took their names from images of black people literally grounds their identities and their businesses in these images. Further, it indicates an environment in which to be seen, bought, and sold is to be black and is, thus, to represent commodity culture itself. The figure of the harlot performs a complementary role, troping the prostitution of all culture in the age of commerce. This visual knowing of African and Afro-Caribbean people as a commodity, a commodified image, and an emblem, by association, of commodity culture shaped, as Dabydeen's novel suggests, self-knowledge on the part of the African as well as the English person.

If we accept these postcolonial investigations into the eighteenth-century configuration of slavery and aesthetics, the century becomes a period in which the "power to see" constitutes the man of taste, judgment, reason, and property; this power defines, in its perceived absence, the person of Africa or African descent as either "naturally inferior" or stalled at an early stage of sensory development and thus lacking the reason, judgment, and taste necessary to the free individual and participant in a civilized public sphere. According to Lloyd, these characteristics then transfer to a "natural" mark, evidenced by color or some other visually perceived physical characteristic which then becomes the measure of the person of color's inferiority.

The anxieties of the upper English and white creole classes are, thus, produced in a colonial relationship dependent on the enslaved and colonized person, whose status as a human being remains linked to the capacity for sight. This status, established philosophically, was then bolstered by eighteenth-century writers who traveled to the Caribbean, such as Edward Long, a Jamaican plantation owner, who testified to the moral, intellectual, and artistic incapacities of the enslaved Africans on his estates. Gikandi has argued that Long's *A History of Jamaica* (1774) provided the evidence European philosophers needed to support an idea of the aesthetic based on the exclusion of Africa and black people from the domains of history, reason, and art. Indeed, it was Long who confirmed the poetry of the black Jamaican Francis Williams as the "slender" and imitative result of an academic education rather than natural abilities.[37]

As Gikandi's work and an earlier essay by Sander Gilman demonstrate, aesthetic philosophies and their dependence on the figure of the black person developed through philosophical crossings and debates between Britain, the Caribbean, and Europe. Crucial moments in these debates appeared in the footnotes. In the same year that Hume wrote in "Of the Standard of Taste" about the refinement of the organ of the eye, Edmund Burke produced an often cited footnote in *A Philosophical Enquiry into the Origin of our Ideas of the Sublime and Beautiful* (1757) that generated a number of responses in Europe. Burke's footnote repeats a story told by William Chelseden, an English surgeon, of a boy who had been blind since birth, but whose sight was restored through surgery. On seeing a black person for the first time, the boy was reportedly terrified. Based on this story, Burke anthropomorphizes darkness, associating blackness and black people with darkness, terror, and the sublime. As Gilman writes: "Thus Negrophobia, irrational in its manifestation, is given an epistemological rationale by Burke, in order to explain, not the nature of the Black, but rather the fear engendered in the mind of the European by the very appearance of blackness. Burke places the Black among those natural forces which can generate the sublime."[38]

In a response to Burke, which drew on additional English publications, Gottfried Lessing figured the black person not as a trope for the sublime, but as an occasion for disgust and ridicule. Though they differed as to its kind (disgust or comedy rather than the sublime), and whether it was innate or learned, even Burke's critics insisted on seeing the European response to the black person in aesthetic terms. Perception, aesthetic and moral sensibility remained capacities of the European mind in response to the black person who became a test case for controversial issues at the limits of the theories under debate.

Both Gilman, in his treatment of Kant's later work, and Dabydeen, in his analysis of the influence of Joshua Reynolds and Joseph Spence on Hogarth, recognize a significant vein of cultural relativism in the late eighteenth century. Derived, in Kant's case, from the influence of Herder and Voltaire, cultural relativism granted the black person and African cultures their own visual agencies and norms of beauty. Gilman claims that at the end of the eighteenth century the black person had attained "the position of an observer rather than an object perceived."[39] However, as Gilman's later work documents, nineteenth-century medical and scientific discourses reconstituted the black and colonized person as object of the empirical gaze of science.[40] Furthermore, the emergence of relativism in the eighteenth century did not obliterate contesting notions of inherent inferiority in "Negroes" as a constituent component of aesthetic philosophy. As a coexisting theory, however, relativism may have prompted, by articulating a moral disturbance, the footnotes haunting the pages of these texts, yet crucial to their arguments. And while liberal intellectuals may have acknowledged the creativity demonstrated by people of African descent or perceived in African arts, the capacity of the African for critical aesthetic judgment has continually been denied. As David Lloyd argues, whether perceived by the European as absent or as yet undeveloped, the lack of a "universal communicability," as evidenced by the formation of a public sphere as forum for critical judgment, structures racist discourses of post-Enlightenment thinkers, whether liberals, such as John Stuart Mill, or extreme conservatives such as Gobineau.[41] This supposed lack of critical judgment then pre-defines the colonized person as inadequate for self-government and incapable of self-sufficiency.

These notions of a developmental or even innate lack persisted in spite of documented evidence to the contrary. Seventy years after Edward Long dismissed the creativity of Francis Williams as a matter not of genius but imitation, evidence emerged that might have established other assumptions as the basis for understanding the art and aesthetic reasoning of people of Africa. Robert Farris Thompson cites, in reports from missionaries who visited the Yoruba capital city of Abeokuta in the 1840s, detailed descriptions of highly developed visual arts and aesthetic principles among the Yoruba. Based on these reports and his own research, Thompson has stated that "[t]he Yoruba assess everything aesthetically – from the taste and color of a yam to the qualities of a dye, to the dress and deportment of a woman or a man."[42] He quotes one of the earliest dictionaries of the Yoruba language, published in 1858, in which the word *amewa* was translated as "knower-of-beauty" and "connoisseur," indicating that aesthetic judgment was a strong concept and practice in this region. These missionary reports of the mid-nineteenth century might have countered earlier notions concerning the lack of an aesthetic vision in people of Africa. The accounts of Bassonge civilization published by Leo Frobenius in 1913 might have provided further counter-evidence.[43] However, as late as 1920, even progressive art critics such as Roger Fry, who appreciated the form and stylistic features of "Negro sculpture," insisted that "[i]t is for want of a conscious critical sense and the intellectual powers of comparison and classification that the negro has failed to create one of the great cultures of the world."[44]

Well into the twentieth century, then, belief in the capacity for a formalized, distanced, and contemplative vision as a racial developmental marker still formed the basis for the denial of full humanity to Africans and people of African descent. In a cultural environment shaped by these ideas about colonized people of color, artists and writers from the colonies attempted to enter the world of art as creators and critics, with the full authority of their own perceptions. They faced an entrenched and, as I argue in Chapters 2 and 3, modernized conception of art that hinged on an imperial, racialized relation with colonized people. The early twentieth-century modernist movements in the arts often replicated, in different versions, eighteenth-century notions of seeing, in, for example, appropriations of "the primitive." Yet these were the movements in which writers and artists from the colonies played a crucial role, adapting the tenets, styles, and forms of modernism for their own countervisual purposes. In doing so, they faced a number of obstacles concerning the artistic practice of seeing. In an essay published in 1963 that turns the tables on art critics such as Fry and his mentor Bernhard Berenson, C. L. R. James contemplates and challenges their aesthetic formulae, proposing new notions of art and new agents of artistic taste, a critique I discuss at length in Chapter 3. I argue that, along with George Lamming, James generates from within European philosophy and aesthetics, the evidence for their blindness.

The colonial relationship is thus one of vision – of seeing and looking – as James, Lamming, and other writers from the Caribbean have repeatedly stressed, and it creates a paradox and double-bind for the colonized artist. The colonized artist and writer is positioned within this visual ontology as lacking the capacity to see and, thus, to create or judge art; yet this position presumably grants the potential of sensory development that culminates in acquiring the full capacity of sight.[45] To become fully human, the colonized person must demonstrate this development by entering the realm of art; such entry, however, threatens the entire system and must be perceived as mere imitation, a perception that again insists on the colonized person as object, rather than subject, of visual contemplation and aesthetic judgment.

Hogarth's *A Harlot's Progress* represents this anxiety of imitation in the figure of the black boy, dressed in orientalist costume, and doubled by the figure in the lower left-hand corner of the monkey, dressed in a lady's finery, though, of course, even those clothes are imitative, belonging not to a lady, but to a "harlot." One editor of Hogarth's engravings even describes Moll in terms of the imitative monkey, stating that "she apes the life style of the class to which she aspires" and also argues that the monkey mirrors the profile and gestures of "the wealthy Jewish businessman."[46] Imitation seems to circulate from one character to another; not one of them can occupy an authentic or original ontological position. It is as if, in order to enter even the fake finery of a harlot's room, the black person must simultaneously imitate the dominant culture (by serving tea as a lady's servant), perform expected stereotypes of the cultural Other (through costume), and then be mocked by a visually twinned figure of the imitative monkey. In spite of Dabydeen's claims on behalf of Hogarth's compassion for black people, and in spite of this particular print's exposé of rampant artifice and greed in English culture, it seems to fix, even more than the era's paintings of black servants, the space of representation for colonized people of color as one in which they are imprisoned in the role of imitators, forever denied creativity and critical reason. However, the very space of art and the ideology of art as an autonomous and disinterested realm may offer a way out of this position. We might follow Gikandi's argument that the representation of black people in the realm of art creates a potential space for their participation as subjects within it. In this part of his argument, the ideology of the aesthetic as a transcendent realm does not just mask its complicity with commerce; it also creates an imaginative, utopian space where people of Africa or African descent may imagine themselves as participants, freed from the economic and political conditions which define them as less than fully human.[47] I contend that gaining the power to see or, as Walcott puts it, "the learning of looking," is crucial to this aspiration; at the same time, it presents the risk of imitation, of being perceived and dismissed as only "parroting" the person of true vision. To confront this problem, twentieth-century writers and artists from the Caribbean do not simply seek acceptance in the world of art; they address vision itself as the grounds on which the modern subject and knowledge of the world are founded.

***

Returning for a moment to the scene which opened this chapter, we can read the movement of C. L. R. James's eyes from the play of cricket to Picasso's painting as a trans-figurative act of seeing. It transfers images of revolt and anguish onto the art of movement embodied in cricket and then back again, crossing boundaries separating nations, races, cultures, high and low art, art and sport, and refiguring as composite and dynamic the images before him. To see becomes a matter, not so much of distant and formalized contemplation, but of active movement "beyond a boundary" as the title of his well-known book on cricket, politics, and art puts it. Most importantly, the movement of his eyes enacts a new subject-who-sees in these crossings, creolized and engaged in a global, transatlantic politics of vision. James was central to this project, but he was hardly alone. Rather, a twentieth-century visual aesthetics of trans-figuration has developed in the work of Caribbean artists and writers throughout the twentieth century.

As mentioned earlier, my argument in this book counters those of cultural critics who stress the importance of sound, orality, and music as resistance to the colonial imposition of literary and visual cultures and to the tyranny of visual epistemologies. In my reading of twentieth-century Anglophone Caribbean writers, they confront vision directly, neither skirting nor rejecting it, and through its transformation as bodily sense, social act, and cultural institution, a new sensory body, beyond sight, yet renewing it, emerges. In the process of creating these sensory transformations, Caribbean writers have contributed to and often anticipated arguments made in contemporary theories of visuality. These arguments are bound up with debates concerning the advent and nature of modernity; they also involve the movements in art and literature that we have come to call, though always with much controversy, modernism.[48]

In the past fifteen years, a field of visual studies has emerged, coalescing what some have called a "pictorial turn" in critical theory, away from the "linguistic turn" of earlier decades.[49] Widening the perspective a little, the late twentieth-century emphasis on visuality in literary and cultural studies includes studies of "representation" following from the theories of Michel Foucault and exemplified in work by critics such as Svetlana Alpers and J. Michael Fried; critiques of "ocularcentrism" also following from Foucault and from Jacques Lacan in a tradition going back to Sartre and Hegel; promotions of philosophical countervisions developed in the philosophy of Maurice Merleau-Ponty and later argued by critics such as David Michael Levin; and critiques of the "imperial eye" formulated most notably by postcolonial critics such as Mary Louise Pratt, Sara Suleri, and David Spurr. Following on Jacques Lacan's theoretical employment of "the gaze" as constituting the subject and on Michel's Foucault's notion of the gaze as producing discourses of knowledge, visual studies addresses everything from traditional poetics to contemporary cinema to commodity culture and the culture of the spectacle. It includes studies of iconography, such as the earlier work of Erwin Panofsky and more recently, W. J. T. Mitchell; of ekphrasis, such as that by Murray Krieger and Françoise Meltzer; and of iconoclasm, such as Huston Diehl's critical study of Reformation drama. One path in the critical theory of vision that has developed recently moves from the "downcast eyes," as Martin Jay has termed a negative Foucauldian notion of vision, to a celebration of a disruptive, "receptive" vision, based in the physicality of the eye, as explicated by Teresa Brennan. This path begins with a strong critique of the Enlightenment emphasis on the sense of sight as the basis for knowledge then points to various countervisions that subvert a dominant and oppressive employment of vision. However, these theorists of visuality rarely link the term "modernity" to the expansion of capital through the slave trade, industrialization, colonization, and the plantation and factory systems. For postcolonial critics such as Gikandi and Gilroy, on the other hand, these imperial and domestic movements of capital constitute modernity and are central to understanding the role of vision and aesthetics in the modern period.

On a path intersecting in some ways with the work of theorists such as Jay, Levin, and Brennan, postcolonial critics such as Mary Louise Pratt resituate the critique of vision within the context of colonialism and offer important ways of understanding colonialist discourses in their deployments of the controlling Western gaze. Pratt, Sara Suleri, Sander Gilman, and David Spurr have all made significant contributions to the understanding of, for example, the natural sciences, medicine, travel narratives, photography, journalism, and notions of the picturesque as imperial practices.[50] In his comments on aestheticization, Spurr indicates the ongoing impact of the eighteenth-century notion of a capacity for distant and contemplative sight as constitutive of a universalized Subject: "I have spoken of aestheticization in journalism as distantiation, transformation, privilege, displacement, consumption, and alienation. Taken together, these terms imply a certain possession of social reality which holds it at arm's length and makes it into the object of beauty, horror, pleasure, and pity" (59). Spurr argues that this "arm's length" view takes possession of social reality itself and can become a "mode of representation by which a powerful culture *takes* possession of a less powerful one" (59). For him, in this context, aestheticization *is* colonization.

In their turns and intersections, these paths in visual studies present tremendous ambivalence towards the visual epistemologies they track, expressing, overall, an anxiety about vision, its promise of beauty or new knowledge coupled with the threat of domination. However, while intent on historicizing their examinations of vision and modernity, none of these critics discuss the contributions of black or previously colonized cultures to disruptions in the hegemony of vision. The Eurocentric approach to visuality neglects well-known studies by, for example, Houston Baker, who emphasizes the "blues geographies of the New World" and "the *sound* and *soundings* of Afro-American modernism,"[51] or Paul Gilroy, who stresses cross-Atlantic flows of music as constitutive of a black Atlantic modernity. Especially for Gilroy, recentering modernity in the experiences of the African diaspora does not simply give another identity to black culture; it transforms Eurocentric ideas of modern culture and the nationalisms that support them.[52] It gives to the black Atlantic a central and definitive role in forging epistemological breaks with the "ocularcentrism" attributed to modernity by scholars such as Levin. And as I contend here, these breaks do not just occur in the realm of sound, orality, and music; they also involve direct encounters with visuality as developed in Western philosophy and aesthetics to offer trans-figurative countervisions in the twentieth century.

TURNER TRANS-FIGURED: WRITINGS BY CLIFF, DABYDEEN, AND D'AGUIAR

Anxieties over the commerce in slaves reached a crisis in the eighteenth century with the mass murder that took place in 1781 on the slave ship, *Zong*. The ship's captain ordered his crew to throw overboard 132 ill, but still living, slaves in order to bill the insurance company for their loss; if he had allowed them to die of natural causes, he and his shareholders would have suffered the loss instead. Claiming that the murders were necessary in order to preserve the remaining "property," the owners of the *Zong* demanded compensation from the insurance company, which refused to honor their claim. Though the court ruled in favor of the *Zong*'s owners, the company still refused to pay, and Granville Sharp began (unsuccessful) proceedings against the crew.[53] The incident shocked the public who were reminded of it again, this time in terms of aesthetic, rather than legal, judgment, when J. M. W. Turner exhibited his vivid rendering of the *Zong* incident at the Royal Academy in 1840, coinciding with the world anti-slavery convention held that year in London. Originally titled *Slavers*

2. Joseph Mallard William Turner, English, 1775–1851, *Slave Ship (Slavers Throwing Overboard the Dead and Dying, Typhoon Coming On)* (1840), oil on canvas, 90.8 cm × 122.6 cm (35¾ in. × 48¼ in.), Museum of Fine Arts, Boston, Henry Lillie Pierce Fund. 99.22, photograph © 2007, Museum of Fine Arts, Boston.

Throwing Overboard the Dead and Dying – Typhoon Coming On, the painting depicts in Turner's characteristic impressionist style the manacled bodies of enslaved Africans thrown overboard during a violent storm at sea.

In the late twentieth century, writers from the Caribbean returned to the *Zong*, re-inscribing Turner's *The Slave Ship* as a site for their explorations of the act of seeing, the commodification of art, and the advent of the modern subject in the epoch of slavery. These literary returns to a visual scene of the Middle Passage indicate an inability to stop looking for what is *not* visible, as much as for what is, horrifically, represented in the painting. In their emphasis on what is only partially present or glimpsed in fragments, Michelle Cliff, David Dabydeen, and Fred D'Aguiar register a subjectivity apparently denied within, yet constitutive of, modernity. Their recently published texts offer an introduction to an aesthetics of trans-figuration that developed in the visual art and literary writing of the Anglophone Caribbean throughout the century. Directing a literary gaze towards a visual work of art, their writings also exemplify the interartistic dimensions of this aesthetics and the importance of literary conventions such as ekphrasis in circum-Atlantic reformulations of the act of seeing.

More than any other in the European tradition, Turner's painting has catalyzed a literary response from the Caribbean diaspora. Paul Gilroy recounts the history of *The Slave Ship* as an abolitionist statement in the year of the world antislavery convention.[54] Tobias Döring has described the many controversies, then and continuing in the present, that surround the painting. While many accept the assessment of Turner's sympathies as sincerely abolitionist, others call him an opportunist who profited from the sensational incident.[55] John Ruskin owned the painting for twenty-eight years; then, when viewing it became too painful, sold it to an American. It has remained in the United States since then, residing at the Boston Museum of Fine Arts and hanging next to other examples of the romantic sublime. As Gilroy points out, Turner's status as master of this genre, his position in cultural constructions of English national identity, and the actual scene portrayed in this painting combine to effect a powerful image of "racial terror, commerce, and England's ethico-political degeneration."[56] Yet, its simultaneous participation in the genre of the sublime and the antislavery movement makes it also a point of departure for an alternate black Atlantic aesthetics. For Gilroy, this alternate aesthetics has taken place in contemporary black British painting and, predominantly, in music; however, in the fiction and poetry of twentieth-century Anglophone Caribbean writers, it takes place in language and the transformation of literary devices for expressing the act of seeing.

Ian Baucom has written of the scene of slaves drowning as a foundational one for Caribbean writers. He traces allusions to this scene from Kamau Brathwaite's line, "[t]he unity is submarine," in *Contradictory Omens*; through Derek Walcott's poem "The Sea is History"; passages from Edouard Glissant's *Poetics of Relation*; a brief mention of the *Zong* massacre in Michelle Cliff's novel, *Abeng*; Fred D'Aguiar's narrative recreation of the scene in his novel *Feeding the Ghosts*; David Dabydeen's long poem *Turner*; and Paul Gilroy's references to the incident in *Small Acts* and *The Black Atlantic*. Though not all of these textual allusions refer directly to Turner's painting, Baucom argues that they, nevertheless, participate in "a cross-Atlantic conversation," a "circular exchange of images and epigraphs as they have borrowed each other's language to orient their collective gaze on this image of the drowning body."[57] We might add to the list of writers and texts that Baucom cites as participants in the conversation Dabydeen's *A Harlot's Progress* in which the captain of the ship *Zong* appears in the character of Captain Thistlewood, the man who "seasons" the child Mungo through repeated sexual abuse. We could add Michelle Cliff's novel *Free Enterprise*, published in 1993, in which Turner's painting occupies central place in a narrative recovery of the women who planned and funded John Brown's raid on Harper's Ferry. Recent poems by M. Nourbese Philip also respond directly to the *Zong* as do paintings by Lubaina Himid.[58] For Baucom this conversation indicates a profound reflection on the relation between value and exchange, depicted in the commodification of drowning human bodies exchanged for an insurance payment, but then transformed in these Caribbean writings to a sense of shared community, new beginning, and an alternative notion of modernity in which time becomes heterochronic and value lies in the insistence of the past in the present.

In my reading of these texts, I stress what may seem at first obvious, and which generates the overall project of this book – the Caribbean diasporic politics of vision developed in these multiple returns to a painting and to the dynamics of seeing it represents and provokes. Though Baucom does not develop this kind of analysis, at times his language indicates its importance. Most importantly for the twentieth-century contributions to theories of visuality that I trace in the work of Anglophone Caribbean writers, Baucom describes the foundational scene itself as "this body, this vanishing but not vanished, drowning but transformed, lost but repeating body" (68). The partial and recurring presence of a lost body constitutes in my argument an aesthetics of resurrection or, to use my previous term, trans-figuration. This aesthetics imaginatively recreates the sensory body, in its both literal and metaphorical meanings (body of writing, body of civilization, transubstantiation of the divine body) through which an alternate sense of time and of modernity itself is experienced. In its fullest development, this aesthetics of resurrection expands to include the apparently vanishing but never disappearing Amerindian presence in the Caribbean, the partial presences within the Caribbean person of multiple racial and cultural antecedents, and the notion of spiritual possession as awakening and re-membering the lost body. It appears most explicitly in Wilson Harris's writing, which I discuss in Chapter 4, but it also appears in varying and more secular forms as an encounter with the notion of vision itself, expressive especially of Afro-Caribbean and Amerindian cultural recoveries, Caribbean nationalist politics, and transnational anti-colonial affiliations.

Returning to the transatlantic conversation that takes as its centerpiece Turner's *The Slave Ship*, we find three very different treatments of this painting in recent work by Anglophone Caribbean writers: Cliff's novel, *Free Enterprise* (1993), Dabydeen's long poem *Turner* (1994), and D'Aguiar's novel *Feeding the Ghosts* (1997). Different as they are in genre, form, style, and setting, all three texts encounter the dynamics of vision represented in the painting to convey an alternate sense of sight, as if seeing beyond and through the eyes to experience vision as indiscrete, composed of movement, rhythm, sound, image, and revelation.

***

Cliff's *Free Enterprise* participates in the project, also undertaken by Dabydeen in *A Harlot's Progress* but in a completely different historical setting, of examining the contradictory interrelations among concepts of freedom, art, and commerce. The title indicates as much and refers variously and simultaneously to the enterprise of slavery as "free trade" and to the enterprise of freeing slaves. Both projects are conducted in this novel by a free mulatto, posing as the captain of a slave ship, and by his daughter, a black woman named Mary Ellen Pleasant ("no stranger to capital"),[59] who uses her successful hotel enterprise to smuggle runaway slaves and to fund revolts, including the raid on Harper's Ferry. In Cliff's title echo all of the following: the name of the black-owned restaurant where Mary Ellen Pleasant meets Annie Christmas, another partner, originally from the Caribbean, in the enterprise of revolt; the phrase Mary Ellen Pleasant gives to her philosophy and an occasion for debate with John Brown; Manifest Destiny (the "greatest enterprise the continent had ever seen" (105)); and the enterprise of freedom itself as more than emancipation, expressed in a visual image linking Mary Ellen Pleasant to Malcolm X. The cumulative effect of the repetition of this phrase in its many diverse contexts is to raise questions about the nature of freedom – as a civil right, an act (political, commercial, or existential), an ideal, an ideology, a collective goal, a social condition – and the means of achieving it ("by any means necessary"). These multiple meanings recall the argument put forward by Orlando Patterson that the development of the concept of freedom in the West has depended on the experience of slavery.[60] Similarly, Toni Morrison has written, "The concept of freedom did not emerge in a vacuum. Nothing highlighted freedom – if it did not in fact create it – like slavery."[61]

Susan Buck-Morss has recently located the contradiction as rooted in the eighteenth-century paradox involving slavery as "the root metaphor of Western political philosophy."[62] As a metaphor, it "connoted everything that was evil about power relations"; however, with a few exceptions, it referred to the slavery of European feudalism, which the Enlightenment bourgeoisie sought to overthrow. Late seventeenth- and eighteenth-century philosophers such as Locke and Rousseau expressed outrage at the condition of slavery but only as a "metaphor for legal tyranny" (826) or basis for asserting the claims of natural liberty (830). Since liberty involved the right to property, and slaves were categorized as property, a perpetual blindness as to the existence and conditions of actual slavery persisted. And it persisted, points out Buck-Morss, in the face of and tested by an unprecedented and successful revolution in the Caribbean, fought by enslaved Africans and their descendants, in pursuit of liberty. This, of course, was the Haitian Revolution, led by Toussaint L'Ouverture and inspired by the very Enlightenment ideals which paradoxically cast him and his people as property to be protected. Buck-Morss asserts that although this revolution, along with other colonial events, inhabits "the margins of European history," its historical placement is profoundly misleading, and we must take into account history from the perspective of Saint-Dominique at the turn of the eighteenth century. She is not, however, the first to make this argument as her copious footnotes indicate with their many references to C. L. R. James's *The Black Jacobins* (1938). James's influential history of this revolution and the play produced in London two years earlier brought to the attention of Pan-Africanists, Marxists, colonial intellectuals, historians, and a diverse London theatre audience the importance of Haiti to the development of notions of freedom in the contexts of slavery and revolution. Caribbean writers of the twentieth century have long referred to this event, its leaders, and its Afro-Caribbean spiritual and artistic practices in their work. Cliff's novel follows, for instance, on writings by James and Lamming, which I discuss in Chapter 3, in exploring the transatlantic development of revolutionary ideas and practice in the aftermath of Haiti.

Free Enterprise interweaves the narrative recovery of the women who helped to organize and fund the raid on Harper's Ferry with another story of abolitionist Bostonians, members of Henry Adams's family, to whose home Turner's *The Slave Ship* finds its way. The character of Mary Ellen Pleasant, at dinner in Alice Hooper's home on the evening of the painting's unveiling, links the two narratives, but the painting itself offers a window onto an extended narrative exploration of art and the dynamics of seeing. The painting generates one aspect of this dynamic, and multiple references to Amerindian arts and to African art forms and images that somehow survive the Middle Passage provide another. In the midst of this narrative deployment of visual art from England, Europe, Africa, the Caribbean, and African America emerge descriptions of well-known works of art such as the Shaw Memorial by Augustus St. Gaudens and his monument for Clover Adams, the wife of Henry, who committed suicide by swallowing the chemicals she used in her own artistic project of photography. Clover's photographs, her subjects, and the process of taking the pictures also carry the narrative and raise questions concerning gender and artistic agency. Through intermittent use of the epistolary form, Cliff imaginatively recreates the images that might have been, but were not, in several of these art works: the faces of the actual African American men who served with Shaw, rather than those of the models St. Gaudens picked at random from the streets; the figure of a former slave "some sort of mixed-blood" (85–86), who quotes Walt Whitman's "Out of the Cradle Endlessly Rocking" but lives homeless on the streets of Washington DC where Clover attempts to take her photograph. These invitations to see behind or more deeply into the actual work of art echo the conflict between ways of seeing marked by the moment of *The Slave Ship's* unveiling in Alice Hooper's home.

On this occasion, members of the dinner party attempt disinterested inquiries concerning the title, the painter, the painting's "form, color," and the best place to hang it. In their attempts at aesthetic distance, we might read the anxieties of the property-owning class when confronted with the interplay of art, property, and the slave trade. The painting's new owner, Alice Hooper, invites Mary Ellen Pleasant to "instruct the company on the incident the painter was illustrating" (74). But Pleasant refuses to play the role asked of her and leaves, prompting an apology from Hooper and a reply from Pleasant: "I think the difference between us may be reduced to the fact that while you focus on the background of the Turner painting, I cannot tear my eyes from the foreground. It is who we are" (80). Clearly who they are shapes how they see. In Pleasant's eyes, Hooper can only be interested in and troubled by the background – the painted background of the ship and the historical background of the art object. Pleasant, on the other hand, sees only the manacled limbs, floating chains, and drowning bodies that compose the foreground.

Pleasant's way of seeing locates the foundational scene of black Atlantic consciousness that Gilroy and Baucom identify and cues us to other black Atlantic visual signs and ways of seeing within the novel. These include the cosmogram Mary Ellen Pleasant's father, Captain Parsons, finds carved on the wall of a jail cell in Montego Bay; a bottle tree constructed by Annie Christmas in the yard of her cabin; and a cloth of patchwork, appliqué, and embroidery made by a South Carolina house slave that portrays a majestic lion with a rifle. In Robert Farris Thompson's documentation of a trans-atlantic visual tradition, created in the crossings from Africa to the Americas, he argues that the Kongo arts were not lost but resurfaced in the Western Hemisphere in the form of the cosmogram and the bottle tree that appear in Cliff's narrative. Composed of a cross, with circles at each end of the intersecting lines, the cosmogram in the novel resembles closely those discussed by Thompson as symbolizing a crossroads and point of contact between worlds – the living and their ancestors, the human and the divine. The circles at the end of the crossing lines represent the four moments of the sun as it travels through space and thus signify a sense of the cosmos as a whole, in motion, and of life as ongoing.[63] Carved on the walls of Captain Parson's jail cell, the cosmogram signals the underground presence of Kongo culture in Montego Bay; it also appears in a scene dreamed by Annie Christmas in 1920 as an image on the disembodied tongue of a snake. She does not recognize the cosmogram, but "it lived in her brain" (22). It lived in the Caribbean and South America also as a major influence in the highly creolized vèvè drawings, made at the beginning of vodun and other Afro-Caribbean spiritual ceremonies. As I discuss in Chapters 3 and 4, these drawings become central to novels by George Lamming and Jamaica Kincaid in their explorations of visual practices and philosophies that offer alternatives to those of neocolonial cultures.

Perhaps most enigmatic of the black Atlantic visual signs in *Free Enterprise* is the holographic image of Malcolm X that accompanies Mary Ellen Pleasant in the Parker House restaurant, invisible to everyone else, but sitting across from her where "[s]he could see his beautiful, as yet unborn eyes before her, could see herself reflected in them" (76). Malcolm, the Parker House waiter, "was waiting on his time, when he would first be called Homeboy, then Detroit Red, then X" (76). Through this holographic act of seeing, the two historical figures recognize one another in a mutually reflective gaze that crosses time, resurrects from the future as it were, an unrecounted history of a relationship between two African-American revolutionaries. Repeatedly, the narrative conveys such temporal crossings, as when Pleasant senses, in her view of the Atlantic Ocean, Turner's painting come to life, "[u]nderneath, underneath right now the painting came to life. The stunning fish, the brown limbs, the chain . . . She felt everyone behind her. In the here and now" (210).

Along with these figures of the black Atlantic, a larger circum-Atlantic countervision emerges in the presence of Caribbean native arts such as bone flutes and the carvings called *zemi*, which are guiding tropes in the writing of Wilson Harris, and which I discuss more fully in Chapter 4. In *Free Enterprise*, all of these descriptions of visual art offer a counterpoint to that of Turner's painting, and often they appear in flashes, momentarily seen, imagined, or dreamed, sometimes only partly understood. Yet their presence accrues throughout the novel, suggesting something more than can yet be fully represented and skewing the temporal pattern of a previously familiar chronological history.

* * *

The significance of partial presences and vanished yet resurrected bodies for altering the experience of time and space comes through also in David Dabydeen's long poem, *Turner*. In a preface to the poem, Dabydeen refers to Turner's painting and to Ruskin's account of it, a critical appreciation which Tobias Döring has argued stands as the central intertext for Dabydeen's poem. Ruskin's essay offers a verbal rendering of the sublime which, arguably, out-masters Turner in its powerful rendition in words of the painting's apocalyptic imagery and was, for many years, the only interpretation of it. Once again, as with the infamous notes in earlier essays on aesthetics by Hume and Burke, a footnote reveals much and becomes target for critique. Dabydeen remarks pointedly on a footnote in Ruskin's essay, the only place in which Ruskin acknowledges the subject of the painting: "Its subject, the shackling and drowning of Africans, was relegated to a brief footnote in Ruskin's essay. The footnote reads like an afterthought, something tossed overboard."[64] Ruskin's footnote and Dabydeen's comment recall Simon Gikandi's remark that Hume's philosophical meditations on taste required, on the margins, a note concerning the inherent inferiority of the "Negroes." In twentieth-century readings, these marginal notes reveal themselves as constitutive of the larger philosophical arguments rather than tangential to them.

The influence of Ruskin's essay and the existence of literary pre-texts as models for the painting lead Döring to analyze Dabydeen's poem as in dialogue, predominantly, with other verbal texts. Though I appreciate this reading, I wish to stress that, like all of the texts I discuss in this chapter, *Turner* is an ekphrastic poem – a verbal representation of a visual work of art. Along with *Free Enterprise* and D'Aguiar's *Feeding the Ghosts*, it participates in a poetic tradition that goes back at least to ancient Greece and the famous description in *The Iliad* of Achilles's shield. I discuss this tradition fully in Chapter 4; however, an important point I should make here is its association, as in the epic, with a nationalist project. The circulation, intertextually and interartistically, of this scene, culminating in an essay and a painting by a writer and artist known for their English-ness suggests another reason for the continual returns made by recent postcolonial writers to the painting and to the fact of the footnote. Through the representational strategies of these texts, they address the visual/verbal composition of England's imperial problematic and simulta-neously its dismantling in order to open the way for new subjects and new ways of seeing in the aftermath of empire.

Organized in numbered sections, and returning throughout to the scene of the drowning bodies, Dabydeen's poem multiplies the identity of the first-person speaker and expands the temporal and spatial settings of the poem so that multiple times, places, and subjectivities interleave with one another. In his summary of the poem in the preface, Dabydeen states that the poem focuses on the submerged head in the foreground of the painting, creating a consciousness formed on this person's imagined awakening from the condition of having "been drowned in Turner's (and other artists') sea for centuries" (ix). The awakening coincides in the poem's first line with the discovery of a baby's body, "Stillborn from all the signs" or "part-born, sometimes with its mother, / Tossed overboard" (1), which the speaker in the poem names Turner, the name also of the slaver and ship's captain. However, the speaker more often refers to the child as "it." "It" has "plopped into the water from a passing ship" (6) and, like a messenger, carries the speaker's consciousness into the past where it becomes a "pod, falling into the pond / In the backdam of my mother's house, . . ." (2). Its arrival at his mother's house coincides with Turner's arrival and the subsequent abduction of the speaker's people. This head/baby/child/still-born birth of consciousness breaks the waters and stirs memories of

forgotten scenes in a half-formed subjectivity undergoing the transformations of a sea change. The speaker becomes pregnant with "[t]his creature"
which "kicks alive in my stomach / Such dreams of family, this thing
which I cannot / Fathom" (16). S/he changes gender, loses skin and
stigma: "Washed clean of the colour of sin, scab, smudge, / Pestilence,
death, rats that carry plague, / Darkness such as blots the sky when locusts
swarm" (16).

In spite of these changes, "it" startles the speaker by recognizing him in
terms of "obscene memory": " 'Nigger!' it cried, seeing / Through the sea's
disguise as only children can" (16). This cry "confirm[s] its breed," that is,
as one of Turner's or of "the other artists" in whose sea he remains drowned
and in whose vision he remains framed. Now he can only remember what
he has forgotten. Turner's parceling of the captives, "children subtracted /
From mothers," (18) has caused the speaker to forget, over many years, her
face, clothing, and ornaments until he no longer calls for her and has "even
forgotten the words" (18).

Forgotten, scenes of his past and his mother appear in terms of the
present moment, the drowning of bodies:

> ... We float like ghosts to fields
> Of corn. All day I am a small boy
> Nibbling at whatever grain falls from
> My mother's breast as she bends and weaves
> Before the crop, hugging a huge bundle
> Of cobs to her body, which flames
> In the sun, which blinds me as I look up
> From her skirt, which makes me reach like a drowning
> Man gropes at the white crest of waves, thinking it
> Rope. I can no longer see her face
> In the blackness. The sun has reaped my eyes.   (22)

The sun is Turner's famous light which, in this re-creation of the painting's
floating bodies, "like ghosts," flaming light, drowning men, and crests of
waves, blinds the speaker. Painted as a body plunged into blackness, he
can't see beyond the sublime scene and style, with its deliberate terror, that
holds him captive.

In the preface to *Turner*, Dabydeen states that "[t]he intensity of Turner's
painting is such that I believe the artist in private must have savoured the
sadism he publicly denounced" (x). Whatever Turner's psychological or
moral disposition, the conventions of the genre in which he paints take
over. The cry of "Nigger!" from the newly born, yet resurrected, head sounds
through time, making it clear that, either way, the speaker remains without

sight of his own, captive to the aesthetic terms in which he is painted, which render him an object of sublime horror in the eyes of those who see him:[65]

> ... "Nigger"
> It cries, naming itself, naming the gods,
> The earth and its globe of stars. It dips
> Below the surface, frantically it tries to die,
> To leave me beadless, nothing and a slave
> To nothingness, to the white enfolding
> Wings of Turner brooding over my body,
> Stopping my mouth, drowning me in the yolk
> Of myself . . .   (39)

As if this were not enough to convince the reader of the poem's decisive conclusion, Dabydeen stresses in the preface that "Neither can escape Turner's representation of them as exotic and sublime victims. Neither can describe themselves anew but are indelibly stained by Turner's language and imagery" (x).

Turner thus names and insists upon the double-bind of a modernity that positions the universal Subject as the one who has developed the capacity for sight, a condition reproduced and sustained by practices of seeing which mark the colonized person of color as excluded from this status. The poem repaints the scene as one in which, as Lamming describes Caliban, the speaker is "denied the power to see." In this ontological economy of vision, the speaker of Dabydeen's poem can never gain new life for it would require that he achieve visual agency. If he fills the child's mouth with imagined scenes of a redemptive past, he only imitates Turner who ". . . crammed our boys' mouths too with riches, / His tongue spurting strange potions upon ours / Which left us dazed, which made us forget / The very sound of our speech" (38). Most importantly, Turner forced, as in the act of rape, his aesthetic on them:

> And we repeated in a trance the words
> That shuddered from him: *blessed, angelic,*
> *Sublime*; words that seemed to flow endlessly
> From him, filling our mouths and bellies
> Endlessly.   (38)

The exercise of transfiguration, in all of its beauty and terror, has been done, on and through the bodies of drowning Africans. In Dabydeen's poem, the consciousness imagined for those bodies can never reinvent the terms through which to escape the scene in which they appear for those terms have already painted them and thus pre-figured them, "endlessly."

Even if the speaker fails, however, we need not read the poem as failing in the effort at trans-figuration. Its very articulation of the entrapment of modernity's visual economy sees through it. Making possible this poetic exposé of the painting and all it represents are the partial subject, the vanishing, only to reappear, head, the floating, still-born, yet awakening consciousness of the speaker, the hidden yet envisioned mother, and the partial-born child. These partial presences inhabit the painting as the limbs, arms, hands, and submerged heads of the drowning Africans, and they also appear as only partially there to someone in the process of losing his sight. They signal the state of metamorphosis and the power of what cannot yet be represented.

The fact that Dabydeen imagines a consciousness for "the submerged head of the African in the foreground of Turner's painting" (ix) signifies the entire poem as a partially absent ekphrasis – that is, an extended verbal description of what cannot be fully seen in the painting, but only imaginatively envisioned through words. The poem counters then, what Gilroy has called "the slave sublime" but from the imagined fragments of a partial, yet multiple, vision. It thus gives subjectivity to those whose drowning bodies and denied subjectivities have made possible the sense of the sublime in men of property. With this resurrected subjectivity, created from what is not fully represented in the painting, develops a renewed capacity to see and, especially, to see through the visual ontological relationship that, paradoxically, keeps the speaker of the poem "... a slave / To nothingness, to the white enfolding / Wings of Turner brooding over my body."

***

Resurrection propels also the narrative of Fred D'Aguiar's *Feeding the Ghosts*. When the slave, Mintah, tossed overboard not because she was "sick and dying" but for insubordination, manages to grasp a rope, pull herself back onto the ship, and appear again below deck, she becomes a god to the remaining slaves and begins a new life for herself.[66] In this novel, the scene depicted in Turner's painting is reconstructed in three parts: as a third-person narrative, taking place during the overthrowing of the slaves; as a courtroom narrative, taking place during the subsequent trial of the ship's captain, Cunningham, accused by the insurance company of fraud and then acquitted; and as Mintah's first-person recollection of her life long after the events on the *Zong*, as an elderly, free and landowning woman in Jamaica. A final chapter returns to third-person narration, followed by an epilogue, once more in the first person, but this time in the voice of an unnamed speaker, both "I" and "we."

Narrated through multiple points of view, the novel portrays moral transformations in all characters, including Captain Cunningham, ironically acquitted due to sympathy he receives when undergoing a crisis in court. At this moment, he hallucinates the court building as a ship and himself as "forced to share the sea with Africans. All the Africans he had ever dumped into the sea, living or dead," and he nearly faints from the pressure.[67] The dialogue and narrative of this courtroom scene expose the legal rationalization of slavery in which a judge might feel uneasy because "131 pieces" (131 living, enslaved Africans thrown overboard) were "too much" (167) but take refuge in the logic of the defense which claims that Captain Cunningham, in fact, protected his property and his investors by carefully separating and destroying the sick and dying so that they might not infect the others. The ledger Cunningham kept, carefully recording each murder, becomes evidence of his responsible and meticulous accounting. Events absent from the ledger are proclaimed in court twice – in the testimony of a young cook's assistant and in a diary the assistant produces which Mintah kept while hiding in the ship's storeroom. According to this evidence, Cunningham forced a reluctant crew to throw overboard living and healthy human beings including children. He also faced a rebellion of the slaves led by Mintah. These accounts, however, are dismissed as "simple-minded" in the first case and "penned by a ghost" in the second (169). Significantly, the fact that Cunningham's ledger does not record either Mintah's "resurrection" or the insurrection on board ship proves, in the court's eyes, that she could not have existed. She could exist only if the man who owned her could see and represent her.

As the narrative of *Feeding the Ghosts* envisions Mintah, she becomes a discrete subject, whose capacity for sight is clearly established as an alternative to the empiricist vision of capitalist accounting. This capacity appears in her talent for woodcarving, an art she learned from her father in Africa. She also, however, emerges in relationship to those who hold her captive and, thus, she exercises a powerful effect on them. In this way, the narrative echoes the multiple and shared identities of Turner in Dabydeen's poem but avoids collapsing them into a prevailing vision of the commodity sublime. Rather, as the elderly Mintah recalls her initial meeting with the ship's First Mate, Kelsal, she remembers that "I was him, he me" (195). This merging of identities took place before she was captured, at a Danish mission where she nursed him during his recovery from fever, calling his name and introducing herself as a way of restoring him. In his confusion he replied, "I am Mintah?" (195). Cunningham's dizzying identification in court with "[a]ll the Africans he had ever dumped into the sea, living or dead" (165) indicates the power of the slaves to affect the consciousness and actions of the slavers. In this way, by momentarily becoming her, they cannot help but see Mintah and even see *as* Mintah.

We might read the intersubjectivity and multiplicity of selves in *Turner* and *Feeding the Ghosts* as effects of twentieth-century literary experiments with subjectivity. However, they relate also to the art Mintah practices when she earns her freedom. In the traditions of African woodcarving she learned from her father and renewed in the Americas appear versions of the "self-multiplying power" portrayed in carvings of the Yoruba god Eshu. Robert Farris Thompson identifies this characteristic of Yoruba art in carvings made in the Americas, a way of seeing that Mintah activates in her woodcarving and that visually echoes the narrative multiplication of selves.[68]

Moreover, the carvings prompt an alternate way of looking that sees art, not as object but active participant in its own meaning. Throughout the first part of the novel, Mintah sees through the eyes of a woodcarver; she herself becomes wood, imagines herself as grained, and names wood as her ally. The rope she grabs to haul herself back on board is "plaited grain," and it saves her (53). Throughout the voyage, she dreams of carving: "Shapes from her sleep were buried in wood for her to find; shapes hidden underground, that were the secrets of the earth, surfaced inside wood and were there for her to uncover" (119). However, Mintah's carvings surprise her by coming from the sea as much as the earth: "They said the wood I worked resembled water in its curves and twists. The very element I sought to escape rose out of wood shaped by me. Trees became waves. Waves sprouted roots, branches and leaves. My carvings exchanged the two and made the sea home, at least in my head" (207). Her cabin is crowded with 131 pieces of wood that make her visitors uneasy. Similar to the unease felt by viewers of Turner's painting, people "love what I do with wood but cannot keep such a shape in their homes" (209). In Mintah's eyes, however, the pieces arise as individuals with names, preferences, breath and, "now today," freedom (210–11).

In a dream, the carved shapes dance, and Mintah recognizes herself in the pattern of a young woman's movements. She realizes that she has misunderstood them and that "[n]ow they were here before me showing me their meaning, and I had helped to shape it" (218). Art transforms in this scene from a still object of the contemplative gaze – bound in its commodity status to the slave trade, and proof, like that of the slave's incapacity for sight, of the man of property's power to see – into an active subject, creator of its own meaning. Still shaped through the figure of the black person, the carvings are bound to Mintah in shared creation and, thus, participate in the "learning of looking" that she continues to experience, learning to see, for instance, her multiple selves in their dance. Crucial to Mintah's visual education is the memory she retains of her father's lessons; she works as his apprentice, not an imitator of the English painter in whose scene she drowns.

Working as her father's apprentice, however, does not mean that she re-creates his art, intact, in the Americas. Rather, the carvings respond to the experiences of the Middle Passage, surprising even Mintah with the changes they undergo. Still linked to her father and to Africa, Mintah nevertheless, participates in the creation of a new and dynamic culture, one she learns to see as she works. This dynamic invokes both the newness of her world and its connection to that of her father where the arts of seeing are highly developed. As Thompson points out, Yoruba art from Western Africa provides ritual contact with divinity and grants the religious celebrant a radiance of the eyes that signifies "the brightness of the spirit" (9). Thompson quotes a Yoruba divination priest:

The gods have "inner" or "spiritual" eyes (*ojú inún*) with which to see the world of heaven and "outside eyes" (*ojú ode*) with which to view the world of men and women. When a person comes under the influence of a spirit, his ordinary eyes swell to accommodate the inner eyes, the eyes of the god. He will then look very broadly across the whole of the devotees, he will open his eyes abnormally.[69]

This art of seeing with both inner and outer eyes, "very broadly" and "abnormally," is central to Yoruba spiritual practices on the African continent and in the Americas, as evidenced by stories told by Yoruba descendants in the Caribbean.[70] In D'Aguiar's novel, fundamental aesthetic practices and ideas survive the Middle Passage; yet in their re-creation, something uniquely Afro-Caribbean emerges. Anthropologists Sally and Richard Price have stressed the specificity and uniqueness of these "New World" cultures; however, they recognize basic aesthetic principles as legacies from Africa, including "ideas about the human body as an aesthetic form, notions about rhythm (in music, in speech, in the visual arts), expectations about dynamism and change in the arts."[71] These qualities bring Mintah's carvings alive, even if only in a dream, as dancers who teach her to see in old and new ways.

The importance of woodcarving in *Feeding the Ghosts* recalls the work of the Jamaican sculptors Edna Manley and Ronald Moody, who exhibited their carvings in the Caribbean, England, Europe, and the

United States throughout much of the twentieth century. In Chapter 2, I discuss the traditions from several world cultures that meet in their work. Their entry into the British art scene in the 1920s and 1930s reshaped modernism in the arts by figuring the colonized person of color as an agent of creative vision. Their work also established precedents in Caribbean visual art for the ekphrastic encounters with visual hegemony in postcolonial Caribbean literary texts such as those by Cliff, Dabydeen, and D'Aguiar.

D'Aguiar's novel, then, does something similar to Dabydeen's poem by creating a character and consciousness unseen in Turner's painting and in the verbal records of the actual incident. As an ekphrastic narrative, it extends the device of ekphrasis to describe that which is absent from visual representation. While Dabydeen's poem escapes the tyranny of Turner's vision by acknowledging it and, thus, seeing through it into the metamorphoses of partial presences and absent figures, D'Aguiar's novel pulls from the Middle Passage an Afro-Caribbean art form, linked to African traditions, in which art itself takes on new meaning. Similar to Cliff's *Free Enterprise* in its images of metamorphic partial presences and glimpses of the arts of the black Atlantic, *Turner* and *Feeding the Ghosts* register a heterochronic temporality, multiple spatial reality, and polysubjectivity coincident with their aesthetic of trans-figuration.

***

Working through vision as a social act; an epistemology; institutionalized discourse of art, aesthetics, and subjectivity; and a trope for spiritual transformation, Caribbean writers thus address the past and remake the sensory body, moving into an experience of space and time that asks us to question and reconceive the temporal chronologies of succession in our repeated use of terms such as the modern, the postmodern, and the postcolonial. It is not just a matter of finding new terms for history, but of thinking about subjectivity, time, and space differently, as Wilson Harris writes, "of extending our senses" and recognizing the stranger within the self and the "organs of the past" within the resurrected body of the present.

In the chapters that follow I argue that writers from the Caribbean have long engaged an aesthetics of trans-figuration, establishing precedents for the current cross-Atlantic conversations among younger writers such as Cliff, Dabydeen, and D'Aguiar about visual art and acts of seeing. Some of these precedents, such as the sculpture of Edna Manley and Ronald Moody, carried forward traditional African and Amerindian arts, rerouted

European primitivism through the African diaspora, and deliberately modeled black figures as seers. To understand with more historical specificity the importance of vision to these artists and to the writers, such as C. L. R. James, Una Marson, Jean Rhys, and Claude McKay who crossed from the Caribbean to Britain and in some cases to the United States, I investigate the cultural environment they encountered as émigrés in the early part of the century. This environment and the creation within and against it of a Caribbean *contra-modernism* form the subject of the next chapter, *Exhibitions/Modernisms 1900–1939*. The convergence in 1919 of intense social contradictions that sparked racial violence often in response to the "sight" of black men in Britain and, in 1924, the display of colonized people as living parts of a popular imperial modernism at the British Empire Exhibition are crucial to understanding the visual cultural politics in which Caribbean émigrés found themselves in the early decades of the twentieth century. Simultaneously, through exhibitions in England, Jamaica, France, and the United States, a transcultural and transnational Caribbean modernism emerged in the sculpture of Edna Manley and Ronald Moody, artists whose work joined with the literary modernism of writers such as McKay and Rhys to lay a foundation for the arts of seeing practiced later in the century by writers of the Caribbean.

Exhibitions/modernisms 1900–1939

In an essay titled "Seeing," the Trinidadian/Canadian writer and film-maker Dionne Brand contrasts her way of seeing and filming black women to that of the white cinematographer and "head of camera" with whom she has worked on various film projects. In her assessment of their visual orientation, they focus on the face and skin, excluding the whole body, its stance and movement. They also want shots angled so that viewers feel that the women in the film see the viewers, not each other. The conflict Brand describes conveys the effects of a certain visual exhibition of black women; it also analyzes the construction of white/black and black/black relationships through different ways of seeing, which include most significantly what is not seen in the gaze of the white cinematographer: "a full Black woman."[1] The power dynamics of the filmic gaze are familiar to critics as a way of reading film narrative and image; here, Brand considers them in the tensions experienced while actually making a film. What strikes me most, however, is the metaphor she invokes as a summation of the power of vision itself: "The eye has citizenship and possessions" (169).

Given the context, we might read the metaphor as recognizing the imagined community of an imperial nation as also an *imaged* nation, an entity made possible through the creation of images that interpellate, through various angles of vision, its citizens and its colonial, racialized others. But another way of interpreting the metaphor is to read the eye itself as exercising the powers of empire. The emphasis shifts in this reading away from images themselves to acknowledgment of the sense of sight. Above all other senses, then, the eye enjoys an imperial power, obligating its citizens and claiming its possessions. Brand's metaphor illuminates the complex intertwining of imperial power and bodily sense that, as discussed in the previous chapter, enabled the construction of the modern subject-who-sees in opposition to the figure of the African. As Brand and other writers and artists from the Caribbean repeatedly indicate, this construction – at the heart of the slave trade's intersection with eighteenth-century aesthetics – lingers in everyday acts of seeing that they must counter in their transformations of the aesthetic principles and subject positions undergirding modernity.

For many Caribbean writers and artists, the aesthetic transformations they effect become also transformations they experience, as their own ways of seeing undergo radical alterations in the course of transatlantic migration from the Caribbean to England, Canada, Europe, or the United States, often back to the Caribbean, and then away again. Writers as disparate as Brand, with her leftist and feminist political orientations, and V. S. Naipaul, with his far more conservative responses to global politics, portray these conflicts and transformations as matters of the eye. In Naipaul's memoir/novel, *The Enigma of Arrival,* he reflects on his experiences on first arriving and the changes he underwent in his first years in England as transformations in seeing – what he saw, how he saw it, and what he could not see. He describes the state of arrival in these terms: "I saw what I saw very clearly. But I didn't know what I was looking at. I had nothing to fit it into. I was still in a kind of limbo."[2] He finds in a book of reproductions a painting by Chirico, titled by Apollinaire *The Enigma of Arrival,* and it becomes the space into which he fits what he was seeing. He casts the changes he experiences as a journey of the eye, and the memoir becomes an extended ekphrastic appropriation of the painting and of the aesthetic gaze. In one passage, he grieves the experience he lost because he was unable to see it, as a writer, during his early residence in London: "I had found, if only I had had the eyes to see, a great subject": "the beginning of that great movement of peoples that was to take place in the second half of the twentieth century – . . . a movement between all continents" (141). Ironically, he believes he was unable to see this subject because of the ideas about becoming a writer that he brought with him, "the ideas of the aesthetic movement of the end of the nineteenth century and the ideas of Bloomsbury, ideas bred essentially out of empire, wealth, and imperial security . . . transmitted to me in Trinidad" (146).

Though Naipaul blames his faulty vision on the colonial imposition of modernist aesthetics and notions of what it means to be a writer, he fails in his analysis to recognize the presence in England of Caribbean and other colonial artists, writers, and intellectuals during the period of the modernist movements. British modernism traveled to Trinidad to influence him, but his émigré predecessors also traveled to Britain to influence it. And, as he perceptively and repeatedly asserts about his own migration and arrival, these were journeys of the eye that prompted transformations in seeing in which he was to participate in later decades. Though Naipaul locates its beginning with his arrival, the "movement between all continents" began much earlier than 1950. By crossing nations, including those of Europe, Britain, and the United States, these transcontinental movements created disturbances of vision, unsettled identities based on citizenship, and questioned the politics of possession. New transnational identities emerged with different ways of seeing and, most importantly, the project of questioning the imperial position long enjoyed by the sense of sight.

In this chapter, I analyze the year 1919, rather than 1950, as a turning point for the many Caribbean émigrés in Britain who, at the end of World War I, experienced the trauma of racial violence. Their increased presence in Britain, the discrimination they faced, and the racial violence sparked at the war's end brought about changes in the notion of Englishness that remapped its cities and towns in racialized visual terms. As if in reaction to these colonial conflicts at home, interwar visual exhibitions, such as those put on by the Empire Marketing Board and the British Empire Exhibition of 1924, reinterpreted England's imperial powers for millions of English men, women, and children through displays of colonial products and "living exhibitions" of colonized people. In the chapter's second section, I focus on the visual media through which Britain reformulated its ideology of empire following the events of 1919, concentrating on the conjunction of modernist aesthetics with popular imperial culture in the 1924 British Empire Exhibition at Wembley.

Addressing this domestic racism and the atrocities of the larger colonial system, Caribbean émigrés analyzed its icons and visual rhetoric politically – through the formation of social organizations, Pan-African conferences, and newspapers published specifically for colonized people of color. They also addressed it through the arts – in sculpture, plays, novels, poetry, and essays. The third section of this chapter brings critical attention to the transatlantic Caribbean modernism created through the exhibitions of Edna Manley's and Ronald Moody's sculpture in England, the Caribbean, Europe, and the United States. Portraying, through a visual medium, people of African descent as visionaries, Manley and Moody countered the "native" stereotypes and colonial gaze of the Empire Exhibition. They also contributed to a heterogeneous modernism in the arts in which black people were gaining what George Lamming later called "the power to see." To engage with British culture in these ways involved a complex shift in subject position for colonial émigrés who intervened in the contradictions of British imperialism as citizens of the empire who were also considered its possessions. The contradictions that pushed them toward this conflicted agency were showing themselves, not just in the distant colonies, but more than ever, within the national boundaries of Britain.

When Horatio Bottomley in 1919 promoted the slogan, "Britain for the British socially and industrially,"[3] he was headlining a postwar campaign to exclude Germans from entry to Britain, an entity ruled by a monarch of direct German descent. To do so, he appealed to an imagined nationality larger than England, somehow a result of nature rather than a history of invasions, conquests, colonization, transculturation, and resistance to such forces. His slogan attempted to constitute a group of people called "British" with a natural and exclusive right to the land on which they then were living. Though many of these Britons, such as the Welsh and the Irish, had different cultural traditions and spoke languages other than English, his slogan attempted to unite them against a newly differentiated "Other."

Bottomley's efforts, against all history and contemporary evidence to the contrary, to construct a purely British identity followed on previous similar attempts to imagine a national identity, even a "race." As a number of cultural critics, including Anthony Appiah, Paul Gilroy, and Ian Baucom have pointed out, ideologies of racial purity have long suppressed a history of cultural mixing in favor of an imagined nation of "Anglo-Saxons." Though the term itself connotes a mix, it nevertheless became associated with something considered "purely" English.[4]

Bottomley's anti-immigration campaign found enough support to result in the 1919 Aliens Act, which restricted the immigration of Chinese and allowed limitations on other immigrants, especially Germans, Eastern European Jews, and "Bolshevik sympathizers."[5] The act was renewed annually until 1971 and allowed governments throughout those years to limit in varying ways and to varying measure the influx of "aliens" to Britain.[6] Passage of the act signals the fact that immigration was perceived as threatening to the nationality called English or British and also that immigration had taken place to some considerable degree before 1919. During the nineteenth century, immigration had indeed changed the demography of England and especially the ethnic composition of London, altering its social geography and its "look." In addition to large groups of workers from Ireland; small groups of entrepreneurs from Germany and Switzerland; political exiles from France, Italy, Austria, and Germany; Jewish people from Central and Eastern Europe; and immigrants from China; those from the distant colonies also sustained a presence throughout Britain before 1919. Peter Fryer and Colin Holmes, among others, have fully documented the presence of increasing numbers of black people in Britain from as early as the third century. The migrations of black people across the Atlantic have not only influenced the social condition we have come to call modernity, but constituted it. As Paul Gilroy's argument in *The Black Atlantic* reminds us, the fortunes that funded the industrial revolution in England depended on the slave trade, and the forced contributions of black people's labor as well as their contributions in politics, philosophy, science, and the arts formed the backbone and much of the consciousness of modern culture.

Focusing on the twentieth century, we can speak of these contributions as extending a *contra-modernity*, to borrow Homi Bhabha's phrase, resulting from the global reach of imperialism, yet countering the assumptions of colonialist discourses, opposing imperial practices, and doing so most effectively through transnational alliances and appeals to Enlightenment ideals of humanism, progress, and reason. In the transcontinental connections made through the Pan-African congresses held in England and Europe from 1900 through the interwar years, or the African Progress Union, or League of Coloured Peoples, colonized people of color became the agents of a resistant, yet still global vision. Their analyses claimed for themselves the reason that eighteenth-century philosophers had conceptualized as based on a capacity for contemplative sight of which they were deemed incapable. Further, their arguments relied on acts of seeing that exposed the imperial system and its injustices. For example, the African socialism espoused by many of the early twentieth-century Pan-Africanists such as Edward Blyden and Marcus Garvey argued for an analysis of labor, production, and consumption that adapted Marx's notion of commodity fetishism to the racial relations of empire and a global economy. In his 1928 speech in the Royal Albert Hall, Marcus Garvey invited his audience to see commodities such as raw cotton differently:

The cotton mills of Lancashire, the great shipping port of Liverpool, tell the tale of what we have done as black men for the British Empire. The cotton that you consume and use in keeping your mills going has for centuries come from the Southern States of the United States; it is the product of Negro labour. Upon that cotton your industry has prospered and you have been able to build a great Empire to-day.[7]

In this speech, Garvey asks his audience to see deeply into the history of commodities and broadly across national boundaries, and specifically, to imagine the transatlantic racialized labor relations behind the surface of industrial success.

Active as these early émigrés were in transforming their own visions and those with whom they organized, they faced intense conflicts, inner and outer, as Caribbean people of African descent residing in Britain. The conflicts, in many ways, galvanized the changes they went through. The career of Dr. Harold Moody, who became a political organizer, typifies the obstacles encountered by educated émigrés from the Caribbean in the early part of the century. Like the somewhat younger C. L. R. James, for example, Harold Moody came to Britain educated by the colonial system to admire everything British and then faced, within the "mother country," the racist discrimination of the colonial system. Though they took different paths politically, Moody and James gained in England a new understanding of the conjunction of racism and colonialism that raised their political consciousness and impelled them to activism. Barred, in spite of numerous academic prizes, from a hospital position, Moody opened instead a private practice and began a long campaign against racist practices in employment and housing. In March of 1931, he organized the League of Coloured Peoples and, in July 1933, published the first issue of the organization's newspaper, the *Keys.*[8] Moody's house at 164 Queen's Road became a center of welcome and orientation for new arrivals from the Caribbean. According to his biographer, David A. Vaughan, however, Moody felt an extreme alienation during his first years in England caused by the racism he encountered. In Moody's case and that of other colonial émigrés, educated to believe in the superiority of British culture, this alienation was compounded by internal contradictions. According to Vaughan, his education led him

to look down on Africans as a species too low in the scale of human development for him to associate with them in any way. He was black indeed, but he resolutely refused in his own mind to admit that he was an African, or that he was in any way related to Africa. This was tragic for him and his race. It involved a dichotomy in his personality. In education and culture he was English but in temperament and colour he was not. Where did he really belong? He found this question almost impossible to answer.[9]

The split in Moody that Vaughan describes went far beyond his own personality to the contradictions between Enlightenment philosophies of freedom and the values of property. Those founding principles of modernity positioned black people as objects of property, undeveloped in their sensory capacities or inherently incapable of such development. Returning to Dionne Brand's metaphor of the eye as having both citizenship and possessions, for Moody and others like him, it would be a question of which of these they could be, citizen or possession.

However, the discrimination Moody faced in pursuing his medical career along with knowledge of similar experiences endured by others led him in very practical ways to recognize the need for unity and organization among people of African descent in England. Significantly, Moody's transformation into an organizer on behalf of black immigrants did not erase his earlier allegiances to English "education and culture"; of necessity, the two existed side by side in his work and identity. Occupying these two apparently contradictory positions transformed them, through practice and example, from oppositional to dynamically linked identities. What seemed a paradox to later generations comprised a difficult but productive tension in Moody's generation and those who came to Britain before him.

Discussing earlier, nineteenth-century immigrants from the Caribbean such as Mary Seacole and J. J. Thomas, Simon Gikandi has made the point that the narratives they wrote occupied two worlds and "seemed to exist both inside and outside the central doctrines of Englishness."[10] Commenting on Thomas's critique of James Anthony Froude's racist doctrine of empire, Gikandi describes Thomas's text as an example of "the ways in which the colonized subject fashioned itself by both questioning and appropriating the civilizational authority of Englishness" (xiv). He notes that identification with the ideals of Englishness did not obscure identification with special, local cultures, in Thomas's case of Trinidad, which had shaped the colonized person's life. Belinda Edmondson has developed this insight, expanding it to an understanding of virtually all Caribbean intellectuals before independence. She argues that the Victorian concept of the Englishman as a "Literary Man" established an association between literary culture, masculinity, and national identity that the Caribbean intellectual internalized and that became also the basis for the development of West Indian and Pan-African consciousness. Also using Thomas's critique of Froude as her example, she explicates the coexistence in his narrative of a West Indian claim to Englishness and a remarkable Pan-Africanist perspective. She sees in the text a fusion of the identities conventionally opposed as Englishness/whiteness and West Indianness/ blackness and concludes, "It is this apparent paradox which is the staple of West Indian discourse of the pre-independence era, and indeed for part of the post-independence era."[11]

While both Gikandi and Edmondson correctly find this apparent paradox in the narratives of writers such as Thomas and stress the coexistence of the two poles of opposition, I would emphasize the physical movement of migration and the inner transformations that led to their writings. Most importantly, I would stress that through this apparent paradox and the transformations they underwent, they were able to intervene in a lingering philosophy and political economy of vision that cast them outside of modernity, as objects to be seen in the construction of the modern European subject.

The impact they made and the changes they effected had much to do with the uncertain location of their subjectivities and also of their actual "place." As they actively engaged it, and as it had already been constructed in the discourses of conquest and colonialism, their exile occupied a space imagined as "elsewhere," neither here nor there, real nor wholly imagined. By historical accident and discursive repetition, the Caribbean and, by extension, the Caribbean person came from a virtual no place. As Belinda Edmondson points out, by "discovering" the wrong place and misnaming it, Columbus fixed the West Indies as a place that could not exist on its own terms: "The West Indies, as the region was (and still is) called, was 'somewhere else': not Europe, not Africa, not India" (20). Edmondson contends that this vague location of elsewhere has shaped an entire discourse of West Indian narrative. For the Europeans, and especially Victorian England, the quality of elsewhere merged with a feminization of the islands in a code that opposed them to an active, masculinized and centrally placed England but did not equate them with the savagery associated with Africa. Rather it designated the West Indies as a place without an identity, lacking or failing in civilization. Edmondson argues that the ways in which the English imagination saw the West Indies, in opposition to the qualities of Englishness epitomized in the notion of a gentleman, in turn shaped the ways in which Caribbean intellectuals saw themselves. She then points to the effects of this discourse on the first generation of Caribbean literary men such as C. L. R. James and V. S. Naipaul: "This relationship with Victorian England in turn affected the first generation of West Indian writers in their efforts to define West Indianness, in which geographical unreality, cultural lack, and racial inferiority all converged to define the terms of writing" (20).

The opposition also shaped the terms in which Caribbean writers would develop their critiques of British imperialism and racism. If we accept Edmondson's argument concerning the English perception of the West Indies as located "somewhere else," we must ask how this perception affected the way West Indian immigrants in England were seen and saw themselves. Though color was an important marker of difference, the difference signified something associated with Africa, yet different from that also. When a black British intellectual, as C. L. R. James saw himself on coming to England, attaches also to an identity of coming from a non-place, "somewhere else," by virtue of being imagined that way, yet is displaced from there to occupy the place, as a British subject, that is England, who, or where, is he? If, like Una Marson, the black intellectual is a woman, from a place coded both "elsewhere" and feminine, how much stronger is the sense of displacement following on mis-identification? These questions, emerging from a complex tangle of colonialist perceptions, policies, and practices, involve a way of seeing that Caribbean writers transform into a narrative critique and reinvention of vision. Crucial to this reinvented vision, as I argue in subsequent chapters, is direct confrontation with the charge of artistic imitation, the charge leveled against the Afro-Jamaican poet Francis Williams by David Hume in the eighteenth century that continued to challenge artists and writers from the Caribbean throughout the twentieth century. As a new valuation of sensory experience, these questions of subjectivity and location have to do with identity but, more than that, with a way of being in the world, experiencing one's body, exercising one's senses, and perceiving oneself in relation to others and the natural world. As a creative dynamic, it began long before World War II, and the conditions in which Caribbean exiles saw and were seen took several turns throughout the century.

The trope of "elsewhere" shaping West Indian narratives and their politics of vision hinged on constructions of Britishness and Englishness that contextualized the entrance into Britain of immigrants from the Caribbean. First used to reconstitute British identity against German, Central European, and Chinese immigrants, the 1919 Aliens Act allowed later governments to restrict immigration from other countries, including the more distant and former colonies. Drawing on Raymond Williams's work as well as that of Edward Said and Linda Colley, Simon Gikandi suggests that we understand Britishness as an identity superimposed over internal cultural differences in opposition to an external, colonized Other that, nevertheless, "was a constitutive element in the invention of Britishness."[12] Ian Baucom has pushed this insight further in his attempt to understand the ideological differences between concepts of Englishness and Britishness. More than notions of "race," Baucom emphasizes instead the value given to *place* in past constructions of British and English identity. Baucom charts changes in legislation governing immigration and nationality that eventually, by 1948, distinguished different kinds of space as British and English:

Englishness has been identified *with* Britishness, which in its turn has been identified as coterminous with and proceeding from the sovereign territory of the empire, and . . . Englishness has also defined itself *against* the British Empire, first by retaining a spatial theory of collective identity but privileging the English *soil* of the "sceptered isle" or, more regularly, certain quintessentially English locales, as its authentic identity-determining locations.[13]

If we pull together the major threads of Gikandi's, Edmondson's, and Baucom's arguments, any description of the "place" of Caribbean immigrants in British society becomes intensely complex. Caribbean immigrants settled in many towns and cities of Britain, often occupying simultaneously a local English place and, as colonial subjects, an imperial, British space – but as outsiders, often of color. Furthermore, they came from a place long imagined as not an actual place but "somewhere else." If they were educated intellectuals or professionals, they identified with English culture and values. Yet they retained some attachment to local Caribbean cultures and, additionally, acquired a regional sense of themselves as "West Indian" that allied them with other immigrants from other countries of the Caribbean. Beyond that, being of African descent, they very likely allied with immigrants from Africa and, being colonial subjects, with immigrants from India and other colonies. As citizens of "British" space, they could expect a place in Britain, but they could not fully occupy it because they were not white and not born on "English" soil. The tension between citizen and possession resulted frequently in dispossession; yet it also prompted political and artistic movements across these exclusionary and shifting boundaries in a creative refiguring of "elsewhere."[14]

The gap between the ideals acquired as citizens of British space, with its "English" notions of progress, enlightenment, and equality, and the reality of a racist local Englishness motivated men like Moody and James in their turn towards political activism. Social and political activism gained momentum and involved many immigrants from the Caribbean during and just after World War I. One reason was the wave of racist violence against black workers in Britain just as the war ended. In the year, 1919, of Bottomley's call for "Britain for the British," acts of collective racially motivated violence broke out all over Britain and spread to the Caribbean. In this year, social contradictions of class, race, and sexual relations intensified, especially in the port cities, such as Liverpool, on British ships, and in the urban neighborhoods where black veterans had begun to settle. The year 1919, more than the post-World War II years of the Windrush or of Naipaul's arrival, thus marks a turning point in the political, literary, and artistic crossings piloted by Caribbean émigrés in Britain.[15] Key figures in the intellectual and artistic life of the black Atlantic, such as Claude McKay and Edna Manley, began work in England that year. Newspapers, such as the *African Telegraph*, published diverse rhetorical strategies for addressing the crisis faced by immigrants of color and deepened their analyses to include the entire scope of the imperial system. The social tensions and racial violence of this year developed from the conditions created, in part, by World War I and, to a great extent, the settlement of immigrants of all kinds who faced, as did the black war veterans, intense hostility and discrimination.

Though middle-class immigrants made an impact culturally and politically, the largest groups of Caribbean immigrants in the late nineteenth and early twentieth centuries were men who had worked on ships and then settled in or near British ports. They served, voluntarily and sometimes by force, the British Empire in World War I, yet were refused equal credit for that effort. The hostility they faced from whites intensified as the war began to wind down and returning white soldiers perceived their place in British society threatened by an increased population of black men. The class tensions of British society compounded with those of colonialism and immigration to further exacerbate the gap between what Baucom has described as "British" space, supposedly inhabited by all members of the empire, and "English" space, belonging to the locally born and characterized by supposedly unique and local traditions.

These contradictions intensified to spark the widespread racial violence of 1919. Though conventionally characterized as a transition from war to peace, this period was marked by extreme nationalism, xenophobia, and racism. Acts of collective violence took place in a number of cities, including Glasgow, Winchester, Tyneside, London, Liverpool, and Cardiff. Including "attacks on Chinese, Greeks, and 'coloured men'" in Cardiff and "an antiblack reign of terror" in Liverpool, the assaults exploded in reaction to racist tensions over employment and sexual relations.[16] In descriptions and analyses of these tensions, we can see how the language of vision and space operate. The "sight" of a black man with a white woman was often identified as the starting point of racial assaults that grew into riots. From individual color bias, perceptions of ethnicity and color developed into racist mappings of entire cities. Colin Holmes comments that, "Once hostility had developed, the targets of White hostility were exposed on account of their spatial visibility. The *Liverpool Echo*, for example, distinguished between what it called 'China town', 'dark town' and 'other alien quarters'. Such spatial separation also tended in itself to create suspicion" (108–109).

The spatial racialization Holmes describes extended well beyond Britain to the colonies where British ships and docks became sites of renewed racial violence. At the same time, in the Caribbean colonies, the demands of labor joined emerging nationalist feelings and the rise of black consciousness. In some cases, these conflicts followed directly from the riots in Britain, even involving some of the same men and thus spreading to the colonies tensions of the newly racialized cartographies of Britain's cities and towns.

Responses to the events of 1919 from middle-class black intellectuals recognized the racialized visual dynamics of space and citizenship and analyzed them in protest against the violence and discrimination at the war's end. Central to their turns towards political activism was discrimination against black veterans. In July, the same month in which demobilized black soldiers, who had been assaulted by whites in Cardiff, fought with British sailors in Trinidad, black veterans in Britain were denied participation in London's Peace March. The exclusion of veterans of African descent from these official peace celebrations provoked debate and protests among writers for the newspapers serving the African and Caribbean communities in England. Issues of the *African Telegraph* dated July–August 1919 and December 1919 reveal the extent of the anger felt by black intellectuals. Numerous articles in the paper during this year reveal the rhetorical difficulty of simultaneously expressing outrage, analyzing the larger significance of the racism and hypocrisy signaled by the exclusion, and also adhering to the paper's stated principles of political moderation.

By negotiating these apparent contradictions, however, the writers do more than protest specific policies; they also position themselves as fully modern citizens well aware of the racial practices and visual rhetoric that persist in casting them as imperial possessions. One editorial, titled "Discrimination and Disintegration," touches indirectly on the visual culture of racism in British art. The article begins by citing the participation of black men in the war on behalf of "the great empires of the world," fighting "splendidly for democracy, for liberty, justice, and freedom." It describes as "specious promises" those "of the freedom and equality and contentment of the New Age" and asserts, "Black men all the world over are asking today: What have we got? What are we going to get out of it all? The answer, in effect, comes clear, convincing and conclusive: '*Get back to your kennel, you damned dog of a nigger!*'"[17] In his choice of hypothetical invective, the author of this editorial, who is unnamed but is probably Felix Hercules, could not be accused of hyperbole. Though the editorial does not allude directly to the many paintings, prints, and caricatures in which black people were portrayed as dogs or positioned, as in eighteenth-century family portraits, to resemble dogs, he refers indirectly to a visual convention long seen throughout Britain.[18] He is well aware of the visual rhetoric that conditions the racist consciousness, and he addresses it through repetition of this iconic association.

Hercules also focuses on the racist vocabulary of sight that had permeated the mainstream newspapers. Denouncing articles in the British press that portray black men "as the most vicious, sensual, and degraded of the human species," he quotes as evidence phrases alluding to the "horror" of the sight of black men with white women. He elaborates especially on this point as a matter of visual perception:

The *Evening Standard* considered it a "detestable sight" for a black man, no matter his position in society, in his own home, or his service to the Empire, to be seen out with a white woman even of the worst class. A retired colonial Governor considered the association of black and white women, no matter how innocent, a "thing of horror." (253)

The selection, for critique, of phrases that echo and obliquely comment on Kurtz's final words in *Heart of Darkness* and the emphasis on visual perception – a "detestable sight" – indicate attention given to the politics of vision on the part of black writers of this period. Hercules' response to this rhetoric of visual perception is a deepened economic and political analysis of imperialism. He analyzes the "horror" felt by the British and expressed in terms of vision as a dynamic of race and gender that supports racism within the entire imperial system. (He does not comment on the class system reflected in his own phrase, "a white woman even of the worst class.") Noting that "the protection of white girls was cited as a reason for keeping the black man in his place," the article states that the real reason is the need to protect "the theory of superiority of the white man" and "a desire to uphold their prestige even at the cost of slandering a whole race" (253–54). He then points out the history of white male / black female relations, the rape of black women by white men, and the illogic of this racial double standard. The mixing of the races is not what is at stake given the many "half-castes" resulting from the assaults of white men on black women.

Additional articles pursue analysis of the visual "horror" aroused in white people, linking it to the rampant materialism of Europe and the use of colonial violence. Though full of outrage, almost all of these articles join a strategy of analysis, exposé, and moral critique with stated principles of conciliation with imperial Britain. One piece that condemns British atrocities while approving British values is signed by Hercules and titled "Shall Violence Win Applause?" Analyzing the "racial riots," Hercules cites as causal factors the British opposition to any sort of relation between black men and white women, racist rumors, and "the thirst for blood" in the crowds of people who attacked individual men, looted and set homes on fire. He states that the British in these instances are no better than southern US whites or Belgians in the Congo. His conclusion, however, conveys a very different tone when he states, "we believe too well in the good sense and in the spirit of fair play and justice of the British people to imagine for one moment that any further deeds of violence will win applause" (263). The discrepancies in tone reflect a tension similar to that found in writings by earlier immigrants, such as Thomas, and by other immigrants of Hercules' generation, such as Moody, and even a little later, C. L. R. James, in their radical Pan-Africanism joined with allegiance to British ideals.

In a position paper titled "What We Stand For," the paper makes clear its loyalty to Britain, listing its principles as "first and foremost ... the maintenance of our connection with Great Britain ... the best and truest friend of the native races within the Empire" and second, "the ultimate goal of political autonomy within the British Empire." In this second principle, the newspaper takes a stand against "vague notions of self-determination" and, in the fifth, distinguishes itself from "irresponsible agitators." On the whole, the five principles express a faith in reason, logical critique, and in individuals as opposed to systems. While mentioning its stand against "disgraceful measures like the Native Lands Act of 1913" and the Pass Laws in South Africa, the manifesto also states its "faith in the integrity of the British people" (271). Though that faith might reasonably have been shaken during the past two years, the newspaper nevertheless restates it in several issues alongside numerous exposés of racist injustice and colonialist violence. Dedicated to the advancement of African peoples of the empire, the newspaper's writers saw the best way forward through stronger protest against colonial injustice and pointed analysis of state-sanctioned racist violence. They also, however, remained committed to their position as British subjects, demanding simply that Britain live up to its own ideals. The apparent discrepancies between outraged protest and faith in moderate political goals perhaps gave the paper and its writers a sharper, rather than blunter, critical edge. The ideals upheld were "British" and, through them, British colonial atrocities appeared not only cruel and excessive but signs of an enormous failure. At the same time, by upholding such ideals, the writers of "What We Stand For" claim their identities as modern, educated subjects, capable of a broad contemplative vision and critical judgment, a judgment aimed against the colonizing forces which would deem them incapable of it. Exercising their own capacity for the formal sight deemed necessary to reason, writers such as Hercules then developed in his 1919 articles the critique of vision as a racialized epistemology.

As Holmes and Fryer have pointed out, black people in Britain gained self-confidence in these years in spite of the difficulties they faced, and they determined all the more to struggle against racist violence and discrimination. Their struggles took the form of political organization, journalistic protest, and also the literary arts. The December 1919 issue of the *African Telegraph* gives a small but significant signal of how black people in Britain and across the Atlantic were imagining their struggle. One of its articles refers to "the race riots in the US" and describes a memo sent to Congress from six bishops of the African Methodist Episcopal Church. The article remarks on the "unusual note of anger" contained in the memo and the fact that the bishops quote "a poem written by a West Indian negro, a native of Jamaica" that the bishops believe expresses the convictions of "a large number of American citizens of African descent." Though the *African Telegraph* does not name the author, the poem is Claude McKay's "If We Must Die," and the *Telegraph* quotes the last lines: "Like men we'll face the murderous, cowardly pack, / Pressed to the wall, dying but fighting back."[19]

From 1919, when Claude McKay arrived in England, Caribbean émigrés participated actively, not only in politics, but also in literature and the arts. Known mostly as a leading figure in the Harlem Renaissance, McKay also worked in England with Sylvia Pankhurst in the Workers' Socialist Federation and contributed several articles to the organization's newspaper the *Workers' Dreadnought*. One of McKay's *Dreadnought* articles protested a racist pamphlet distributed by an otherwise left-wing editor, E. D. Morel. Though credited with helping to end the atrocities of Leopold's regime in the Congo, Morel propagandized against the use of black troops in occupied Germany, calling it a "Sexual Horror Let Loose by France on the Rhine" and accusing black soldiers of brutally raping white women. McKay objected to "this obscene, maniacal outburst about the sex vitality of black men" and proceeded to challenge the assumptions and stereotypes proclaimed by Morel.[20] McKay took refuge from the racism he experienced in England at a club for black soldiers and another, the International Club, where he met socialists, Communists, anarchists, trade unionists, writers, and journalists from all over the world. At the same time he published a collection of poems, *Spring in New Hampshire*. In the next decade, C. L. R. James and Una Marson exemplified the activist intellectuals who engaged simultaneously in political organizing, journalism, and the arts. Others, such as Ronald Moody, Edna Manley, and Jean Rhys were mostly occupied in England with the arts, though Manley was also engaged in the emerging nationalist politics of Jamaica. Their sculpture, poetry, plays, journalism, and works of fiction appeared everywhere, from art exhibits of the London Group to West End theaters, important newspapers, and major publishing houses.

The active presence of these artists and writers in interwar Britain and the public exhibitions of their work exerted an impact on what we have come to call modernism. Especially through their emphasis on the politics of vision, whether in visual art or works of literature, these exiles from the Caribbean contributed to modernism and laid the groundwork for later postcolonial literatures. The trope of "elsewhere" attached by the British to the West Indies becomes a pivotal element in their work, allowing them to redefine the seen and the unseen and to empower their creativity in many ways. The artistic and literary life of the interwar years, which we have come to know as the period of British high modernism, clearly included the work of a number of Caribbean émigrés, many of them in close contact with English writers, artists, and intellectuals, and all of them involved in the exploration of vision as a social and artistic relationship. To understand their work, it is important to consider the cultures of modernism and ideologies of empire that evolved in the years after World War I and that they encountered when they arrived in Britain. In the next section, I examine the 1924 British Empire Exhibition at Wembley as one of the main cultural events in which modernist visual aesthetics are coupled with a revised notion of the British Empire.

As the social landscape of cities and towns became racialized during and following the war, efforts to mark public space with new ideologies of empire were underway. We can read the British Empire Exhibition of 1924 as a reaction to the 1919 violence and protests against it through revival of British imperial hierarchies at home, in the London suburb of Wembley. By relocating a miniaturized empire in domestic space, British authorities superimposed upon English soil a larger imperial Britain, transforming the contradictions of 1919 into mass entertainment promoted by modernist aesthetics.

EMPIRE EYES: POPULAR IMPERIAL MODERNISM AT WEMBLEY

In the years following the end of World War I, the British government, trade organizations, leaders of nationalist youth movements, and various commercial firms engaged a number of enterprises to aid the British in re-imagining their identity as an imperial power. Some of these were launched by single organizations or individuals and then promoted through government sponsorship, advertising, and in the schools. The most successful of these movements was Empire Day, founded by the Earl of Meath, who also chaired the Duty and Discipline movement. Meath launched Empire Day in the early 1900s as a state school holiday to be spent, in Meath's words, "by the children in exercises of a patriotic and agreeable nature."[21] The holiday became official almost everywhere in England so that, by 1922, 80,000 schools held an Empire Day holiday, and in 1928, one newspaper claimed that 5 million children had participated.[22] This event took advantage of the new sound technology, using the radio and gramophone to further its propaganda. However, it also relied heavily on visual media including plays, pageants, film and slide lectures, posters, displays of empire products, flags, and picture postcards of the empire's industries.[23]

Visual media figured significantly in the promotion of interwar imperial ideologies in other venues as well. Jeffrey Richards has documented the emphasis on imperialism evident in films of the 1930s. He argues that, while propaganda in this period stressed the positive benefits of empire in trade and the circulation of commodities, popular films also continued to emphasize the hard work and self-sacrifice demanded of individuals taking up "The White Man's Burden."[24] Another operation that depended on visual media was the Empire Marketing Board (EMB), formed in 1926 as a political compromise in response to debates over tariff reform. The EMB used all available popular media and advertising methods to promote the consumption of Empire products within Britain. In addition to nation-wide public lectures and, by 1933, an estimated 10 million leaflets and pamphlets, the EMB used billboards and brightly colored product packaging; it displayed the slogan "Buy British" from airplanes and on banners and enormous boards everywhere. Obviously, this particular construction of "British" included the entire empire and was synonymous with it. John Grierson's legendary documentaries educated the English public about "Cargo from Jamaica" (bananas), "Windmill in Barbados" (sugar), and "Drifters" (herring fleets in the North Sea). These films were shown even in the daylight in railroad stations and one film about milk evidently attracted so many viewers at Victoria Station that "it disrupted the running of the Southern Railway and had to be temporarily abandoned" (210–211). Not only talented filmmakers contributed to the cause, but also well-known artists, who designed posters for the campaign. Among these were McKnight Kauffer, Charles Pears, F. C. Herrick, Paul and John Nash, and Clive Gardner. Gardner's "strikingly modernist" (211) sequences of industrial scenes provide one example of how empire propaganda conscripted the modernist aesthetics of the prewar art scene.

The coupling of modernist visual aesthetics with a revised notion of the British Empire was best evidenced, however, in the British Empire Exhibition held at Wembley in 1924. With education as its explicitly stated purpose, this exhibition urged upon the British public a new way of seeing the empire and colonial hierarchies. Celebrated as a "Family Party of the British Empire," the exhibition represented each of the colonies as "neighbours at Wembley."[25] Numerous large pavilions displayed carefully arranged manufactured goods and handcrafts from the colonies. As in previous empire exhibits, these displays included reconstructed villages or artisans' shops inhabited by living people engaged in supposedly typical daily activities, "natives" who made weavings, danced, and otherwise performed for the 27 million visitors to Wembley. However, the education received by those visitors encompassed more than information about empire products or "natives" and their activities. Framing that information and winding its way into the exhibition guides, a rhetoric of visual aesthetics educated the British masses in the principles of modernist aesthetics as formulated in England before the war. To a certain extent, previous imperial exhibitions also relied on visual spectacle and linked modern manufacturing with the decorative arts. However, the guidebooks for the 1924 Wembley exhibition join the language of specifically modernist aesthetics with the rhetoric of empire to showcase the entire exhibit. Through this rhetoric the modern subject-who-sees expands to include the masses of working- and middle-class visitors to the exhibition. The guides coach them in the repeated practice of viewing aestheticized objects that David Hume, as discussed in Chapter 1, believed necessary to educate the eye in the acquisition of taste. Since that practice included viewing the colonized people on display in the exhibit's pavilions, it constructed the masses as modern subjects through the exclusion of "natives" from the same visual education. However, the colonized people on view at Wembley also contributed, through their performances, to its project of education. Their ambivalent status belongs to and extends into new cultural venues a long history of black people in Britain perceived as spectacles and entertainment, specimens of exotic lands under rule of the British crown.

In *Black Edwardians*, Jeffrey Green documents the presence of black people in Britain between 1901 and 1914, noting the numbers of imperial exhibits on both small and larger scales that displayed black people as entertaining spectacles during that time. These ranged in kind from enactments of the warfare between British settlers and the Ndebele in a show called "Savage South Africa" that employed black actors, to Edward's coronation parade in 1902 which displayed the battles and human spoils of empire in the "kings, rajahs, presidents, chiefs, emperors and prime ministers" called to witness it and in the generals and troops from all over the empire who marched in it. As Green points out, all of these shows participated in "the centuries-old tradition of parading captives from foreign lands as evidence of military success."[26] He adds that "in Edwardian Britain displays of Black people also supported the widespread belief that White people in general, and Britons in particular, were superior" (3). John M. Mackenzie supports this view, extending it to all the British imperial exhibitions from the 1870s through the 1930s and arguing that they displayed colonized people in "native villages" in order to perform only "one function, to show off the quaint, the savage, the exotic, to offer living proof of the onward march of imperial civilization."[27]

However, even in the prewar context, colonized people of color did not occupy a simple position as objects of the imperial gaze. Rather, the racist stereotypes to which they were subjected became, in some cases, opportunities for cultural and economic agency. Green documents an engagement at the 1904 City of Bradford Exhibition of a large group of men, women, and children from Somalia, who lived on the grounds throughout the summer "carrying out, in public, a range of activities that were pictured on at least nine postcards sold at the show." These include the activities of a "native" doctor, a "native family," a school day, and "washing day." However, they were not simple villagers but "seasoned entertainers" who had made enough money as actors in France and England to acquire and insure a significant household of goods stored in their apartments on the grounds. When they departed for Liège at the close of the show, the local newspaper remarked on the "English suits" the men wore and their "astonishing" facility with English. Immediately preceding their departure, the actors also claimed civil and economic rights, petitioning the town hall for compensation over what they saw as unfair payment for their work (5). Green describes numerous shows featuring Somalis, living in their "villages," on the grounds of various exhibitions and gardens throughout Britain, especially between 1908 and 1910. A group billed as "the Dahomey Warriors" toured Britain from 1905 through 1909. Sometimes described in blatantly racist terms by journalists, who wrote, for example, of "large eyes [that] roll at you from ebony faces," they were actors, "seasoned travellers and semi-professionals," employed and paid by promoters who hid their occupational status from the public.

The instability of their status as objects of the imperial gaze derived from the gaps between their actual occupations and the image they presented. It was generated in the contradictions between racist stereotypes and the claims such individuals and groups could legitimately make to the rights of workers and citizens of the British Empire. The ambivalence of their identities differs from but complements that analyzed by Homi Bhabha as constituting the subjectivity of the colonized person. Bhabha's notion of colonial mimicry refers to the process that made C. L. R. James, for instance, a black British intellectual. Though never granted the full status of an Englishman, the colonized person of color who perfectly acquires English manners, dress, and education exposes to both his or her own consciousness and that of the colonizer the fact that this identity is a constructed one. Such mimicry subverts the rationale for imperialism based on a natural hierarchy of authentic and natural differences between colonizer and colonized.[28] The mimicry engaged by these touring Somali "villagers" and "Dahomey warriors" is that of the minstrel's mask, the oppressed person who imitates the stereotypes of his own identity, exposing them also as constructed.

The status of Caribbean people as visual objects at the Wembley exhibition of 1924 was also complex and uncertain resulting from their roles as actors, "acting" as themselves. Performing, moreover, in an aestheticized space designed as a "great educational opportunity,"[29] their roles extended the unstable subject position of black actors in the Edwardian period into new cultural domains. These included the relief of imperial anxieties through the promotion of modernist aesthetics.

If, as Peter Fryer has claimed, white British people soon forgot the "riots" of 1919, the exhibition indicates deeper anxieties in that forgetfulness that prompted a deliberate, elaborate, and expensive spectacle of colonized people, apparently tamed, domesticated, and on "view" within England. Rather than overcrowded, impoverished city neighborhoods, docks, and ships (scenes of the 1919 racial violence), the carefully staged tropical palms, coconuts, bananas, ginger preserves, and planters' punch of the West Indian Pavilion created a new visual background for the perception of Caribbean émigrés, while members of the West India Regiment Band, the West Indian "market woman" called "Sunny Jamaica,"[30] and the women weaving "jippa jappa" hats provided reassuring examples of what West Indian people did, cordoned off from the visitors who observed them. In addition to addressing fears of immigrant settlement and racial mixing in England, the exhibit addressed anxieties resulting from intensified doubts, following the war, about the strength of Britain's empire abroad. For some, the doubts were moral, prompted by reports of oppressive and brutal colonial practices. Creating an artificial whole that claimed to represent the totality of empire, wherein all of its dynamic parts functioned safely and smoothly as "neighbours" and as "one," the exhibition contained and assuaged such anxieties.[31] Relief came in the form of visual displays of imperial achievements meant to educate the ordinary English person as to his or her citizenship within a vast global network of imperial trade and communication. Offering "The Wise Way to See Wembley," the guidebooks aided English visitors in re-imagining the empire, not as an exercise of military might and governance, but as a friendly, global arrangement of goods and peoples. Positioned as visual evidence of that friendly arrangement, displayed in poster and magazine images and presented live in the exhibition pavilions, the "natives" on display gained a muted cultural agency in relieving these anxieties; from a small, domesticated podium, they were enlisted in the cause of instructing the British public in a revised imperial history even as they continued to bear the imperial gaze.

The education offered the British public by the 1924 Wembley exhibition included repeated lessons in modernist aesthetics. The new curriculum developed out of a shift in the rhetoric of empire from invasion, conquest, and governance to communication, trade, and education; from military domination to aesthetic appreciation. The "British Empire Exhibition Guide" repeatedly recommended to the visitor such modernist qualities as harmony, subordination of parts to a dynamic whole, and the lines of connection within the whole as ways of seeing particular buildings and their relationships within the exhibition. For example in describing the Palace of Engineering, the guide explains why it is so pleasing to the eye:

The explanation of the harmony that prevails is to be found in the fact that the fancies of individual exhibitors have been subordinated to the plan of the whole, agreed upon by a group of forty architects. The result is a triumph, and the wonder of construction and arrangement break gently upon the visitor instead of beating him flat with their noise, as is so often the case. (48)

The first thing we might note in this passage is the reference to a group of architects, whose collectively planned design overrides the "fancies" of individual exhibitors. Artistic form, then, on a grand, collective, and structural scale matters far more than the content of the exhibits. That a group came up with "the plan of the whole" recalls prewar artistic activity in the form of groups: the London Group, Bloomsbury Group, Camden Town Group, Omega Workshops, and the Vorticists, to name a few. We might note also the guide's promotion of certain aesthetic qualities. In addition to its approval of subtle harmonies, the guide also approves of light, order, and splendor while rejecting any appearance of what might be considered Victorian clutter:

> The long spacious, light avenues within the building, the pillars stretching far into the distance like forest trees, the flattened arches that support the glass roof, the magnitude and order of the whole, strike the mind with an impression of splendour. Mere size, particularly if the foreground is filled with fussy detail, is too apt to be depressing. The contrary effect is produced by this great harmonious place with its satisfying arrangement of indoor parks partitioned off and entered by porticos from the corridors. (48–49)

While the emphasis on splendor, harmony, and order in the description of the Palace of Engineering may recall classical rather than modernist aesthetics, we should remember that English theories of modernist art developed from a deep appreciation of Renaissance classicism. As seen in the rejection of "fussy detail" and emphasis on the "satisfying arrangement" of parts within an ordered whole, the passage repeats the key terms of English modernism. As part of the dynamic whole of the exhibition, and granted muted cultural agency as educators, the colonized people on display thus unintentionally participated in teaching the British public aesthetic values that echo those promoted by Bloomsbury elites Clive Bell and Roger Fry in the first decades of the century.

Fry, especially, was influenced by his study of Renaissance art, which he appreciated for the arrangement of shapes and forms in overall harmonious wholes. In an essay titled "The Art of Florence," Fry praises artists for their ability to "construe these distinct forms into such a coherent whole as will satisfy the aesthetic desire for unity."[32] In a discussion of a painting by Baldovinetti, "architectonic harmony" becomes a reference point for the kind of unity and wholeness he has in mind (133–134). The language of architectural unity and structural wholeness reappears in the Wembley exhibition guide's description of the Palace of Arts where it celebrates the capacity of this building's design to convey visually "the Art of the whole of the British Empire."[33] Here the concepts of architectural harmony, unity, and wholeness, perceived by Fry within one work of art, take on imperial dimensions while retaining their reference to aesthetics. To appreciate this new version of the empire, visitors are trained in viewing from "a wider standpoint."[34]

Another key modernist term, that of "significant form," underwent a similar adaptation. Both Fry and Bell emphasized the formal elements of a painting – rhythm, line, volume, space, and color – as far more significant in creating an aesthetic effect than any "realistic" reference to a world outside the imagination. They insisted that the greatness of any work of art had nothing to do with morals, ethics, or social life at all; it belonged to the imagination and was thus free to create its own world.[35] Given the exhibit's ideological mission, it is not surprising that both of the exhibition guides suppress any reference to the history of slavery, indentured labor, revolts, and mutinies in the colonies and any questions as to the morality of empire. It is also interesting to note, however, that neither of the guides attempts to persuade visitors that the representation of the empire they are touring resembles anything in the real world. Rather, they repeatedly stress the patterns, lines of connection, and unities created by and within the representation itself. In this emphasis on form, the guides echo the Bloomsbury concept of "significant form," defined by Bell as a sense of arrangement or connection "according to certain unknown and mysterious laws" that moved the viewer to experience the high sensibility of an aesthetic emotion.[36]

Profoundly moved by the significant form they saw in the work of Cézanne and other "post-Impressionist" European painters, Bell and Fry had exhibited their work to the British public in 1910. However, neither the public nor the critics responded well to the 1910 Post-Impressionist Exhibit, some comparing it to child-like scrawls and others to pornography.[37] Two years later, Fry attempted to correct what he perceived as viewers' expectations for "the descriptive imitation of natural forms," arguing that the post-Impressionists, on the other hand, "do not seek to imitate form, but to create form; not to imitate life, but to find an equivalent for life."[38] His explanation for how they do this calls again on the language of unity and structure ("the clearness of their logical structure, and . . . their closely knit unity of texture") and asserts that the distinguishing characteristic of all the painters shown is "the markedly Classic spirit of their work."

We might read the British Empire Exhibition and its guides, twelve years later, as presenting in modified form these aesthetics to a now highly entertained public. It was a public, not of art lovers and critics, but of the expanding middle classes, caught up in a popular spectacle that renewed the ideologies of imperialism through the lessons of modern art. The aesthetics of significant form, especially the emphasis on arrangement of forms, lines of connection, and movement, appear everywhere in the exhibit and the language of the guides.

Perhaps most remarkable is the way that the guide teaches visitors how to perceive the connections that shape the larger whole of the exhibition.

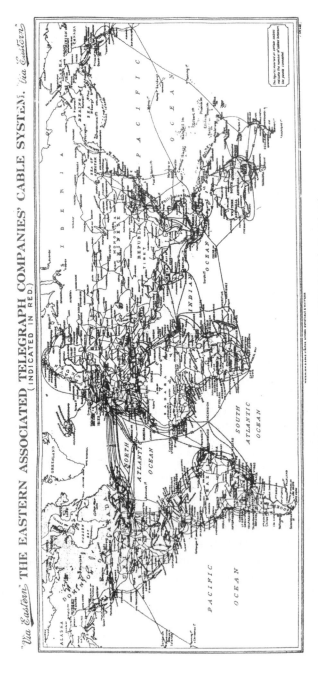

3. *The British Empire Exhibition, 1924, Official Guide,* British Library.

From the beginning, the "British Empire Exhibition Guide" joins modernist principles of art with the excitement of recent technological innovation and commercial advertisement. Facing the guide's cover appears an ad for the Eastern Associated Telegraph Companies. It states that "Their Cables and their efficient Service are the connecting Links binding the whole World." A list of telegraph stations unfolds to a three-page map of the world. Here we find a significant visual change in the cartographic representation of the British Empire. Viewers accustomed to identifying areas of the world ruled by Britain through red or pink shading saw, as expected, these areas colored in pink. However, the telegraph cables connecting them appeared in much stronger red. The telegraphic lines of *connection* are thus most visually prominent and, signaled by their coloring in red, stand more significantly for the totality of the British Empire than the colonized lands that they connect. These connecting cables, displayed visually as marking and unifying the whole world, lead the way at the front of the guide, providing a model for visual apprehension of the miniature Wembley empire. Thus, the ordinary English citizen learned to "see with Empire eyes" a world mapped by modern communications technology and perceived according to modernist visual aesthetics.

The prewar Bloomsbury aesthetics which stressed the dynamic connections of significant form left their legacies in other postwar cultural events, especially the modernist novel as practiced by Virginia Woolf for whom Clive Bell and Roger Fry had served as mentors. In Woolf's case, we find similar formal aesthetics as those made popular and imperial at Wembley, and a comparison demonstrates just how modernist these elements of Wembley actually were. Woolf's concerns, like those of the Wembley organizers, lay also with the postwar reconstruction of social meaning, but unlike the organizers, she was concerned with a counter-imperial potential in the arts. In *To the Lighthouse*, she reflected on and departed from the aesthetics promoted by her Bloomsbury friends.[39] Considering the significance of the connecting cables in the Eastern Associated Telegraph Company advertisement, readers of Woolf's *To the Lighthouse* (1927) might recall the problem faced by Lily Briscoe as she attempts, after the war, to finish a painting that she started before the war began: "It was a question, she remembered, how to connect this mass on the right hand with that on the left."[40] Though Lily (and Woolf) address the question with an agenda quite different from that of the 1924 British Empire Exhibition, similar formalist principles are involved. Lily refers to masses of shape and color, similar to those representing the regions of the empire on the imperial map, and she finds ways to connect them that resemble

closely those employed at Wembley. These include the narration of simultaneous and parallel journeys, different kinds of temporality, a "telegraphic" communication that mysteriously crosses immense distances,
and the transformation of the narrative subject who occupies past and
present simultaneously.

In the final sections of *To the Lighthouse*, Woolf, as author, takes on her
character Lily Briscoe's artistic project of connecting "this mass ... with
that" and creating a structured, dynamic whole. One way she does this is
through a cinematic aesthetics of narrative simultaneity. The novel performs this simultaneity through parallel narratives that connect Lily's
artistic "vision" with the voyage of Mr. Ramsay and his children to the
lighthouse. The exhibition guide also presents parallel and simultaneous
journeys as a portrayal of the experience of touring Wembley. The
Foreword to the guide announces that while visitors tour the exhibits,
"A Special Service Squadron of the Navy is now completing a tour of the
Empire." Visitors can thus imagine themselves on a parallel journey with
this squadron, seeking along with the sailors an education in empire:

Its ships have touched at every great port where the Union Jack flies, seeking to
educate our peoples in the glories of their heritage. It is sober truth to say that, with
the Empire in microcosm before our eyes at Wembley, we have an equally great
educational opportunity as the sailors on those ships, and can learn to understand,
with them, that our Empire stands for justice, progress and liberty.

The parallel journey taken by Wembley visitors, like those of Woolf's
characters, occupies different temporalities simultaneously, as depicted in
the guide's celebratory description of the "Wembley Ways." This includes
all the "ways to Wembley" – by rail, tube, tram, and omnibus – governed
by speed and efficiency: "The usual bus service is a four-minute one. At
rush times a bus will leave every fifteen seconds" (12). It also describes "The
Ways About Wembley," one of which is the "Never-Stop Railway," a train
that never stops moving, though it slows at the stations to allow passengers
to enter and leave the train. The celebrations of speedy modern travel
contrast with the section titled "The Wise Way to See Wembley." This
section urges a leisurely rather than rushed tour of the exhibition and
promotes the model of the Grand Tour. The public is then to imagine
themselves as aristocrats slowly touring the miniature empire as if it were
the Old World (imagining five days as if it were five years perhaps) and
doing so by means of the most modern (and inexpensive) modes of mass
transportation. As they tour, they are to see most vividly the lines of
connection and the arrangements of parts in harmonious wholes among

and within the exhibition buildings. These lines of connection would correspond in a logic of formal simultaneity to the global web of the Eastern Associated Telegraphic Company's red cables.

Both of the narrative voyages in *To the Lighthouse*, the inner voyage taken by Lily and the journey taken by Mr. Ramsay and his children, actually began ten years earlier and, in that sense, represent an extended or, rather, postponed narrative time in contrast to the immediacy of the simultaneous moment when both journeys reach their conclusion. This dual temporality, like that of the Wembley guide, brings the past into the present as an act of the imagination – while Wembley visitors imagine an aristocratic Grand Tour, Lily Briscoe conjures the dead Mrs. Ramsay, and the Ramsay children, with their father, complete a voyage that Mrs. Ramsay had inspired long ago. The simultaneous completion of the Ramsays' voyage on one land mass and of Lily's painting on another connects those two narrative masses. It also "telegraphically" connects the separated characters who simultaneously incorporate the past into the present as they separately and together resurrect the spirit of the dead Mrs. Ramsay. Through this multiple telegraphic connection, Lily Briscoe has her "vision."

On opening day, the British Empire Exhibition added to its own cinematic sense of simultaneous journeys and the emphasis on telegraphic lines of connection with yet another performance of the aesthetic of dynamic unity, offering a decidedly imperial vision. The exhibition formally opened on St. George's Day, April 23, 1924, with the announcement by the King, "I declare this exhibition open." Though the words were hardly notable, the form in which they were communicated was spectacular. Not only was this the first time that the King had spoken to the British people by radio, his words were also "flashed around the world, received again at Wembley and borne in a white envelope by a telegraph boy to the King eighty seconds later."[41] This brief opening speech performed in one dramatic and ritual moment the near simultaneity possible in sending and receiving a telegraph message. But most important, it impressed upon the Wembley crowds the knowledge that words in the English language had encircled as a whole and in an instant the world the British wished to reclaim. Language and the culture it represented thus symbolically remade the empire. As both sender and receiver, the British king managed to occupy two identities at once and to, thus, appropriate the heightened literary self-consciousness of modernism in a dazzling display of modern communications. The motion of the words in the pulsing of the telegraph signals, like parallel voyages of the crowds at Wembley and the Special Squadron, literally signaled to all present or listening on their radios that the new unity of the empire was a dynamic one. As in the modernist aesthetics of Fry and Bell, the power of Britain, as portrayed at Wembley, lay in its capacity for simultaneous movement and dynamic connections among the large masses of land that constituted the empire. Millions of English citizens learned to see a world constructed and perceived according to modernist visual aesthetics. It was as if the entire empire had been subjected to the brush of Cézanne, electrified, and displayed to the masses by Roger Fry.

Woolf's novel, on the other hand, employs similar techniques to trace the creative legacies bequeathed by an Edwardian wife and mother of eight to a young, unmarried, woman painter. Three years after the Wembley organizers sought to reassert in modernist terms the symbolic power of the military and the monarchy, Woolf characterized a feminist matrilineage, all but rubbed out by the patriarchal and imperial forces that resulted in war.[42] Woolf destabilizes the aesthetic view, displacing the gaze of judgment with that of an inner vision at the same time that the novel formally relies on a narrative aesthetics of significant form. The colonized people on display in the various pavilions at Wembley perhaps unintentionally destabilize, though in a different way, the hierarchical relations of seeing with "empire eyes." Presented as displays within the aestheticized space viewed by the exhibit's visitors, they, nevertheless, performed the "native" stereotypes that confined them, suggesting the constructedness of their interwar imperial identities.

In the process of learning "the wise way to see Wembley," working- and middle-class English people were also imagining *themselves* in new and somewhat contradictory ways. Touring Wembley, they became simultaneously aristocratic and middle class (the "Grand Tour," "within reach of all," cost only eighteen pence). Relocated, mostly from London, to a suburb, they became "neighbours" of the colonies, all gathered in "one place," and part of the same "Family." They were seeing themselves in relation to colonized people, connected by lines of trade, telegraph, rail, and language. The empire thus became a visibly coherent and domesticated neighborhood, no longer separated by vast distances or fractured domestically into separate Chinatowns, "dark towns," and "alien quarters." The British public was learning about it in a dollhouse version constructed inside their own home so that British imperial space could not threaten the preserves of "English" space. Yet many visual cues reminded them of colonialist hierarchies. Thus resituated, and with the lens of modernism before their eyes, they learned how to re-imagine their imperial history, reinterpret their recent war experiences, and reaffirm their racial identities. In each case formalist visual aesthetics helped to suppress certain elements in favor of others.

One display, the British Government Pavilion, reinterpreted for the British public the recent losses and catastrophes of World War I. The edited version of the guide describes the Pavilion as presenting an electrically animated map of the world on which ships "mysteriously and invisibly propelled, pursue their path from port to port." The description recalls Clive Bell's definition of significant form and the "mysterious laws" that propel the arrangement of forms in a great painting. The guide instructs visitors to be impressed with this constant motion, portrayed by "ever-changing lights which indicate the growth of this mighty empire." Beyond the map appears a theater, where the dramatic arts and the feats of modern engineering combine to offer

various models of the Western front, including the Battle of Ypres, and some of the fighting on the Somme, while the Military and Air Force Authorities in combination present an attack on London by night, a spectacle sufficiently vivid to send every visitor away with the determination that the Air Force shall lack nothing that it may need for the country's defense.[43]

This literal theater of war, enacting a cinematic aesthetics of simultaneity, seems deliberately designed to transform the painful memories of Ypres and the Somme, where hundreds of thousands of men lost their lives for virtually no military gain, into renewed military fervor, suppressing the bitterness actually felt by many returning soldiers.

Renewed nationalism accompanied renewed racialist categories. Though urged to see themselves in close proximity to and connected with colonized people, visitors to the exhibition could also reaffirm their identities as "white." The guide constantly intones the "need for settlement in the distant parts of the Motherland." A Gallery of the Overseas Settlement provides visual evidence for this need in a "frieze round the wall illustrating the economics of Empire" accompanied by guidebook statistics of the numbers of "white folk" in the distant colonies. Assumptions of racial purity are at work here, suppressing increasing evidence and fears of racial mixing within England and the British Empire. At the same time, the postwar ideology of empire as family re-shuffles the relation between local English and imperial British space, providing reassuring visions of settler life in the colonies. As a campaign for increasing "white" settlement, it renews imperial adventure plots in a more domesticated framework. If the empire could appear at "home" in Wembley, settlers might well feel at home in the distant empire. Furthermore, just as the different parts of Wembley were linked to one another and to one's own living room by lines of instant communication and rapid transit, so would one's more distant new home in the colonies be linked to the grand dynamic whole of England and its empire. The adventurer, voyaging out into the colonies, would simultaneously reach a larger, expertly organized, home.

Though imagined and constructed for the benefit of a "white" British public, this artificial neighborhood of Wembley also granted a contradictory cultural status to colonized people within Britain. As object of a domesticated imperial tourist gaze, their visual presence was now required, as "natives," to actively instruct millions of English men, women, and children in new lessons about the empire and themselves. The culture of empire, already constructed through the sense of empirical observation, now incorporated modernist aesthetics as its way of seeing. At the same time, it reclaimed the colonized person as a sort of "Indian in the Cupboard," transporting him or her to England, to help create these newly modern "Empire eyes." Into this complex, newly imperialized visual environment, came sculptors, writers, and political organizers from the Caribbean bent on claiming the "power to see" and addressing, by necessity, the role of vision in constructing the modern subject.

EDNA MANLEY AND RONALD MOODY: TRANSATLANTIC
CARIBBEAN MODERNISM

The 1924 Empire Exhibition at Wembley did not escape criticism, protest, or ridicule. Whatever muted agency I might ascribe over eighty years later to the colonized people on display at Wembley, colonial subjects living in England at the time saw in the "living" exhibits grounds for protest. Several groups filed formal complaints including the Union of Students of Black Descent.[44] Additionally, in 1925 a Yoruba law student, Ladipo Solanke, organized the West African Students Union (WASU) directly as a response to the exhibit.[45] The group grew in England and extended to four branches in the four British colonies of West Africa, attracting Paul Robeson as a sponsor, and in the 1930s, becoming "a hive of intellectual and political activity."[46] When Italy attacked Ethiopia, WASU took an anti-imperialist position, working closely with the Fabian Society's Colonial Bureau to bring African grievances before Parliament. Solanke and WASU also became important figures in the emerging Nigerian nationalist movement.[47] That such an influential international organization formed as a direct result of the 1924 exhibit indicates the power of visual politics in this era. It was the "wholly degrading way in which Africans were presented" – that is, the way in which they were visually displayed – that sparked Solanke's political activism and motivated the growth of a significant political organization.

Various segments of the English public also criticized the exhibit, often mocking the event as mass commercial entertainment. *Punch* published a cartoon by H. M. Bateman characterizing the exhibit as a roller coaster and asking "Do You Wemble?"; a society formed calling themselves the WGTU (The Won't-Go-to-Wembleys); and P. G. Wodehouse and Noel Coward mocked the exhibit and its crowds in their writing.[48] One of the more substantive critiques appeared in a brief essay by Virginia Woolf, titled "Thunder at Wembley," in which she cast an ambivalent glance at the hordes of British attending the exhibit. Turning her gaze on the masses of middle-class visitors, she asks a question to express the contradiction she sees:

Each is beautiful; each is stately . . . Indeed they are the ruin of the Exhibition . . . As you watch them trailing and flowing, dreaming and speculating, admiring this coffee-grinder, that milk-and-cream separator, the rest of the show becomes insignificant. And what, one asks, is the spell it lays upon them? How, with all this dignity of their own, can they bring themselves to believe in that?[49]

Ultimately, she turns her reflections, which she admits are "so chill and so superior," away from the crowds, to the falseness and impermanence of the exhibit's monuments and to the folly of its organizers. A thunderstorm brings it all to ruins:

The pagodas are dissolving in dust. Ferro concrete is fallible. Colonies are perishing and dispersing in spray of inconceivable beauty and terror which some malignant power illuminates . . . Clergy, schoolchildren, and invalids group themselves round the Prince of Wales in butter . . . the Empire is perishing; the bands are playing; the Exhibition is in ruins. (186–87)

Staging an act of nature to throw into relief the fragility and artifice of the exhibition, Woolf implies that the actual empire is also being shaken by forces beyond its control and, despite the music and propaganda, is, nevertheless, perishing. Crucial to her subversive response are the dynamics of the gaze, which she turns away from the show of colonies and their people to study the crowds instead and, from them, to her real targets, the Duke of Devonshire and Lieutenant General Sir Travers Clarke. She writes that "we would fain credit" (187) them with forethought since they have failed to keep out the crowds, who distract from the show, or the forces of nature – birds, insects, bushes, sky, and finally, the thunder – that destroy it. The implication, of course, is that forces beyond their control are destroying the actual empire, and lack of forethought on the part of the aristocracy and military is responsible for the chaos.

Mackenzie argues that responses from British intellectuals to the popular culture of imperialism between the wars do not represent the views of the working and middle classes. He points out that some of the biggest effects of the exhibit were the creation of pride in being British, an identification with the empire, and a longing among immigrants, from Eastern Europe, for example, to be truly British. But as we have seen, not all immigrants responded in this way. That the WASU worked in alliance with the Colonial Bureau of the Fabian Society, of which Leonard Woolf, Virginia's husband, was a leading member, indicates the links forged across racial and cultural boundaries in opposition to imperialism and its propaganda.[50] Most importantly for this study, the groups linked in shared opposition recognized the power of vision in constructing social relations of colonialism and set themselves the task of creating alternatives. We might view the Pan-African congresses of the 1920s that took place in London as a political countervision to the artificial visual whole of the empire created at various imperial exhibitions and culminating in Wembley.[51] At these congresses, representatives from Sierra Leone, Grenada, Liberia, Haiti, Nigeria, Angola, South Africa, the East African countries of Uganda and Kenya, Guadeloupe, the Belgian Congo, Madagascar, Trinidad, Guyana, Swaziland, Jamaica, Martinique, the French Congo, the Philippines, India, and the United States saw themselves together as a group, "neighbors," to echo the language of Wembley, and unified in their opposition to imperialism and racism. The 1921 Congress adopted unanimously a manifesto, demanding "the recognition of civilised men as civilised despite their race and colour" and claiming the legitimacy of land held in common against the acquisitive greed of capital.[52] It advocated an equitable distribution of world income and explicitly condemned colonial rule for "uprooting ruthlessly religion and customs, and destroying government, so that the favoured few may luxuriate in the toil of the tortured many."[53] The 1923 Congress, held for two days in London, urged socialist economic policies and demanded, for "the civilised British subjects in West Africa and in the West Indies, the institution of home rule and responsible government."[54] These claims for autonomy from British imperial control, worldwide equality among nations and races, and unity among African peoples took the protests, expressed, for example, in the *African Telegraph* following the exclusion of black veterans from the 1919 Peace March much further in their anti-imperialist political and social vision.

The "empire eyes" created at Wembley to see the empire as a whole thus generated a countervision in the efforts of colonial subjects, represented at Wembley as objects of the voyeuristic imperial gaze, to become active agents in re-envisioning themselves and the social relations of empire.

The artificial whole of empire gave way, through their activism, to the notion of a cross-colonial community, intent on reshaping the world as free from colonial rule. Edna Manley and Ronald Moody, two sculptors from Jamaica, contributed directly to this countervision with works of visual art that, by the end of the 1930s, established a transatlantic Caribbean modernist aesthetic. Coextensive with Jamaica's movement toward independence and, at the same time, an influence on British and international modernism, Manley's and Moody's sculpture addressed directly, through the medium of visual art, the act of seeing.

***

In 1924, the year of the British Empire Exhibition at Wembley and protests against it, Edna Manley was accepted to membership in the Society of Women Artists and exhibited in London her first Jamaican work, *Beadseller*. Just three years earlier, Manley had married her "coloured" cousin Norman Washington Manley and subsequently traveled with him and their infant son in 1922 to live in Jamaica. Jamaica became her home by marriage, but it had also been her home through her mother, who was born and raised there. It was her mother who, on her marriage to a Methodist minister from England, had emigrated to England from Jamaica in 1897, and Manley grew up therefore in an émigré household. Writing of her connections to Jamaica, Rex Nettleford quotes Manley as saying, "When I came to Jamaica I was totally and absolutely inspired. Don't forget my mother was Jamaican and I'd grown up with the most nostalgic stories of Jamaica, and I just felt I'd come home."[55] So, when Manley traveled in 1923 to England, her country of birth and education, it was, nevertheless, as a citizen of Jamaica, whose art was newly inspired by its land and people.

Until the making of *Beadseller*, Manley's work had been most heavily influenced by Romantic art. In a comprehensive and illuminating study of her work, David Boxer describes all the pieces she had done before leaving England, which were either studies of animals or portrait heads, as "romantic-realist." Depicting the change her work underwent following her move to Jamaica, he writes,

> We are hard put to explain the tremendous aesthetic leap . . . It was as if in one fell swoop, nearly a hundred years of sculptural development had been bridged; we were suddenly transferred from the language of Delacroix, Barye, et al., to the world of the Modernists: Brancusi, Gaudier-Breszka, Zadkine, Picasso. (17)

Identifying symbolism and cubism as the two styles at work in *Beadseller*, Boxer declares the work "entirely European and consciously modernist,"

4. Edna Manley, *Beadseller* (1922), bronze (unique cast), H. 16½ in., National Gallery of Jamaica, courtesy The Edna Manley Foundation, photograph Maria La Yacona.

then narrows the field of influences to focus on Picasso (17). Boxer describes the lines of the piece as "a carefully geometricized composition of a kneeling figure bent backwards" and notes the subjugation of details to a "strict planar and linear articulation," all of which point, for Boxer, to the formal methodology of Picasso's analytic cubism (17).

I would second much of what Boxer sees in *Beadseller*, especially his appreciation of the beauty of the hands, the detailed relief of the beads, and the figure's prayerful attitude. Yet, there is some irony in describing the strong influence of Picasso's cubism as "entirely European." Even if we do not agree with the position taken by a number of critics in the late 1980s and 1990s that European "primitivism" such as that evidenced in Picasso's supposedly first cubist painting, *Les Demoiselles d'Avignon*, "is the result of theft," its reliance on the tribal arts of Africa is undeniable.[56] Sieglinde Lemke has argued for an assessment of *Les Demoiselles* as a hybrid work of art, one in which the cultures of Africa made a distinct contribution.[57] More recently, Simon Gikandi has extended her argument and that of others, such as Clifford Geertz and Hal Foster, to challenge Picasso's centrality in the modernist art canon and in the formalist aesthetics of modernism. He claims that Picasso's elevated status enables the continuing ideology of modernism, reproduced throughout the twentieth century by art historians and museum curators, in which it "encounter[s] the Other in its ugliness and terror and then purif[ies] it so that it c[an] enter the modern art world as part of its symmetrical economy."[58] Thus, African art is appropriated and contained, while its influence, as art, is denied. For, as I would add, to acknowledge such debts would be to acknowledge the African person as capable of the kind of vision that constitutes the modern subject-who-sees, an ontology that hinges on, as discussed in Chapter 1, the exclusion of Africa and Africans. Gikandi describes this containment of difference as the "hauntology that has come to define the moment of modernism" (458). Like the footnotes haunting the texts of the eighteenth-century aesthetic philosophers, the figure of the African as visually creative persists on the edges of the modernist project. As I shall argue, Edna Manley's work and the critical controversies surrounding it complicate this already complex dynamic in a number of ways specific to Jamaica's movement for independence and its continuing nationalist project.

Reading beyond *Les Demoiselles d'Avignon*, it seems clear that, through Picasso's cubism and other "primitivist" works, African cultures made powerful contributions to what we have previously considered wholly European art. In light of such modernist hybridity, Edna Manley's words concerning the total and absolute inspiration she received on coming to Jamaica may help to explain the "tremendous aesthetic leap" that puzzles Boxer.

Boxer recognizes that the subject of *Beadseller*, composed from drawings Manley made of market women in Mandeville, "was a clear declaration that Jamaica and its people were to be the young artist's basic inspiration" (17). However, this inspiration, received from people of African descent, coincided with Manley's evident recognition of the power within a modernism that only appeared European, but was actually a configuration of forms and styles hybridized from European, Iberian, Egyptian, Asian, and to a very large extent, African sources. Once away from an England increasingly influenced by this hybridized modernism and surrounded by

Afro-Caribbean people and their cultures, modernism emerged suddenly, but I would argue, differently, in Manley's work. Europe's "preference for the primitive," as E. H. Gombrich has recently phrased it, is nearly always all about Europe. In the case of modernist primitivism, an aesthetic frequently derived from masks and carvings contained in ethnographic museums, European artists were often seeking an exotic and energizing alternative to Europe's cultural fatigue and sometimes imagined the "primitive" as bearing traces of Europe's own pre-industrial and tribal past. Manley's modernism signals something else – a turn to the African diasporic *present* as a source for her art. Her Jamaican modernism transforms the appropriations of African tribal art in her European influences and returns them to re-inhabit the sites of her early education in London with a newly inspired Caribbean creativity, neither all about Europe, nor I would argue, solely about Jamaica, emerging, rather, in the passages between.

The move Manley made from England to Jamaica and the journeys she continued to make between the two countries throughout the 1920s and 1930s put her in a unique position as an artist. These movements gave her a mobile aesthetic vision and creativity generated from connections she was forging between colony and metropole. In the years following *Beadseller*, her art changed rapidly and dramatically, incorporating influences still from Europe and England where she continued to receive critical praise, but also becoming increasingly in touch with Jamaican cultures and movements for social change and political independence. From 1924 through 1929, Manley exhibited a total of seven works in four different shows in London. Her work gained notice first in France, in articles published in *La Revue Moderne* and *Les Artistes D'Aujourd'Hui*. By the summer of 1929, she had received reviews in the British press as well. Her greatest successes in England, however, came during the 1930s, beginning in 1930 with three separate exhibits and election to the London Group. Of the pieces shown during this year, the seven-foot carving in mahogany titled *Eve* drew the most attention. *Eve* had appeared the year before in the Goupil Galleries Summer Salon Exhibit and received lengthy praise from the *Morning Post* reviewer.[59] It then traveled with several other pieces to a number of exhibitions, including shows put on by the Women's International Art Club and the London Group; throughout 1930–31, *Eve* continued to merit considerable attention from reviewers and critics.

David Boxer describes *Eve* as "a technical tour-de-force" (20). The turning action, or *contraposto* of *Eve* conveys a sense of physical motion within the stillness of wood that lends dynamic strength, especially in the full limbs and torso, in the figure of a young woman. As Boxer points out,

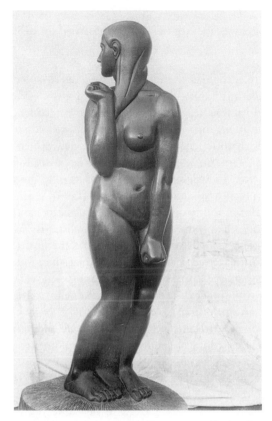

5. Edna Manley, *Eve* (1929), wood (mahogany), H. 84 in., Sheffield Galleries and Museums Trust, courtesy The Edna Manley Foundation, photograph Maria La Yacona.

this turning action shaped *Beadseller* and its companion piece, titled *Listener*, and became "a marked stylistic trait of the young artist, one in fact that [would] persist throughout the twenties and thirties" (16). He sees in this trait the expression of both personal experience and a philosophy in which opposing dualities rule not only her life but the universe (18).

While Boxer focuses on the psychological and philosophical significance of the dynamic motion shaping these pieces, a critic at the time stressed their "pure art spirit." In *The Art of Carved Sculpture* (1931), Kineton Parkes referred to the modernist quest for pure form and celebrated what he saw as Manley's superior vision:

she sees more in Sculpture than Form-research. She wants more than the obvious external form-mounting. She wants to get beneath the surface to find the spirit which prompts and is never tired . . . Edna Manley, away from London and Paris and glad so to be away, produces a naive unsophisticated art, an outpouring of the pure art spirit.[60]

Parkes seems to recognize the unique perspective Manley has found in Jamaica and the inspiration she has received there as revitalizing a tired modernism. However, he cannot move, in his assessment of her work, beyond the primitivist rhetoric that opposes sophistication to naïveté, ideas to nature. This rhetoric recurs in his critical review of her work when he describes her as "Untrammelled . . . by the currency of modernistic ideas" and also in a letter, in which he depicts her as having "got away from the shackles of sophistication and . . . down to God's earth again."[61] For Parkes, as for Boxer, modernism is "wholly European"; and they both see something more than pure modernist formalism in Manley's work. However, Parkes celebrates what he perceives as the unshackled opposite of metropolitan modernism, failing to recognize the modernist dependence on images of the "primitive." Associating her work with that of Picasso and attributing to it complex psychological dimensions, Boxer remedies the naïve primitivism of Parkes's early assessment, but he, too, fails to recognize the Africanist contributions to the modernism he values. I would argue that Manley's education in London, her affinities with Epstein, Gaudier-Breszka, and Dobson as well as Picasso, had made her sophisticated, and she did not cast aside her ideas on arrival in Jamaica. Nor did she repeat them with all their primitivist assumptions. Rather, she transformed them as her work moved in new directions, influenced as I shall argue, by Afro-Jamaican and indigenous traditions of visual art.

In spite of Manley's clear indications that she was deeply affected by Afro-Jamaican spiritual traditions, rituals, and ways of seeing, the prevailing criticism of her work perceives it in the primitivist dichotomies set up by the aesthetics of modernism. For example, Wayne Brown reads the shift in Manley's work from the linear planes of *Beadseller* to the rounded curves of *Eve* as a rejection of her London influences, specifically of the advice she received from a London teacher, who urged her to " 'look for the planes' " (156). Like Parkes, he sees the change in style as a "conscious rejection of contemporary metropolitan culture" (156) and a decision to plunge the "intellectual depths of her own nature and . . . the sensuous non-cerebral life of the island" (157). David Boxer, on the other hand, attributes the shift to Manley's adoption of "the prevalent tenets of 1920s neo-classicism which had invaded British sculpture," especially in the work of Frank Dobson. Again, Boxer cites Picasso as the major influence, particularly in Picasso's revival of his own earlier "Rose" and "Iberian" styles (20). If we are cautious, however, in accepting the oppositions of modernist primitivist rhetoric, we can see in Manley's work a rerouting of these styles in all of their hybrid complexities through her commitment to Jamaica, not as site of the natural and sensuous in opposition to London's metropolitan sophistication, but as a contemporary location of African diasporic cultures.

In considering the turning motion of *contraposto* emphasized by Boxer, the more general sense of "pure art spirit" noted in Parkes's earlier reviews, and the dramatic changes in Manley's Jamaican works, we can again attend to her words, quoted earlier, in which she describes the total and absolute inspiration she received from Jamaica. Manley's interests in the Afro-Caribbean cultures of Jamaica and her involvement in the independence movement, as wife of a Jamaican political leader, put her in the midst of uniquely Caribbean "movements" in several senses of the word: the individual and collective movements of cross-Atlantic migration; arts movements that appeared revolutionary in their context; and upheavals in racial, class, and colonial relations that developed into full-scale movements for national independence. C. L. R. James, who migrated from Trinidad to England in 1932, became intensely fascinated with the concept of "movement" – as an element of formal aesthetics, as a social and political force, and as a trope for the development of human consciousness. As I discuss more fully in Chapter 3, James's essay, "What Is Art?", published as a chapter in *Beyond a Boundary* (1963), transforms the formalist concept of "movement" from something perceived in a painting to a political *and* aesthetic force, one that exerted its cultural power in unexpected, popular places.

The "movements" of aesthetic emotion, social change, and personal development that James articulated in *Beyond a Boundary* were beginning in the 1930s and were represented in Manley's art. I see in *Eve* a similar configuration of a modernist aesthetic, perhaps influenced by Picasso's "Iberian" style or Dobson's neoclassicism, perhaps speaking of a philosophical sense of contraries working in unison, perhaps reflecting a dual sense of home and circum-Atlantic affinities, certainly expressing a newly found inspiration from Jamaica, but also representing through the human figure a unique crossroads of styles, forms, and cultures, all in motion, turning with history and with the personal development of the artist.[62] In her pieces from the 1930s, especially *Negro Aroused, Prophet*, and *Pocomania*, these movements, in all senses of the word, become even more apparent and coincide with the influence of Afro-Caribbean and indigenous art forms.

6. Edna Manley, *Negro Aroused* (1935), wood (mahogany), H. 25 in., National Gallery of Jamaica, courtesy The Edna Manley Foundation, photograph Maria La Yacona.

Judging by the titles of these carvings, Manley has turned away from the Western universalizing and symbolic names given to earlier pieces such as *Eve, Dawn, Demeter, Youth,* and *Adolescence* in favor of explicit references to local spiritual traditions and political movements. The motion conveyed through these forms does not depend as much on a spiraling shape as on forces that pull simultaneously toward the sky and the earth and on the combined expression of inward enlightenment and physical power. In *Negro Aroused,* the sense of enormous physical strength in the curving arm and back create also lightness in the opening between the bent arm and torso. Similarly, as the large joined hands press downwards, they support the extreme bend of the neck and uplift of the head and eyes as if in reverence toward a vision of something above. David Boxer gives a full and eloquent description of this carving. He mentions first the influences of "a particular figure type of William Blake where the heads in profile are raised upwards in some response to the divine" and the influence on Blake's design of "Michaelangelo's Victory" and "another famous Michaelangelo image, the Adam of the Sistine Chapel" (24). Boxer states that crucial to the power and impact of *Negro Aroused* as "the very icon of an age," was its "absolute clarity of meaning through form" (24). Its symbolic power arose within the context of labor uprisings, black power, and nationalism in which Manley created it. Noting its "system of structural tensions," he states that "the figure seems to surge upward in some sort of insistent appeal" (24). He adds, "The half figure of an unmistakably *black* man, his gaze turned skywards, is a symbol of a search; a vision of a new social order, a *New Day*" (24).

Negro Aroused became an icon for Jamaica's nationalist spirit and, in 1937, Manley wrote of the effort it took to make it: "*Negro Aroused,* etc. was trying to create a national vision, and it nearly killed me, it was trying to put something into being that was bigger than myself and almost other than myself. It has taken me weeks to stop – being the Negro Aroused!! Ah well – badly put but you'll understand."[63] Much later, in 1984, she recalled the circumstances in which it emerged:

I have never really known just how *Negro Aroused* was born. But I know that the fact that I had been able to do it gave me a new sort of confidence. It seemed to be an expression that flowed from the trips I was taking at night listening to the Pocomania meetings – watching the political meetings on the Parade. I felt something coming, very definitely something coming.[64]

Manley's words describing the creation of *Negro Aroused* contrast with Boxer's assessment of it in ways that help to explain recent controversies over the development of Jamaican art history and the place of Manley's work within it. In Boxer's assessment, European and English artistic influences (Michaelangelo and Blake) combine with the forces of Jamaican nationalism and black consciousness to generate the work and its significance. He does not credit any local cultural forms with influencing the work. However, Manley clearly recalls "the trips I was taking at night listening to the Pocomania meetings." Judging by a later entry in her diary, Manley was becoming a lifelong and trusted visitor to those meetings. She writes in 1979 of taking "to their first pocomania meeting" a number of visitors, including Zora Neale Hurston.[65] The language she describes in 1937 as "badly put" – "being the Negro Aroused" – evokes the notion of possession by something "bigger than myself and almost other than myself," words that might also describe Afro-Caribbean religious rites of possession such as those undergone by Pocomania celebrants.

The influence of the Pocomania meetings seems to have been a powerful one, making valid any speculation as to the significance of their ritual practices on Manley's work in this period. In her doctoral dissertation, "Fine Art as an Expression of Religion in the Jamaican Culture," Nadine Althea Scott has pointed out that enslaved Africans brought to the Caribbean strong traditions in visual art, which were suppressed by the planters and colonial governments. Works of art such as altars, masks, ceremonial clothing, and other ritual objects were no longer permitted, and creativity emerged instead in orality, song, and dance.[66] We can read Scott's point as further confirmation of the overall argument concerning the advent of modernity with which I have been working in this book. In their suppression of African diasporic visual arts, the colonial governments reconstituted themselves as modern subjects who had developed the capacity for sight on which depended reason, judgment, and aesthetic values. Visual traditions, such as watercolors and landscapes, became the provenance of the European planter class; however, some self-taught local artists emerged, especially in the twentieth century, such as John Dunkley, Henry Daley, and Malica Reynolds (known as Kapo), whose works express spiritual traditions adapted from African cultures in the Caribbean. While the work of these artists might trouble the dynamic excluding them from the visual arts, as Annie Paul has recently pointed out, a set of categories distinguishing these "intuitives" from the "mainstream" painters has prevailed in Jamaican art history and curatorship.[67] Two points are important here: first, the exclusion of Afro-Caribbean religious and folk cultural practices from the category of "art" and, second, the separation within the category of art between "intuitives," inspired by spiritual traditions from Africa, and "mainstream" artists, positioned within Anglo-European aesthetic contexts.

An alternate notion of what constitutes art, such as that developed by Robert Farris Thompson, for example,[68] would include the altars and religious objects, even the ritual gestures and dances of the Pocomania ceremonies Manley visited, and could acknowledge African diasporic artistic influences in *Negro Aroused*. It would resituate Manley's work in relation to the "intuitives" of Jamaica but also in a wider, transcontinental and circum-Atlantic context of African diasporic modernism. Even Manley's choice to carve in wood, as Veerle Poupeye has noted, indicates a "revival of African traditions in Jamaican culture that accompanied cultural nationalism."[69] Manley deliberately chose to engage this tradition in the visual arts in spite of the hostile reaction on the part of the Jamaican upper classes to the small collection of African carvings she brought with her when she moved from England to her new home in 1923. African traditions of woodcarving continue their influence in the literature of the Caribbean, evidenced by their centrality in novels such as Fred D'Aguiar's *Feeding the Ghosts* which I discuss in Chapter 1. Manley's choice to work in wood carried this tradition forward and made it an iconic medium of Caribbean movements for independence and sign of an aesthetics and way of seeing that crossed the Middle Passage to be reshaped in the Americas.

In addition to rerouting African traditions through European primitivism to the diasporic present of Jamaica, Manley's work may have incorporated Amerindian traditions of carving already established in Jamaica when she arrived. Indigenous Jamaican sculpture had existed for centuries before the European conquest in the form of Arawak zemi carvings, available to Manley in brochures put out by the National Institute of Jamaica. There was also a tradition of woodcarving sustained by the descendants of the Maroons, slaves who escaped the plantations and established surviving communities in the remote and, for British soldiers, inaccessible mountains of central Jamaica. Namba Roy, a sculptor who worked with Manley and exhibited in London during the 1950s, came from the Maroon village of Accompong where he descended from a lineage of official woodcarvers. In addition to making his sculptures, he published an epic romance, *Black Albino*, which took place during the Maroon Wars of the eighteenth century. Maroon history and culture were legendary, and Manley's interest in local cultures suggests that she would have been aware of their carving tradition.

It seems clear that, on completion of *Negro Aroused* in 1935, Edna Manley's work constituted a full expression of Jamaican modernism, uniquely shaped by her education in England, her personal interests in Afro-Caribbean spiritual traditions and the folk cultures of Jamaica, and her position as wife of a political leader in a country undergoing tremendous social change. *Negro Aroused* appeared with over twelve other sculptures including *Prophet* and *Pocomania* in her first one-person exhibition, held in Kingston in January of 1937 and again that year in March at the French Gallery in London. This solo show, located almost simultaneously in Jamaica and England, marks a moment of crossing cultures in modernism that reaches across the Atlantic to shape both the colonizing country's art world as well as that of the colonized.

Recent controversies over Jamaica's art history ignore the emergence of Manley's art in these passages between England and Jamaica and neglect the impact of her work outside a strictly Jamaican context. In an article published in *Small Axe*, a leading journal in Caribbean cultural studies, Annie Paul has accused leading figures in the Jamaican art world of having "manufactured an art history spanning seven decades, a linear narrative intertwined with the story of Jamaica's nationhood" in which "Edna Manley bestrides the national canvas like a Marvel Comics superheroine – Artwoman."[70] Paul's argument is not so much with Manley's work as with its iconized status within what she considers a tightly controlled "production of art history," which leaves no room for any form of visual creativity that does not fit the "formalist-modernist framework in which [Jamaican art] is embedded" (75).

A point of tension within this narrative of Jamaican art is located in the discrete categories of "mainstream" and "intuitive," mentioned earlier, which recall previous oppositions of "civilized" and "primitive" and evoke in their current use anxieties concerning African influences in Jamaican art. David Boxer's introduction to the catalogue for the 1987 National Gallery exhibit, "Fifteen Intuitives," suggests the reasons for the persistence of the opposition. Here he expresses his hesitation to use the term "primitive" because it "would have placed too much of an emphasis on an admittedly important aspect of our Intuitives, who *are* essentially Black people descended from Africa, namely the African retentions which are clearly evident in the work of some of the Intuitives."[71] The statement makes several contradictory moves, suppressing, yet openly, the "admittedly important" African influences in the work of these artists, while with the possessive "our," keeping them narrowly confined to Jamaica's national art history and within the terms of that history. Veerle Poupeye, who has worked with the National Gallery of Jamaica for many years and published on Jamaican and Caribbean art, has acknowledged a mainstream Jamaican ambivalence toward notions of the "primitive," which she sees as an unresolved tension in Jamaican art.[72]

Boxer's introduction to the "Fifteen Intuitives" exhibit does suggest that the "intuitive" artists, such as John Dunkley and Kapo, may have influenced the more "mainstream" artists, such as Carl Abrahams and Edna Manley. If this question were pursued, the "Intuitives," with their African influences might be repositioned in leading roles, shaping the "mainstream" and not just discovered, encouraged, and supported by it. Paul argues for the potential in this view and also urges opening the nationalist model to international movements in art. However, in her discussion of Manley, she remains within the nationalist paradigm she critiques.[73] She does not consider Manley's work significant anywhere but in and for Jamaica; nor does she consider Manley as part of a larger, international modernism, or as a sculptor whose work participated with other artists in a cross-Atlantic Jamaican modernism. This is partly because neither the Jamaican art histories she criticizes nor histories of English modernist art recognize Manley's role in these movements. Rather, they see her work in national terms.

If we consider Manley's art work in other contexts, as some art historians are beginning to do, such as that of a larger art history of the Caribbean region or a history of diasporic black art and culture, the nationalist narratives on both sides of the Atlantic open up, and the Africanist presence becomes part of a larger picture. For example, *Rhapsodies in Black*, a book on the Harlem Renaissance, published in 1997, recognizes Manley's and Ronald Moody's contributions to this art movement of the black Atlantic. Books by Richard J. Powell on *Black Art and Culture in the Twentieth Century* (1997) and Veerle Poupeye on *Caribbean Art* (1998) also discuss Manley's work alongside that of the Harlem Renaissance artists. In Jamaica, one year after the *Small Axe* issue appeared, a volume edited by Petrine Archer-Straw, *Fifty Years – Fifty Artists: 1950–2000, The School of Visual Arts*, celebrated the fiftieth anniversary of the Jamaican School of Visual Arts. Essays by Boxer and Archer-Shaw in this volume reassess Manley's work as linked to English modernism, such as that of the Bloomsbury Group, to the Harlem Renaissance, and to her observations of Jamaican life.[74]

Though helping to open the nationalist paradigm that Paul has critiqued, these narratives retain limited definitions of visual art and do not fully appreciate the extent of Manley's translations of the "primitive" in modernism. They also assume that the influences across the Atlantic traveled only in one direction, from metropolitan center to colony, and do not ask what impact Manley's work or that of other Jamaican modernists, such as Ronald Moody, might have had in London, Paris, or New York. In *Caribbean Art*, Veerle Poupeye notes resemblances between the

7. Aaron Douglas, *Into Bondage* (1936), oil on canvas, 60⅜ in. × 60½ in., Corcoran Gallery of Art, Washington DC. Museum purchase and partial gift from Thurlow Evans Tibbs, Jr., The Evans-Tibbs Collection, 1996.9.

work of Harlem Renaissance artist Aaron Douglas and that of Edna Manley, implying that Douglas's murals may have influenced Manley.[75] Poupeye does not mention specific works by Douglas, but if we consider the murals titled *Aspects of Negro Life*, created in 1934, we find figures that resemble in style and shape the figure of *Negro Aroused*, completed by Manley a year later and indicating a possible influence from Harlem on her carving. Moreover, the central figures of Douglas's *The Creation*, completed in 1935 when Manley finished *Negro Aroused*, and *Into Bondage*, completed a year after, repeat even more closely the lines of the head and shoulders of *Negro Aroused*, suggesting that influences may have operated in both directions during these years.

Recent critiques of what Joseph Clarke calls "Creole modernism" also point to anxieties around the "Africanist presence." In an article on Jean Rhys's 1934 novel *Voyage in the Dark*, Clarke argues that this Creole modernism requires an ambivalent representation of "black bodies" to construct a white or creole identity, struggling for self-definition.[76] Following Clarke's critique, we might easily read the alliance of Manley's work with a nationalist political movement and her representation in *Negro Aroused* of what Boxer describes as an "unmistakenly *black* man" as helping to secure the position of the "coloured class" as the leaders in what was to become a new nation.[77] Later in this chapter, I present an alternate reading of the "black bodies" figured in Manley's work; however, Clarke's argument indicates a problem in the nationalist discourse which positions the Africanist presence in Jamaica, not as the image of a new citizen or political leader, but as that of the inspiration behind the new citizenship of Jamaica.

While recognizing Manley's involvement with a nationalist political cause, I am arguing here that this was not the only "movement" in which her work gained significance; nor does it provide the only source for understanding the "meaning" or impact of specific works. First of all, it is important to keep in mind the local colonial policies that gave rise to Jamaica's labor and political movements of the 1930s. For example, in the year that Manley completed *Negro Aroused*, the Colonial Office was busy supporting the United Fruit Company's attempts to incapacitate the Jamaican Banana Producers Association. Declaring the small peasant land-holder of Jamaica unfit, by reason of "temperament and by his degree of education," for cooperative agricultural production, colonial officers relied on racist ways of seeing Afro-Caribbean people to proclaim them incapable of self-determination.[78] Countering this construction of the Afro-Caribbean person, Manley portrayed for Jamaicans a black man as the individual agent of a far-reaching vision. Second, as I have already argued, this figure echoed and probably influenced the figures created simultaneously in New York by Aaron Douglas and thus visually joined Jamaica's emergent nationalist movement with that of the Harlem Renaissance. Finally, and as I will now more fully discuss, the work of other Caribbean modernists in both art and literature becomes a significant context in which to assess the value and impact of Manley's sculpture.

In order to fully appreciate the scope and potential impact of Caribbean modernism, it is important to view Edna Manley's work alongside that of Ronald Moody. Viewing their work together, we can revise the idea of Jamaican modernism in yet another light, one that illuminates the epistemology of the visual that these sculptors addressed. In the process, we can reply to a key question raised by the *Small Axe* issue. In the preface, the editors ask why the newly independent Caribbean states invested in visual art as a means of developing a national culture. They state that this investment, rather than in publishing houses or scientific laboratories, illustrates "how closely colonial models were followed in most of the region producing bodies of work whose conformity to high modern notions of 'art', 'taste' and 'beauty' have persisted thirty years after independence" (v). Yet, what becomes especially evident when viewing Manley's work alongside Moody's are very different reasons for an emphasis on visual art in the context of decolonization. In both Manley's and Moody's sculptures of the 1930s, we find reflections on the act of seeing itself created through the medium of visual art. Because colonialist images and assumptions about colonized subjects depend on an epistemology of the visual, countering those assumptions requires a visual medium.

***

The year, 1923, that Manley traveled to England with her Jamaican work *Beadseller* was also the year Ronald Moody emigrated from Jamaica to England. Ronald Moody was the brother of Dr. Harold Moody, who had already established a private medical practice in England and who, later in 1931, founded the League for Coloured Peoples in London. Intending to practice dentistry, Ronald Moody began studying at Kings College and became an avid reader of philosophy. He was especially drawn to eastern philosophies of China and India, interests that lasted throughout his life. He also began working in plasticine and clay during the 1920s. The event that seems to have been most pivotal in his development as a sculptor, however, was his viewing in 1929 of Egyptian art in the British Museum. According to his niece, Cynthia Moody, he was "transfixed by 'the tremendous inner force, the irresistible movement in stillness, which some of the pieces possessed'" and, from that moment, determined to become a sculptor.[79] While still making a living as a dentist, Moody began, in 1934, to work in wood. In that year, he completed one woodcarving, *Wohin*, and began another, *Johanaan*; by 1937, he had produced enough work and achieved sufficient recognition to hold his first solo exhibit in Paris. This was the same year in which Edna Manley held her dual one-person shows, first in Jamaica and then in London and becomes, therefore, even more significant as the year in which Jamaican modernism received international recognition.

The next year, 1938, Moody went to live and work in Paris and held a second one-person show in Amsterdam. In 1939 he had twelve pieces on exhibit in the United States in a show titled "Contemporary Negro Art" that opened in both Dallas and Baltimore. It is ironic that Moody was a British subject who lived in England and completed most of the pieces exhibited in Europe and the United States while in England; yet his work appeared only twice in England during the 1930s and then as one or two pieces shown in large group exhibits.

One of these British exhibits is significant, however, not only for including Moody's work but for the kind of cultural statement it attempted to make. Titled "Negro Art," the exhibit was held at the Adams Gallery in 1935, the year Manley completed *Negro Aroused*, and it showed ninety-five different works, mostly paintings and sculpture. The catalogue opens with a preface by Michael Sadler who had edited, along with other "members of the Art Sub-Committee of the Education Committee of the Colonial Office," a book, *Arts of West Africa*, which was then appearing from Oxford University Press.[80] Sadler describes the exhibit as bringing together three kinds of art "which can be studied together with advantage." These were first, "a selection of negro works such as are usually seen under museum conditions as ethnographical specimens." Sadler emphasizes that, rather than showing them as ethnographic artifacts, he chose them as "pure works of art" to be displayed "as in an exhibition of contemporary work." The second category was "some painting and sculpture by living negro artists." The third was "paintings by contemporary English artists some of whose works have been inspired by an interest in negro life or art."[81] In displaying these three categories of art side by side, Sadler moves beyond the European primitivist assumptions concerning African art. Especially in recognizing contemporary "negro artists," he grants them an equal position and the status of the fully modern subject. In acknowledging the inspirations from "negro life or art" in the work of English artists, he recognizes the crossings of cultures in modernism. Further, he honors and showcases artists from Africa and the Caribbean as the inspirations and, by implication, teachers of English artists such as Jacob Epstein, Mark Gertler, and Eileen Agar. Unlike exhibitions held in the United States and Europe in the 1980s that suggested "affinities between the tribal and the modern,"[82] this exhibit listed African artists by individual name, named also their teachers and colleges in Africa, and gave detailed information about the context in which a work was produced and the context in which it might be viewed or used. Providing this information, Sadler displayed African art as emerging from the creativity of educated individuals in civilized societies, shaped by traditions of critical judgment that Europeans had long denied existed in Africa. Sadler retains the modernist language of formalism to describe

African art, subsuming it within the aesthetics of modernism; however, he does so as an alternative to their usual status as ethnographic data or examples of handcraft. The show marks an attempt to change the perception of African diasporic arts in England, in decided contrast to Roger Fry's earlier ambivalent admiration of carvings produced in what he considered uncivilized cultures and also in contrast to the imperialist ideology governing the exhibit of African arts at Wembley in 1924.

Even so, it is interesting to note that, while one example of Moody's work is included in the exhibit, Edna Manley's is completely absent. This is surprising, given that Manley had long been exhibiting with the London Group and had received praise in the British press for her work since the showing of *Eve* in 1929 at the Goupil Galleries. Perhaps the categories in use did not work for Manley's situation. Manley had, in fact, messed with categories of race and nationality when she married her "coloured" cousin and moved to Jamaica, but more significantly when, in 1931, she declared herself the descendant of an African ancestor and, therefore, "coloured."[83] Her identification with Africa appeared in an interview published in an English newspaper and set some members of her family there against her. In Jamaica, it further allied her with the ascendent political class and supported her husband in his political goals. In England, it may have complicated the critics' views of her. She appeared to be a "white" woman, born and educated in Cornwall, and so did not fit exactly the category of "living negro artist," nor was she a "contemporary English artist," having moved to Jamaica thirteen years earlier and recently identified herself as of African descent. Even in this well-meant attempt to honor the achievements and influences of African diasporic art, the identifications of "negro" (meant apparently to cover every thing and person now or at one time in the past from Africa) and "English" remained vague yet separate. As a man of color from Jamaica and a British subject living in England, Ronald Moody apparently belonged. However, it is not clear in what category he was placed since the works were not displayed by category but combined, with the hope, as Sadler states "that a relationship between them is made more vividly apparent."

Ronald Moody described his work in an interview conducted after World War II:

My past is a mixture of African, Asian, and European influences and, as I have lived many years in Europe, my present is the result of the friction of Europe with my past. This has not resulted in my becoming an ersatz European, but has shown what is valuable in my inheritance, which I think shows in my work.[84]

Like many of Manley's pieces, his are massive and, like Manley's, his work has been compared to that of Jacob Epstein. Though Moody created many fine pieces of sculpture, including the monumental work of public art called *Savacou*, commissioned for the campus of the University of the West Indies at Mona, I would like to discuss his most well-known piece of the 1930s, *Johanaan*, along with Manley's works of the 1930s, for I believe that in these internationally recognized works of Jamaican modernism, Caribbean artists were beginning to address directly, through the medium of visual art, the act of seeing.

***

Finished in 1936, *Johanaan* was one of only two works by black British artists chosen to appear in the Tate Gallery's retrospective exhibit, "RePresenting Britain, 1500–2000." Though it appeared in his two solo exhibits in Europe in 1937 and 1938, as far as I can tell, it never appeared on exhibit in England until after World War II. Carved in elm, it stands taller than a man, though it represents only the head and torso of a male figure. The display caption in the Tate refers to "Moody's understanding of Eastern philosophies and their expression through art." It also mentions the influence of Egyptian sculpture and compares Moody to Epstein in his ability to exploit "the properties of his chosen material to present a monumental and universal image of man."[85] Another description of *Johanaan* also stresses the universality of the figure and appears in the catalogue accompanying the Hayward Gallery Exhibit of 1989–90 titled *The Other Story*. Rasheed Araeen first places Moody as a member of "the native middle class" who can accept and assimilate bourgeois humanism. He adds, "this of course takes place through a complex social process, the ambivalence of which enables the repressed desires of the colonized to be expressed as the universal human predicament."[86] Araeen then explains the feeling conveyed by *Johanaan* through this psycho-social analysis of the artist's repressed position in colonialist society: "The serene silence or calmness of a Buddha-like face can camouflage the intensity of inner state of mind or feeling, and it is this feeling that seems to be profoundly expressed in the work of Ronald Moody" (16). Evidence from Moody's writing supports the notion that he was interested in portraying a universalized humanity. He felt that this was the artist's job. And it is possible that repression of social and political desires could result in the profound calm conveyed by Moody's work. Moody was also, however, as many sources acknowledge, drawn to the spiritual traditions of the east; he was a member of the Gurdjieff Society for a number of years beginning in the 1940s, and he had developed notions of the self that

8. Ronald Moody, 1900–1984, *Johanaan* (1936), wood (elm), © Tate, London 2006.

did not necessarily conform to bourgeois humanism, especially if we consider the bourgeois self to be based on assumptions of an autonomous individual with a discrete inner subjectivity. In fact, notes he made concerning his works indicate that he viewed the bourgeois self to be a form of spiritual imprisonment. Commenting on the symbol of the wheel in his work, he wrote of "the ceaseless repetition of the selves and their actions which can lead to a state of self-imprisonment and a belief that this is 'myself.'" He referred to a larger "Self" that "can be overshadowed by the many selves and appear not to exist."[87] In another document, he wrote that his idea for *Johanaan* was that of the "Spiritual Man."[88]

If we read the "serene silence or calmness" that Araeen notes in *Johanaan* in the context of Moody's philosophy and the transcultural influences shaping his work, another interpretation emerges that focuses on the representation in *Johanaan* of the act of vision. Most striking, apart from the figure's size and its square-shouldered posture, is the head with its large eyes and peaceful expression. The shape of the head and ears do resemble the heads of Buddha in sculptures from Asia. The eyes, however, though large, are not directed at anything, nor are they focused downwards as in many portrayals of the Buddha. Undelineated by iris or pupil, they project openly and directly forward. While looking straight ahead or perhaps slightly upwards, they appear simultaneously to gaze within. Or perhaps, it is better to say that they gaze beyond the immediately visible world. Wondering what and where they see prompts the imagination of the viewer also to see differently, and perhaps more, to reconsider the meaning of sight and the kind of world one can construct through vision.

The title *Johanaan* refers to John the Baptist, the visionary and prophet. The power of his seeing is conveyed through a tension similar to that shaping Manley's works of the 1930s: an intense and even rigid physical strength shaped in the warm, heavy matter of wood out of which arises the visionary head with its gaze directed beyond the material world. The Spiritual Man conveyed through this figure may be a universal, meditative self, and it may emerge from a colonial psychology; however, we might also associate it with the "elsewhere," discussed earlier in this chapter, occupied in the British imagination by the West Indies. That is, we might see in this act of seeing a transformation of the fantastical and even monstrous image of elsewhere ascribed to the Caribbean (not China, not the Indies, not Africa, but elsewhere) into another act of the imagination, creating an alternate elsewhere. Interestingly, this alternate elsewhere evokes images from China and India, and also from Egypt. Composed of many cultural selves, it nevertheless projects a larger "Self" and seems to transcend the body's rigid or potentially imprisoning posture. Portraying this new universality in the figure of a male torso, Moody retains the masculinity of the modern subject-who-sees; however, the near military stiffness of the body indicates perhaps its limitations, especially in contrast to the transcendent vision conveyed through the eyes and head.

Johanaan portrays the "power to see" elsewhere on English soil by an artist who is both Caribbean and British, occupying a displaced, self-consciously multicultural position. As with Manley's works, it represents a profound Caribbean diasporic movement, lived in the artist's life of emigration from Jamaica to England and later Europe and back again,

9. Edna Manley, *Prophet* (1935), wood (mahogany) H. 30¼ in., National Gallery of Jamaica, courtesy The Edna Manley Foundation, photograph Maria La Yacona.

deeply enriched by the development of his consciousness through the ancient arts and philosophies of several world cultures, and emerging at a time of political change in the Caribbean. The impact it registers, along with Moody's other carvings on exhibit in England and Europe and those of Manley simultaneously on exhibit in England and Jamaica, is the transformation of the colonial "Other" from object to agent of vision. But even more, it offers a transformed vision of the act of seeing itself through a truly transcultural modernist imagination.

In Manley's *Negro Aroused, Prophet,* and *Pocomania,* we find similar representations of alternate acts of vision. Vision in these works crosses the

10. Edna Manley, *Pocomania (Vision)* (1936), Hoptonwood Stone, H. 23½ in., Wallace Campbell Collection, Kingston, Jamaica, courtesy The Edna Manley Foundation, photograph Maria La Yacona.

threshold of material and spiritual realms by embodying the act of seeing, through figures of seers, visionaries, and mystics. The gaze of the *Negro Aroused* turns directly skyward, as toward the divine, but also as David Boxer describes it, as an expression of the Jamaican people's "yearning for a better existence."[89] Boxer sees *Negro Aroused* and *Prophet* as companion pieces, the first representing a contemplative posture, in "concentrated repose"; the second representing the aroused black man "moved to action"(25).

The stance of the *Prophet*, standing straight on rounded thighs, powerful arms stretched high, with hands joined, suggests a forceful moment in a larger action.[90] The head, in contrast to that of *Negro Aroused* turns slightly downwards, and the eyes stare straight ahead. Wide open, they radiate the force of the body's strength, directed at the world. Yet, as the eyes of a prophet, they see elsewhere, to the action that is coming. They portray, perhaps, Manley's sense at the time of "very definitely something coming" through the political movements and spiritual traditions of the Afro-Caribbean people of Jamaica. With *Pocomania*, Manley shapes a figure in distinct contrast to *Negro Aroused*. While one arm curves softly toward the chest embracing the downward spiral of the head, the other arm reaches high above the head. Rather than upward, the eyes gaze downward into the crook of the arm, the cup of the hand, even the place of the heart, that is covered by the hand. Though made of gentle curves, the figure's power comes from the tension between this intense inwardness and the outward thrust of the other arm. We might read the action of that other arm as reaching upwards, toward the divine as in the gaze of the *Negro Aroused*, or as pulling forcefully, almost violently, downward. It is a moment of stilled spiritual and physical action, the moment of divine possession. If these rounded curves represent the influence of English neoclassicism, they have given it profoundly new significance through the portrayal of local Afro-Caribbean spirituality as a vital, contemporary Jamaican culture.

 Prophet and *Pocomania* become companion pieces to Moody's *Johanaan*, which is sometimes titled *John the Baptist* and was completed in England in the same two years. Though they offer very different portrayals of the act of seeing, all three represent, through visual art, the act of a seer and a moment of transfiguration. All three contribute to modernism a transcultural Caribbean aesthetic that is about vision itself.

***

What was the influence of Jamaican modernism in England? This is a difficult question to answer. In general terms, it inaugurated the continuing shift in British art of the position of the colonized person of color from that of object of the aesthetic gaze to subject. It made evident, for those who could read the visual signs, a transcultural modernism that was already in effect but not recognized. The exhibit of "Negro Art" in 1935, for example, made a strong gesture, with the help of Moody's work, toward recognizing as art and on equal terms the Africanist sources borrowed by European and British modernism. Its influence was also evident in the turn taken by Manley's work to the African diasporic present, and then re-turn to the sites of unacknowledged but nevertheless hybrid modernism in England. These sites included the Goupil and Burlington Galleries, where Manley's work appeared in the London Group exhibits, the Suffolk Street Galleries, where she exhibited with the Women's International Art Club, but it also included a large and well-publicized exhibit in 1930 on the rooftop of Selfridges Department Store. In this exhibit, Manley's work reached a wide audience, becoming accessible to the middle classes who might not frequent art galleries but who could be drawn from their business or shopping to the rooftop exhibit. She fared extremely well in the number of pieces chosen for the exhibit – six, including *Eve*, compared to three by Moore, four by Hepworth, one by Epstein, and one by Dobson.[91] Her success is reflected in her election that year to the London Group and the praise she received from critics in the press and in Parkes's influential *Art of Carved Sculpture*. This success opened the borders of English visual art. Even though critics did not move beyond the language of primitivism in their assessments of Jamaican modernism, Moody's and Manley's explicitly Caribbean and circum-Atlantic translations of that element in European modernism unsettled the dichotomies of "civilized" and "primitive" that shaped critical discourse. Furthermore, their work repeatedly invited viewers to consider the question of vision and thus to consider ways of seeing beyond the color-coded and racially motivated nationalisms that insisted on those dichotomies.

Manley's and Moody's transatlantic Caribbean modernism in the visual arts joined with Caribbean modernism in literature during the late 1920s and 1930s, especially in questioning primitivist and formalist aesthetics. For example, Claude McKay's *Banjo* (1929) and Jean Rhys's *After Leaving Mr. Mackenzie* (1931) portray the relationship between artist and model, prompting reflection on the colonial relationship in visual and aesthetic terms. Composed of episodes in the lives of migrant dockworkers and sailors who are living for the moment in Marseilles, *Banjo* continues the story of Ray, a character who appeared in McKay's previous novel *Home to Harlem*. Ray comes from Haiti and has been partly educated at Howard University. In the chapter, "Storytelling," he recounts a time in Paris when he posed for an art school and then for individual artists. McKay makes immediately clear the sexuality projected onto the black man, who is made to pose "naked on a little platform with a stout long staff in my hand and a pretty Parisienne in the nude crouched at the base."[92] The owner of the studio who poses him in this way requires an assurance that, as a member of "a savage race," Ray can behave himself. Ray claims never to be tempted otherwise though the students take great liberties in touching and posing him. He describes the students as "fierce moderns," who discuss with him "the African Negro sculptures," "primitive simplicity and color and 'significant form' from Cezanne to Picasso" (130). Ray shows his understanding of the contradictions involved in the scene when he comments humorously, "Their naked savage was quickly getting on to civilized things . . ." (130). He then pursues a critique of "significant form" in a daydream that takes him back to Harlem and a "sea of forms of such warmth and color that never was seen in any Paris studio." However, his fantasies of Harlem, rather than the presence of French female students, disturb the scene, threatening his sense of himself not as civilized, but as a man: "And – good night! My staff went clattering to the floor and it was refuge for me." Immediately following what appears to be an unintended erection, Ray decides "that only the other sex was qualified for posing in the nude" (130). As a civilized person, Ray clearly does not wish to be seen in what could only be read as a "savage" posture; his conclusion concerning the qualifications for posing indicates that only women should occupy such a sexualized position. In this decision, Ray refuses to provide modernism with its racialized, eroticized Other.[93]

While a scene of posing in McKay's novel questions "significant form" and comments on the display of black bodies as crucial to the formation of modernist aesthetics, Rhys's narrative directly confronts primitivist painting as a genre that dispossesses women of citizenship and subjectivity. In *After Leaving Mr. Mackenzie*, the protagonist Julia Martin also tells a story of posing for an artist in Paris. The novel's framing devices expose the way she, though apparently white, has been recast by the primitivism of modernist European painting as an exoticized colonial Other, dispossessed of any visible or internal signs of identity. The scene of this dispossession is that of an artist's studio where, as Julia poses, a woman in a reproduction of a painting by Modigliani claims to be even "more real" than Julia.[94] As I discuss more fully in Chapter 4, this novel portrays a crisis of representation in the life of a homeless woman with uncertain nationality. While her subjectivity is increasingly muted, the painting speaks to suggest an untold story haunting the narrative even as the "dark" face with "animal" features of the painting usurps Julia's own voice. Julia tries to sustain an inward gaze but fails in her attempt to "grapple with nothingness" (130). In this narrative, visual primitivism has dispossessed the woman it claims to be or demands to represent. The doubling of the viewer of the painting with the woman figured in it and the blurring of subject and object created through the painting's claims to *be* its viewer, an apparently "English" woman, along with the instability of that English identity, unsettles dichotomies of civilized and primitive.

The scenes of posing represented in both novels portray the anguish of the colonized person conscripted for the modernist aesthetic project. They portray also the frames through which the colonized person was seen and the subsequent threat to that person's subjectivity. In a story told by Aubrey Williams, the painter from Guyana who exhibited his work in England, Europe, and the Caribbean from the 1950s through the 1980s, these were the frames through which, on their meeting, Picasso saw him. As recently recounted by Simon Gikandi, Albert Camus introduced Williams and Picasso, a meeting to which Williams had looked forward but which cruelly disappointed him:

I remember the first comment he made when we met. He said that I had a very fine African head and he would like me to pose for him. I felt terrible. In spite of the fact that I was introduced to him as an artist, he did not think of me as another artist. He thought of me only as something he could use for his own work.[95]

Picasso's inability to see Williams as anything but a "very fine African head" recalls the vocabulary of Bloomsbury and the London Group, the influential circle of artists led during the 1930s by Duncan Grant and Vanessa Bell and to which Edna Manley was elected in 1930. In a letter from Grant to Bell written in 1930, he comments, "Your Negress sounds lovely. I hope you are doing lovely things of her. Are you putting her into your life?"[96] It also recalls Virginia Woolf's remark published in 1928 in *A Room of One's Own*, "It is one of the great advantages of being a woman that one can pass even a very fine negress without wishing to make an Englishwoman of her."[97] Meant to criticize the patriarchal colonial mentality and belief in English superiority, Woolf's remark nevertheless claims the power to see and judge as "very fine" a black woman. This language of visually claiming and judging the black person, positioning her or him as a body to be used in one's argument in the case of Woolf or one's art in the case of her friend, Duncan Grant, permeated even the more progressive circles in England in the late 1920s and 1930s and retained its currency well into the period of decolonization. Rhys's and McKay's novels reveal the haunting of modernism by the transnational and circum-Atlantic subjectivities it suppresses. They join Manley's and Moody's visual modernism in making visible the cultural hybridity on which modernism depends.

We might even argue that Jamaican visual modernism asked viewers to reconsider their images of the Caribbean as an elsewhere of no significance, a no-place, and to consider instead the promise of an alternate elsewhere in the visions of prophets and seers shaped by artists from the Caribbean. Again, I would mention Rhys's novel in support of this cultural effect. As her character fails to find a way to represent herself to others, she feels her life and self "float way from [her] like smoke" (53), and we feel that whatever self she has exists elsewhere, for it cannot exist there. This trope of elsewhere recurs more explicitly in Rhys's later writing of the 1960s as it does in the writing of a number of Caribbean writers in the independence era. I make this interartistic comparison to suggest that in their representations of the visionary gaze, Manley and Moody were embodying a trope that writers from the Caribbean also addressed and represented in their own ways to counter the British colonialist imagination. But much of this is analysis in retrospect. Actual evidence of such general cultural influence is difficult to find, as is actual evidence of specific influences.

For example, what were the influences on artists with whom their work appeared? On the London Group? On sculptors such as Hepworth and Moore, or on painters such as Vanessa Bell, Mark Gertler, and Duncan Grant? Oddly, Manley is sometimes described as having been born in Yorkshire, which was Barbara Hepworth's birthplace, as if the two women became mixed in the minds of critics and journalists. Elected in the same year, along with Henry Moore, to the London Group, they were evidently on equal footing as artists in the London art scene in 1930. Judging by the greater number of Manley's works chosen for the Selfridge's Exhibit in 1930, she was receiving even more attention and praise than either Moore or Hepworth that year. Many reviewers and critics in England found their work to be not only similar but of equal artistic quality. Yet, I find no mention of Manley or Moody in art histories of the period. For example, in Frances Spalding's *British Art since 1900*, there is much discussion of Roger Fry's influence on Moore and the general influence of Fry's essays on "Negro Sculpture" and "Art of the Bushmen," published in 1920 in *Vision and Design*. Spalding credits Fry with contributing to the move away from "the hegemony of the Greco-Roman tradition" in British sculpture. While Spalding emphasizes the influence of African art and also of Mayan art on British sculptors such as Moore, she does not mention Manley or Moody. She characterizes the period in general as a conservative reaction to modernism as evidenced by the Seven and Five Society, which proclaimed themselves against "pioneering" and in favor of expressing their feelings in intelligible terms.[98] Charles Harrison's *English Art and Modernism, 1900–1939* focuses more closely on the modernist period and the decades in which Manley and Moody were actively exhibiting their work. Yet in this lengthy (385 pages) book, which includes a chapter on "The Development of Modernism in Sculpture," there again appears no mention of either Manley or Moody. This chapter and another one on

"The Early Thirties: Unit One" discusses at length the work of Eric Gill, but most of all, Hepworth and Moore. Rather than stressing the conservatism of the period, Harrison discusses at length the attempts of Paul Nash and the Unit One group to revive the avant-garde and distinguish itself from the London Group.[99]

Even the catalogs from the exhibits themselves, which often include photographs of a number of artists' contributions, do not show photographs of Manley's or Moody's works. Most puzzling is the catalog from the "London Group Jubilee Exhibition" held at the Tate Gallery in 1964. None of Manley's pieces appear in this retrospective for the decade of the 1930s, during which she exhibited with the London Group as a member six times, preceded by two exhibitions in 1929 as a non-member. Between 1928 and 1939, the London Group held thirteen exhibits, and Manley's work appeared in eight of them.[100] However, the only place her name appears in the catalog is in its list of "Past and Present Members of the London Group," given according to dates of election. In the "Historical Note" by Dennis Farr and Alan Bowness, a paragraph on the 1930s which lists artists who exhibited in the 1930 Open-Air Sculpture show at Selfridges omits Manley's name even though six of her pieces appeared in the show.[101] Others, such as Hepworth and Moore, who had fewer pieces on exhibit, do appear on the Selfridges list.[102]

The 1964 retrospective of the London Group appears to be a moment when Edna Manley's name and her work are erased from British art history. If it were not a retrospective, organized according to decades, her omission might not seem so odd, given that she ceased to exhibit in England after 1938. However, to serve the aims of this particular show, her fairly significant presence on the English art scene in the 1930s should have been acknowledged.

We can only speculate as to why Manley's exhibition history with the London Group was excised in this show. Two years earlier, Jamaica had achieved independence from England. For twenty-six years Manley had been exhibiting almost exclusively in Jamaica, building an art movement and educating young artists there. Perhaps the colonial politics of her presence in the 1930s and then absence during the movement for independence was something to which the organizers did not want to even allude by including her. This decision, however, suppressed representation of transnational and cross-cultural movements in the arts by adhering to a revisionist nationalism, rendering the "London" of the London Group an English, rather than a cosmopolitan, city.

I can only suggest that the need for a singularly British art, whether conservative in its reaction to modernism as with the Seven and Five

Society or experimental in its desire to reformulate the avant-garde as with Unit One, was so nearly desperate in the period between the wars that artists, such as Moody and Manley, whose cultural and racial backgrounds belied the nationalist and racial categories in operation, were excluded even while their work received critical praise. As discussed earlier in this chapter, "Britishness" as a cultural identity has depended on the construction of colonial alterity and also on a notion of "Englishness" as defined by location on English soil, a spatial distinction motivated by racial ideologies. The need for a British art was really a post-World War I need for English culture and identity – not "British" then in the imperial sense, but in the sense of "English," located on English soil. This need for cultural identity in many ways motivated the 1924 British Empire Exhibition at Wembley which, though projecting a picture of imperial power, did so on English soil, in the suburbs, for the entertainment of the English masses. And the same need seems to filter into the arts groups of the time, so often designated by their place names: Camden Town, Bloomsbury, London. This association of Englishness with specific locations would exclude Manley after her move to Jamaica and declaration of herself as "coloured"; it would exclude Moody by virtue of his birth "elsewhere" in Jamaica and also his color. In Manley's case, it is possible that, following Jamaica's achievement of independence from British colonial rule, the attempt was made to erase Manley's entire history with the London Group.[103]

I want to argue, nevertheless, that their presence in England, troubling as it may have been to the racial and national categories necessary for institutionalizing British art, mattered. Indirect signs of such influence on the London Group may appear, for example, in the change, between 1920 and the early 1930s, in Roger Fry's writing on African art. In 1920, Fry praised the aesthetic qualities of African sculpture; however, he asserted emphatically that, lacking a critical intelligence, "the negro has failed to create one of the great cultures of the world."[104] In the early 1930s, however, Fry acknowledged the great civilizations of Benin and Ifey, praised the spirituality of African art, and credited it for making modernist European art possible.[105] Manley's work, a visual reminder of the contemporary African diaspora in the work of a colonial artist, on exhibit with the London Group (which Fry is said to have "dominated") from 1929 through the year of Fry's death in 1934, may well have contributed to this change.[106] Taking a longer view, the recent recognition of black Atlantic cultures, including the international scope of the Harlem Renaissance, and the continuing recovery of figures central to this transatlantic movement, attests to the shaping influence of artists such as Manley and Moody on a wider modernism.[107] The presence of their work in the galleries and homes of England opened the borders of English art to these broader, international and African diasporic cultural movements.

As evidenced in Claude McKay's and Jean Rhys's novels, Caribbean modernism developed as an interartistic as well as transatlantic movement beginning as early as 1930. Artists and writers cited one another's works and engaged in professional and personal relationships with one another. Caribbean modernism was also closely linked to the political movements and organizations on behalf of colonial independence and against racism in Britain. These interartistic and political associations developed in the 1930s, grew steadily during the 1940s and 1950s and took organizational form in the founding and flourishing of the Caribbean Artists Movement (CAM) during the 1960s and 1970s. In Chapter 4 of this study, I discuss more fully the period of CAM in the development of Caribbean visual politics. In the next chapter, I discuss the work of three émigrés from the Caribbean, Una Marson, C. L. R. James, and George Lamming, whose literary and theatrical productions of the 1930s through 1960 shaped, along with the visual art of Manley and Moody and the narrative fiction of McKay and Rhys, an exilic Caribbean modernism addressing the politics of vision.

3

Exile/Caribbean eyes 1928–1963

The 1930s in British literary and cultural history are conventionally portrayed as a turn away from modernist aesthetics towards a more politically oriented art, as if the two were mutually exclusive. The poetry of Auden and his "generation" has stood for this turn, and the anti-fascist movement has been seen as its prompt. Recent feminist criticism, however, has disturbed the neatness of this chronology by arguing for the anti-fascism within, for example, Virginia Woolf's modernist aesthetics, and revised notions of modernism itself as both spatially mobile and temporally plural (including "geomodernisms" and "late modernism") have further compli-cated the divide. Considering the modernism of the Harlem Renaissance or of the later Négritude movement which it, in part, inspired, extends our acknowledgment of modernist aesthetics into, definitively, the movements against fascism and colonialism. As my previous analysis of the Caribbean modernism of Edna Manley, Ronald Moody, Claude McKay, and Jean Rhys demonstrates, such transatlantic modernist arts intervened in British culture of the 1920s and the 1930s. Following Homi Bhabha's notion of a "contra-modernity," we might think of their simultaneous participation in and sometimes resistant transformation of the tenets of modernist aesthetics as a *contra-modernism*. Adapting Bhabha's description, such a contra-modernism "may be contingent to modern[ism], discontinuous or in contention with it."[1] This concept can help to locate the constitutive alterity within modernism, the ways in which colonial émigrés shaped and re-circuited the aesthetic, political, and ideological projects of the interwar years and after. Rethinking modernism in this way is not just a matter of recovering lost or suppressed writers and artists; rather, it is a matter of recognizing the unassimilated as necessarily so – to acknowledge their significance as, to adapt another of Bhabha's phrases, "otherwise than modernism."

Such an alterity, simultaneously within and outside of modernism, cer-tainly crosses the line between the 1920s and the 1930s, the self-consciously aesthetic and the political, in Britain. Alongside Edna Manley's and Ronald Moody's exhibitions, Jean Rhys's novels, and Claude McKay's poetry and fiction, Una Marson and C. L. R. James made contributions to the visual cultures of England and the Caribbean that also countered the "empire eyes" promoted by the 1924 Wembly exhibition and institutions such as the Empire Marketing Board throughout these decades. Through fiction and poetry they explicitly examined the class, gender, and racial dynamics of the social acts of seeing. Their contributions as playwrights altered London theatre history by bringing, for the first time, all-black casts to the stage in serious drama. Perhaps most importantly for the development of later Caribbean literature, they directly confronted the double-bind of colonial imitation, the dilemma faced especially by artists of color from the colonies in the wake of assertions by eighteenth-century philosophers such as Hume that their efforts resembled those of "a parrot, who speaks a few words plainly." As I demonstrate in this chapter, James and Marson present this problem as one of vision itself in order to work through it, to *see through* colonial imitation into a freer, self-reflexive, and politically charged modernist aesthetic of the 1930s. In the first section of this chapter, I work with James's early short fiction and his novel, *Minty Alley*, and with Marson's three volumes of poetry to distinguish their methods of *seeing through*, in all senses of the phrase, English literary traditions and the social hierarchies of colonial society. In the second section, I analyze their plays, considering the ways they stage, as visual and visionary acts, Afro-Caribbean movements for freedom. In very different ways, James and Marson confront the dynamics of seeing as inherent in colonial relations, and both work through those dynamics to pose and resolve the dilemma of colonial imitation.

With the growth of independence movements in the Caribbean through the 1950s and, simultaneously, increased emigration to Britain, the traditions of Caribbean modernism begun in the 1920s extended further into a new transatlantic fictional aesthetic in the work of George Lamming. In the third section of this chapter, I explicate Lamming's fiction as influenced by the work of earlier Caribbean modernists such as Jean Rhys, so that the problem of colonial imitation is mitigated by the recognition of an established transatlantic Caribbean contra-modernism. Through strong visual tropes, Lamming's novels explore racial and sexual tensions in the lives of Caribbean emigrants and in struggles for Caribbean independence, and they do so in a prose style of fragments, collage, and shifting points of view. This Caribbean contra-modernism inserts a troubling temporal multiplicity, the sense of a "time-lag," to continue with Bhabha's terms, which keeps alive, in the midst of modernism's dictum to "make it new," the making of the past. To conclude the chapter, I turn to C. L. R. James's "What Is Art?" a crucial essay in his genre-bending work *Beyond a Boundary* (1963), which highlights in its carnivalesque turn-about of prevailing modernist aesthetics, an alterity within them. As if acknowledging the constitutive otherness of Caribbean modernism and its impact during the first half of the century, James promotes West Indian cricket as the model for modernist art and the responses of cricket fans as a superior critical sensibility. All of these contributions to an otherness within and extending modernism depend on the experience of exile undergone by increasing numbers of Caribbean immigrants and the transformation, through exilic alienation, of the body and its senses, most importantly, the sense of sight.

C. L. R. JAMES AND UNA MARSON: SEEING THROUGH COLONIAL IMITATION

In 1932, Marson and James, both well-established writers involved in progressive social causes, left their countries for England. At age twenty-seven, Marson had already achieved celebrity in Jamaica for her writing, including two collections of poetry, but especially for her play, *At What a Price*, which critics in the *Jamaica Times* and the *Daily Gleaner* praised highly. James, too, had made a name for himself. At thirty-one, he had already published a short story in the British *Saturday Review* which had then been reprinted in *Best Short Stories*. In Trinidad, he had participated in the growing labor movement, coedited the literary journal *Trinidad*, and contributed to its successor, the *Beacon*. Marson had worked as a social worker, secretary, and journalist. The feminist magazine she set up in 1928, the *Cosmopolitan*, made her the first woman editor-publisher in Jamaica and gave her a forum for her developing political views. Through the *Cosmopolitan*, she hoped to organize women workers, promote feminist consciousness, bring positive attention to the racial politics of Marcus Garvey, and urge social and economic improvements for Jamaica's poor. James had helped to organize theatrical groups, spoken publicly on behalf of the labor activist Arthur Cipriani, and written on cricket for the *Labour Leader*. Having published successfully, both arrived in England with literary ambitions and a few connections. Marson's were with Dr. Harold Moody, whose home became her refuge during her first two years in London when, in spite of her many skills and talents, she faced open racist discrimination in her search for lodging and a job. She ended up working for Moody as secretary of the League for Coloured Peoples and editor of its magazine the *Keys*. James's intense interest in cricket led to an invitation from Learie Constantine, the famous cricket player from Trinidad, who was then living in northern England, to help with work on Constantine's memoirs. Following his move a year later to London, James's career took off in several directions, in journalism, literature, and politics.[2]

We can read James's fiction and Marson's poetry as explorations of what, for James, involved repeated motions of colonial mimicry that could only be altered through critical self-reflection on the part of middle-class colonial intellectuals and, for Marson, comprised a "slavish" imitation of English literary traditions that she sought to expose and undermine. Between 1928 and 1936, in Trinidad and then England, James intervened in the double-bind of colonial mimicry by transforming the narrative conventions of English and European fiction through forms borrowed from Trinidadian street culture, black Atlantic and international proletarian aesthetics, and scenes of religious visionary practices. Working also in the 1930s, traveling between Jamaica and England, Marson portrayed acts of vision to employ and, simultaneously, undercut the traditions of English poetry.

Their work, before coming to England, on magazines devoted to literature, the arts, and social issues set points of departure for their writings and provide contexts for understanding their literary projects. James's participation in the *Beacon* group began around 1927 and put him in the center of debates around national independence, the labor movement, and socialism. The *Beacon* published often conflicting and controversial points of view, especially concerning the labor movement and its leader Arthur Cipriani. Reinhard Sander has commented on the failure of the group's socialist ideals when some of its members entered the political arena in the late 1930s, citing their contradictory ideological positions and middle-class intellectual backgrounds. He states also, however, that the literature they produced "marks an important turning point in the cultural history of the West Indies."[3]

Perhaps because of these contradictory and conflicting positions and the class background of the *Beacon* members, the relationship between the educated middle classes and those of the working and lower classes became one of the group's chief concerns. Emphasizing the impact on the group of the Russian Revolution, Hazel Carby stresses the influence of Soviet social and cultural policies on the literature they published.[4] A central requirement of proletarian literature demanded that writers abandon the position of independent observers and become, instead, participants in the lives of the masses. These aesthetic guidelines inevitably posed the problem, for the middle-class writers of the group, of their separation from the working and lower classes of Trinidad. Most significantly, they challenged the status of the educated colonial man as a modern subject constructed through an assumed capacity to see – to observe from a formalized distance. Recognizing that the complexities of the colonial relationship were central to altering class hierarchies in Trinidad, James indirectly shifts the emphasis in his short fiction to the self-representation of the educated colonial. Rather than assuming that he could simply renounce that class status and its position of distant observer, he makes it the subject of narrative irony in his short stories. In his novel, *Minty Alley*, he then brings the middle-class intellectual to a point of critical self-observation that presents in visual terms the problems of dependency and colonial imitation.

Carby argues persuasively for placing James's short stories and *Minty Alley* within an international context that includes the proletariat literature of the 1920s and 1930s and the art and literature of the Harlem Renaissance.[5] I agree and argue, further, that writing in this broader transnational context about class, ethnic, and gender relations in Trinidad, James goes to the heart of the paradox constituting the modern subject. In this paradox, the European subject is constructed as modern by casting Africa as "pre-modern" and as the object of European contemplative reason and judgment. Afro-Caribbean intellectuals such as James are caught then in an ambivalence toward, not only the lower classes and their adherence to Afro-Caribbean folk cultures but the self-representation of the educated and, hence, modern, Afro-Caribbean individual. James's ambivalence toward folk cultures shapes the narrative dynamics of his short fiction and provides a critical lens through which to reposition the hierarchies of "modern" and "pre-modern" as competing systems of knowledge.

James's ambivalence stemmed from an intellectual orientation developed through his colonialist education and increasing adherence to what Paget Henry has termed an historicist perspective. Henry argues that James was an overwhelmingly historicist thinker, one who proudly claimed European "modern" philosophies, including their influences on Marxism and Pan-Africanism, and insisted on the Caribbean and the Caribbean subject as historically constituted through social discourses and practices. James rejected as grounds for knowledge the philosophies and spiritual traditions of what he considered "pre-modern" Africa, including their contemporary versions in the Caribbean. As Henry puts it, "In James, the self is radically historicized, which leaves it without mythic or religious dimensions."[6] In this respect, James's attitudes were secular and Eurocentric. However, I would add that this philosophical orientation, in conjunction with his commitment, while a young man in Trinidad, to social change and the creation of a local literature, led him to a dilemma that shapes all of his literary writing. As a modern subject, he was obligated to reject Africa and its diasporic formations long constituted as either pre-modern or inherently incapable of modernity and, therefore, inferior. Yet as a socialist and historical thinker, James was aware of the development of the self, as Henry puts it, within specific historical and social relations. The dilemma is one of sight: James claimed the status of the modern subject-who-sees – a distant, formalized view of history that, paradoxically, allowed him to see the conditions in which subject-formation takes place. It gave him a political problem to address and also an aesthetic project. Adhering to the socialist-oriented aesthetic of realism and respect for the oppressed "folk," James could not, as a creative writer, ignore the inherently interesting and complex dynamics of spiritual traditions that came from, not only Africa, but also India, Amerindia, and Europe, coexisting in the same country, the same neighborhood or "yard," and often in the same person. In fact, his fiction plunges directly into these elements of lower-class culture, as if through them, he might see more clearly the heart of the system that divided the middle-class intellectual from the masses.

James's first published short story, "La Divina Pastora," turns on the contrast between the narrator's explicitly stated belief in "the essential facts," which he promises to record, and the belief, on the part of the story's female characters, in the power of a religious icon.[7] Sacrificing a small gold chain to La Divina Pastora, Anita Perez prays to the image for the love of her neighbor Sebastian, whom she wishes to marry. Later, dressing for a date with Sebastian, Anita wishes she had the chain back so that she might wear it that evening. In a twist at the story's end, however, we learn that, not only has she been given Sebastian's love but, as if to prove the power granting that love, her second wish – for the return of the gold chain – has also, mysteriously, come true. Home from her date, she undresses and puts some pins in a cigarette tin on her table. The narrative then shifts to Anita's mother who, "lying on the bed and listening with half-closed eyes to Anita's account of the dance, was startled by a sudden silence followed by the sound of a heavy fall" (27). We learn the reason for Anita's fall as her mother turns to the table for some smelling salts and sees "in its old place in the cigarette tin, .. a little chain of gold" (28).

The vision of the gold chain, mysteriously returned to its tin, appears to Anita but also to her mother, confirmed then by two sightings, and by the telling of the story as one composed of "essential facts." Fact and faith intertwine, and the twist takes in the narrator as much as the characters, undermining his distanced reportage and reliance on fact. However, though the narrative irony targets more than the characters with the story's surprise ending, the ironic tone remains to raise more questions and to promote ambiguity as an epistemological device and aesthetic virtue. Importantly, this ambiguity rests on the power, not of the saint so much as the evidence of the vision, the sudden appearance of the wished-for object, seen and then confirmed by another act of seeing so that it can become an element of faith in the world of empirical facts.

James's treatment of this creolized religious practice places the question of class relations in Trinidad in the realm of competing knowledge systems and ways of seeing. His critique of the separation between the classes comes through in the turn-about he enacts through the surprise vision, a turn-about that redirects the irony towards the presumably educated middle-class narrator and the reader. Some readers may associate narrative irony with the European literary tradition, and the surprise short-story ending even more specifically with the "O. Henry twist."[8] However, as Reinhard Sander points out, these elements were prevalent in the calypso forms popular in Trinidad in the 1920s and 1930s. Sander cites Gordon Rohlehr who describes the calypsonian pose of "a disinterested listener, or of a newspaper reporter who is always on the spot, or of one who had been told hot news by a reliable source or a barrack-room dweller who cannot help but overhear what is going on in bed next door" (10). Sander attributes to the calypso form also the "element of ironic reversal in their surprise endings" (10). James's story, thus, offers a hybrid or creolized genre, influenced by popular local street culture, proletarian literature, the Harlem Renaissance, and "modern" short-story conventions. In the self-reflexivity and epistemological uncertainty of these narratives, the social realism of the *Beacon* group's aesthetic principles transmutes into a creolized modernism. Nevertheless, through the pose of the outsider, listening in and reporting what he hears, or distantly observing the minute details of lower-class households, James examines the problem posed by the *Beacon* group concerning class relationships and social change, while the creolized elements of the narrative enact an artistic response to the problem. And by placing in contest with one another "modern" secular orientations to knowledge and those of "pre-modern" Caribbean spiritual practices, the narratives sustain an ambivalence at the heart of the class relationship.

An ironic ambivalence toward Caribbean folk religions appears also in "Triumph," embedded in the turnings of a more complex plot, which involves several main characters.[9] Though portraying the rivalries of three poor women struggling to survive in a barracks "yard" in Port of Spain, "Triumph" is also very much about religious practices. Each turn in the plot follows on a religious ritual, and its main events take place on religious holidays. When one woman, Irene, puts a "black spirit" (30) on another, Mamitz, Mamitz's fortunes immediately decline. Determined to help Mamitz, a third neighbor, Celestine, gives her a ritual bath and, just as immediately, Mamitz's romantic and financial luck change for the better. As Celestine puts it, "the power of the bath held good" (36). She and Mamitz then conspire to flaunt Mamitz's new prosperity in Irene's face. When Irene approaches Mamitz's doorway following an Easter Day feast, Celestine and Mamitz fling the door wide, revealing a startling sight: "– and then she saw. Both halves of the door were plastered with notes, green five-dollar notes, red two-dollar notes, and blue dollar ones, with a pin at the corner of each to keep it firm. The pin-heads were shining in the sun" (40). As the women taunt her, Irene "[can] find neither spirit nor voice to reply" (40).

Ending with a materialist and vengeful twist on the Epiphany, pinheads "shining in the sun," the story also puts a secular spin on Easter with the resurrection of Mamitz's fortunes. The story's "triumph" consists of a humiliating revenge on a woman blamed for doing something in which the educated reader ought not to believe, putting a "black spirit" on her neighbor, and yet it results in depriving her of her "spirit" and "voice," a psychological effect the reader might easily accept. James portrays an intertwining of Christian and Afro-Caribbean spiritual beliefs and practices in the everyday lives of the women; further, he makes those beliefs crucial to the "facts" of the narrative and confirms them through a materialist vision: the sight of money enshrining a doorway.

As with "La Divina Pastora," the ironies of the plot are generated through the narrative voice. Positioned as a distant observer, one educated enough to mention Kipling, Shaw, and figures of Roman mythology, the narrator can describe not only the history and culture of the yard but the intimate details of the residents' lives. Again, the narration belies the narrator's position, at least what readers might assume as an educated person's dismissal of folk religion. In the story he tells, "the power of the bath h[olds]," and yet the modernist irony remains to distance both readers and the narrator from actual belief in the rituals that bring about Mamitz's resurrection and the defeat of her enemy.

In his only novel, *Minty Alley*, James re-frames the questions posed in the earlier short stories, making more explicit the relationship between the educated middle classes and the lower classes of Trinidadian society. While the short stories portray, through a distanced observing narrator, spiritual practices as a way in to the epistemological barriers separating the classes, *Minty Alley* highlights that distant observation as the pose of its main character. An entirely absent third-person narrator describes Haynes, the young middle-class protagonist of the novel, in the act of living among and spying upon the working-class lodgers of a boardinghouse; that act of participant visual observation thus comes under narrative scrutiny. Although obeah and Christianity mix in the lives of many of the novel's characters, it is not surprise moments of religious vision that challenge the modern subject's worldview, but an ongoing secular motif, that of a peephole. In *Minty Alley*, seeing as a social act and, more specifically, an act of voyeurism, organizes the entire plot and characterization. Portraying the act of middle-class voyeurism, James's novel, described by Eric Keenaghan as "social realism with a modernist twist,"[10] presents and questions a complex social dynamic involving class and gender divisions, colonial imitation, and the narrative conventions of coming-of-age plots.

Minty Alley opens and closes with scenes of voyeurism, and throughout the narrative voyeuristic scenes mark turning points in the plot and development of the main character. An educated young "creole," Haynes distinguishes himself from the boardinghouse located at No. 2 Minty Alley and all who reside inside the house when he first arrives on the doorsteps and peers "[t]hrough the open jalousies."[11] His detailed surveillance of the interior establishes the house on Minty Alley as the object of Haynes's penetrating gaze. From then on, he struggles to maintain this superior position, but it becomes an increasingly ambiguous stance, as he is drawn into the life of the boarding house and as its lodgers begin to penetrate his personal space.

Once moved inside his own room, Haynes must struggle to maintain his privacy and determines, in a fit of boredom and restlessness, to leave the "blasted place" (36). He changes his mind, however, when he discovers a gap between the wallboards of his room, through which he can see his landlord, Benoit, forcing kisses on the servant girl. As Haynes continues to peer through the crack in the wall, things get even steamier when Benoit and another woman, who works as a nurse, passionately embrace. Feeling that "[t]he stage" is "set for a terrific human drama," Haynes tells his former servant Ella that he thinks he "shall get to like it very well" at Minty Alley.

At age twenty, Haynes has had no experience with women outside of books and "often experienced difficulty in looking young women fully in the face" (37). With his peephole he no longer needs to look directly at a young woman, risking her return gaze, in order to satisfy his sexual curiosity; furthermore, he may exploit the transgressions of others for his own excitement while keeping himself distant from any moral responsibility. Haynes, thus, resembles the viewer of pornography in his role as Peeping Tom. He also occupies the position of the tourist peering behind a camera lens, this time one who has gone "slumming" in his own neighborhood. H. Adlai Murdoch has argued that Haynes's gaze represents "an integral part of colonial domination," one mediated by the fact that he is black, an Afro-Caribbean colonized subject who is the most culturally assimilated to colonial society of all the characters.[12] Aldon Neilsen has written that, "In effect, Haynes literalizes the panopticon effect of social hierarchy in the colony. His is the surveying eye of middle-class morality enviously scanning the daily lives of the lowly" (29). Haynes certainly acquires a furtive sense of power through his peephole sufficient to support his eventual rise to a figure of authority within the household. However, these descriptions miss a key visual dynamic of the narrative: the other boarders are hardly passive objects of his gaze. Haynes's "surveying eye" counters their invasions of his own privacy and, by enacting a visual exchange, gives him several opportunities for growth beyond that of adolescent voyeur.

Indeed, Haynes progresses from a sexually innocent young man, dependent on the maternal Ella, and intellectually detached from the "life" of the working classes, to an involved member of the household who, upon his sexual initiation, becomes "master of the house."[13] However, by positioning Haynes's coming-of-age within the context of scopophilia, James exposes the blindness of the middle-class intellectual to his own dependency on the labor of the working class and to colonialist conventions that keep him in a social impasse, repeating rather than changing the conventions of colonial society. The modern, educated subject-who-sees is actually sight-impaired. He cannot see his exploitation of others; nor can he see his own complicity with and colonial imitations of the "master."

In an excruciatingly painful scene following Haynes's discovery of the hole in his wallboards, the nurse savagely beats her small son, and Haynes, though knowing that "he should have saved Sonny," does not interfere. Positioned as a "cruel mother," who appears white, "dominates the house," is frequently absent, and alternately steals from its resources while bestowing gifts on special occasions, the nurse occupies a colonizing position at Minty Alley. Her character allows James to criticize the ideology of the colonial relationship as protectively maternal and to expose the related and hypocritical construction of whiteness in the Caribbean. Haynes's inability to resist her casts him as dependent, still a child within the colonial class and color system of Trinidad.

Thus, if Haynes grows up in this coming-of-age plot, it is not through moral action. Rather, he matures through sexual initiation. And even this step towards maturity reveals his dependence, this time on a young working woman, Maisie, who is the niece of his landlady, Mrs. Rouse, and on the promiscuous and exploitative Benoit, who coaches Haynes as to the moves he should make: " 'Hold her and kiss her,' Benoit had said. So he held her and kissed her, and then to his astonishment did what he liked with her" (168). Only after Benoit has left Mrs. Rouse and married the nurse, leaving a vacancy in the role of male head of household, does Haynes begin to feel his confidence increase. The women turn to him, and he begins to feel "a sense of responsibility" (154). But it is mostly a "sense" dependent on their admiration of him and on their labor. Miss Atwell, for example, is his "abject slave" (154), and though he might be late with his rent, "[m]orning, noon, and night everything was ready punctually on the table for him" (137). Ambitious on Haynes's behalf, Maisie advises him to seek a higher salary, a suggestion he follows with success. "And after that he was the master of the house" (173).

In presenting the complex slippage of this role, from the historical plantocracy to the nurse and Benoit, then to Haynes, James anticipates Bhabha's later theoretical insights into the ambivalence of colonial relations. As Bhabha has written concerning the "mimic men" produced by colonial education, they are "appropriate objects of a colonialist chain of command"; yet they emerge as " 'inappropriate' colonial subjects."[14] In the relations between colonizer and colonized, they become a partial representation of the colonizer, able to return a "gaze of otherness" and threaten the entire system by making the observer the observed and challenging any notion of essential identity. In the context of Minty Alley, Haynes partially represents the colonizer in his educated manner and taken-for-granted superiority; however, he desires another kind of education which the previous "master" Benoit and the women of the house can give him. Attempting to remain distant while learning from them, his surveillance breaks down when they return his gaze, enter his room, and bring him into their lives. The colonial relation repeats, differently, in each interaction, its ambivalence exposed as racial, class, and gender identities become increasingly indiscrete through visibly "inappropriate" relations. Yet they follow a pattern by which Haynes does accede to the position of "master."

As this plot line develops, a second direction of Haynes's growth begins to emerge, again, portrayed through acts of seeing. In this alternate narrative line, Haynes begins to see the members of the household differently, becoming aware of the domestic economy in which he benefits from his class position and the work they do for him. Haynes is shocked, for example, to discover that the rest of the household often goes without food while his meals appear regularly, and he wonders about the sacrifices they make. After he has lived in the house nearly a year, he enters the kitchen "for the first time" and, submitted to the heat of the enormous stove and the sun on the galvanized roof, feels "that he [is] in the mouth of hell" (187). This sudden sight of "hell" causes Haynes to see Mrs. Rouse differently, to notice how thin she has become and to see her courage. He also sees the "Indian" servant Philomen in a new light, "getting thinner and thinner," in part from problems with her lover, but also from endless hours of work. Haynes sees all of this independently and directly, through his own action of entering the kitchen, where the main business and labor of the household take place.

However, Haynes's dependence on women and especially on women of the servant class does not alter at all; in fact, as the household breaks up, he returns to the care of the woman who worked for his mother and, thus, to a childlike relationship that his role as "master" of No. 2 Minty Alley had only temporarily altered. Haynes may have gained a few insights into the labor of the women with whom he has lived, but they have not prevented him from relying on their labors once again. Though willing to advise Mrs. Rouse in her financial affairs, he is still eager to leave what he now calls "this damned house," repeating his initial angry response to "the blasted place," back again where he started.

Only the concluding scene suggests a potential within the second narrative thread – that of the possibility for self-reflection. This scene, too, seems to take Haynes back where he started, outside No. 2 Minty Alley, looking inside the windows, occupying his old position of Peeping Tom. The difference is that the house has been sold and is now occupied by a middle-class family.

The front door and windows were open, and from the street he could see into the drawing-room. Husband and wife and three children lived there and one of the children was sitting at the piano playing a familiar tune from Hemy's music-book. Over and over she played it, while he stood outside, looking in at the window and thinking of old times. (244)

The scene he views resembles a vision of his own future, caught in a fishbowl of middle-class conventionality.[15] He has previously given up a real relationship with Maisie for a dream, "the girl of his dreams, the divine, the inexpressible she whom he was going to marry one day" (212). His romantic dream requires marriage, and he now sees in the same place previously occupied by the unmarried partnership of Mrs. Rouse and Benoit, a respectable, middle-class marriage, a model of its kind with three children and piano lessons. He has dreamed of this future, but what he really sees is a child playing "[o]ver and over" "a familiar tune" (244). The figure he focuses on is not the husband or the wife, but a child, repeating something familiar. In focusing on the child, he looks at himself perhaps for the first time and sees the repetition of convention and the dependence on others that has blocked all potential for change, growth and maturity. He sees, also, the replacement of a strong folk culture by the rise of the black middle class, repeating colonial conventions of respectability rather than enacting any real change in the social life of the island. Though outside, he sees *into himself* and his future and, thus, his return to adolescent voyeurism ironically opens (and literally in the portrayal of doors and windows as open) the possibility for more mature self-examination. James suggests that only by observing himself as part of a class system and by truly seeing his dependency on others and complicity with colonial conventions can the young middle-class man gain any self-knowledge or hope to effect any social change. Haynes must see through the imitative gestures with which he has constituted his adult self. In this *seeing through*, the repeated motions of colonial mimicry are both the lens and the object of critique as vision reflects on itself. James leaves Haynes poised on the threshold of that vision. In that liminal position, Haynes is also crossing from the position of voyeur to that of self-reflexive prophet, occupying an unstable epistemological ground no longer securely scientific or secular.

* * *

As James's literary project took off from his participation in the *Beacon* group and their debates concerning class relations in Trinidad within an international context, so did Una Marson's poetry respond to a circle of writers and intellectuals and a magazine that attempted to extend its cultural reach beyond the boundaries of Jamaica while celebrating the specificity of Jamaica's heritage.[16] In the *Cosmopolitan*, which Marson founded and edited, we can read what may seem in retrospect conflicting ideologies concerning class, racial, and cultural relations in a colony yet to experience the labor revolts and independence movements of the late 1930s. However, its over-arching concern for an internationalist perspective prefigures Marson's later activism, writing, and cultural work in England, Europe, and Asia.[17] For her early poetry, this internationalist orientation offers a context for a different critique of colonial imitation, one that moves laterally, across the empire, rather than following the slippage of the colonial chain of command that James charts in *Minty Alley*. Further, its idealist visions of a "world-wide commonwealth" draw on popular cross-colonial spiritual movements to reframe the question plaguing James of folk religious practices and the "modern."

Reading Marson's poetry in the context of the *Cosmopolitan's* stated philosophies and articles, it becomes clear that even in her earlier poems, Marson imitated conventional lyric and sonnet forms but did so in order to implicitly subvert sexist and colonialist hierarchies. She also uses those forms to question her own colonial imitations and gesture toward a freer poetics. Additionally, she inscribes a transcultural, cross-colonial orientalism that locates inner vision as a means of personal transformation. Finally, by portraying the racism enacted through social practices of seeing, her later poetry explicitly challenges the foundational relations of colonialism and extends her verse forms in creolized invocations of the blues.

Before she left Jamaica for England, Marson published two collections of poems, one in 1930 titled *Tropic Reveries* and a second, a year later, called *Heights and Depths*. In 1937, following her four-year stay in England and return to Jamaica, she published a third volume, *The Moth and the Star*. We can read a number of developments in her poetry over these seven years, perhaps most notably the move from what her biographer refers to as poems of "pure Romantic derivation"[18] modeled on the sonnet or lyric form, to poems written in dialect, often explicitly evoking the blues. However, the early love poetry appeared alongside poems explicitly designated as "parodies" of Shakespeare and Kipling, suggesting that, though writing within the traditions of English verse, Marson also took her distance from them. As Alison Donnell has pointed out, even the early sonnets, though not explicitly parodic, nevertheless, subtly undermine their own apparent message.

With their recurring images of feminine enslavement to a lover, these sonnets can be especially puzzling to readers who know of Marson's feminism. The metaphor of slavery is all the more disturbing given Jamaica's history. Donnell argues, however, that much in these sonnets suggests ambiguity especially in their subversive turns of phrase. Arguing for a counter-discursive reading of Marson's sonnet, "In Vain," Donnell highlights the contradiction in the troubling line, "as thy slave to come into my own." She claims that "Marson's poem reveals how taking control of submission can be an act of transgression" and argues further that, by thus undermining the subordination of the feminine speaker, Marson subverts also the relationship between "In Vain" and the European sonnet tradition.[19]

If we read this trope of enslavement alongside an important 1928 *Cosmopolitan* article titled "The Value of Right Reading" by J. E. Clare McFarlane, the significance of the troubling "slave" relationship becomes more clear and historically concrete. McFarlane, who headed the Jamaican Poetry League of which Marson was an active member, figured the literary education as a romantic quest and writes of wandering until "there comes a time when we stand face to face with a view that stirs our inmost souls"; here "the questing spirit" meets his master, "the directing force destined to be its guide through life."[20] However, McFarlane is not content to remain a dependent in literary matters, and the crucial turn in his argument comes at this point in the "road": "It is all well to discover a master and to learn all that he can teach; but this having been done we should not permit our intellects to become slavish and imitative" (100).

As an argument schooled in the canons of English literature that he recommends for the beginning student, yet coming from the colony which served, in the eighteenth-century writings of Edward Long, as evidence for the notion that an actual slave could become only an imitative poet (see Chapter 1), McFarlane's essay invites a double reading. It inserts itself in between the two sides of a split in the language of freedom and slavery that marked the Enlightenment. Homi Bhabha has described this split as it appears in Locke's *Second Treatise*: one side upholds the right to property, "the locus of a legitimate form of ownership," as a marker of freedom; the other refers to the tyranny of feudal slavery and becomes "the trope for an intolerable illegitimate exercise of power."[21] McFarlane's essay follows both sides of the split by adhering to all the visual tropes of distanced contemplative sight deemed necessary since the eighteenth century to the aesthetic judgment exercised by the free man. His motif of a wandering quest leading to "a view that stirs our inmost souls" fully deploys that vocabulary of seeing and sensibility. His language of slavishness might, therefore, allude to Enlightenment protests against the slavery of feudal Europe, the "intolerable illegitimate exercise of power." However, coming from a colony steeped in the legacies of the African slave trade, the home of the enslaved poet Francis Williams, whom Long had accused of merely parroting the poetry he had learned, McFarlane's language of slavery also refers to a no longer "legitimate form of ownership," the rights to property that legitimated slavery in the eighteenth century. Creating within that side of the split a new colonial subjectivity, McFarlane translates emancipation into the realm of literature. There, he is unwilling to be "slavish and imitative"; further, he asserts his power to govern his own intellect in not permitting it to become so.

Returning to Marson's poem, "In Vain," we might read it as inserting a similar turn of subjectivity within the canonical forms of English literature. In addition to the subversion of gendered identities that Donnell finds in the sonnet, its final couplet sustains a doubled reading *by virtue* of the sonnet form. The third stanza signals this way of working through the sonnet in order to be emancipated from it with a play on the words "heart" and "art": "But thou, king of my heart, art far away."[22] In this distance between her heart and what might be read as the king's art, emerges the possibility for artistic alterity. Finally, the paradox of being bound to sonnet conventions while undermining their codes finds its perfect formal expression in the sonnet's required couplet:

> In vain one boon from life's great store I crave,
> No more the king comes to his waiting slave. (128)

The lines suggest simultaneously nearly opposite meanings. The first, in keeping with the rhetoric of the preceding stanzas, emphasizes the title phrase "in vain" and repeats the suffering of waiting in vain for the lover's (or literary "master's") return. In a second reading, however, the couplet makes full use of the sonnet form to express a radical turn of thought: the emphasis shifts from that of suffering "in vain" and falls instead on the "one boon" craved by the speaker. In this reading, the couplet's final line explains that *boon* as a situation in which "[n]o more the king comes to his waiting slave." Read beyond the theme of love and as a comment on the colonized woman writer's bondage to the traditions of English poetry, "In Vain" expresses within those conventions an intense desire for freedom from them.

The contradictions between a desire for a freer art and the continued attachment to Britain, especially the ideals of art and civilization represented by English culture, appeared also in representations of the British Empire as still en route towards its own stated ideals. This trope appeared in a poem written by McFarlane and directed toward a major event of the British Empire Exhibition at Wembley in 1924. Titled "The Fleet of the Empire (Reflections on the visit of the Special Service Squadron) July, 1924," the poem alludes to the special squadron sent by the exhibition's organizers to all the regions of the empire (See Chapter 2) and its arrival in Jamaica. Though the poem celebrates "Britannia's way," it repeats over and over in the refrain that "Our Empire plunges thro' the deep / Into the dawn of a greater day."[23] While the exhibition guides urged visitors at the exhibition to "see with Empire eyes" the unity of the whole presented in miniature at Wembley and to imagine themselves as, like the special squadron, taking their own tours of the empire, British imperial citizens of the Caribbean represented themselves as also "like them" but in a different way:

> Like them, the great Dominions wait –
> Great units of a greater whole –
> The promise which the years unroll:
> The consummation of their fate.   (49)

Rather than sightseeing around the empire, the colonies wait, like the ships in the ports, for a "greater day." Marson's "In Vain" also expresses this theme of waiting, apparently for the lover or king, but more significantly, for the moment in which the speaker comes into her own. That waiting is hardly a passive act; rather, it involves complex turnings in the split invoked by the discourses of freedom and slavery. Marson's early "imitations" of the English lyric and sonnet forms were thus deliberate performances of the expectations for colonial writers in which she apprenticed herself to her "master," exposed the "slavery" of imitation to view, and found a way through it to suggest the possibility of a freer poetic voice.

* * *

To explain how vision works in Marson's poetry, I wish to call attention now to other ways in which *Tropic Reveries* took its distance from English love poetry. At least two of these poems, "Summer Days" and "Renunciation," indicate the influence of "Indian" love lyrics, most explicitly a popular Victorian orientalist poem, and also, indirectly, the devotional lyrics of Bengali poet Rabindranath Tagore and the Indian *kirtan* tradition. When we read the two poems as expressions of spiritual longing, a Christian version of the longing expressed in Tagore's *Gitanjali* poems and one that coincides with the desire for artistic freedom, we can see the elements of visionary writing Marson incorporated into her early poetry. Also evident is a cross-colonial literary interaction that shifts the usual postcolonial emphasis on cultural relations between colony and metropole to a much wider and more complex rerouting of cultural influences across colonies and across the divide of high and low cultures.

Even if we agree that many of the poems Marson wrote in the 1920s and published in *Tropic Reveries* in 1930 and *Heights and Depths* in 1931 were, on the whole, influenced by English Romanticism, even that Romanticism suggests another, transcultural, line of influence. Erica Smilowitz has pointed out lines Marson adapted from Shelley; these include Shelleys's opening line to "The Indian Serenade" which Marson used as an epigraph to "A Dream" in *Heights and Depths*.[24] But as the title to Shelley's poem reminds us, the Romantics were steeped in an orientalism that often focused on India. W. B. Yeats's poems, often associated with modernism but certainly tied to Romanticism, included in his early years some "Indian" poems that led him to a more serious interest in India and friendships with Indian writers, including Rabindranath Tagore. It is clear that, by 1937, Marson had read Tagore and looked then to his work on behalf of Bengali culture in India as a model for the development, through the arts, of Jamaican national identity. Delia Jarrett-Macauley quotes from a piece Marson wrote for the Jamaican journal *Public Opinion*: "In the end Jamaica . . . would be judged 'not so much by its "sugar and rum," as by the products of its great minds. Gandhi, Pandit Nehru and Rabindranath Tagore are better known than the financial magnates and the gold-laden maharajahs of India'" (117). Though I've not found explicit evidence that Marson read Tagore's poetry in the 1920s, it would be surprising if she had not. Following his receipt of the Nobel Prize for Literature in 1913, Tagore traveled extensively and gave many interviews. His writing won him global fame and admiration, and among English speakers, his status was enhanced by the fact that Yeats wrote an introduction to the prizewinning *Gitanjali*. His influence in the Caribbean was apparent by 1932 when he published an essay in Trinidad's the *Beacon*. Marson's membership in the Poetry League of Jamaica, her job on the *Jamaica Critic*, and her interests in Jamaican nationalism would most likely have led her to his writing during the 1920s. Further, similarities in theme and language suggest this alternate way of reading some of her love lyrics.

In the poems "Summer Days" and "Renunciation," religious longing and earthly, romantic love converge in ways that recall not only English Romantic poetry, but also the spiritual songs of Bengal introduced to the English-speaking world by the translation of Tagore's *Gitanjali* in 1913. "Summer Days" invites readers to make this connection with a footnote, urging us to read the poem "To the tune of the Indian Love Lyric 'The Temple Bells.'"[25] While her note most likely refers to a popular song, it nevertheless confirms that an orientalist influence guides the poem. Though the theme differs, "Summer Days" echoes the rhythms of Laurence Hope's poem "The Temple Bells,"[26] and many readers might argue that Marson borrowed sentimentality as well as stereotyped "Indian" poetic themes directly from Hope. Such stereotypes were popular in Jamaica in the late 1920s and early 1930s, as evidenced by a review published in the *Cosmopolitan* of a performance of the musical play *Kismet* by a writer who goes by the name "Artistic" and declares her-/himself as "[l]oving all books and plays and scenes eastern."[27] If Laurence Hope's poem does indeed shape the rhythm of Marson's "Summer Days," we find an ironic instance of an Anglo-Indian woman (her real name was Adela Florence Nicolson) attempting highly popular imitations of stereotyped "oriental" themes, that are then referenced in the colonial "imitation" Romanticism produced by Marson in Jamaica. Here is yet another version of the rampant slippage of imitation in the colonial chain of command, to the point that it becomes a twisting series of uneven relays, resulting in what most critics read as pretty bad, "imitative," poetry.

However, when we recognize that the *kirtan* tradition of devotional poems in which Tagore wrote was also shaped in India by the importation of British poetic traditions, some of them formed through orientalist inspiration, the relays become less a matter of "authentic" devolving into derivative poetry and more a tangle of transcultural and cross-colonial influences. These include the rerouting of myths of the Other back through the Other's culture. Moreover, I find in Marson's "Summer Days" versions of poetic conventions found in Tagore's *kirtan*, which do not appear in Hope's poetry. Even if the influence did not come directly from Tagore, acknowledging these conventions in Marson's poem recognizes a cross-colonial circuiting of poetic traditions that leads us to a new perspective on Marson's poetry. It allows us to locate the crucial moment of vision that generates the poem's dynamics of grief, desire, and continually renewed anticipation.

As the title of "Summer Days" indicates, this poem joins the seasonal cycles with the theme of love, a familiar convention in the Vaishnavan tradition adapted by Tagore. Many of Tagore's poems were actually songs, or *kirtan*, which Mary Lago has described as exploring "the endlessly puzzling relationship between man and his Creator ... in uncounted numbers of lyric variations upon a single controlling metaphor: the love of Krishna, the eight incarnations of Vishnu, and Radha, his favorite among the *gopis* or milkmaids of holy Vrindavan."[28] In their divine and simultaneously sensual relationship, "[t]he ceaseless cycle of their meetings and separations stands for the relation between God and the human soul."[29] In Marson's "Summer Days," the initial grief of separation from a lover turns to an ecstatic anticipation, "He is coming my beloved, / Coming now to see his love," which then turns to an apparent reunion, "Oh my darling thou art come, /My poor heart has ceased to moan." However, almost immediately the lines resume the future tense and an attitude of blissful anticipation, "For you'll soothe my every care, / You'll dry my every tear" (12). The poem resides now in a zone marked by both closeness and separation in which the speaker is still waiting for the lover, "Oh come to me, my love, / I am waiting here for thee, . . . // Come, ah, come to me my love, . . ." (13). The turn from grief to the ecstatic sweetness of anticipation generates the emotional intensity of this poem. The reader wonders, though, about the plot. If the lover has, indeed, "come" so that the speaker's heart "has ceased to moan," why must the speaker immediately resume waiting for the lover?

One response is that the speaker only imagines, through visionary anticipation, the act of joining with the loved one. The repetition of "Come oh come . . ." // "Come, ah, come to me my love" in the final stanzas echoes then the conventional appeal of the *kirtan*. Tagore expresses it in number 45 of the *Gitanjali* poems:

> Have you not heard his silent steps? He comes, comes, ever comes.
>   Every moment and every age, every day and every night he comes, comes, ever comes.
>   Many a song have I sung in many a mood of mind, but all their notes have always proclaimed, "He comes, comes, ever comes."[30]

The song Tagore describes in this self-reflexive poem might describe also Marson's "Summer Days," which continually regenerates, through imagined union, the occasion of a lover who "ever" comes.

Thus, to read Marson's "Summer Days," with its reference to an "Indian Love Lyric," means to read the influence of an often "orientalist" English Romanticism, as circuited through Tagore's modern adaptation of an ancient Bengali lyric tradition and, also, a popular Victorian imitation, in Hope's "The Temple Bells," of ancient "oriental" themes. This complex relay of cultural influence, "Eastern" and "Western," "high" and "low," from colony to metropole to colony, and also across colonies, offers a model for understanding the cultural formation of colonial subjectivities far more complex than that found in the usual postcolonial focus on relations between colonizer and colonized, however ambivalent they may be envisioned. Elleke Boehmer has departed from the colony–metropole model in *Empire, the National, and the Postcolonial, 1890–1920* in which she argues that nationalist resistance to colonialism emerged in cross-colonial interactions.[31] Boehmer does not consider the Caribbean or Caribbean writers in her model, which is based largely on Indian, Irish, and South African examples. The presence of "East Indians," however, in the Caribbean, dating from their immigration as indentured laborers in the mid-nineteenth century gave Caribbean writers an immediate interest in the anti-colonial movements in Bengal and later all of India. The *Beacon*, especially, offered regular columns reporting on events in India, and the *Cosmopolitan* based its philosophy and title on the cross-empire migrations between colony and metropole and across colonies. In an important editorial on "The Colour-line," published in the *Cosmopolitan* in December 1929, Marson turns to the American-based Ghanian educator, James Emman Kwegyir Aggrey, as a cross-colonial model for the ideal political activist, describing his life as exemplary of the "wide wisdom and dauntless courage" necessary to create worldwide harmony between black and white. In an earlier *Cosmopolitan* article, published in August 1928, the Reverend J. Leslie Webb writes of the entire world coming to Jamaica through the circulation of culture. He mentions commodities, transportation, and the promise of television, but he stresses the spiritual implications of this large circulating "world-wide commonwealth," in which "[w]e are members of one another."[32] On this vision of a potential world unity, he bases his definition of "[t]he true cosmopolitan" who "holds that these gifts [of each nationality] are to be pooled for the benefit of all, and that each nation should make its own commonwealth. He has the 'international' mind, which must be carefully distinguished from the merely nationalist and from the 'non-nationalist'" (165). Both defining the philosophy of the magazine and appealing to a broadly conceived notion of spiritual connection, this reverend seems to expand the Christian worldview he represents to embrace all nations and cultures and the dynamic interactions among them. Reverend Webb's notion of a worldwide spiritual commonwealth echoes Ezra Pound's earlier praise for Tagore's *Gitanjali* as inaugurating a new period of "world-fellowship."[33]

Such cross-colonial literary, political, and spiritual interactions appear also in "Renunciation," a sonnet that begins, as does "Summer Days," with a catalogue of the delights of nature (all "for me") and ends, similar to "In Vain," with the apparent desire for enslavement:

> But not for me what most I crave –
> To call thee mine, – to be thy slave.[34]

As with the concluding couplet of "In Vain," this couplet invites a double reading. In the first reading, the speaker must accept that, though she can claim all these earthly pleasures, she cannot have what she most craves, which is in itself a contradiction: "To call thee mine, – to be thy slave." In this first reading, she desires the contradictory act of possession coupled with the condition of being, herself, possessed. In the second reading, she actively renounces the craving, asserting in contrast to the previous lines that this lover is *not* "for [her]." In either case, as in the *kirtan* tradition, contradictory ideas coexist – the pleasures of earth's beauty enjoyed "for me" and the visionary self-sacrifice that, in the second reading, brings a deeper kind of self-development through freedom from craving, possession, and enslavement. The complex relays of orientalist influence insert another axis of difference in the Afro-Caribbean/European relationship of colonial Jamaica, which presumes a progression from "pre-modern" Africanist cultural practices to those modeled after European culture as a necessary movement toward modernity and both cultural and political independence. Inserting the orientalist vogue through echoes of popular English songs or the influences of Tagore's poetry destabilizes and confuses such colonialist hierarchies and assumptions. It invokes a model of cross-colonial influence, permeated also by colonial imitation, but imitation so laterally dispersed and circuitous that notions of authenticity and derivation lose their meaning and the charge, since the eighteenth century, of slavish imitation loses its force.

If these early poems allowed Marson to develop a transcultural aesthetics of visionary or mystical experience, her later poems published in 1937 as *The Moth and the Star* turn the rerouted impulses of English Romanticism in new directions. In these poems, the act of seeing is exposed as one of cruel dispossession. Titled for Shelley's poem of the same name, this volume offers poems such as "Quashie Comes to London," "Gettin' De Spirit," "Brown Baby Blues," "Canefield Blues," "Lonesome Blues," and "Kinky Hair Blues" that reflect clearly the influences of Claude McKay's dialect poetry and the blues poems of the Harlem Renaissance. Phillip Sherlock wrote in his introduction to the volume that Marson's poems expressed a "new note which is so characteristic of the work of some of the great Negro poets of to-day," and he compared lines from "Kinky Hair Blues" to lines from poems by Gwendoline Bennett, Countee Cullen, and Lewis Alexander that reflect pride in being black.[35] Many of the poems address directly the racism of British society, including the poem titled "Nigger," first published in the *Keys* in 1933. Creating a scene in which a white child utters the epithet, tracing its history, and expressing its profound psychological effect on the subjectivity of the person of color, this poem anticipates the theme and the spirit of Fanon's famous lines in *Black Skin, White Masks*, "Dirty nigger!" Or simply, "Look, a Negro!"[36]

As in Fanon's words, the social relationship and psychological condition constituted through the racialized gaze ("Look, a Negro!") drives this new period in Marson's poetry, one that Denise deCaires Narain depicts as a modernist turn.[37] Along with the shifting perspectives and fragmented forms that deCaires Narain notes, Marson adds to her poetry the "new note" that Sherlock celebrates by exploring the social act of seeing. In poems of varying style and voice, Marson portrays the stares aimed at a "Little Brown Girl" in the streets of London, "[a] city of coated people"; the feelings of "Quashie," who catalogs the delights and oddities of London only to claim, finally, that he is "sick fe see white face"; and the emerging confidence of a "very black" woman who replaces "[t]his white lady's picture" with a mirror through which she "begin to be real proud / Of my own self."

If we read several of these poems alongside one another, a rich dialogue of female voices emerges, all engaged in questioning, deploring, surrendering to, or proudly defying the cultural eye that determines feminine beauty through racist standards. As if in response to the "very black woman" in "Black Is Fancy," who prefers her own image in the mirror to that of a white woman's portrait, the voice in "Kinky Hair Blues" argues with herself about straightening her hair and bleaching her skin. Three verses of the six stanza blues song praise "dis kinky hair" and "me black face" before giving in to the pressure of the other voice, "Now I's gwine press me hair / And bleach me skin." However, she does so with protest ("I jes don't tink it's fair") and a final question, all blues: "What won't a gal do / Some kind of man to win" (91).

In "Cinema Eyes," Marson frames a clichéd ballad plot of lost love, jealousy, and murder within a mother's response to her daughter's request to attend the cinema. The mother refuses her daughter's request because of her own tragic past, the misery and death chronicled by the ballad, all of which result from "a cinema mind." As the mother tells her story, she refused to marry a black man who was "good and true," marrying instead her "dream lover" a light-skinned man who fit the "ideal built up in my heart" through "cinema eyes." In reality, however, he "tortured" her "in hell" and could not see the beauty in their dark daughter. The final tragedy occurs when her first lover returns, only to be shot and killed by her husband. She concludes by telling her daughter,

> Come, I will let you go
> When black beauties
> Are chosen for the screen;
> That you may know
> Your own sweet beauty
> And not the white loveliness
> Of others for envy.   (87–88)

In this poem, Marson locates in the most popular of visual cultures, the movies, the source of an internal colonization that brings tragedy to women's lives. She makes specific to women's lives the growing awareness in the 1930s of the effects of racism on black self-perception. By framing the traditional ballad plot within an analysis of a particular cultural institution, she subverts the assumptions guiding the ballad form that love and jealousy reside universally in the hearts of men and women. The tragedy and its clichés recede as the framing dialogue shifts the central relationship of the poem from the traditional heterosexual romance to a mother–daughter relationship and, furthermore, presents that relationship as the site for social and psychological change. But what most interests me is that Marson accomplishes all of this by focusing on the act of seeing. The title of the poem, "Cinema Eyes," and the accompanying phrase, "cinema mind" condense into brief phrases her insight about the complexities of vision as a social relationship, institutionalized in the technology of film and then repeatedly reproduced in the social life organized around the cinema ("Yes, I know you are eighteen, / I know your friends go, / I know you want to go."). She portrays through this mother's reflections on her past the ways in which the social act of seeing transmits racist values that undermine a black woman's self-esteem and judgment, reshaping her mind, creating false desires, and influencing her decisions. The mother's refusal of her daughter's request becomes a call for a new kind of cinema and a celebration of her daughter's "own sweet beauty" seen through eyes guided by a newly awakened "pride of race."[38] If we read this poem, as we did the earlier sonnets, as a comment on colonial imitation, Marson has voiced clearly her refusal of any poetic form but one that creates, like the new cinema imagined by the mother in "Cinema Eyes," a new black poetics.

I do not see Marson's poetic career, then, as a development from purely derivative verse to more progressive experimentation with the blues. Rather, I see different methods through which Marson explores the twinned questions of imitation and vision in all of their colonialist forms. Marson's early poetry explores the slip joining spiritual and human love through a complex re-circuiting of transcultural and cross-colonial orientalist imitations; these poems also undermine the colonialist imitation of British verse conventions, calling attention to the "enslavement" involved in imitation itself. In her later blues poems, the emphasis shifts to explicit critiques, through the folk poetic forms of the ballad and the blues, of the self-destructive internalization of colonialist values and racist standards of beauty.

Both James, in his fiction, and Marson, in her poetry, engaged the paradoxes of colonial mimicry, and both of them created creolized modernist forms. Situated as they were in colonial societies that valued imitation but with increasing ambivalence, they performed their abilities to write successfully within English and European traditions; at the same time, they used those traditions to explore opposition to the assumptions and hierarchies of colonialism. Both began to *see through* colonialist imitation in both senses of the phrase; they worked with and through the conventional forms while they questioned the act of imitation, seeing through it to the possibilities for a freer literary experimentation. Further, they created this doubled discourse by representing acts of vision. In their plays, as I will argue in the next section, James and Marson stage acts of vision and, as with James's short stories, ambivalence toward Afro-Caribbean spiritual traditions motivates their dramas, this time in the context of emerging nationalist movements and struggles for social emancipation.

MARSON AND JAMES: BLACK VISIONARIES ON STAGE

Una Marson's play *At What a Price* and C. L. R. James's *Toussaint Louverture*[39] mark significant moments in the visual culture of Britain between the wars. *At What a Price*, which had brought Marson critical praise in Kingston, was staged again, in 1934 at the Scala in London, as a benefit for the League of Coloured Peoples. Though it did not make a profit, it made (or should have made) theatre history as the first black colonial production to appear on a London stage. James's play, *Toussaint Louverture*, also written and acted by black émigrés, appeared at the Westminister Theatre two years later, performed under the auspices of the League for the Protection of Ethiopia. These two plays presented London theatre audiences and African diasporic communities in Britain with a new visual experience. Rather than watching black actors performing, as they did in music halls or at imperial exhibits such as Wembley, as tribal "natives," they saw them, in the case of Marson's play, as well-educated, middle-class people, caught in social, psychological, and moral conflicts. In James's play, black actors, including Paul Robeson as L'Ouverture, enacted the complex struggles involved in the first successful revolution against slavery and European colonization.

While these plays presented an alternative to the stereotyped roles previously enacted by black performers, Una Marson's two subsequent plays, produced in Jamaica in 1937 and 1938, confronted and reframed colonialist performances of "native" and "folk" stereotypes directly, highlighting them as performances rather than identities. Once highlighted, the staged performances became a means for the exploration and refashioning of Afro-Caribbean women's social identities, while offering Jamaican audiences the opportunity to "see" through multiple, transatlantic, spectator positions.

Performed for Jamaican audiences at Kingston's Ward Theatre, these plays, in very different ways, were influenced by Marson's years in England, and both represented, in the dramatic visual format of the stage, socially critical and inwardly visionary experiences. *London Calling*, produced in 1937, portrayed Afro-Caribbean drama students in England performing as stereotypical tribal "natives," and through that performance, undergoing a revisionary self-fashioning of their identities as West Indians in England. Through self-conscious, explicit, and deliberate mimicry of a colonial stereotype, Marson thus staged a solution to the dilemma of colonial imitation that her poetry had already addressed, while portraying a new identity and process of identity-formation for Caribbean women.

One year after the production of *London Calling*, *Pocomania* appeared to much acclaim. It presented a young woman torn between two cultures: a female-centered, folk culture of Afro-Caribbean spiritual traditions, which promises transcendent visionary experiences, and a conservative, middle-class and male-dominated Baptist culture, which offers a conventional marriage. *Pocomania* enacted, in a contemporary, rural Jamaican setting, the cultural forces of African spiritual traditions that played such a powerful role in the Haitian Revolution and that James had explored in his fiction and reproduced on the London stage in *Toussaint Louverture*. By appropriating some of James's thematic concerns and theatrical devices from *Toussaint Louverture*, Marson suggests in *Pocomania* that the liberty and equality of young women are as important, in 1938, as the contemporary labor struggles that led later that year to the strikes in Jamaica at the Frome plantation, or as the struggles against fascism and colonialism that James's play intentionally evoked. Through the staging of ritual and ceremony, she also highlights the role of performance in creating social identity.

James's *Toussaint Louverture* resides at the chronological center, 1936, of this brief theatrical history and also occupies an inspirational position for Marson's two later plays, especially for *Pocomania*. Though Marson followed in James's lead in 1938, appropriating some of the dramatic elements of *Toussaint Louverture* for *Pocomania*, she led James four years earlier in crossing the "colour bar" of London's theatre world. Her play, *At What a Price*, created for the first time a place for black actors in England to perform other than in musical halls and imperial exhibits, and roles to perform other than those of "native" stereotypes. It also changed the direction of imperial cultural flow by bringing Jamaican theatre to London, assuming and helping to create a "cosmopolitan" audience on both sides of the Atlantic. This audience was envisioned as familiar with the British literary tradition, popular English fiction, contemporary Caribbean fiction, and Jamaican folk culture. Through these multiple cultural allusions within the play, Marson appealed to and also outlined the dimensions of the transatlantic Caribbean identity that she developed further in *London Calling*.

Though *At What a Price* led the way, credit for breaking this new ground usually goes to James whose play starred Paul Robeson as Toussaint and, like Marcus Garvey's historical dramas produced earlier in Kingston, Jamaica, portrayed events of momentous historical action.[40] In contrast, Marson's plays dramatize the social, psychological, and moral struggles of young women of color. Their situations appear relatively domestic, and the marriage plot governs the outcomes of their struggles. At first glance they may appear to fit the category slighted by Kole Omotoso in his critical history of Anglophone Caribbean drama as set in the sitting room of the "salariat class."[41] However, the conflicts of the plays depend on a larger context in which women are seeking independent lives and a place in the public world.

At What a Price portrays a young woman who yearns for independence and, through its self-reflexive plot and language, it joins with *Voyage in the Dark* by Jean Rhys and *Banana Bottom* by Claude McKay to shape a Caribbean contra-modernism focused on women's lives within a colonial and transatlantic context. The script follows the formulaic plot of an innocent girl seduced and abandoned in the big city, but does it critically and self-reflexively. We can thus read it alongside Rhys's *Voyage in the Dark*, a novel published in the same year of 1934, as critically refashioning a melodramatic convention and shifting its point of view to that of the young woman, who is of the Caribbean. In *At What a Price*, Ruth Maitland leaves her village in rural Jamaica with her parents' blessings for a job as secretary in Kingston. She also leaves behind a respectable young man who truly loves her and to whom she returns at the play's end. In the intervening acts, she is seduced and abandoned by her employer, supported by her best friend, and received back home by her parents. Though pregnant, she refuses at first to marry her previous fiancé because she believes he acts out of pity and duty. However, he convinces her that his love is true, and so the play ends. As does *London Calling*, this play resonates with Rhys's portrayal in *Voyage in the Dark* of a young woman from Dominica who has left her home to follow an acting career but is disinherited by her stepmother when her father dies and so left impoverished and without resources. Her seduction and subsequent abandonment by an older and wealthy man leave her pregnant with few alternatives, and the novel ends tragically, though, in spite of the melodramatic plot, not sentimentally. Rhys's modernist style and appropriation of Caribbean elements within the narrative make *Voyage in the Dark* very much a part of twentieth-century emergent postcolonial literature. The similarities with Marson's play are important here because the novel and the play, written by Caribbean women who had emigrated to England, portray the longings for adventure and independence in young women and the obstacles to their development as individuals within a colonial, patriarchal society. The play, with its recourse to the marriage plot, demonstrates that marriage is the only safe place for intelligent women; the novel, by refusing the marriage plot, makes the point clearly that those women who do not have recourse to marriage meet tragic ends.

While riven with different kinds of class and color contradictions, Marson's play and Rhys's novel both present young women who are vulnerable to the sexual advances of men because they have left their homes and families to attempt life as independent working women, and both comment self-reflexively on the cultural scripts of the fallen woman. When Ruth's employer arrives at her boarding house, he brings a book, *The Green Hat*, which Ruth has already read, saying that he was "sorry for the girl" but "didn't like the book a bit."[42] A popular (and scandalous) novel of the 1920s, *The Green Hat* tells the story of a declassé society girl, deemed "fallen" because she indulges in sexual affairs. However, she does so for reasons that turn out in the end to reveal her true nobility and purity of character. As the plot develops, it incorporates a resounding critique of English patriarchy and the upper class. In Marson's play, Ruth's employer does not explain his dislike of the novel; however, the exposure of male hypocrisy in *The Green Hat* suggests that Marson alludes to a critique of his own character, which he is unwilling to face. The play makes several other references to the cultural script it re-inscribes. In one scene, Ruth replies to her employer, "A very pretty speech, Mr. Fitzgerald. I have read of this in books. I have seen it on the screen, now I experience it . . . Big Boss loves little typist!" (III.2).

By incorporating these references to the fallen (modern) woman narrative, *At What a Price* imitates it, but in a mocking, dialogic way. Marson highlights her character's cultural knowledge and her own through this self-reflexivity, and in other scenes emphasizes their literary educations, again in playful ways. Ruth's Kingston friends quote Wordsworth, mention Byron, and criticize each other jokingly for "[m]ixed metaphors" and "exhibition[s] of verbosity" as "both superfluous and redundant." At one point Rob, Ruth's fiancé, displays his dual facility with English literature and Afro-Caribbean folk sayings by quoting Lewis Carroll, "The time has come, the Walrus said / To talk of many things . . .," then commenting, "Time longer dan rope" (III.2). Marson's Afro-Jamaican characters perform their class standing through their voices, showing themselves masters, not just imitators, of the English language and literary canon through their ability to treat both playfully. They thus model a Caribbean modernist treatment of language as composed of fragments of various traditions, crossing class and national borders, and signifying on one another. In the context of English expectations for costumed "native" entertainments, these black characters, played by actors from England, West Africa, Jamaica, St. Lucia, Bermuda, British Guiana, and India,[43] also made a powerful visual statement, countering colonial stereotypes that persisted well past Wembley.

In a decade noted for its class politics, the play insisted on middle-class values but portrayed marriage and sexuality as class relations, offering a response to the fallen-woman script in a celebration of middle-class rural Jamaican life. Finding its resolution in a return home to rural Jamaica and a marriage, Marson's play resembles the plot of Claude McKay's novel *Banana Bottom* (1933). McKay's character, Bita Plant, has been raped as a girl, taken under the wing of the parson, and sent to England for her education. When she returns, she reconnects with the peasant life of her home by marrying, in the end, a working man from her village. One of the differences is that, in McKay's novel, the marriage crosses class lines, as Bita marries an uneducated working man. In Marson's play, Ruth Maitland returns, pregnant, to sympathetic middle-class parents and a fiancé who still wishes to marry her and clearly respects her. Their enlightened views demonstrate a strength of their class and also of the rural home they represent.

Though Marson's *At What a Price* first broke through the "colour bar" in London theatre and though it resonated with both McKay's and Rhys's novels, James's *Toussaint Louverture*, performed two years later, received far more attention than Marson's play.[44] I will discuss *Louverture* and Marson's two later plays at the end of this section. But first, a survey of the reviews of James's play will indicate the effects on theatre audiences of seeing, for the first time, all-black or nearly all-black casts in serious dramatic productions on the London stage. The reviews of *Toussaint*

Louverture appeared in papers of all political leanings, but virtually all of them are permeated with colonial and racial ambivalence. Some reviewers recognize the political points James hoped to make. However, more often, the reviewer disapproves of the political questions raised by the play as when M. Willson Disher writes in the *Daily Mail*, London, "Worthy as this may be as propaganda, the theatre, alas, would give a more cordial welcome to the blood-and-thunder part of Haiti's history."[45] In addition to controversies concerning the play's politics, almost all of the reviews reveal the extent to which London theatre audiences struggled to accustom themselves to the sight of an almost all-black cast on a London stage in a serious drama. In these comments the visual effects of the play come into sharp relief. Even when critical of the white actors, reviewers tend to single them out by name while omitting any reference, even in praising them, to black characters or actors as individuals. The sole exception is Paul Robeson, often noted, however, not for his acting, but for "the place which [he] has gained in London's affection."[46] Perhaps the most mixed-up and ambivalent of the reviews appeared in the *Observer*, written by Ivor Brown. Brown begins with a reference to Wordsworth's sonnet, makes a joke about the Duke of Marmalade's name, and states that only because Toussaint himself is interesting does the play remain interesting. He praises "the pulse of righteous indignation," but finally concludes that:

Probably poetry would better have honoured the great and magnanimous figure of ebony which Mr. Paul Robeson presented like some tremendous tree defying hurricane . . . If Mr. Auden had been part author, we might have ended with a real Hymn of Haiti to voice what triumph the negroes retained; as it was, the surge of emotion came through in Mr. Peter Godfrey's production, to which the coloured actors contributed far more of value than the white. With the exception of Geoffrey Winicott's Napoleon, the white men, as enacted, were something of a burden, whereas the simplicity of the insurgent blacks, while it did not involve great performance, had its own natural humour and charm.[47]

The review mires in illogic and contradiction, unwilling to take James seriously as an author and unable to see individual black actors. Even when judging them fine, this reviewer cannot credit their acting as an achievement of talent or training, but can only rely on primitivist clichés of black "emotion," "simplicity," "natural humour," and "charm."

The ambivalence of these reviews echoes an unease with black actors expressed a year earlier in New York City in reviews of the Orson Welles production of *Macbeth*, also set in late eighteenth-century Haiti. While the setting and recreation of vodun ceremonies link the two plays, Welles set his play later, at the court of the Emperor Henri Christophe, emphasizing the "blood and thunder" desired by English reviewers of *Toussaint Louverture*, rather than the revolution's liberatory beginnings as did James. The theatricality of "voodoo" appealed to Welles, and the play was a tremendous success, its fame spreading beyond the theatre world. After its New York City performances, it toured the United States, drawing 100,000 people to see the show. James must have read about it, and he may have been influenced by what he read in his decision to stage *Toussaint Louverture* the next year. His motives for producing his play and his attitudes toward its subject matter were, of course, quite different from those of Welles who evidently could not refrain from addressing the leader of the African drummers hired for *Macbeth* as "Jazbo."[48] In spite of their different motives and the different effects of their plays, reviews of this *Macbeth* also expressed racialized ambivalence concerning the black cast, placing tremendous emphasis on the color of the actors' skins, the new kinds of make-up required, and the special fabrics and lighting used due to their complexions (41–42).[49]

These reviews, especially those of *Toussaint Louverture*, reveal much about the racialized visual environment in which Marson and James were working. Their decisions to produce serious plays about Afro-Caribbean people, employing large casts of black actors for the first time in London theaters suggest a strategy of directly confronting British colonialist attitudes through visual means. Even if the reviewers failed to give black actors and playwrights their due, they nevertheless were forced to directly address the fact of serious Afro-Caribbean drama on English soil, to adjust their play-viewing eyes and begin to see differently.

* * *

In addition to challenging visual expectations for the London stage, Marson and James offered colonial émigrés a theatre which represented their psychological and domestic concerns as well as their revolutionary history. Further, in choosing the theatre as their medium, they engaged one of England's greatest cultural traditions and also the cultural heritage of the Caribbean, dating back to the beginnings of carnival and incorporating Afro-Caribbean religious rituals and folklore. In his study of Anglophone Caribbean theatre, Kole Omotoso praises playwrights such as Derek Walcott for their use of a Caribbean pre-theatre heritage that includes religion, myth, carnival, and the Anancy trickster tale. Though Omotoso omits Marson from his theatre history, the traditions he values are precisely those Marson incorporates into both *London Calling* and *Pocomania*. Further, her plays make the most of the theatrical visual effects possible through those pre-theatre traditions.

Though *London Calling* was performed in Jamaica in 1937, Marson began writing the play while still in England in 1934.[50] In the intervening years, Marson underwent profound changes in her understanding of colonialism and of the importance, to people of African descent, of African cultures and traditions. Her work with the League for Coloured Peoples, which introduced her to C. L. R. James, was instrumental in beginning these changes, as was her meeting in 1934 with a king from northern Ghana, Ofori Atta. Marson's biographer, Delia Jarrett-Macauley, has stressed the impact on Marson of Ofori Atta's politics and cosmopolitan personality: "[s]he came to the realisation that Africa mattered: that its cultures, people and wisdoms equalled those of Europe and that, without the persistent attention of African people, its history would be lost, neglected and denied."[51] We can discern this transformation and the rise in Marson's confidence and sense of authority in her political activism and also literary writing of the period. But more than reflections of personal development, her plays and poetry offer a focused cultural analysis of the struggles engaged by women of color through literary representations of the dynamics of vision.

One of the events in which Marson first participated on her arrival in London in 1933 was a week-long celebration of the William Wilberforce Centenary in Hull. Apparently believing that she would be helping to further the cause of racial understanding, Marson participated in a "mock Victorian exhibition of freaks and objects, including slave relics" (53). She also acted in a tableau performance as a "lifelike reproduction of a West Indian market seller" (53). This is an interesting choice since Edna Manley had exhibited in Kingston, Jamaica, her sculpture depicting a market woman, titled *Beadseller*, just a few months before Marson left Jamaica for England. The image of a West Indian market woman might well have held ambivalent connotations for Marson – gesturing towards the new cultural movement in the arts just emerging in Jamaica when she left but also reflecting familiar, clichéd images of Caribbean women. The context, however, suggests a bizarre fixity and immobility to the role as she was filmed alongside a wax figure of Wilberforce from Madame Tussaud's. Only one year after her arrival in England, then, Marson encountered the visual culture of the imperial exhibits, not as a visitor, but as an object of the colonial gaze, a West Indian woman, performing the clichéd image of a West Indian woman.[52] That she believed her part in this filmed tableau was beneficial to herself and other people of color in Britain demonstrates again the ambivalence and confusion surrounding these exhibits. That at least a part of the show involved a "mock exhibit" highlights the self-reflexivity already possible concerning imperial propaganda and also indicates the potential cultural agency of the performers. In this case, that creative agency was soon fully realized in Marson's plays. In *London Calling*, Marson staged for the Jamaican theatre audience another "mock exhibit" of stereotypical "natives"; however, she used it as a farcical play-within-a-play to reflect on the complexities of West Indian identities in England.

London Calling takes place in London during the winter of 1934 and spring of 1935. The main characters are educated middle-class émigrés from an imaginary Caribbean island called Novaka. Studying drama in London, living in Bloomsbury, these students' lives echo those of Jean Rhys and Louise Bennett, who journeyed from the Caribbean to study drama at the Royal Academy of Dramatic Arts in Bloomsbury. They also echo, in their theatrical mimicry of "native" performances, the occupations of many colonized people brought to England as entertainers, who performed themselves as "natives." However, by drawing on traditions of masquerade and the turn-about associated with Caribbean carnival, *London Calling* stages a parodic performance, meant to imitate to excess and thus ridicule the colonial social order. Moreover, by exporting the subversive mockery of Carnival, the play-within-a-play in *London Calling* becomes a means for the main character, Rita Fray, to reconceptualize her identity as a colonial émigré to whom, finally, London does call.

The play opens by introducing the problem of imitation in opposition to authenticity and makes clear the significance of that dilemma for these actors who are also colonial subjects. When Alton Lane describes his brother Frank as talking "so much like a Yankee one would never believe he belonged to Novaka," Rita replies, "Just the type to ape anything – . . ."[53] Distinguishing here between acting and "aping," or art and imitation, Rita also seems to be criticizing Frank for denying or disguising his West Indian identity. But the language she uses resonates with racist associations. In the United States, immigrants from the Caribbean were called "monkey-chasers," and in England, colonial subjects were ridiculed by the English for "aping" the manners and dress of English and European cultures. As a metaphor for imitation, the term dehumanizes the colonized person while excluding him or her from the status of the universalized modern Subject capable of reason, original thought, and aesthetic judgment. A few lines later in a discussion of "society folk," Rita confesses to an impulse of her own to imitate or "try . . . for a spell" their luxurious lives (I.1, p. 3). Clearly, these drama students of African descent are caught in and have partially internalized a historical bind that frames their efforts at art as imitation. Rita's remark, however, suggests the importance to their social identities of the distinction between art and imitation, and it foreshadows the trick the students later play to upend its racist dimensions.

The trick begins when, asked to perform a sketch of their native lives, one of them asks, "What do they take us for? Cheap entertainers?" Alton replies, "That's an idea" (I.1, p. 9). The idea takes concrete shape as they plan a masquerade in which they play the roles often played by "cheap entertainers" from the colonies. Their performance thus positions them in two roles simultaneously – as serious drama students acting as "cheap entertainers," and as entertainers "aping" native stereotypes by wearing invented tribal dress of blankets and beads and speaking broken English. The dynamic between imitation and art is further complicated by that of cultural mimicry and authenticity when they receive coaching for their act from Prince Alota. A friend from an African country, Alota sympathizes with what the students describe as Novaka's solely English customs, advises them as to costume, and teaches them African dances. In this way, Marson makes a clear distinction between Afro-Caribbean culture and that of Africa, but it is evident that, to the English, the students will appear as natives of Novaka because they are black and dressed as "natives." At the same time, the play indicates the affinities felt between Afro-Caribbean students and émigrés from Africa, suggesting that, instead of "only English" cultural influences in Novaka, the Novakans and the African prince share some cultural connections. Though the play never makes these connections explicit, it alludes to the "back to Africa" movement of Marcus Garvey when one of the students asks whether Prince Alota is taking them all back to Africa. The script thus acknowledges, in a humorous way, the potential significance of the mock impersonation of African "natives" for Afro-Caribbean people.

The students perform their new roles twice, once at the International Society, where they impress their friend Larkspur's cousin Elsie Burton, and again at the aristocratic Burtons' residence where they go for a Christmas visit. Only the second performance appears on stage, and the script implies that it reproduces the first, but with implications beyond those of the usual second night. Now they are imitating their own performance but carrying it beyond the previously staged "sketch" into the realm of their actual social lives where it becomes an extended improvisation, blurring the lines between the play and the performance within it.

Imitating their previous entertainment in a performance improvised on Christmas Day, the performers might recall for Jamaican audiences traditional Christmas festivities held during slavery (and continued in various forms through the present day) and associated, in Jamaican history, with subversive pleasure, mockery, and revolt.[54] Rita and her friends reproduce those performances by entering, in costume, the home of British aristocrats just as, in earlier centuries, the slaves had "thronged into the Great House on Christmas morning, singing and dancing and beating their gumbays, . . . in all their finery."[55] That the celebrants, in this case, are actors recalls also the carnival character of Actor Boy performed during these Christmas "Jonkonnu" festivities.[56] An Afro-creole tradition, the Jonkonnu combined masked performances from different African nations with English theatrical elements such as mumming plays and often included modified, sometimes anti-colonial versions of Shakespearean plots and recitals of Shakespearean monologues.[57] Actor Boy, a carnival character who then acts another role in a play, thus highlights the potentially subversive role of the actor and the act of creative, creolized mimicry. These historical and cultural allusions deepen an already complexly framed dramatic performance in Marson's play, taking its significance beyond the confines of the play itself and inviting the audience to reflect on their position within these historical points of interconnection.

Just as the plantocracy held mixed feelings towards the Christmas carnival festivities, the Burton household is depicted as conflicted in their attitudes towards their guests. Elsie represents the open-minded liberal young person who is interested, curious, and willing to treat them as equals. Her brother expresses a "Tory" attitude of open prejudice, while her mother worries about what their friends will think, and her father insists that they must all behave as hospitable and gracious hosts. None of them, however, sees through the masquerade. When Larkspur unexpectedly arrives, he plays his own joke by arranging to have photographs taken of the actors on a balcony with the Burtons. The photos are then published in a newspaper and prompt furious letters from the Burtons' acquaintances, who complain of "the sight of Douglas with that black wench" and of "Elsie being attended by those two burley negroes" (II.2, p. 1).

With these photographs and the responses they elicit, Marson reproduces and reflects on the significance to the British in the period between the wars of "the sight" of racial mixing. The words of these staged letters echo almost exactly the letters quoted in the *African Telegraph* following the racial violence of 1919. As discussed in Chapter 2, one editorial in the *African Telegraph* quotes a letter published in the *Evening Standard* that described the association of black men with white women as a "detestable sight" and a "thing of horror." The *African Telegraph* writer then analyzes this "horror" felt by the British and expressed in terms of vision as a dynamic of race and gender that supports racism within the entire imperial system. With these actual quoted letters as precedent, the letters in Marson's play invite a similar analysis. One of the letters Marson writes into *London Calling* protests "the sight of negroes as guests in your old and respected home" (II.2, p. 1) and thus highlights the threat, perceived visually by the British, to the class system and its carefully marked social spaces. An alternative response comes in a letter from the International Society, praising the Burtons for their courage and hospitality in welcoming "coloured guests into their home" (II.2, p. 1). Ironically, however, the joke fools the International Society and liberal Elsie, too, indicating that even the most tolerant British remained ignorant of the people to whom they extended their benevolent welcome.

But the play's largest irony appears in the development of Rita Fray's character and resolution of her conflicts. One conflict concerns her disillusioned feelings for her new residence in England, caused by the racism and discrimination she has experienced and which has made her homesick for Novaka (with its supposedly all-English customs). The other involves her feelings for Alton Lane, who wishes to marry her. These conflicts are apparently resolved in a quick succession of events following the masquerade. The actors reveal themselves as "native" self-impersonators and exchange apologies with the Burtons, and Larkspur asks Rita to marry him. Rita, however, plays her own joke on everyone by suggesting to her friends and the Burtons, who come to visit her, that she intends to accept Larkspur's proposal. If she were to do this, she would indeed be "trying" the life of "society folk" as she had previously acknowledged wanting to do. However, a farcical turn-about ensues that demonstrates Rita's determination to "act" on her own. As Alton approaches the flat during Larkspur's visit, Rita asks Larkspur to hide behind a curtain. By coincidence, all the other characters are also present and hidden under sofas or behind screens. All are therefore listening when Rita accepts, not Larkspur's proposal, but Alton's renewed suit, and all express in unison the play's final line, "WHAT?" (III.1, p. 12).

Characters listening behind curtains, the repetition of a "joke," and Rita's "acting" as if she intends one thing rather than another in the play's final act makes return to farce the means of ending the play. It also suggests that Rita's conflicts are resolved through making a choice in marriage. However, I would argue that in the doubled performance of the second act something else happens that allows Rita to re-imagine herself in England: an inner recasting of her identity takes place *through* the impersonation of clichéd images of African tribal people. By acting the roles of "cheap entertainers," they confront the exploitation and racist damage done by such entertainments. With the help of Prince Alota, they also "ape" or imitate African "native lives," but as a performance framed by their own decision to act. In discussing their plans for the masquerade, one of the students protests, "They think us fools enough without adding to it of our own free will" (I.1, p. 10). But the opportunity to exercise their "own free will" is precisely the point. Confronting the stereotypes and the exploitation by mocking them, the students assert their capacity for free and reasoned judgment based on the ability to see through the stereotypes and to challenge, through performance, the colonial relations that have required them to enact those stereotypes over and over. In this performance, they act in the sense of an original social action, critiquing colonialist assumptions and, simultaneously, making their own connection with Africa through the Prince, a friend and another colonial émigré of color. Thus they reconnect with Africa on their own terms by mocking the terms of the stereotype. At the same time, they assert their difference from Africa. This renegotiation of the relationship between Afro-Caribbean people and those from Africa, through interrogation of the "native" stereotype, intervenes creatively in the images of Africa promoted through black actors in British popular culture during the mid-1930s and in the ideology of Garveyism.

Appearing in Kingston to an audience that very likely had seen or at least knew about Marcus Garvey's pageants, produced in the same city in 1930 and 1932, *London Calling* provided a complex and entertaining reflection on the African identity urged by Garvey on people of African descent. It also offered an alternative to the kind of theatre Garvey produced – the sweeping historical pageant with large casts of actors – and that produced by James in *Toussaint Louverture* with its emphasis on great men of action. Further, in its mockery of the "native" stereotype, *London Calling* addressed a dialogue with the star of *Toussaint* that took place during the mid-1930s in the *Keys* in articles critical of the stereotyped roles Robeson had been playing. One of these reviews specifically targets *Sanders of the River* for its depiction of Africans as "hordes of angry savages" and "ignorant black children" ruled by "the strong, silent white man." Praising Robeson's acting, the reviewer then states emphatically, "As Bosambo he is completely wasted."[58] Subsequent articles praise Robeson when, as a member of the Unity Theatre, he returns to the stage in a play titled *Plant in the Sun* in which he plays the role of a strike leader. Marson's *London Calling* dramatizes the dilemmas facing not only the famous Robeson but also lesser-known actors and drama students from the African diaspora, living in England. Placed dramatically in the hands of the actors and presented as farce, the masquerade becomes a carnivalesque occasion for turning their visual objectification and imitation of a colonial stereotype into fully realized cultural agency. It puts into quotation marks the return to Africa, allowing Marson both to distinguish Afro-Caribbean people from Africans and to suggest the importance of Africa to their diasporic identities. When Rita chooses her long-time suitor Alton, also from Novaka, and at the same time, finds success in her work and at least a temporary home in England, she is asserting her newfound ability to creatively envision an original and cosmopolitan identity for a Caribbean woman on English soil.

According to Macauley, *London Calling* enjoyed a moderate success compared to the high praise that Marson's next play, *Pocomania*, received. The plays seem strikingly different from one another. However, by suggesting an *in*sight, gained through performance, through which Rita Fray recasts her identity, *London Calling* does share a structural element with *Pocomania*. In *London Calling*, the insight we might imagine Rita experiencing is successful; in *Pocomania*, an expected and yearned for inner vision fails to take place.

* * *

Pocomania is structured dramatically around absent visionary experiences. Set in rural Jamaica in 1938, the play begins and ends, at least until the concluding lines, with the drum music of Pocomania ceremonies. Throughout the play, characters sing entire songs, dance, and talk against the background of music and of drums. Rhythmic sound, rather than vision, seems the predominant sense to which this play appeals, as the drum music becomes a virtual character, responsible for developments in the other characters and in the plot. Yet I suggest the expectation of a vision, in the spiritual sense, and its failure to appear structures the play, gives it tension and suspense, and provides its resolution. The expected visionary revelation, promised by Pocomania, links this play to the sculptures of Edna Manley (one of which is titled *Pocomania*) and, to a certain extent, those of Ronald Moody. Marson might have seen Moody's work while she was still in England, and she would certainly have been aware of Manley's sculpture by 1937 since Manley had been exhibiting in England all through the 1920s and 1930s. In 1936, when Marson returned to Jamaica, Manley was carving *Pocomania*, and in January of 1937 held her first one-person exhibition in Jamaica in which *Pocomania*, then actually titled *Vision*, was shown.[59]

Similar to other Afro-Christian Jamaican religions such as Revival, Pocomania combines the Afro-folk spirituality of Myal with the Christianity of Jamaica's Great Revival of the early 1860s. Often referred to as Pukumina, the creolized religion emphasizes healing and spirit possession. As Leah Rosenberg points out in her analysis of Marson's play in the context of competing ideas of nationhood, Pocomania appealed to the poor, who could not afford to marry, and thus became associated with sexual immorality. The apparent loss of physical control experienced by the predominantly female worshippers during the rites of spirit possession contributed to this association. Its practices, along with those of obeah and other folk religions, were often banned or outlawed. Furthermore, as Rosenberg notes, in 1938, Pocomania was a strong force in the West Kingston neighborhood most identified with poverty and labor resistance. She emphasizes the significance of Jamaica's growing movement for independence alongside increasingly intense labor rebellions during the 1930s and culminating in 1938, the year of the play's production, with strikes and riots in Kingston and throughout the countryside. Marson does not explicitly address these labor struggles, and in her attempt to convince middle-class Kingston audiences that they share a culture with the working class, she also, as Rosenberg states, "rejects the legitimacy of Pocomania's central rite, spirit possession."[60]

I agree with Rosenberg's reading of the Pocomania ceremonies in the play as modified to present "a cleaned-up version" (38). However, this description applies mainly to the lengthy ceremonies performed on stage in the final scenes of a Ninth Night Celebration, a service in honor of the deceased and beloved Pocomania leader Sister Kate, which, without her guiding presence, ends in chaos. This ceremony consists mostly of hymns and folk songs until interrupted by fights between men who have drunk too much rum. In contrast, the play's first scene gives us a brief glimpse of a ceremony conducted by Sister Kate in which a girl works "herself up to frenzy," while the other celebrants sing hymns, dance, and shout (I.1, p. 9). Between this initial, brief ceremony and the lengthy final scenes of the Ninth Night Celebration, the play's central scenes are constructed around Pocomania ceremonies, led by Sister Kate, that are *not* portrayed on stage. These ceremonies are clearly associated with the ancestor worship of spirit possession and with the visionary experiences of such rituals. In this respect, Marson does present a version of Pocomania palatable to the middle class, but she also signals far more important, off-stage, and therefore, doubly forbidden ceremonies which the play's main character yearns to experience.

The quest for inner vision motivates the protagonist, a young middle-class Afro-Caribbean woman named Stella Manners. Throughout the play,

Stella is torn between two religious communities – that of the female-centered Pocomania celebrants and that of the Baptist church in which her father serves as Deacon. Though the plot seems to decide in favor of the middle-class Baptist men and Stella's marriage within the church, a crucial scene undermines that conclusion by positioning the Pocomania practitioners as more knowledgeable than the educated, middle-class characters. This scene stresses the cultural legacies of Africa in the drumming of Josiah, who learned drumming from his father, who learned it from Josiah's grandfather, who came to Jamaica on a slave ship from Africa. The conversation in creolized Jamaican nation language among Sister Kate, Sister Mart, and Broder Kendal extends linguistically the African connection made through Josiah's inheritance, emphasizing the importance of the ancestors to their speech, beliefs, and celebrations. But most important, the cultural insight and folk wisdom the speakers express position them as centers of knowledge even though they remain marginal figures in the larger social world of the play. In fact, it is by virtue of their marginal positions, that Sister Kate, Sister Mart, and Broder Kendal can analyze the class divide, express their sympathy for the "better class" who must hide all their feelings "because dem is respectable," and critique the system in which "dem wot hab money kep we so poor dat dem gals and young man no married."[61] When Sister Kate considers Stella's interest in Pocomania, she remarks that, "It is not possible to be respectable and common at de same time." Sister Mart corrects her, claiming, "But we not common, we is destant," and Kendal repeats, "We is quite destant" (II.1, p. 18).

Their "destance," identified and performed in this central scene, suggests that, as spiritual leaders, they are positioned to see, understand, and analyze the social system from a contemplative (and marginalized) distance while administering to the needs of the poor and, at the same time, sympathizing with the middle class. The scene invites the audience of the play to at least partially align themselves with these characters for they "see" more and understand more than the middle-class characters of the play. The audience of the play is thus allowed to eavesdrop on a conversation not meant for middle-class ears; at the same time, they are invited to consider the superior vision of these spiritual leaders.

The knowledge of the Pocomania leaders contrasts to that presented in the next scene in dialogue among the men of the middle-class Christian community. These include David, the young man who wishes to marry Stella. The men discuss the meaning of Pocomania – "little madness" – and express their concern over Stella's interest in it. David, the more liberal of them, explains that Pocomania appeals to the people because of its vitality and its inclusion of the many Jamaicans who live together outside of marriage and are, therefore, excluded by the Christian church. However, he agrees that "there is too much that is base and erotic" (II.1, p. 22).

This conflict between a male-dominated, middle-class, "cold" Christian church and a female-centered, inclusive folk spirituality represents, in the social world, the internal struggle experienced by Stella who seeks something more in her life than the obedient domesticity of her sister Dawn. In an alternate version of the play, Stella states explicitly to David that she feels "trapped, bound and imprisoned in this dull house and this boring village" (Alternate II.2). She explains that rebellion has long been "swelling up" and that she envies the peasants their freedom to love "without all this business of a conventional marriage" (Alternate II.2). Her experiences in the Pocomania celebrations have brought her ecstasy, fear, and finally a great relief that she compares to the condition of a boy from whom Jesus had cast a devil.

As in *London Calling*, *Pocomania* incorporates imitation and performance as a means to explore possible identities for a young Caribbean woman. In her attempts to explore the alternative offered by the Pocomania community, Stella implicitly acts the part of an actor, wearing a wrap and turban as disguise so that she may attend their ceremonies, dressed as they do, and go unrecognized by her family. Seeking another kind of female identity, like Rita in *London Calling*, she adopts a costume, but Stella's disguise frees her to explore actual African diasporic identities. Unlike the masquerade of *London Calling*, in which Rita enacts a stereotype against and through which she imagines a new identity, Stella's disguise gives her the identity of the person she longs to be, a spiritual visionary, free from the conventions of an imitative, middle-class colonial culture.

However, the actual ceremony is absent, not performed, and therefore whatever Stella experiences remains a mystery. The audience has only David's description of it as "foul – indescribable," and his words are undercut by the folk wisdom of the Pocomania leaders, spoken in the earlier scene. They acknowledge that Pocomania rituals might make "respectable" people ill; however, this is not because the ceremonies are "foul," but because the "upper classes" "can't understand it" (II.1, p. 18).

Nevertheless, David's version of the ceremony prevails in the main action of the play. David makes Stella promise never again to attend a Pocomania meeting or to see Sister Kate. Still yearning with curiosity and now mourning Sister Kate, who has died from her illness, Stella begs to attend the Ninth Night celebration for Kate. When David says that she will be able to hear the singing and drums from her house, she insists that "it won't be the same as seeing them" and repeats, "I do want to see the Ninth Night" (III.1, p. 27). Her insistence makes clear that, beyond the drumming and music, or rather, called by them, Stella seeks a vision, something she expects to be revealed to her through the act of seeing the ceremony and through the act of seeing itself. Overhearing their argument, Stella's father, the Deacon, forbids her to go under any circumstances.

But Stella does go, hiding in the bushes during the second scene of Act II, which is devoted entirely to the Ninth Night celebration. This scene stages all of the songs, mostly hymns and many sung in full, the drum and banjo playing, memorial speeches, food and drink. As Rosenberg notes, it does not portray spirit possession but resembles a relaxed Christian service. However, it is this service which exerts so little hold on the participants that they drink too much, couples go off together, and fights break out. In the confusion, Stella stands up, senses David nearby, and runs to his arms. The concluding lines replace the "little madness" of Pocomania with that of their love, substituting the Christian male's "rescue" for the salvation of spiritual vision. Thus, Stella's quest ends. On one level, it seems that the more tolerant faction of the male-dominated Christian middle class has won the conflict presented by the play, and the woman's quest for fulfillment has been sacrificed to social requirements of marriage and respectability. The Afro-Christian ceremony has been exposed as an unruly crowd, fallen into sexual promiscuity and drunken brawls. However, what the audience sees is a drunken brawl prompted by a mostly Christian service. In that confusion, not one induced by Pocomania, Stella joins David, and both of them acknowledge that the chaos took place because Sister Kate was no longer there, and the "spirit" she offered had been lost. With this admission, the grounds of the conflict shift. Stella's original quest becomes a valid one, and it becomes possible to imagine that, had Sister Kate lived to guide her, she might have achieved the vision she sought.

This absent vision, then, is central to the play's structure. It allows the actual marriage plot to develop and admits an alternative, shadow plot. In the actual plot, a young woman is prevented from acting independently, from exploring the African elements of her cultural identity, and from seeking a revelation that would position her differently, not as a dutiful daughter or wife, but as a leader and visionary in the community. Around the absent vision, however, turns an alternate plot in which the authority of Jamaican nation language, women leaders, African drumming, and ancestor reverence guide the development of what remains an unseen, alternate female Caribbean identity.

Delia Jarrett-Macauley sees the play as "an early literary attempt to reconnect Africa with the Caribbean" (135). I agree, but I want to argue for another connection, one that reveals Marson's politics in *Pocomania* as more revolutionary and feminist than an initial reading or viewing would suggest. Crucial similarities between the staging of *Pocomania* and that of James's *Toussaint Louverture* indicate that Marson's dramatization in Jamaica of Pocomania rituals alluded to the eighteenth-century struggle, on the part of black Caribbean slaves, for "Liberty, Equality, and Fraternity." The play makes a connection not only between Africa and the Caribbean but, as I will show in comparing it with James's *Toussaint Louverture*, between two Caribbean countries in two different revolutionary moments – Jamaica on the eve, in January 1938, of a black laborers' revolt and Haiti, 137 years earlier, in its successful revolutionary defeat of three European powers. Furthermore, Marson makes that connection through the social and psychological struggles of a young woman, linking her quest for something more than an oppressive, feminine domesticity with the contemporary labor movement and the historical quest of the Saint-Dominiquan slaves for freedom. Marson also addresses questions of class relations that motivated James's fiction, by presenting a middle-class black woman who feels a spiritual kinship with the female leader of a "folk" religion. Rather than alienating the educated middle-class person from the lower classes or exposing their relationship as one of voyeuristic observation, Marson's play suggests a tragedy for the middle-class woman of a cross-class female relationship that is never allowed to develop.

James's play was produced in London in March of 1936, six months before Marson left England for Jamaica. This was a year of significant events in the world and in Marson's life. The invasion of Abyssinia, now called Ethiopia, by Italy and refusal of England to defend the world's only continuously black-ruled country from fascism outraged many black and also white leftist intellectuals. Marson was already working in London for the Abyssinian minister, Dr. Charles W. Martin, in 1935. She met Abyssinia's ruler, Haile Selassie, when he arrived in London in June of 1936, and she then accompanied him later that month to Geneva, where he unsuccessfully put his case before the League of Nations. Like Marson, C. L. R. James protested England and Europe's lack of response to the invasion. In the early months of 1936, his article "Abyssinia and the Imperialists" appeared in the *Keys*. But of most importance, in terms of its impact on the British public, was his decision to produce *Toussaint*

Louverture as a benefit for the Abyssinian cause. According to his editor, Anna Grimshaw, James meant to dramatize this nearly forgotten event in black history as "an intervention in the debates surrounding the Ethiopian crisis" and also in order to demonstrate "that the colonial populations were not dependent upon leadership from Europe in their struggle for freedom, that they already had a revolutionary tradition of their own."[62] He focused the play on the Haitian Revolution's leader, Toussaint L'Ouverture, and the conflicts he faced – with other leaders, with the British, French, and Spanish, and in his relationship with the masses of uprising slaves.

The exact version of the play produced on March 15 and 16, 1936, at London's Westminster Theatre, is not, to my knowledge, anywhere in print. Most critics who write about the play refer to the version titled *The Black Jacobins* in *The C. L. R. James Reader*, edited by Anna Grimshaw, and published in 1992. However, this is the script from a production directed in 1967 by Dexter Lyndersay at the University of Ibadan, Nigeria, and it differs greatly from the two typescripts of the 1936 play that I have been able to locate. By comparing the playbill from the 1936 London performances with these two original typescripts and a scene from the play published by James in the same year, it is possible to approximate the performance script of the 1936 productions.[63]

Though very different in character, setting, and plot, *Pocomania* appropriates key elements of *Toussaint Louverture* to make political points of a more domestic and feminist kind. In Marson's dramatizations of Pocomania ceremonies, she borrows from James's staging of vodun rituals; in her distinctions between religious leaders, she echoes James's distinct portrayals of revolutionaries; in the conflict of cultural identity that Stella faces, Marson refashions the conflict between loyalty to France and to his "people" that Toussaint L'Ouverture faces; and, in her portrayal of an absent Afro-Caribbean spiritual vision, she inverts the central vision of James's play, a profoundly European and secular scene, imagined by all the characters, of the French Republican Committee in Paris.

The first of these similarities appears in the opening of both plays with the staging of religious ceremonies and conflicts. Just as Marson's play opens with the sound of drums late at night disturbing a young girl in her middle-class home, James's play also opens with the sound of drums. In *Pocomania*, it is Sister Kate's yard, and the drummer is young Josiah. In James's play, it is the slave encampment at La Grande Rivere in April 1793, where all the leaders of the revolt are gathered. These include Bouckman, the houngon or vodun priest, Toussaint, Jeannot, and Dessalines. The stage directions state that "All through the scene there is the steady beat of drums" (I.2, p. 8). Accounts of atrocities recently committed by the French turn the crowd away from Toussaint, who urges them to present the Colonial Assembly with a petition, and toward Dessalines, who stirs them to violent rebellion. Boukman, as priest, leads the crowd in rejecting the Christian God and invokes instead "Our God who is good [and] orders us to revenge our wrongs" (I.2, p. 10). He rips off his neck a cross hanging from a chain and ceremonially passes a vessel, from which the other characters drink, and "There is a great rattle of the drums" (I.2, p. 10) as it becomes clear that the vessel contains blood. In this way, they all bind themselves to their plan, including Toussaint, who drinks only when all of the "kneeling Negroes call to him to drink" (I.2, p. 11).[64]

Though it is not certain how much James actually knew about vodun rituals, he did know what cultural historians and anthropologists continue to affirm, that vodun played a major role in the Haitian Revolution. He apparently knew that Dessalines engaged in ceremonies before battle, and he recreates vividly the role of vodun in resisting slavery and symbolically enacting liberty from European colonial oppression. Marson has domesticated the revolutionary impulse in Afro-Caribbean spiritual traditions, locating the ceremonies in Sister Kate's yard, rather than the forest, making their leader a woman, who is tolerant and wise, and at the same time, stressing the links between the Caribbean and Africa and emphasizing the desire for freedom that the drums represent. In James's play, the scene establishes the difference in character between a violent, self-indulgent Dessalines and the more thoughtful, moderate Toussaint that develops throughout the play. A similar division among the Pocomania celebrants in Marson's play positions Sister Kate as the wise and guiding spirit in whose absence self-indulgence, fighting, and chaos prevail. Kate's essential nobility is affirmed at the end of the play in contrast to the chaotic dissolution of the Ninth Night celebrants, just as Toussaint appears tragically honorable in contrast to Dessalines. This parallel in characterization accompanies other similarities between the two plays that indicate to me the influence of James's play on Marson and, more importantly, the extent to which she appropriated his historical play about revolution in the Caribbean to explore the conflicts facing a Caribbean woman who seeks independence and freedom of the spirit.

Both James and Marson present in their plays the conflict of identity experienced by an educated, colonized subject. In each case, the colonized person is torn between the culture and education associated with the colonizing country and a resistant culture of her or his "people," one associated with the Afro-Caribbean spiritual practices of the islands. Even Toussaint's name signifies the dilemma. At the beginning of his leadership in the revolt, he rejects his slave name Breda and adopts Louverture, meaning "opener of a way for his people" (LL, p. 8) and referring to the opening chant in vodun ceremonies, yet a French name.[65] In Marson's play, Stella seeks an opening; she desires freedom, and she longs to realize her vision. In contrast to the day's beginning represented by her sister Dawn's name, Stella's name indicates that she occupies the more risky world of the night and dreams and, as Carolyn Cooper notes, is "starry-eyed."[66] In creating these parallels between her play and James's, Marson proposes that Stella's quest for freedom and vision extends that of the slaves of Saint-Dominique.

Marson also appropriates for her feminist purposes a political point made powerfully in James's play. When Toussaint has successfully defeated the British army for the French, the French and the British convene to sign a truce. However, they end up plotting together against Toussaint to ensure continued European authority on the island. As the British commander Maitland puts it, "I have spoken, not as an Englishman, not as an enemy of France, but as a white man and a representative of a colonial power with the same interests as yours" (LL, p. 7). Two of the Frenchmen present remind the French commander of their debt to Toussaint; he, nevertheless, asserts that if Toussaint wins his next battle, "this Negro is nominally our servant, but virtually master of the island. And the problem then is no longer French but concerns all who rule in these colonies, French, British, and Dutch" (LL, p. 8).

Marson's play reflects a feminist version of the political point James makes in this scene. In Act II Scene 2 of *Pocomania*, the men in Stella's life convene to discuss the "strangeness" of her attraction to Pocomania. Though they disagree about the role of the Christian church and the reasons for the appeal of Pocomania to the people of Jamaica, the men, nevertheless, come to an agreement based on the need they both feel to control Stella's sexuality. They agree to "save her from herself" and from the "base and erotic" elements they perceive in the ceremonies. In this scene, Marson represents men overcoming fundamental disagreements in order to join forces in regulating the sexuality of a young woman and confine her to a middle-class marriage. Like the competing French and British, these two very different men ally with one another (and implicitly with her father who holds even stronger convictions) in order to ensure that Stella does not follow Sister Kate and emerge as another female leader, out of their control, as the generals fear Toussaint will become, on the island.

These similarities indicate the influence of James's play on *Pocomania*. However, the central vision of freedom guiding each play differs radically.

In the two typescript versions of James's play, he includes a scene that appears to have been omitted in the actual performance. Marson, therefore, could not have seen it, and it could not have influenced her play. However, it does indicate to us now some key differences between their attitudes toward Afro-Caribbean spiritual traditions as inspirations for Caribbean revolutionary movements.

In *Pocomania*, the play stages, twice, everything but the actual visionary experience associated in Stella's mind with freedom. In Act II, she dons a disguise and escapes to the Pocomania ceremony; however, this ceremony does not take place on stage but remains an absent scene. Stella's expected visionary experience also remains either unrepresented or thwarted. The omission of the expected Pocomania ceremony as a scene in the play also denies the audience the opportunity to see for themselves the guiding power of Sister Kate. In those absent scenes resides an Afro-Caribbean spiritual vision that Stella was willing to disobey all of the men in her life to experience. In its absence, it represents the longed for "destant" perspective of Sister Kate and her colleagues, one that "sees" clearly and from a distance the class, gender, and racial social relations of Jamaica. In contrast to the riot that ends the Ninth Night Ceremony, it represents a visionary bridge between the middle and working classes, men and women.[67]

In *Toussaint Louverture*, the scene of freedom appears in Act I, Scene 4 on a stage within the stage, as Colonel Vincent begins to describe the historical moment he witnessed while in Paris. Instead of Vincent's continued narration, an inner curtain rises to reveal the scene in Paris when the President proclaims the "liberty of the Negroes" without the "dishonour of discussion." Notes on the manuscript indicate that "(This is an almost verbatim report of the sittings of the 3rd and 4th of February, 1794.)." In keeping with the record, James portrays three deputies from San Domingo, one black, a mulatto, and a white man. He presents, as dialogue, the historical speech:

Since 1789 the aristocracy of birth and the aristocracy of religion have been destroyed: But the aristocracy of the skin still remains. That too is now at its last gasp, and equality has been consecrated. A black man, a yellow man, are about to join this Convention in the name of the free citizens of San Domingo. (I.4, p. 42)

This historical moment in which the slaves of the French colonies win the freedom for which they have long struggled is, thus, portrayed as a vision – a performance within a performance that the characters of the framing play "see." It is the central and turning point of the play, for following his vision of the proclamation, Toussaint sends his sons "whom

I treasure most on earth" (I.4, p. 45) to France to be educated as a sign of his confidence in the Republic. While James positions the central vision of freedom as located in France, a moment in colonial history that turns into betrayal, Marson points to a vision that was never allowed, one sought through an Afro-Caribbean female-centered folk culture. Its loss, by implication, signals a loss for her character, in spite of the "happy" ending. Furthermore, by following James's play, Marson's *Pocomania* seems to deliberately suggest that the liberty and equality of young women and their development into full human beings requires both "modern" ideas of marriage *and* cross-class female alliances.

In this respect, *Pocomania* bears reading alongside Virginia Woolf's *Three Guineas*, also appearing in 1938. In this book-length essay, Woolf makes a case for understanding war and fascism in Europe as inextricably tied to patriarchal hierarchies in England. To develop her argument, Woolf refers repeatedly to nineteenth-century feminists such as Josephine Butler, who led the movement against the Contagious Diseases Acts which denied civil rights to working-class women. Butler and her cause represent for Woolf an historical instance of female cross-class alliance, and she gives her a special place among other women whom she considered her foremothers, such as Florence Nightingale and Emily Davies. Interestingly, these three women are among those Jarrett-Macaulay names as important references in Marson's *Cosmopolitan* articles of the 1920s (31). In these articles, addressed especially to white-collar working women,[68] Marson may have anticipated by a number of years Woolf's location of the crucial struggle for women's freedom from domestic tyranny in the political acts and writings of nineteenth-century feminists. Through their historical understanding of class divisions, Marson and Woolf also target middle-class conventions of respectability as barriers to political and social connections among women. In *Three Guineas*, Woolf refers to "the daughters of educated men"; however, exploring a theme similar to that in Marson's play, she makes continual reference to the values of chastity and respectability which prevent women from making cross-class alliances. In *Pocomania*, it is precisely male insistence on their perceptions of Stella's chastity that unite them in their efforts to "save her" from Sister Kate.

To catalyze in their readers' or viewers' minds a larger picture and broader critical analysis, both Marson and Woolf deliberately activate a visual imagination as the central act of their argument. In *Three Guineas*, Woolf makes extensive use of visual media, reproducing a series of photographs depicting professional men – judges, dons, generals, and archbishops – in full regalia of hats, capes, medals, and horsehair tufts waving from their braided shoulders. These photographs, which bear no commentary, contrast implicitly with the photographs Woolf asks her readers to *imagine* – of ruined houses and dead bodies in war-torn Spain. Like Marson's play, Woolf's argument depends on the dynamic between what actually appears in the text or on the stage and what remains an absent visual image. Woolf argues in *Three Guineas* that the tyrannies of fathers over the lives of their daughters, the exclusion of women from education and the professions, and the sexual subservience of women to husbands in a patriarchal society were no different from the tyrannies of dictators abroad and, furthermore, encouraged militarism and war. This was a difficult argument to make in 1938 when many leftists considered women's issues a relic of the suffragist past, trivial matters compared to the anti-fascist cause. And *Pocomania* hardly makes such an argument outright. However, by echoing James's play in its recreation of Afro-Caribbean spiritual traditions, setting them in the life of a rebellious young woman, who yearns for independence and spiritual vision, Marson connects the cause of women's free social development with that of movements in resistance to colonialism and fascism.

Adopting the theatre as their medium, Marson and James staged, visually, the powerful historical and domestic struggles of black visionary figures. They also engaged a performative tradition that, obviously, involves more than the visual. Unlike painting or sculpture, the theatre engages all of the senses, taking advantage of the actor's entire body in movement, speech, and song. The viewers must respond with their eyes, and also their ears and the kinetic sense responsive to dramatic gesture, dance, and scenic movement. In this way, and also through their work in the 1940s and 1950s with radio and television, Marson and James take their politics of vision beyond the visual, providing a precedent in Caribbean modernist arts for the representation in later postcolonial Caribbean literature of a radically reoriented sensory body.

GEORGE LAMMING AND C. L. R. JAMES: EXILE,
CRICKET, AND MODERN ART

The precedent set by Marson and James in dramatizing the revolutionary visions of Afro-Caribbean people joined the Caribbean modernism of Edna Manley, Ronald Moody, Claude McKay, and Jean Rhys as influences on the work throughout the 1950s of George Lamming who, in turn, influenced the later writing of James. World War II and its aftermath brought new waves of Caribbean immigrants to Britain, including

Lamming who arrived on the same ship as Sam Selvon in 1950. Lamming later identified 1950 as part of a longer history of West Indian migration, but "really the beginning for writers."[69]

The year 1950 did mark such a beginning, but it was for writers whose identities collectively transformed into "West Indian" or "Caribbean" in the new context of significantly increased immigration. The writers, such as James, Marson, Rhys, and McKay, who preceded Lamming's generation had not yet identified predominantly as belonging to a group or community of West Indians. Their creative and political affiliations were varied and ranged from mainstream English writers and artists, such as the Bloomsbury and London Groups, to groups organized on behalf of colonial émigrés, to Marxists, feminists, and Pan-Africanists from diverse regions of the empire. While Marson and James met through the League for Coloured Peoples and its journal the *Keys* during the 1930s, McKay, who wrote for the socialist-feminist *Workers Dreadnought*, had already departed England in 1921. Rhys, as a white creole, may not have encountered those of predominantly African descent, and to my knowledge, had no contact with Edna Manley. Nevertheless, Rhys's and James's writing of the 1930s and Marson's work with the BBC in the early 1940s all had a profound effect on Lamming's writing and that of others who began to publish in the 1950s. It is important to acknowledge these predecessors, along with those who usually receive credit in Lamming's case, such as Frank Collymore and Henry Swanzy, because they created models for literary and historical writing and provided media opportunities for the new emigrant writers of the 1950s and 1960s.

These post-World War II writers arrived in Britain along with hundreds of other West Indian men and women, often skilled workers, recruited by advertisements promising employment in all occupations.[70] From different islands, emigrants of different classes, colors, occupations, and nationalities met one another on board ship and, after arrival, in the port cities, trains, and the metropolitan center of London in encounters through which they began to reconfigure their identities as "West Indian" and "Caribbean." Reflecting on his own journey, Lamming has written:

No Barbadian, no Trinidadian, no St. Lucian, no islander from the West Indies sees himself as a West Indian until he encounters another islander in foreign territory. It was only when the Barbadian childhood corresponded with the Grenadian or the Guianese childhood in important details of folk-lore, that the wider identification was arrived at. In this sense, most West Indians of my generation were born in England.[71]

Lamming's writing, especially his novels of the 1950s and his collection of essays, *The Pleasures of Exile*, published in 1960, were, along with Selvon's fiction, among the first to reflect on and interpret this exilic formation of a new regional consciousness. In doing so, they extended the project begun by Marson in her play *London Calling*, from the recasting of individual Caribbean identity in England to that of a larger collective.

An important conduit for this reconfiguration of identity was the radio program Marson produced during the war, "Calling the West Indies." Through this popular program servicemen from the Caribbean who were stationed in England could "call" back home. Eventually Marson transformed the program into a cultural and literary venue, promoting the work of Caribbean artists and writers.[72] Following her work with George Orwell on a program called "Voice," Marson changed "Calling the West Indies" to "Caribbean Voices" and featured, among other items, selections from *Focus*, the magazine edited in Jamaica by Edna Manley, and from *Bim*, the literary magazine from Barbados edited by Frank Collymore. Thus, "Caribbean Voices" created cross-island identifications in England and also within the Caribbean. Owing to the input of "Caribbean Voices" along with its emphasis on and active search for materials of literary accomplishment, *Bim* unexpectedly created cross-island identification even for readers and writers in Barbados. According to Lamming: "Because by the time you get the Trinidad contribution coming, by the time Jamaica comes, by the time it's being fed also by Caribbean Voices, the things that are coming to it and so on, Collymore finds, really, that he has spawned a regional project, which was not part of his original agenda."[73] Sometimes "Caribbean Voices" focused on specific writers or interviewed well-known figures such as Ronald Moody and Learie Constantine. The program ran throughout the 1950s, first under Marson's direction and then that of Henry Swanzy, and provided what Kamau Brathwaite has called "the single most important literary catalyst for Caribbean creative and critical writing in English."[74] It brought to the attention of England and the entire English-speaking Caribbean the work of writers in Jamaica, Barbados, or Trinidad, and it fostered connections among émigrés from those different islands. The voices heard and promoted on this program traversed the distances between islands, the Caribbean region, and England with such important effects that we might argue for the sense of sound as the predominant sensory vehicle for the reconfiguration, in exile, of discrete island affiliations into a broader regional nationalism.

Yet even in this period of radio, the men since canonized as the first generation of West Indian writers emphasized acts of seeing and the eye itself as the foundations for creativity in language. In the novels of George Lamming the sense of sight explicitly constitutes the new emigrant as West Indian, part of a newly forming community of men and women beginning to see themselves differently in relation to each other and the rest of the world. Lamming and James, along with other émigré writers of the 1950s such as Andrew Salkey, Michael Anthony, and Sam Selvon, helped to form a regional Caribbean identity in exile; they also created what David Ellis has referred to as a "literature of education" by informing the British public about Caribbean life.[75] In this way, they took into their creative hands the mission previously undertaken in the interests of empire by exhibits such as the 1924 Wembley exhibition, where colonized people posed as stereotypes of "natives" in the guise of educating English people about the colonies. These writers gave those muted actors a radical voice, portraying instead the experiences of colonialism and racism from the point of view of the Caribbean person.

Beginning with his first novel, *In the Castle of My Skin* (1953), Lamming depicts the subjectivity of his characters as a social relationship in which the eye becomes a cage; subsequent novels of the 1950s deploy visual tropes and acts of seeing as methods of turning the plot and developing character. The next decade of the 1960s begins with the publication of Lamming's book of essays, *The Pleasures of Exile*, and his novel, *Season of Adventure*. In this decade, which marked the political independence of several Caribbean countries, also appeared C. L. R. James's remarkable book – a cross between memoir, sports essay, and meditation on art and history – *Beyond a Boundary* (1963). These three books by two Caribbean men of letters who were, by then, well known in England and the Caribbean, expound on "a way of seeing" as the epistemological ground for the regeneration of language and critical revision of history. In *The Pleasures of Exile*, Lamming revisits James's narrative history of the Haitian Revolution. Titled *The Black Jacobins* and published in 1938 as an extension of the 1936 play *Toussaint Louverture*, James's book had gone out of print during World War II, and Lamming intended to introduce it to a new readership. In Lamming's commentary, Toussaint becomes Caliban, the slave "denied the power to see," who nevertheless, creates a new vision through which he "orders history." Lamming's novel, *Season of Adventure*, makes visual art central to revolutionary politics, while James's chapter in *Beyond a Boundary*, "What Is Art?", turns the tables on bourgeois modernist aesthetics, returning the power to see and judge art to the people, the masses of cricket spectators all over the world. This emphasis on visual art and aesthetics signals the emergence of the Caribbean Artists Movement, where intense interactions among artists and writers and debates over aesthetics took place throughout the late 1960s and into the early 1970s on both sides of the Atlantic. It also previews what would become a revisionary return in Caribbean literature to the epic convention of *ekphrasis*, the verbal description of visual art. The predominance of visual tropes in the writings of Lamming, James, and later, Wilson Harris and Derek Walcott suggests the importance in the 1950s and 1960s of re-imagining the sense of sight in concert with the newly heard voices of Caribbean émigrés.

* * *

Lamming's first two novels, *In the Castle of My Skin*, published in 1953, and *The Emigrants*, published in 1954, develop a tradition of Caribbean modernism begun by Jean Rhys in the 1920s and 1930s. Like Rhys's novels, Lamming's depart from realist conventions to portray the effects of migration and exile on the sensory body and subjectivity of the Caribbean emigrant. However, unlike Rhys's depictions of isolated female figures, Lamming's novels portray the relationships among Caribbean émigrés, their emergent sense of a regional identity in exile, and transatlantic connections to nationalist movements in the Caribbean. *In the Castle of My Skin* is set in an imaginary Caribbean village amid the nationalist uprisings of the 1930s, and it is written in what many critics agree is either a "modernist" style or, at least, one that refuses realism. *The Emigrants*, set in London during the 1950s, also deploys a style that often seems fragmentary, unstable in point of view, and shaped through a collage of voices and discourses, shifting at times from prose to verse to dramatic dialogue, and from third-to first-person narration and back again. Critics have long recognized and debated these modernist elements in Lamming's writing. Gordon Rohlehr, for example, has noted the significance in Lamming's work and that of other Caribbean writers of "its ambivalent swing between folk/oral and Euro/modernist aesthetics."[76] Some critics, however, such as Michael Thelwell, oppose any use of narrative techniques resembling modernism on the grounds that they eschew "history and cultural reality."[77] Merwyn Morris has criticized *The Emigrants* as "not at all a good novel," especially due to the slow pace of the beginning and the contrived neatness of its plot. Nevertheless, he appreciates, without calling it modernist, the "prose poem" of the novel, a passage offering "an impressionistic patterning of fragments of speech, thought, feeling and incident on the train."[78] On the other hand, Morris finds lack of realistic character motivation a serious flaw in several of the novels and criticizes *The Pleasures of*

Exile on a number of counts including a lack of coherence. In contrast, Peter Hulme considers what he calls the awkwardness of Lamming's prose as "not a sign of failure to adhere to a norm but, rather, a symptom of a breaking away from that norm toward a new way of writing (and reading) which has yet to be fully formulated, at least in the case of the Caribbean."[79] Hulme positions Lamming's writing as somewhere between realism and postmodernism, but oddly, does not mention modernism. Others, such as Simon Gikandi and A. J. Simoes da Silva, acknowledge the Eurocentrism of the term "modernist" but nevertheless consider it of critical importance in understanding Lamming's work. Gikandi identifies modernism in two ways: first, as including "what one may call a Third World modernism distinct from the prototypical European form" – close to what I have termed in this chapter, a contra-modernism – and second, with writing that emerged after the decades associated with European modernism.[80] He thus extends Lamming's affiliation with modernism to include the work of other writers from the 1950s through the 1980s such as Paule Marshall and Michelle Cliff. Crucial, though, to Gikandi's analysis and that of others who place Lamming in a modernist context of some kind, are the effects of the colonial situation on language and of creolization in subverting narrative realism.

I wish to add another dimension, the significance of visuality, to the analysis of Lamming's unique narrative dynamics as creolized, contra-modernism. Attention to predominating visual tropes helps to situate Lamming's work in the intersections of modernism, anti-colonial trans-nationalism, and literatures of exile; it also illuminates one of the more debated aspects of Lamming's writing, the portrayal of women. By exploring the act of seeing as one that constitutes and is also, therefore, foundational to changing the colonial relationship, Lamming glimpses, almost by accident, the subjectivities of women and recognizes their importance in the processes of social change.

Lamming's narrative exploration of vision works with two shaping influences: the tradition of existential philosophy associated with Jean-Paul Sartre and the Haitian vodun ritual of the Ceremony of Souls. As Janet Butler has noted, Lamming became acquainted with Sartrean existentialism while living in Trinidad before he emigrated to England.[81] In a recent interview with David Scott, Lamming states that "my Caribbeanness begins in Trinidad, not in Barbados" and speaks of his time in Trinidad as "the decisive moment in making directions and choices."[82] If we place this statement concerning the significance of Trinidad in forming his regional identity alongside his statements concerning the regional nationalism created through *Bim* in

Barbados and his earlier declaration that "most West Indians of my generation were born in England," we perceive a three-point itinerary of the
development of Lamming's consciousness of himself as "Caribbean" or
"West Indian." By locating the "decisive moment" in Trinidad, he also
points to the moment when he was teaching at a Venezuelan college and
reading the literature of Spain, Latin America, and the Hispanic Caribbean
alongside that of existentialism. In this same interview, Lamming describes
his continued and avid reading of "everything by Sartre, everything by
Camus, everything by de Beauvoir, all of the debates going on [among]
the French" during his first years of exile in England (III). So, at the
culminating point in the process of becoming West Indian, Lamming is
also turning to the French, just as at the decisive moment in Trinidad,
he turned to the Spanish and Hispanic Caribbean. In other words, his West
Indianness was not just a regional identification; it extended well beyond the
Anglophone Caribbean and well beyond both the Caribbean and England to
absorb European intellectual thought along with the Africanist elements
of négritude and of the arts movements of the 1940s in Trinidad. In 1956,
Lamming spoke at the First International Congress of Black Artists and
Writers, sponsored by the journal *Présence Africaine*, along with Richard
Wright, Frantz Fanon, Aimé Césaire, and others whose philosophies of
négritude were shaped by existentialism.[83]

The Sartrean concept of the Self–Other relationship as constituted
through the look ("le regard") permeates Lamming's narratives, giving
rise to conflicts among characters and also, in my reading, disturbing
transformations in the sensory body of the emigrant. These threatening
alterations in the characters' ways of seeing, even in the physical eye itself,
signal potential for either the annihilation of self-conscious agency (in
existential terms, freedom) or the creation of new vision and the renewal
of language. Though seeming at times misogynistic in his portrayal
of women characters, positioning them as obstructions to emancipation,
Lamming cannot avoid recognizing the construction of women as objects
through the eyes of the colonizer and in the eyes of men. The deep
ambivalence toward women represented in his novels expresses this perhaps unintended consequence of his narrative exploration of the sense
of sight. Furthermore, it destabilizes gender identifications in ways that
threaten masculinist hierarchies of both England and the Caribbean,
resulting in a modernist, gender-bending subjectivity reminiscent of
Claude McKay's writing. Such gender ambiguity, however, remains threatening and sparks the brutal violence against women portrayed especially in
Lamming's early novels.

The second of these two visual tropes central to Lamming's essays and fiction comes from Haitian vodun. Lamming visited Haiti in 1956 where he witnessed the vodun ritual called the Ceremony of Souls. This was the same year that he visited the newly independent Ghana, so that the trans-atlantic connections, political and cultural, both linking and differentiating the Caribbean and the countries of West Africa became important to his thinking. His visits to Haiti and Ghana developed further the interest in African cultural "survivals" and in Afro-Caribbean arts such as steel pan, carnival, and calypso that was active among intellectuals and artists during his four years in Trinidad.[84] Vodun is the key element of Caribbean influence shaping the modernism of his narratives and, as in the writing of Marson and James, allows him to explore cross-class and -color relation-ships. Echoing Marson's and James's plays, discussed in the previous section, Lamming opens his portrayal of Afro-Caribbean spiritual rituals with the music of drums. However, in both *Season of Adventure* and *The Pleasures of Exile*, the focus moves to the visual art of the vèvè, drawings made by women on the *tonelle* floor in outlines of corn meal that invite the presence of the gods.[85] These vèvè, described by one character in *Season of Adventure* as "the source of all the visual arts in San Cristobal,"[86] prefigure the novel's central visual trope, that of painting. In *The Pleasures of Exile*, they emblematize Lamming's repeated metaphor of "a way of seeing," as the sensory catalyst for revolutionary change and creativity in language. In contrast to C. L. R. James's earlier ambivalence toward Afro-Caribbean spiritual traditions in his short stories of the 1930s, Lamming draws on both "pre-modern" and "modern" elements of the Caribbean experience. These two elements – Haitian vodun and existentialism – intertwine in Lamm-ing's work to give philosophical and, at the same time, concrete historical significance to the visual as a way of exploring the dynamics of national, racial, and gender conflict in this first generation of specifically "West Indian" writers.

The echo of Lamming's engagement with existentialist philosophy begins in *In the Castle of My Skin* with the characterization of the head teacher. Meditating on the subtle encounters between teacher and student or teacher and teacher, the head teacher thinks,

Deep down he felt uneasy. He had been seen by another. He had become part of the other's world, and therefore no longer in complete control of his own. The eye of another was a kind of cage. When it saw you the lid came down, and you were trapped. It was always happening ... in the cinema before the lights were dimmed. You walked down the carpeted path with all those people sitting above and around you, sitting snugly and critically between their ears and their neighbours. It seemed the whole cinema like the public square had turned into one enormous eye that saw you. A big cage whose lid came down and caught you.[87]

In this passage, the move between the individual "eye of another" to that of a public "enormous eye" indicates the significance of this act of seeing for both individual subjectivity and a larger system of social relationships. The larger system is that of a colonial society in which the Sartrean notion of a self in conflict with, yet constituted by, the look of the Other[88] expands to a larger sense of social surveillance. The image of "one enormous eye that saw you" recalls the advertisement for the 1937 Exposition Internationale des Arts et Techniques dans la Vie Moderne in Paris, which provides the setting for Jean Rhys's novel, *Good Morning, Midnight* (1939). The ad appeared on the cover of the May 1937 issue of *Vendre* and consisted of one eye, occupying the entire width of the page, its pupil an image of the European half of the globe, with a dot marking the location of Paris. The words Exposition Internationale curve over the top and bottom lids of the eye, the letters appearing as its lashes.[89] All of the world could be seen at the exposition, implies the image, but also the exposition is the eye that captures all of the world. That Lamming's character perceives a similar enormous eye in the cinema of a colonial village fits the theme of the exposition, which celebrated the commerce and technology of modernity as well as the arts of modernism. As an image of colonial surveillance, caging the colonized individual's self-perception, the enormous eye also alludes to earlier explicitly imperial exhibitions, such as the one at Wembley in 1924, suggesting the imperial reach of their visual displays in shaping the colonized mind and nervous system.

Lamming had apparently read Rhys's novels, for he makes allusions to them in his next novel, *The Emigrants*, in which the look, glance, or eye of the Other permeates the narrative, sets the conflicts between characters, and causes an alteration in the actual eye of the main character. *The Emigrants* follows in Rhys's footsteps, especially those set by *Voyage in the Dark*, her 1934 novel about a young West Indian woman in pre-World War I England, not only in theme but also by improvising a narrative style of Caribbean modernism. In the early pages of *The Emigrants*, the main character alludes to both Rhys's novel and the project of reinventing the novel as a genre. The first-person narrator of this chapter describes reading a book titled *The Living Novel* and reports, "I read it as though by habit, page after page for several hours. The Novel was alive, though dead. This freedom was simply dead."[90] The novel as a genre thus takes part in an existential project of freedom, and the passage cues us to read the specific

11. Cover, *Vendre*, No. 162 (May 1937), reprinted from *Paris 1937: Worlds on Exhibition* by James D. Herbert, © 1998, Cornell University, courtesy Cornell University Press.

novel in our hands as one that begins with such philosophical and narrative self-consciousness. The passage, which continues to describe a dialogue between the narrator and a friend, drinking together in a rum shop, ends with a near quotation from Rhys's *Voyage in the Dark*: " 'At least one can try to start all over again.' We knocked the glasses and finished the last drink. / '. . . start all over? . . . again . . .' " (14). These lines echo the last lines of Rhys's novel, "And about starting all over again, all over again . . ."[91] They signal a debt to Rhys, and also an intention to renew the novel, to bring it alive as Caribbean literature, making 1950, as Lamming said in the 1972 interview quoted at the beginning of this chapter, "the beginning for writers" who have become self-consciously and collectively West Indian.

The Emigrants portrays this process of identity re-formation as fraught with visual tensions, acts of seeing that, however subtle, constitute epistemological violence and lead to physical brutality. Throughout the novel, detailed descriptions depict the lines of sight between and among groups of people or between two people, eyes meeting or not, glances thrown one way or another, eyes turning one way or another. Becoming West Indian or Caribbean involves seeing and being seen, and these visual dynamics put the body of the Caribbean person at risk.

Violence – epistemological, physical, and sexual – erupts in Lamming's novels, both those set in England or *en route*, as are *The Emigrants* and *Water with Berries*, and those set in the Caribbean, such as *Age of Innocence* and *Season of Adventure*. The brutality against women and their ambiguous roles in the narratives have, in particular, created controversy among critics. Lamming's remarks in an interview with George Kent in 1973 further spark the debate. Speaking of *Water with Berries*, the novel that most closely responds to Shakespeare's *The Tempest* and also alludes to *Othello*, Lamming states that the rapes and murder of white women in this novel are a price paid:

That horror and that brutality [of colonial history] have a price; which has to be paid by the man who inflicted it – just as the man who suffered it has to find a way of exorcising that demon. It seems to me that there is almost a therapeutic need for a certain kind of violence in the breaking. There cannot be a parting of the ways. There has to be a smashing.[92]

Several critics have questioned Lamming's apparent support of a necessary and therapeutic violence against women.[93] Lamming's language recalls the work of Frantz Fanon, especially in *Black Skin, White Masks*, where Fanon discusses the transference of the desire for colonial power on the part of the colonized male into desire for the white woman, who substitutes for the white man as an object of violent revenge through rape. However, in several of Lamming's novels, Afro-Caribbean women become the targets of rape, beatings, and murder perpetuated by Afro-Caribbean men and sometimes by white men. These incidents complicate critical questions concerning the portrayals of women and invite us to reconsider their larger roles in the narratives. Are they, as various critics argue, represented as sites of danger, obstructions to emancipation, negligible figures in a masculine nationalist quest, recipients of the loathing and fear felt for the colonizer, peripheral anti-colonial voices, or in some cases, important to, but not creators of, political change? How are differences of race and class figured in their characters and relations with others?

Focusing on *The Emigrants* and *Season of Adventure*, I argue that representations of existential acts of seeing and the visual art of Haitian vodun ceremonies combine to bring forward the subjectivities of women, their oppression, and their central position as agents of political change. By developing characters through moments in which they perceive themselves *as seen* by others, Lamming represents the subjectivities of women, or the feminized Other, in *The Emigrants*; in *Season of Adventure*, he positions Afro-Caribbean women as bridging class divisions, making political revolution possible. The negative, alienating effects of seeing in the Sartrean existentialism that influences these narratives lead to a sense of despair at the conclusion to *The Emigrants*. However, we can read the dialogue with the past made possible by Afro-Caribbean spiritual practices represented in *Season of Adventure* as an alternative vision, one that surpasses the sense of sight in its interartistic performance, to offer a more positive view of community and social change. Through the vodun vèvè of the Ceremony of Souls, Lamming locates women as creative agents in the dialogue with the past that he considers crucial to an ongoing transformation of the colonial relation.

In *The Emigrants*, women per se do not receive positive treatment. They become prostitutes or lesbians (and this last is clearly presented as a negative change), endure unwanted abortions, betray men, and are continually objectified in the eyes of the male characters. In the concluding scenes, a man brutally assaults his emigrant wife. However, these portrayals of female degradation intersect with threats to the male characters' sexual identities, constituted through the act of seeing and residing at the heart of the emigrant male's condition. By portraying the emigrant male as a feminized Other, Lamming depicts the experience of *being seen* as a sexual object in a racist colonial environment as an assault on one's being that obstructs the formation of a West Indian consciousness and collectivity in 1950s England.

The potential for this formation of a new Caribbean identity begins to unfold while the emigrants are still on board ship, and it is portrayed explicitly as a matter of seeing. In this scene, a group of emigrants from various islands fall asleep in the afternoon sun. In a dialogue written as if it were a playscript, involving characters whose names are often only "the Jamaican" or "the Barbadian," they have been discussing who they are.[94] Reflecting on the historical explosion that is taking them all, "searchin' and feelin'," to England, the Jamaican stresses their new name:

We never hear so much talk till lately 'bout the West Indies. Everybody sayin' me is West Indian. We is West Indians. West Indian this, West Indian that . . . A good name. Them is West Indians. Not Jamaicans or Trinidadians. Cause the bigger the better. Them' is West Indians … Them all provin' something. An' is the reason West Indies may out o' dat vomit produce a great people, 'cause them provin' that them want to be something.[95]

Moving out of dramatic dialogue into third-person narrative prose, subsequent passages portray the nap that soon overcomes the group as a threshold sensory experience. Falling asleep as they approach England, they can no longer see as they have seen before. Though sleep makes them vulnerable, it gives them the opportunity to suspend their sensory habits and to transform the meaning of their relationships with the "objects" of the world.

In sleep they were without a relation which the others now experienced. They couldn't *see*. The habit that informed them was suspended, … It seemed possible that the habit which informed a man of the objects he has been trained to encounter might be replaced by some other habit new and different in its nature, and therefore creating a new and different meaning and function for those objects. (83)

Though on the threshold of giving new meaning to the objects they encounter, the emigrants are, themselves, vulnerable to objectification. In fact, they may appear as nothing more than "heavy black flesh" or even "shapes of land growing out of the deck." Unable to see, they are unaware of the process they themselves are undergoing, "the sway that rocked them," and "it would have been possible to convert them into objects" (83). However, on awakening, they seem to have undergone a change: "They were together. He seemed to suspect the strength of an increased group" (85). In response to a question about " 'what sort o' place this Englan' is?' " a character named Tornado reminds them that " 'God give every man two eyes to see with' " (85).

In England, however, the process of transformation must continually incorporate the assaults of being seen by others, to the point that the main character's eyes are damaged:

Collis drank some more whiskey, and rubbed his eyes. They were worrying him again … Sometimes he felt as though he might lose his normal sight. It was as though his imagination had taken control of his vision, and faces lost their ordinary outline. He couldn't recognize the nose as nose, or the eye as eye. The organs kept their form, but somehow lost their reference. They became objects. (212)

The damage done to Collis's eyes recalls the extreme alienation experienced by Roquentin in Sartre's novel, *Nausea*, published in English in 1949.[96] At one point, Roquentin states, "my eyes were empty," hoping that he is now delivered from the obstacle of vision, but the sense of sight returns to delude him.[97] Similarly, Collis seems on the threshold of some other way of seeing, but his altered vision only objectifies the features of the faces of other people, and it creates a dizziness or nausea that causes Collis to deliberately alienate himself from other West Indian emigrants.

The deterioration of Collis's vision intersects with the experience of another character, Dickson, whose body disintegrates under the sexually objectifying stares of two Englishwomen. In the development of Dickson's character, we find the metonymical development of a woman's subjectivity and a vivid representation of the complex ways in which gender and race transmute through one another in a colonial relation. Believing that one of the women has invited him to her room because she had chosen him out of all the other emigrants as the one with whom she wished to have a relationship, Dickson is suddenly caught, waiting with his clothes off, by both women:

And he heard her say: I beg your pardon. She said they only wanted to see what he *looked* like. He was lying on the divan, his clothes uncouthly thrown in one corner, and he sat up, rigid and bewildered, in his vest. The women were consumed with curiosity. They devoured his body with their eyes. It disintegrated and dissolved in their stare, gradually regaining its life through the reflection in the mirror. (256)

On a very personal level, this scene repeats the display of the colonized body institutionalized throughout the nineteenth and into the twentieth century in the English and European imperial exhibits. In this case, the colonial relation enables a reversal of the usual gender dynamics of the sexual gaze, so that rather than a male gaze objectifying the body of a woman, these white Englishwomen have the power to see and, by seeing, destroy the male: "after that experience with the women, which often in his sleep was revived, it was a torture to see and be seen simultaneously. A degradation beyond anything he had known before, more shattering than anything he would experience again" (237). The sense of extreme degradation Dickson experiences recalls the vulnerability of the body, "*degraded* consciousness" and "shame" that Sartre describes as resulting from being seen by others.[98]

Dickson's experience is especially humiliating because he had gone to the woman's room believing that something special about him had attracted her:

out of them all she chose me perhaps the doctor was telling her about me she could understand nothing like the intelligence it can reduce all difference the understanding she and me the doctor and me and what could have happened to make him befriend me to make her choose me the common language of a common civilisation reason she could see he could see. (254)

As this passage exemplifies, the narrative frequently shifts in this scene into an interior monologue, portraying the effects of this visual humiliation on the inner consciousness of the character, who at first believes that a bond of "intelligence," "common language," and "common civilisation" draws the woman to him. The alternation between third-person narration and interior monologue depicts the shock he undergoes and the irony of having been chosen by the woman:

> The light was turned on and his eyes hurt.
> You chose
> The moon had sneaked away.
> I don't understand. Come in. Your sister *too* . . .
> . . . He couldn't recollect what had happened. Now he was in the street.
> His shirt was flying outside the pants, and the wind lashed his face.
> out of them all. me. the man is mad. out of them all. me. me.   (256)

Caught in a glare of light, his eyes hurting, Dickson flees. His mind becomes a chaos of voices colliding and remaking the meaning of his illusory belief in having been chosen for qualities of his mind and cultural upbringing. The passage conveys the process by which his sense of self, "me," has been redefined by the terrifying "radical metamorphosis" involved in being seen.[99] Later, in the bar, Collis describes what has happened to his eyes, triggering Dickson's anguish all over again:

"I can understand it at certain times," he said. "In sex, in the sexual act.". . . "My relation is that of a subject to an object. That is true. I see the body as an object. You understand? I'm sure you understand. And I wanted to ask some women . . . but I couldn't. That would be beyond me." He had turned his eyes on Dickson. "Have you ever felt that you were *seen* in this way?" . . . Dickson was stumbling blindly through the swaying crowd . . . Azi and Phillip saw . . . They looked at Collis and the Jugoslav with incredulous eyes. Phillip was rubbing his forehead and the sockets of his eyes . . . (265)

Dickson's terror is thus renewed and drives him through the crowd, blinded again, among "incredulous eyes." The passages portraying Dickson's degradation by the Englishwomen deploy modernist devices to convey the unreality of his experience, which has altered his deepest sense of himself as a person in time and space. It has recolonized and feminized him, twisting his gender and temporal location by putting him in a place reminiscent of the woman named Saartjie Baartman and called the Hottentot Venus, who was exhibited throughout England and Europe in the early nineteenth century, a captive object of curious imperial eyes. As Sander Gilman has documented and Anne McClintock has also discussed, curiosity about Baartman focused on her sexual organs, which were displayed even after her death.[100] Jean Rhys alludes to this case, identifying Baartman with Caribbean women when the characters in *Voyage in the Dark* refer to Anna Morgan as "the Hottentot." By portraying a black male emigrant in a similar situation, Lamming follows Rhys in exposing the complexities of gender, race, and colonial relations whereby, in Rhys's novel, the white creole woman may become a racialized Other and, in Lamming's novel, the colonized man may become a feminized Other through the colonial gaze. When Collis speaks of wanting to ask women about their experience of being seen in the sexual act and then turns to ask Dickson if he has been "*seen* in this way," he inadvertently places Dickson in the place of a woman. This threat to the masculinity of the Caribbean male subject results from being seen as an object and leads, in the conclusion of the novel, to an act of brutal violence against a Caribbean woman.

In the novel's concluding pages, a character known only as the Strange Man appears outside a club where West Indians gather. A stowaway on an emigrant ship, the Strange Man has brought a large group of new arrivals, reminding the club owner of earlier promises to "always stick together" as West Indians (168). However, the owner, whom everyone calls the Governor, feels "no loyalty towards the crowd outside," and when appealed to, Collis states, " 'I have no people' " (270). When the Strange Man brings in his girlfriend, the Governor recognizes her as his own wife from home who had already betrayed him there with a "Yank." He cannot control his rage: "He kept his eyes on the woman, two sparks emitted from the points of daggers. 'Get out.' The woman stood where she was, no longer human. She was a fact" (270). The Governor proceeds to kick the woman across the floor. She "howl[ed] like an animal" and "made a pool of blood on the floor" (270). The novel ends with the characters either waiting or dispersing, cleaning "the mess," or in the case of Collis, looking out the window.

The language of the passage in which the Governor assaults his wife evokes more than the realist anger of personal and political betrayal. His eyes become daggers, a cliché, but one with philosophical weight in a novel driven by existential acts and metaphors of vision. His dagger-point eyes physically dehumanize the woman. The act of looking and the act of kicking her across the floor become inseparable in her degradation to a howling animal. In *The Second Sex*, published in English two years before *The Emigrants*, Simone de Beauvoir argues that, through violence, men establish the complete alterity of women. Violence marks a woman as Other and thereby affirms her status as a possession whereby the male claims another man's property and reaffirms his own masculine difference from her. Derived from the theories of kinship developed by Claude Lévi-Strauss and inflected with an existentialist notion of the Self–Other relation, de Beauvoir's analysis rests on the idea that "The reciprocal bond basic to marriage is not set up between men and women, but between men and men by means of women, who are only the principal occasion for it."[101] Given Lamming's intense reading of works by Sartre and de Beauvoir during the late 1940s and early 1950s, this perspective can help to explain the significance of the scene. The Governor's violence against his wife speaks of his previous claim but does so by highlighting her status as object, passed from one group of men to another, from himself to the US soldiers, to the new group of emigrants. She represents the conflicts between these groups of men and, through her, the Governor can refuse any affiliation with the Strange Man and his group. By kicking her, he caps his rejection of the entire group of recent West Indian emigrants, indicating the change wrought in him and Collis since their arrival in England. They no longer feel any loyalty to West Indians as their people; their eyes have been so damaged that they can no longer see themselves in these recent arrivals. Moreover, the humiliations, misrecognitions, and objectifications that the Governor's and Collis's group of emigrants has endured strike at their masculine identities to the point that a woman, not the Strange Man, becomes the target for rage and violence. The Governor may want revenge against his wife, but he also needs to prove in this same moment that he is no longer one of the group she represents in her need for help. Simultaneously, he acts for Dickson, asserting a male identity against the feminizing of black men as sexual objects in England. He makes her fully Other, dehumanized into a "fact," and an animal. The act portrays the failure of this great project of "searchin' and feelin'" with its promise for the transformation of the sensory habits of the body and the new meanings that this group of emigrants might have found for their lives. Instead of granting them a revelatory new vision, their eyes no longer see individual features on the face of human beings but perceive them only as objects. Their solidarity as West Indians has deteriorated into a disavowal of any associations with one another.

The novel offers, however, an interpretation of how such objectification happens and with what effects on the consciousness of the objectified Other. Though Lamming does not seem interested in portraying these effects on the women characters, he does portray them in the experiences of the men. Through Dickson, a glimpse of the subjectivity of a woman emerges. In the modernist alternation between interior monologue and third-person narration that conveys the moment when he occupies the position of a captured and colonized woman, the narrative portrays metonymically the subjectivities of women, "*seen* in that way." The novel's ending may express a narrative outbreak of misogynistic violence, but it also appears as a logical outcome of the violence against men and women whose expectations for seeing with their own two eyes and creating new meanings for their identities in the world have been cruelly denied.

The glimpse of feminine subjectivity that the novel offers through its portrayal of Dickson is developed more fully in *Season of Adventure*, published in 1960, which centers on a young Caribbean woman in the midst of a social revolution. Again, feminine subjectivity develops through an incident in which a major character reconstitutes herself *as seen*, but this time she also sees from the outside, herself, or someone nearly herself, in the act of being seen, and this dynamic act of social vision propels her towards self-knowledge and significant political action. Moreover, the initial sensory experience which launches her quest revolves on the visual art of Haitian vodun rituals and develops further through the work of a Caribbean painter. Lamming's interest in Haitian vodun surfaces in 1960 in this novel and also in *The Pleasures of Exile*, published in the same year. Both place in dynamic dialogue with one another the negative existential philosophy of vision guiding Lamming's portrayals of the social act of seeing with the promising insight gained through Afro-Caribbean spiritual practices by invoking the Haitian Ceremony of Souls. This interaction allows the narration of sensory transformation and also opens the way for a new vision of Caribbean history and identity. Lamming's "Introduction" to *The Pleasures of Exile* describes the ceremony as a ritual communion with "the Dead" and a dialogue, therefore, between the present and the past that makes the future possible. Lamming stresses the importance of dialogue here, which becomes a narrative model for the book's essays and also for the shifting discourses of his novels, in which dramatic dialogues often intersperse with narrative prose. In explaining the ceremony as a practice resistant to colonial rule, Lamming focuses on the visual art, or "*ververs*," of the ritual. When the ceremony is outlawed, the celebrants leave the *tonelle* and instead practice their religion in the streets:

The ceremony is simple. You make certain *ververs* in the dust, and whenever two or three are gathered together by the sign of the *ververs*, the gods are there. It is that sign, like a cross, which reminds them of their need. Then the Law arrives. The police arrive without warning; but no charge can be made. For the worshippers stand to welcome their protectors, the police, and at the same moment their feet have erased the signs of invocation which they had made in the dust. The god is not there, for his cross has gone. But the moment the police depart, the signatures will be made again; the god will return, and prayer will assume whatever needs those peasants whisper.[102]

As Lamming states elsewhere, documentary or ethnographic details of the actual Haitian ceremony are not so important as the symbolic value of its ritualistic practice. In the collection of essays that comprise *The Pleasures of Exile*, it becomes a trope for re-visioning history in dialogue with the past, denying the authority of British cultural institutions, and establishing instead the authority of a "Caribbean way of seeing." By calling the *ververs* (or *vèvè*) signatures, Lamming indicates their importance as a visual language, an Afro-Caribbean spiritual art form that signs on behalf of the gods and the people.[103] They provide the link between seeing and language, which is the central theme of this book, and which Lamming expresses most explicitly in a passage describing the transformation of the Caribbean slave from an object or tool used by others to an active subject of his own life.

Lamming figures the Caribbean slave as Caliban, and, as Sandra Pouchet Paquet points out in her illuminating foreward, Caliban transforms in Lamming's writing from the ignorant savage of Shakespeare's play to Toussaint L'Ouverture, the heroic revolutionary leader of the Haitian Revolution, and then becomes representative of the contemporary resistant Caribbean writer. In this series of transformations, Caliban, who received language from his master only to curse him, becomes a creator with and through language.[104] Inseparable from this transformation through language is Caliban's acquisition of the power to see. Caliban thus figures the twinning of active vision and language that shapes all of Lamming's work. Lamming defines Caliban as, initially, a creature without a self; he is only "a reaction to circumstances imposed upon his life" (107). Most importantly, "Caliban is never accorded the power *to see*. He is always the measure of the condition which his physical appearance has already defined" (107). This condition is that of a slave in relation to his colonial master. Writing about James's *The Black Jacobins* and the relationship between slaves and their owners, Lamming states:

in the eyes of their owners, they had no language but the labour of their hands. If these hands, like the prongs of the plough, showed signs of weakening, the property was disposed of; buried or burnt while it was still alive . . . We may guess the age of a man; but a plough, like the land it opens cannot evoke a similar interest. For it was not human, but the category of nature to which masters had relegated these savage and deformed slaves. (120–21)

Yet a paradox arose for the master in that the slaves remained, nevertheless, human, and the property owners were therefore forced to treat their own property without proper care, for they must brutalize the slaves in order to insure their submission and thereby the safety of the master. This paradox had its effect on the slave, too:

Imagine a plough in the field. Ordinary as ever, prongs and spine unchanged, it is simply there, stuck to its post beside the cane shoot. Then some hand, identical with the routine of its work, reaches to lift this familiar instrument. But the plough escapes contact. It refuses to surrender its present position ... More hands arrive to confirm the extraordinary conduct of this plough; but no one can explain the terror of those hands as they withdraw from the plough. *Some new sight as well as some new sense of language is required to bear witness to the miracle of the plough which now talks.* For as those hands in unison move forward, the plough achieves a somersault which reverses its traditional posture. Its head goes into the ground, and the prongs, throat-near, stand erect in the air, ten points of steel, announcing danger. (121) (my emphasis)

In this mysterious and revolutionary act, the ontological basis for knowledge turns upside down. That which has seemed a part of nature has actively refused a relationship which has also seemed intrinsic to the natural order. His refusal has given him speech so that all who witness the "miracle of the plough which now talks" require "some new sight as well as some new sense of language." Lamming's description of this act recalls Edna Manley's sculptures of the 1930s, especially *Negro Aroused*, *Prophet*, and *Pocomania*, which portray the act of seeing as revolutionary. However, Lamming transforms these mute figures into creative agents themselves by recognizing their articulation of a new language.[105]

In *Season of Adventure*, the novel published alongside *The Pleasures of Exile* in 1960, Lamming again experiments with the language of the novel to investigate the dynamics of a Caribbean society in the midst of revolutionary change.[106] The turn of the living plough into a speaking man portrayed in *The Pleasures* indicates the necessity for, not only new language and vision, but also a radical alteration of the entire sensory body in creating social change. In *Season*, the colonized body and mind come under the powerful sway of the arts of the vèvè, the steel drum, and the paintings of a Caribbean artist. In this novel, Lamming places the arts at the center of political change. While many characters, male and female, undergo such physical and inner transformation, the character of Fola, a young middle-class woman, remains crucial to the narrative even, I would argue, in its second part when the focus shifts to Chiki, a painter from the lower class who has been to college, traveled in the United States, and returned to his home in the impoverished community of the Forest Reserve.

Season of Adventure takes place on an imaginary island, San Cristobal, two to three years after it has achieved political independence. Sandra Pouchet Paquet has interpreted San Cristobal as representing all of the Caribbean, and the novel's characters and plot as composing a critique of the failures of the post-independence elite, their corruption and greed, and the oppression of the poor under their governance. It opens with the sound of the drums playing in the Ceremony of Souls, a ritual frowned on by the governing class, but to which Fola, adopted daughter of the Chief of Police, has come with her teacher. Her experience at the ceremony completely alters Fola as she shakes violently, becomes incontinent, goes into a trance, and falls under the persistent "glance" of an old woman in the chaos of spirit possession. When the women make the vèvè, Fola's teacher tells her they are "the source of all the visual arts in San Cristobal. Just shapes of fish, fowl and whatever the gods favor."[107] He mentions Chiki, the painter from the poor village called the Forest Reserve, who "helped me understand how the ceremony is every man's *backward glance* . . . Only the dead can do it, Chiki says, and the living who are free" (49). The ceremony and its visual arts launch Fola on her own quest for freedom and knowledge of her past. As she writes in a note to Chiki, responding to his initial hostility towards her: "That you of all men should deny a woman the right to make her *own backward* glance!" (225). She is determined to free herself from what she perceives as the lies lived by her family and class; her quest then focuses on the identity of her real father, whom no one has revealed to her. Fola becomes "Fola *and other than.* This Fola had started on a history of needs whose details she alone would be able to distinguish: a season of adventure which no man in the republic could predict" (185). The phrase "Fola *and other than*" conveys the potential of a self in a moment of existential negation necessary to the development of freedom or agency.[108] Fola thus becomes the central questing character of the novel, occupying a liminal social position full of possibility. Located by adoption within the ruling elite, she nevertheless feels strong affinities with the poor people of the island. The mystery of her paternal origin allows the possibility that she may belong to more than one social class or may become a bridge between them.

As Fola begins her quest, she is deeply alienated from her mother; however, Agnes, too, is undergoing a transformation related to the Ceremony of Souls. In an allusion to the water from which the dead spirits come, Agnes feels "water . . . like an ocean around her" (154). Though each woman undergoes transformations separately, they come together in a bond toward the novel's end. The submerged mother–daughter plot develops through the combined experiences of *seeing/being seen* and of summoning the past in psychological and spiritual transformations that drive the novel's plot, creating conditions for the re-formation of the self and for political change.[109]

This revolution happens through the two women's actions and in relation to the development, in the novel's second part, of the character of Chiki, the painter who is working on three canvases, each a depiction of a biblical story which "are now transformed into an opposite vision that has grown like weather from the Forest Reserve" (188). Along with this oppositional vision, the novel generates images of the male body and the senses in states of extreme alteration. For example, as the result of a brutal beating endured while he was in the United States, Chiki's face is "unjustly ugly," his lips are broken, and he has lost an ear. Chiki's missing ear parallels his friend Gort's inability to read. Twinning again the ability to see with the acquisition of language, Lamming makes Gort, the steel pan drummer, illiterate: "he shares a total darkness with the blind whenever his eyes see words on paper." Chiki, however, has been to college and can certainly read, but he cannot, in his painting, "transmute the sound of Fola's voice, or the magic of Great Gort's drum" (241–42). One of Gort's closest friends is a literally blind Englishman who, for a time, allows Gort to spare him some of the inconveniences of his blindness. This circuit of senses among individuals and between eye and ear is represented in Chiki's painting on the center of Gort's drum, "delicate with lines like a human navel . . . which doesn't tear the steel, yet opens like a womb under each line" (52). When Gort looks into the distance, "it is Chiki's hand that guides him as he watches a distance of colour climbing from the tree-tops to the sky." Through Chiki's art, Gort reads the world around him, and through Gort's music, Chiki's painting opens as if in the process of giving birth. This interartistic genesis, through extreme alteration of the body and re-circuiting of the senses, echoes the transformations Fola underwent in the *tonelle* and that her mother, we may suppose, experiences in the "ocean" that surrounds her.

When Chiki assesses his own work, he sees with pleasure his ability to create the sense of movement. "Movement, . . . movement is my greatest gift" (230). This aesthetic value derives from a formalist concept of "significant form," which C. L. R. James addresses in his essay "What Is Art?" As I discuss in the next section of this chapter, James appropriates the aesthetic value of movement and turns it about to undermine the authority of bourgeois art institutions and to grant "the people" the right to make and judge art. Lamming does something similar in this novel. A movement of the people arises on San Cristobal when the police raid the Forest Reserve, destroying Gort's drum by "punctur[ing] the navel of the drum" with their rifle butts. Looking for the murderer of a government official, the police have targeted the entire village, and the government subsequently outlaws steel pan playing. The "revolt of the drums" performs with music and the movement of the people a raising of the dead previously enacted in the Ceremony of the Souls and in Chiki's painting of Lazarus: "They had seen the *tonelle* transformed into a real, familiar tomb; and the corpses like Lazarus climbed back to life, denying the power and the permanence of the grave" (360). Chiki's canvases have scripted the revolt: "Chiki stood at the window, collapsed with tears as he saw his canvases come to life" (360).

The crisis that leads to the revolt of the drums also takes Fola to knowledge of her origins, and that, too, requires one of Chiki's paintings in order to unfold. However, most importantly, it requires from Fola an act of existential freedom. Claiming that her father committed the murder and that they can find his face on a portrait in Chiki's studio, Fola acts as "other than" the Fola she was brought up to be. She defies Piggott, who is her stepfather and the Chief of Police, and she looks both to the past and the future of San Cristobal by leading them to Chiki's portrait. The narrative puts it in existential terms: "Fola had been restored to that freedom which now ordered her to put an end to Piggott's authority" (271). However, the portrait is difficult to read precisely because of the artist's gift for "movement":

The painter's hand had preserved the naked outline of a murder and a man: a face which had been caught in every line and movement of its features . . . The eyes looked suspicious and alert in different ways. The left eye seemed more nervous, more reluctant to open up as though afraid of what it saw, glancing backward from the corner of its socket. But the right eye was wide and fierce, a triumphant glare of certainty dazzling its surface. The eyes seemed to compete for an exclusive vision of what confronted them; fixed, hard and determined, as though they were in private agreement about two different ways of seeing. (293)

The duality of vision and elusive motion of the painting become prophetic, not only of the island's destiny, but of the father Fola finally discovers. In a narrative revelation that, for some critics, appears as awkwardly deferred to the novel's end, Agnes tells a story of two possible fathers: though both of them forced themselves on her, one after the other, the first was familiar and attractive to her, the bishop's blond nephew; the second was a stranger, a black "native of the soil" (343). Fola was conceived in a "double father-hood," through violence, desire, and fear as, the narrative suggests, was the island. This honest "summon[ing of] the past" (335) finally engaged by Agnes, rather than the lies previously perpetuated by Fola's family and by the First Republic, is necessary to the country's future.

The future requires a new language and also new forms of social relations, including those between men and women. A more conventional or sentimental conclusion would script a romance or marriage between Fola and Chiki; however, by a strange twist in which Chiki's brother may be the black man who raped Agnes, this becomes impossible.[110] We might read this an incestuous enclosure and a denial of possibility. Or, we could see that because their relationship thus falls outside of the conventional marriage plot, it remains to be created. However, as Sandra Pouchet Pacquet has pointed out, in this novel and others by Lamming, the agents of such creativity are always men.

The structure of *Season of Adventure* supports Pacquet's point. Though the novel begins with Fola's quest and centers on her development, the second part focuses primarily on Chiki and the performative role of his art in concert with that of the drums. Fola's story and that of her mother become more of a supporting subplot. Furthermore, Fola endures a brutal rape, attempted murder, and beating that recall the violence against women in Lamming's previous novels. She seems, in this respect, more an object and occasion for the men to act out their parts.[111] Even so, a number of critics, like Supriya Nair, see Fola as "one of the strongest female characters in Lamming's novels" (118). Simon Gikandi even sees Lamming's portrayal of Fola as opening the way for later feminist writers such as Michelle Cliff.

Though cathartic male violence against women in the colonial setting permeates the narrative, the feminine position of being "seen in that way" also yields the possibility for self-realization and freedom in existential terms. Through seeing herself as seen by Others, Fola engages her "*own backward* glance." Following her experience in the *tonelle*, the next major step in this journey of vision occurs in a scene in which Fola sees her mother as the object of the gaze of other men. Seeing her mother as *seen*, she also sees someone resembling herself being *seen in that way*, for her mother is wearing one of Fola's dresses, looks as if she might be Fola's age, and is mistaken by the men for Fola's sister. Fola sees her mother, almost herself, as *seen*, and the experience recalls the Ceremony of Souls:

It was the way *this woman*, who happened to be her mother, had been *seen* . . . Fola now saw her mother through their eyes. She had placed a similar meaning on her mother's presence; and every recollection of her mother persuaded Fola to this certainty: her mother was *a whore, a whore, nothing but a whore*. That's what she wanted to say. She was the child of a whore . . . She was losing her hold on what she knew: like the night she felt her reason slip and sink into the improbable realities of the *tonelle*. Her mother's presence seemed to drag her back to that experience of the *Houngan's* voice in dialogue with the dead souls in the tent; drag her back into the accusation of the old woman's glance. (152–53)

Far from resting here, in this vision of her mother as the men see her, Fola's backward glance leads her to connect with women across the class divide. She sees herself, daughter of the mother who is seen in that way, as a bastard. But she also sees herself in the prostitutes at the hospital who come for help with abortions and are abused by the same man, a doctor who courted her at a dance and through whose eyes she was forced to see her mother. She, thus, undergoes the degraded consciousness experienced by Dickson in *The Emigrants*, recognizes a self other than the self she had previously been, yet moves through this "radical metamorphosis" into a larger sense of community that, for the narrative of *The Emigrants*, is impossible. It is the doctor who constructs all of these women as whores and who screams, hypocritically, about "standards" when a poor woman begs for his help at the hospital. Listening, Fola "thought there was some connection between those women and herself" and again, "she was Fola, and *other than* . . . she would be active and free from the outside" (175). In Part Two of the novel, the section apparently devoted to Chiki's art and the "revolt of the drums," she is free to cross the forest and the pond into the Reserve where she is "restored to [her] freedom" by her act of intervention in her stepfather's arrest of the Forest Reserve men. This is the moment when she leads them to Chiki's portrait of her doubled, dual-sighted "father." Without this action, the mass movement of the people in the revolt of the drums could not have taken place.

Fola asserts her freedom at great risk and suffers the consequences in brutal assaults by men. Lamming has made clear that, in this case, he has not represented violence against a woman as a price paid by the colonizer (or his postcolonial agents) displaced onto the woman. Speaking specifically of Fola, he explains: "*Season* is a book of extremes and the journey that the woman has to make in class terms is considerably more difficult than the male would have to make. When a woman crosses those bridges, much, much more is involved. There is likely to be much greater punishment and much greater scales of rejection."[112] Fola's free actions spark male rage, yet also gain her respect from another male character who realizes that "a miracle happened when he started to think of Fola in her own right."

With a reminder "to think again about their relation to the *tonelle*," the novel's conclusion gestures towards the creativity of the women who drew in cornmeal the signs of the vèvè described at the novel's beginning as "the source of all the visual arts in San Cristobal." If we read the novel with this backward glance to its beginning, we can discern the strong possibility for the creative agency of women, not just in the ritual ceremonies of the past, but in the new society to be developed. The possibility develops from their work as visual artists of and participants in Afro-Caribbean spiritual trans-formations, in which they demonstrate a power to see that recalls the visions represented earlier in Edna Manley's sculptural portraits of male prophets and seers.

* * *

Three years after the publication of *The Pleasures of Exile* and *Season of Adventure*, C. L. R. James also located visual creativity in the West Indian person, both as individual and collective, in his book about cricket, *Beyond a Boundary*. As Lamming's *The Pleasures of Exile* had been shaped by James's *The Black Jacobins*, so James's writing about art in *Beyond a Boundary* built on Lamming's descriptions of painting and his association of political movements with an aesthetic of "movement" in *Season of Adventure*. James picks up on the exploration of Western art and aesthetics that Lamming offers in his fiction, turning to the modernist aesthetics that dominated discussions of art in the early and mid-twentieth century. Looking back at modernism, James does not abandon his interest, expressed in his earlier writing, in the lower classes and popular culture of the Caribbean. Rather, he supplants his earlier, ambivalent fascination with Afro-Caribbean religious practices with a focus on cricket. In this globally popular sport, James finds a cultural practice that embodies, literally, a deep engagement with the class, racial, and colonial conflicts of English and Caribbean history; furthermore, by presenting cricket as art, he challenges dominant institutions of art and art criticism. In this respect, James becomes a crucial figure in the formation of a new "way of seeing" that Lamming theorized in his essays and fiction.

Indeed, as exemplified by the story with which I open Chapter 1 of this study, James becomes, for other intellectuals and writers from the Caribbean, an icon for that new way of seeing. Told by Stuart Hall, the story characterizes James by his dynamic eye: "James would take a postcard of *Guernica* to cricket matches, and during intervals when play stopped he would take it out and study it. When play resumed, he would put it away."[113] In the movements of his eye, James created a visual bridge linking the historical forces of tyranny, resistance, and creative transformation that he saw in Picasso's painting to those he saw in the play of cricket.

James wrote *Beyond a Boundary* during what Stuart Hall refers to as the fourth phase of his life's work, spent primarily in the Caribbean in the years when Trinidad and Barbados gained independence from Britain. For part of this time, James was active in nationalist politics, but a falling out with Trinidad's prime minister, Eric Williams, and a near-fatal automobile accident sent him back to England in 1963. That same year *Beyond a Boundary* was published by a British company. Most readers of James's work value this remarkable genre-crossing text – neither autobiography nor critical study yet both, somewhere between philosophy, aesthetics, and sports writing – as the culmination of his life's interests and a path-breaking work in what we currently call cultural studies.[114]

In *Beyond a Boundary*, James characterizes significant events and moments in his life by the pattern of movement they trace, and he often devotes pages to celebrating movement – in cricket, his travels, in theatre, painting, and politics. He describes his movement as a six-year-old boy in Tunapuna, turning from the window in his room, from which he watched for hours the cricket matches on the field outside, to the books on the top of the wardrobe next to it as setting "the pattern of my life."[115] Writing about the West Indian cricket player, Learie Constantine, who first invited James to England, James celebrates movement as what really matters, a personal trajectory intertwined with social change. James credited Constantine with raising his consciousness about racism, helping him to see the necessity for West Indian independence, and prompting him to break out of his nineteenth-century intellectualism. In James's writing about painting and sculpture and in his appropriations of modernist British aesthetics, he finds a cluster of metaphors, especially those of movement, through which to question the empiricist epistemology of imperialist discourses. He also extends our ontological notions of the visual out of the exclusive realm of sight to a kinetic, intercorporeal dynamic. Finally, as traced in Hall's portrait of James's way of seeing, we can discern in James's writing a dynamic link between our perception of the everyday world and the imagination through which human beings creatively transform themselves and represent their world. Like Lamming's writing, however, James's essays in *Beyond a Boundary* raise questions concerning the agents of the newly evolving sensory dynamic, more specifically, the gendering of this creative agency. Locating it in cricket, James moves from the often woman-centered world of Afro-Caribbean spiritual practices in his earlier writing to a gentleman's sport that only peripherally and belatedly includes women as players.

Probably the most extensive meditation on movement appears in the chapter titled "What Is Art?" in which James argues that "cricket is an art, not a bastard or a poor relation, but a full member of the community."[116] To make his case, James turns to the aesthetics of Bernhard Berenson, the powerful American socialite, connoisseur, and art critic, who influenced, among many others, Bloomsbury aestheticians Clive Bell and Roger Fry and, through them, the work of E. M. Forster and Virginia Woolf. As if in reply, not only to their "high" modernism but also to the popular imperial version promoted by the Wembley guidebooks, James discusses in *Beyond a Boundary* the concept of "significant form." As James describes Berenson's definition, "significant form" denotes "the movement of the line, the relations of colour and tone ... It was the line, the curve, its movement, the drama it embodied as painting, the linear design, the painterly tones and values taken as a whole: this constituted the specific quality of visual art" (200). According to James's rendition of this philosophy, the second characteristic of significant form, after "tactile values," is "movement," an artistic quality observable in the "perfect flow of motion" of the Spanish bullfight or the West Indian cricketer's "style": "Another name for the perfect flow of motion is style, or, if you will, significant form" (206).

James makes his most important move, however, when he redefines significant form, making cricket the measure of its adequacy, rather than the other way round:

What is to be emphasized is that whereas in the fine arts the image of tactile values and movement, however effective, however magnificent, is permanent, fixed, in cricket the spectator sees the image constantly re-created, and whether he is a cultivated spectator or not, has standards which he carries with him always ... On the business of setting off physical processes and evoking a sense of movement in the spectator, followers of Mr. Berenson's classification would do well to investigate the responses of cricket spectators. The theory may thereby be enriched, or may be seen to need enrichment. To the eye of the cricketer it seems pretty thin. (205)

James turns around the equation that positions the elements of European painting and sculpture as the measure of the art of any sport. He suggests instead that critics of European painting can find solutions to the theoretical problems facing them in cricket and, more specifically, in "the responses of cricket spectators."

Turning the tables on the famous art critic allows James to position cricket, a sport in which West Indians excel, as the arbiter and measure of artistic value. We might question the logic of James's argument by pointing out that most art forms such as painting are representations of something experienced or felt in the real world, while cricket *is* a real-world experience. A cricket play might be portrayed, for example, in a photograph or film which, as representations, would qualify as candidates for art, but not the play itself. For James, however, cricket as an art form re-presents crucial aspects of real-world experience.[117] It embodies, literally, movements of Caribbean history, colonialism, and resistance to imperialism, and in Britain, resistance to social forces of industrialization. Cricket began and evolved as a popular sport in England between 1778 and 1830, played then by rural artisans who were not subjected to the work order and regulatory time of the factory system. In this period of modernization – the transition from an agricultural society to an industrial one – the play of cricket offered resistance to social forces that blunted the mind and imagination.[118]

The turn in James's argument thus locates the formation of a *contra-modern* vision in the play of cricket by "men of hand and eye." Further, it links the formation in England of a popular rural game, expropriated later by the Victorian bourgeoisie, to the successful appropriation by black West Indians of a sport played at first in the Caribbean among members of the planter class. In this last transatlantic, cross-class development of cricket, James sees forces of decolonization at work in spite of the fact that he first learned the sport as part of a colonial education meant to instill British ethics and notions of manliness. He argues that the contradictions of racism also played themselves out on the cricket field, educating black players as to the political nature of the game and making evident the contrast between their abilities and their lack of freedom.

James's rhetorical turn gives a different identity to the eye that sees and the gaze that judges in the process of defining art. It is no longer the individual eye of a bourgeois art critic but that of a collective, "the local masses of the population," first rooted in villages and towns but now spread across the world. Appealing to his readers' inner eye, James writes in an essay of 1969:

Visualize please. Not only in the crowded towns and hamlets of the United Kingdom, not only in the scattered villages of the British Caribbean people were discussing whether Sobers would make 200 or not. In the green hills and on the veldt of Africa, on the remote sheep farms of Australia, on the plains of Southern and the mountains of Northern India, on vessels clearing the Indian Ocean, on planes making geometrical figures in the air above the terrestrial globe. In English clubs in Washington and in New York, there that weekend at some time or other they were all discussing whether Sobers would make the 200 required from him for the West Indies to win the match.[119]

More than an acknowledgment of the global popularity of a sport, James's analysis of cricket under the question taken from Tolstoy, "What Is Art?", resets the terms of modernist aesthetics and recasts the agent of critical vision and judgment. James puts cricket in the place of the high art of Western civilization and relocates the masses of local populations as the purveyors of the gaze which orders civilization. He concludes with an image of an historically integrated vision: "We may some day be able to answer Tolstoy's exasperated and exasperating question: What is art? – but only when we learn to integrate our vision of Walcott on the back foot through the covers with the outstretched arm of the Olympic Apollo" (211). The idea of an integrated vision, in which images of the cricketer's movements join those of the ancient games and the classical art of Western civilization, recalls Hall's portrait of James, his eye moving from the play of cricket on the field to the reproduction of *Guernica* in his hand, integrating the two in his unique way of seeing.

Both James's image of an integrated vision and Hall's portrait of James raise questions about the nature of this integrated vision, about what it includes in its movement and what, inevitably, it does not or cannot see in creating its coherence. Considering James's emphasis on collective, creative "movement" in "What Is Art?" we might ask, for example, how *Guernica*, the product of a single European painter's efforts, can be linked to the collective historical forces that made cricket such a dynamic form of art for James.

Hall's essay gives us the beginning of an answer in a conversation with James concerning the historical significance of individual artists:

I once asked James about the three great moments in which he could see a single artist speaking on behalf of a whole historical revolutionary moment. He told me about the Acropolis, even though its architect is unknown. He told me about Shakespeare, and he told me about Picasso's *Guernica*. He said, "Look at Picasso. Look at *Guernica*. It is about the energies of the Spanish revolution. When you look at *Guernica* you see the whole movement, the whole maelstrom of the Spanish revolution encapsulated in an esthetic form." (15)

In James's response to Hall's question, the phrase "the whole movement" condenses at least two meanings of the word "movement": its meaning as an aesthetic element, the dynamic effect of a combination of lines and shapes, and as a political force, the revolutionary effect of a combination of historical contradictions. It brings together the modernist aesthetic and the Marxist analytical value on "wholeness" as a dynamic interplay of various elements and thus conveys the democratic values that James wished to interject in the discourses of art. Further, it indicates the Hegelian notions of art and totality that guide his analysis.[120] Most important, in his directions to Hall, " 'Look at Picasso. Look at *Guernica*,' " he expresses the interplay among the individual artist, the work of art, and the "whole maelstrom of the Spanish revolution" that he could see in the painting because he saw those same elements in the play of West Indian cricket.

However, we might wonder about the liberatory extent of this vision since it seems to encompass an exclusively masculine field, both in cricket and in art. In *Beyond a Boundary*, James neglects to mention the increasing numbers of Afro-Caribbean women playing cricket or their attempts to form associations and overcome sexist discrimination in the sport.[121] The gender politics of cricket in the Caribbean were closely tied to its importation by the English plantocracy and its role in movements for national independence. Hilary Beckles has described the early formation of cricket in the West Indies as positioning women "well 'beyond the boundary' " (224). For the English planters who brought cricket to the Caribbean, it was a sport in which Victorian British ideals of manliness were constituted and reflected. As Beckles notes, "The struggle for the democratisation of this elite institution within the undoubtedly superordinate patriarchal colonial West Indian world, therefore, was socially understood as characterised by rivalry between men – the politically enfranchised of European descent and the dispossessed of African descent" (224). During the movements for national independence, West Indian identity was asserted and claimed, in part, through the West Indian team's success and especially in their wins over England.[122] The English players were even mocked as effeminate by some of the masked characters among the "cricket carnival" audience.[123] James clearly avoids these complicated nationalist gender issues in his writing about cricket in the period of the independence movements.

In later years, however, the "integrated vision" created in the movement of his eye from cricket match to *Guernica* changed, expanding to incorporate the paintings of Jackson Pollock and, simultaneously, a more inclusive notion of "man." In these writings, the importance of the individual artist to James's "integrated vision" also becomes clearer. Celebrating his perception in Pollock's apparently abstract paintings of "the sense of feet walking along" and the representation of "the beginnings of humanity in that men, or rather, human beings, walked," James again celebrates motion in the same breath that he explicitly refigures the gender of humanity as inclusive of all. The trope of movement is crucial to this expanded view of both humanity and "high" art, a way of seeing already shaped through the interrelated movements of highly individualized bodies in motion on the cricket field (Leary, Sobers, Worrell), a kinetic intercorporeality experienced as part of everyday life among black West Indians in Tunapuna. In moving his eye between an actual cricket game and *Guernica* and then between *Guernica* and Pollock's walking feet, he finds a way to integrate in a postcolonial countervision the experiences of everyday perception ("Walcott on the back foot through the covers") and those of the artistic imagination ("Look at Picasso. Look at *Guernica*"; the "sense of feet walking"). The "sense" he refers to in his description of Pollock's painting remains unnamed; it suggests collective kinesis more than individual sight, something inclusive of the whole body in human history that taught him to perceive this aesthetic of "movement."[124]

James's postcolonial countervision moves actively between intersecting notions of modernity: modernity as hegemonically European and visual and modernity as centered in the experiences of the African diaspora and movements in the Caribbean for national independence. In "What Is Art?", James counters European ways of seeing by subverting modernist art criticism; his notion of movement as an aesthetic element of significant form exceeds the fixing, ahistorical gaze of colonialist and aesthetic discourses. It counters the ocularcentrism of modern Western philosophy, ultimately leading us out of sight as the dominant and dominating sense to kinetics, a sense of movement as experienced, not simply viewed, in the interplay among West Indian players on the field of cricket, the "eye of the cricket spectator," the artist's imagination, and revolutionary players on the field of history.

4

Ekphrasis/diasporic Caribbean imaginations
1960–2000

The transatlantic Caribbean modernism forged by Edna Manley, Ronald Moody, Claude McKay, Jean Rhys, Una Marson, C. L. R. James, and George Lamming addressed colonial relations that they recognized as inextricably bound to concepts and practices of seeing. Entering the realm of art from which the discourses of colonialism excluded the possibility of their participation, they nevertheless sculpted acts of visionary sight, staged visually the dilemma of colonial imitation, cast individual and social change as matters of the eye, and appropriated modernist visual aesthetics in order to break through the boundaries set by a philosophical orientation in which vision reigns as the predominant sensory experience. Their contributions in art and literature shaped a transatlantic modernism while building a more specifically Caribbean movement in the arts. This movement emerged officially in the 1960s as CAM or the Caribbean Artists Movement, and alongside the achievement of independence by a number of Caribbean countries, it sparked intense interactions among painters, sculptors, textile designers, poets, playwrights, fiction writers, and critics from the Caribbean. In this context and following on the work of Jean Rhys and George Lamming, the poetic device of *ekphrasis* – the verbal description of a work of visual art – became a central figure for the continued exploration of vision in Caribbean literature.

Conducted by Derek Walcott and Wilson Harris and taken up again by a younger generation of writers including Jamaica Kincaid and Michelle Cliff, this exploration of sight extends the diasporic Caribbean imagination into the past and across the globe, recovering "lost" traditions of indigenous and African arts in conflicted dialogue with modern European aesthetics. Through recurrent, revisionary, and extended ekphrastic writing, Walcott and Harris engage in a poetics of painting. In my analysis of their work of the 1960s and early 1970s, the most significant differences between these two writers result from their contrasting approaches to the Amerindian presence in the Caribbean, and these differences emerge through their divergent ekphrastic poetics. Some of these differences concern the problems of imitation and reproduction, and certainly, the process of creativity itself. Harris also reflects on and resignifies the gendered discourses of European conquest and postcolonial nationhood, a concern that links his work to that of Kincaid and Cliff who (with Jean Rhys as a crucial precursor), refigure the feminized "elsewhere" long associated with the Caribbean. Finally, in Harris's remarkable prose, the "art of seeing" resurrects, through the poetic devices of not only ekphrasis but synaesthesia and apophasis, all of the senses in kinetic, transfigurative "bodies" of knowledge and civilization.

DEREK WALCOTT AND WILSON HARRIS: THE POETICS OF PAINTING

In the final section of Derek Walcott's long poem *Tiepolo's Hound* (2000), the poet's persona and "I" narrator of the poem describes a painting by Giambattista Tiepolo:

> ... Tiepolo has painted himself,
>
> painting his costumed models, on the floor, what must be
> his mascot: a white lapdog revels in the wealth
>
> of Venetian light. Alexander sprawls in a chair.
> An admiring African peers from the canvas's edge
>
> where a bare-shouldered model, Campaspe with gold hair,
> sees her myth evolve. The Moor silent with privilege.[1]

This passage exemplifies the poetic device of ekphrasis; moreover, it appears within a poem composed of numerous similar ekphrastic passages, structured as a dual quest: for a particular remembered painting and then for the epiphanic moment of seeing experienced on first viewing that painting. As a painter himself and a playwright who has worked for many years in the theatre, Walcott continually explores the relationship between the visual and the verbal arts. In his ekphrastic poems, Walcott reveals interconnected patterns in global histories of conquest and migration, especially those of the Mediterranean and the Caribbean, through which figures of his own poetic persona emerge, refracted through the past, imaged on the canvas, and ekphrastically framed in verse.

The poetic tradition of ekphrasis has its source in the epic poem and it, thus, figures in the formation of a national consciousness. It also gestures toward creativity: by crossing sign systems, ekphrasis highlights the act of representation and, by representing the more "natural sign" of visual art, it offers a glimpse of the apparently divine powers involved in creation itself. To better understand these features of ekphrasis, it will help to recall the example to which virtually all epic poets and their critics in the European tradition refer, which appears in the eighteenth book of *The Iliad*. In these passages, Achilles' mother Thetis helps him to prepare for battle against the Trojans by presenting him with a shield made especially for him by the god Hephaestus. In this passage, the narrative action of the poem appears to cease, replaced by a spatial orientation in the extended description of Hephaestus' art. The shield is marvelous; on it appear images of the heavens, the earth, the gods leading men to battle, the cities and their peoples in celebration, and the countryside and all of those living and laboring within it. As Murray Krieger has argued, such representation of visual art within poetic narrative creates an illusion, both "mirage" and "miracle": the illusion of visual art appearing before us, yet in words; the mirage of narrative action suspended by a spatialized, yet nevertheless narrated, visual object; and the miracle of access to a reality beyond language, yet represented within it. In representing, through words, another representational language – that of the visual – ekphrasis represents representation itself.[2]

However, as Krieger also argues, the language of visual signs has traditionally seemed a more "natural" language, closer than words and their arbitrary linguistic relations to the "real." Thus, while representing representation, ekphrasis appears at the same time to lend access to the realm of divine, rather than human, creation where signs are "natural." In the combination of these apparently contradictory functions, ekphrasis becomes a rhetorical strategy for constituting social power.[3] The interplay between the arbitrariness of verbal language and the relatively natural signs of visual art constitutes and then naturalizes Achilles as hero, human and superhuman. On a formal level, the verbal has overtaken and incorporated its semiotic other, the visual and its "natural" signs. However, the illusion of the natural sign created by this incorporation gives divine sanction to Achilles' power. Thus armed, symbolically possessed of the cosmos and all creation, Achilles' anger increases, and divinely conjured as Greek, male, and heroic warrior, he enters battle.

Among many other examples of the rhetorical device of ekphrasis, one important to understanding the gender dynamics of the trope appears in numerous poems, Henry James's well-known novel, and Robert Browning's famous monologue, the "portrait of a lady" or "my last duchess" trope. Here a device that seems to celebrate a woman's beauty actually represents and comments on the social relationship whereby a man possesses a woman through the possession of her image. Again, masculine identity consolidates through a verbal mirage. By representing verbally a work of visual art, which in turn represents or compares to a woman, both of whom may belong to a man, ekphrasis combines the two kinds of property relations and naturalizes the gender identities constituted through them. As W. J. T. Mitchell notes, although works of art and the women portrayed within them are both often feminized as mute objects of beauty, the difference of gender is only one among many possible constructions of difference performed by ekphrasis.[4] Racialized figures in paintings, such as the African in Tiepolo's portrait of *Apelles Painting Campaspe*, also signal property relations of ownership and dispossession. In its mirage-making capacities, ekphrasis enacts transcendence of language through language, lending an aura of divinity to and naturalizing the social power it constitutes. At the same time, by representing verbally the painting and woman or figure of racial difference in it, ekphrasis reframes them and, thus, comments on the social relationship of possession that they signify.

Ekphrasis, then, has to do with social power as acquired or denied through forms of possession in several ways: the consolidation and possession of naturalized, divinely sanctioned, national, and masculine identity; the dispossession of female and racialized identities; and, on a more exclusively formal level, the attempt by writing to possess the image by rendering it verbally.[5] Writers from the Caribbean such as Walcott, Wilson Harris, Jamaica Kincaid, David Dabydeen, Fred D'Aguiar, and Michelle Cliff employ the device repeatedly, building on precedents established by earlier writers such as Rhys and Lamming, and pushing the trope to its limits in order to critique its foundations in narratives of conquest and colonialism. Furthermore, because ekphrasis is a trope of the visual sign, its obsessive repetition as a poetic and narrative device allows Caribbean writers to enter the realm of the visual, examine its epistemological claims, and critique its institutionalization in empirical science, the commodification of art, and the philosophy of aesthetics.

In the passage from *Tiepolo's Hound* which I've quoted above, Walcott not only employs the convention of ekphrasis with all of its historical weight and postcolonial possibilities, he uses it to describe a painting in which the aesthetic experience he seeks is literally framed as the history of conquest. The presence of a sprawling Alexander, his mistress Campaspe, and the peripheral African depict the relations of conquest in the ancient Mediterranean world. Further, the painting within the painting of Campaspe alludes to the story of the artist Apelles who fell in love with

Campaspe as he painted her and to whom Alexander then gave her as a gift. Conquest, the possession by European men of Africans as slaves and servants, their possession and exchange of women, and the aesthetics of an evolving myth of beauty are all framed within Tiepolo's painting and again within Walcott's poem. The protagonist of this history and its art is constituted through these visual dynamics as a masculine composite – Apelles/Alexander, Walcott/Tiepolo – in joint possession of both paintings and the human beings represented within them.

However, by reframing Tiepolo's painting in his poem, Walcott unsettles this composite masculine identity. An earlier line has expressed his poetic quest in military terms: "If I pitched my tents to rhetorical excess, / it was not from ambition but to touch the sublime, // to heighten the commonplace into the sacredness / of objects made radiant by the slow gaze of time" (98). Invoking the martial in his description of an aesthetic goal – the pursuit of the sublime – Walcott touches on the history of the sublime as a philosophy developed in tandem with the pursuit of profit through the slave trade and the ambitions of colonial conquest. As a subsequent line makes clear, he is framed in at least two ways within Tiepolo's painting and the history it suggests:

> If the frame is Time, with the usual saffron burning
> of his ceilings over which robed figures glide,
>
> we presume from the African's posture that I too am learning
> both skill and conversion watching from the painting's side.   (129)

Here Walcott positions himself in "the African's posture," at "the painting's side," but he is also with Tiepolo, who has "painted himself" as the poet does in words. If we view the actual painting along with its ekphrastic representation, we may note also the resemblance between the painter Apelles and the image he paints of Campaspe, a resemblance suggesting that the masculinity of the composite subject also refracts. Both faces turn toward the model or "real" Campaspe and both eyes open wide as if startled by what they see.[6] Mirroring their twinned faces, Alexander's profile doubles that of the model, his mistress Campaspe, as they both gaze toward the painting. The central space of the painting remains open, as if occupied by the crossing of these lines of sight, making the act of seeing the subject of the painting.

The poet thus addresses the "art of seeing" by occupying several postures, including one that parallels the life of Camille Pissarro, the Impressionist painter who was born on the island of St. Thomas and left the Caribbean to pursue his ambitions in France, becoming the friend of

12. Giovanni Battista Tiepolo, Venetian, 1696–1770, *Apelles Painting Campaspe before Alexander* (or, *Apelles Painting the Portrait of Campaspe*) (*c.* 1725–26), oil on canvas, 57.4 cm × 73.7 cm, Montreal Museum of Fine Arts, Adaline Van Horne Bequest. 1945.929, photograph Montreal Museum of Fine Arts.

Gauguin and the less famous teacher of Cézanne, his paintings remembered as "ordinary" (155). From a Sephardic Jewish family, forced to flee first Portugal, then France, before settling in St. Thomas, Pissarro brought with him to Europe an ancestral history of exile and migrancy. Further, as Walcott suggests, he brought to the Impressionist movement "the noise / of loss-lamenting slaves" which "tremble in the poplars of Pontoise, the trembling elegiac tongues he painted" (158).

In imagining the influence of the Caribbean, and especially the songs of Afro-Caribbean slaves, on a post-Romantic European art movement, Walcott suggests two important points – that Europe's artistic and intellectual history owes much to the people enslaved and colonized in the New World, and that even the more scientific optics of Impressionist landscapes carry within them the horror of slavery. Through both of these revisionary notions, Walcott explores the historical conditions that generate his quest and articulates the constraints they place on him as an artist. One of these

constraints positions him, like the African in Tiepolo's painting, as "learning / both skill and conversion watching from the painting's side" and
forces him to address, as Walcott has done throughout his career as poet,
the limits and possibilities of colonial imitation. In this, he continues the
"conversion" through mimicry that catalyzed much of Una Marson's
poetry and plays, and his poetics acknowledge and celebrate the process,
claiming, as C. L. R. James did, English and European literary traditions as
his own inheritance, through which he is free to create. The conditions and
aesthetics of that freedom, however, remain bound to the history of slavery
in the Caribbean. In this "frame," Walcott's poetry, especially in *Tiepolo's
Hound*, approaches and then dwells, with almost mournful resignation, in
the realization that the sublime moment he seeks depends on his own
inscription, as a man of African descent, in the modern aesthetics that
require blackness as its constitutive Other.

In another telling passage of doubled identities, the poet imagines Pissarro
and his tutor Fitz Melbye sketching and feels himself "being drawn, /
anonymous as my own ancestor," (138) in their unsigned and lost drawing:

> I felt a line enclose my lineaments
> and those of other shapes around me too,
>
> . . . I shrank into the posture they had chosen,
> . . . keeping my position as a model does,
> a young slave, mixed and newly manumitted
>
> last century and a half in old St. Thomas,
> my figure now emerging, ...   (140–41)

Following another tenet of the ekphrastic device, the sketched portrait of
himself as his own ancestor actually speaks, putting him in dialogue with this
ancestral double. As Françoise Meltzer points out in her study of ekphrastic
portraits in literature, "The Greek *ekphrazein* means 'speak out,' 'to tell in
full,'" (21) so that when an apparently static work of art is described within a
narrative two things happen: first, the main narrative appears suspended
(what Murray Krieger calls the "mirage" of ekphrasis) and, second, what
seems to be a spatially fixed object – the work of art – becomes the site for the
intercalation of another narrative, the story the work of art speaks. Walcott
makes this figurative "speaking out" a literal dialogue in the poem in which
his ancestor laments Pissarro's failure to become "our own pioneer" (142).
The poet then regrets that "St. Thomas stays unpainted" and proclaims it all
"unfair" (145). The powers of representation – here, the multiple narratives
and dialogues performed through ekphrasis – coincide with the theme of the
failures of representation. This theme of failure haunts the poem, even as it

continually frames and reframes the act of representation through these extended ekphrastic passages. Near the concluding passages, the Walcott persona describes "another book that is the shadow / of my hand on this sunlit page, the one // I have tried hard to write, but let this do; / let gratitude redeem what lies undone" (158). The resolution in gratitude remains forlorn, dwelling in loss and "the remembered past" which is acknowledged as an imagined, visually invented past. Walcott's poetic persona is caught here in the very dilemma that he illuminates, the history of a racialized aesthetic that developed in the transatlantic crossings of the slave trade and Caribbean plantation economy.

In Simon Gikandi's discussion of the development from the eighteenth into the nineteenth century of twinned notions of the aesthetic and of race, he places philosophical treatises by Kant, Hume, Hegel, and Burke alongside a reading of Edward Long's *History of Jamaica*, a work in three volumes published in 1774. He argues that Long's work, testifying to the moral, intellectual, and artistic incapacities of his slaves, provided the evidence needed by European philosophers in formulating ideas of the aesthetic based on the exclusion of Africa and of black people from the domains of history, reason, and art. Citing Long as a "native informant," who gave authority to statements based otherwise on lack of knowledge and experience, Gikandi emphasizes "the connection between the plantation ideology and the aesthetic ideology in 18th–19th-century debates on modernity."[7] In a statement that recalls Walcott's portrayal of himself in the position of an African "watching from the side of the painting," Gikandi asserts that "the crisis afflicting modern society, and the mode of stabilization which art was supposed to establish, were directly linked to the racialized figures whom we see drifting on the margins of European cultural texts" (10). This formulation of aesthetics through the peripheral figure of "the black" as "Other" creates a paradox for any artist of African descent who attempts to claim authority within a field whose very existence emerged in the conditions of his or her subjection.

However, Gikandi finds in the eighteenth-century notion of art as an autonomous realm a counterpoint to the racial subjection necessary to the development of Western art. While representations of black slaves or servants in family portraits signified the wealth and status of the family, on another level, the portrait as a work of art within the newly developing aesthetic philosophies offered a

utopian possibility that the artwork might detach itself from bourgeois capitalism and play a redemptive role. It is this utopian possibility, the dream that the work of art might actually be separated from the slave economy that sustained it, that made the aesthetic central to the slave's attempt to claim the central categories of bourgeois culture, including freedom, morality, and subjectivity. (11)

Gikandi's statement resonates with Walcott's reading of the sidelined, attentive Moor in Tiepolo's painting as ambiguously "silent with privilege" (129).

Theoretically, all Caribbean artists and writers face the dilemma of entering a field in which they are already imaged and whose very foundations intertwine with the history of slavery that haunts their present and even motivates their ambitions. But those writers who, like Walcott, Harris, Dabydeen, D'Aguiar, Kincaid, and Cliff, return again and again to the representation of visual art in their fictional or poetic narratives are highlighting the problem and reflecting on it as they work through its visual dynamics. By signifying verbally on visual art and the realm of the aesthetic, they move it, transfer its figures, and transform its assumptions. Their ekphrastic narratives also transform the device of ekphrasis itself by simultaneously extending it to excess and grounding it in the history of the Caribbean, the site, as Gikandi argues, of evidential support for the aesthetics their works explore and counter.

***

Ekphrasis as a major trope in Walcott's poetry appeared much earlier than *Tiepolo's Hound*. Tobias Döring has argued that *Omeros*, published ten years earlier, "is at heart ekphrastic"; the figure of Achilles as a major character certainly prompts such a reading even though the poem does not directly or centrally focus on visual art.[8] Even earlier, in 1973, Walcott's first long poem, *Another Life*, explored the relationship between painting and poetry as a practice of seeing. In this emphasis on the "sister arts," he reflected on his own dual gifts and career decisions. However, in making painting the central trope of his poem, he also shared an accelerating emphasis on visual art with another writer from the Caribbean, Wilson Harris, who left what was then British Guiana for London in 1959 and published in the next year his first novel *Palace of the Peacock*. Though working in different places – mainly Trinidad for Walcott and London for Harris – and under different cultural influences – national theatre in Walcott's case and the Caribbean Artists Movement in Harris's – these two writers gave central place in their poems and fiction of the 1970s to painting.

In this section of the chapter, I establish a context, during the late 1960s and 1970s, for the increasing emphasis on visual art in Harris's and

Walcott's work and argue that, though ekphrastic narratives become central to their projects during this time, they differ in their literary effects due to Walcott's focus on autobiography and European traditions of art and Harris's turn toward the epic and indigenous Caribbean arts. If the shaping device for Walcott is the multiple-framing of an extended ekphrasis, for Harris, it is the process of expanding and blurring the frame, allowing the act of painting to rewrite history and the present moment through what he considers the obscured resources of the Caribbean. Harris thus reconceptualizes history and subjectivity from within an "eclipsed" potential of an unrealized or unnarrated Caribbean past and insists on the possibility of an "original epic." Walcott reconceptualizes the individual, but within the "frames" of the aesthetic dilemma his poetry exposes and illuminates; accordingly, he retains an ambivalent stance toward the epic form. Both writers explore, through ekphrasis, the significance of seeing for a history of conquest and the resulting creolization of peoples and cultures. For Walcott, the exploration involves mainly European and Afro-Caribbean cultural elements; for Harris, it depends fundamentally on the visual art of indigenous peoples of the Americas.

Harris's work of the late 1960s and early 1970s developed within close interactions between writers and visual artists from the Caribbean, living in England. His active participation, along with that of the Guyanese painter, Aubrey Williams, in the conferences and art symposia held by the Caribbean Artists Movement in 1967 and 1968 and the publication in 1968 of his novel *Tumatumari*, titled for the painted rocks of the Guyanese landscape, signal the importance of both visual art and Amerindian cultures to his writing. At the First CAM Conference in 1967, Williams spoke on "The Predicament of the Artist in the Caribbean," and at the Second CAM Conference, Harris gave a talk titled "The Amerindian Presence in Guyana"; both presentations stressed the indigenous arts of the Caribbean as sources for contemporary creativity and identity. These events took place in what was increasingly felt as the exciting emergence of an exilic Caribbean community of artists and writers, claiming the authority of their own perceptions in tandem with the achievement of political independence in several Caribbean nations, and generating new kinds of fiction, poetry, painting, and sculpture, grounded in the cultures of the Caribbean, in dialogue with Anglo-European traditions.[9] Together, Williams and Harris brought into the arts and critical debates of CAM the significance of Amerindian cultures for any postcolonial understanding of the region.

In *Tumatumari*, Harris responds indirectly to the events leading to Guyana's recent independence through a reflection on and narrative performance of the rewriting of history. The dominant tropes for this re-visionary process are those of Amerindian culture, including a Mayan ceremonial well, or *cenote*; the Olmec heads of Mexico; the Guyanese legend of Chief Kaie; and the "sleeping," painted rocks, or *tumatumari*, of the title. Harris interweaves these figures with allusions to classical Greek and medieval European arts of memory, Afro-Caribbean traditions of spirit possession, and critiques of narrative realism as the model for national history. The interplay of such diverse elements defamiliarizes and reconfigures them through a dynamic, culturally syncretic prose.

Harris's critiques of the realist novel are well known by now to readers of Caribbean literature; however, the place of visual art, especially the arts of Amerindia in his creolized texts, are crucial to understanding the often difficult narratives that he creates in his move beyond the conventions of realism. In *Tumatumari*, the protagonist Prudence dreams of carving on the rock lid of a well a date found in papers written by her father, who has held the Chair of History. However, her pen slips, and the numbers are transposed to create a "rock of association – primitive gateway" through which she inadvertently links her family history with "the earliest exploring steps ... taken by the Mediterranean world."[10] This "primitive gateway" reconnects Prudence to the conquered peoples of Amerindian, African, and Asian descent haunting her own psyche and lineage: her dark-skinned brother whom her father had hidden away, her sister Pamela's black baby, given up for adoption in the United States, and an "East Indian" woman, struck down in an accident with her father's car. Seated on the "Chair of the Well," she occupies her father's previous position; carving, with a slip of the pen, lines of ancient history on the rock, she unlocks the past that his familial and nationalist narratives had suppressed.

In this experimental novel of 1968, we find a gesture similar to the ekphrastic passage quoted at the beginning of this chapter from Walcott's *Tiepolo's Hound*. In the painting described in that passage, the conquering Alexander with his "admiring African" cohabits with the painter and his model an image of the conquest resulting from, to borrow Harris's words, "the earliest exploring steps ... taken by the Mediterranean world." The self-reflexive visual and verbal framing of these colonizing steps highlights the implication of art and its myths in that history. Positioning himself doubly as the painter and the African, Walcott employs a painting within the European tradition as his "gateway" to obscured ancestral connections. Similarly, Harris's Prudence activates the pen and academic Chair of European culture, but she occupies the physical posture of ancient Amerindian artists, ancestors of the tribes who populate the landscape in which she lives and whose rock art signifies a past crucial to the new history she writes. These "sleeping rocks," more often in Harris's work referred to as *timehri*, possess Prudence and lead her through a ritual "memory theatre" where, for example, she sees an "East Indian" woman named Isabella, linked in imagination to the Spanish Queen and sponsor of Europe's early appropriations of the Americas but also a woman almost killed by Prudence's father in an automobile accident. The connection, made through the gateway of the *timehri*, indicates a suppressed ancestral link across cultures and a disruption of fixed dichotomies of victim and victimizer. It requires a new way of seeing, represented in the memory theatre by an "Eye" that appears on the "Rock-Face of the Well." Prudence identifies the Eye as the presence of divinity and as simultaneously a sign that conversations with previously obscured figures of the past have resumed. The ekphrastic passages in this novel, then, lead to direct representation of divine vision and creation. Through this cross-cultural and cross-temporal dialogue, Prudence releases forces of translation and metamorphosis, healing ancient wounds and reassembling the "buried living cultures" of Amerindia, European arts of memory, and New World African spiritual traditions.

More than any other Caribbean writer, Harris has long stressed the crucial significance of Amerindian arts to a vision of the Caribbean and its potential. The talk he gave in 1968, "The Amerindian Presence in Guyana," drew on the supposed historylessness and rootlessness of surviving Amerindian tribes as a source for reconceptualizing character in the novel and altering the fixed narratives of history. By bringing forward the broken ancestry of the Caribbean as a present yet destabilizing force, the solidity of history and consolidation of powers within it might be disrupted, allowing space for a "new and profound order of compassion within the novel" and a "new radical art of fiction."[11] Harris has followed this talk with numerous others in which Amerindian arts, such as *zemi* carvings, and ritual practices, including the Carib bone flute, become points of departure for recovery of a complex and multilayered past which alters taken-for-granted notions of identity and history, space and time.[12]

His meeting, in 1967, with Aubrey Williams, who had been showing his paintings in England and Europe since the 1950s, underscored and intensified Harris's interest in indigenous sources for the Caribbean creative imagination. Williams shaped his canvases and murals through a number of influences, including those of abstract expressionism, the Mexican muralists, and the music of Shostakovich, but probably most important was his experience living with the Warrau Indians of Guyana. At the

First CAM Conference, also in 1967, Williams spoke of the importance of indigenous art for the contemporary Caribbean artist, arguing that it came from a "naturally 'abstract' " environment. He reminded his audience:

It is a very strong landscape and the primitive art that came out of this landscape remains unique. We should be proud of our non-figuration. We should be proud of the essences of human existence that the people from that neck of the woods have produced in the world. We should be proud of people like Tamayo from Mexico. We should be proud of people like Matta from Chile. We must become more involved with the visual output of our artists in the Caribbean because they are going to change the real seeing of the world. They are going to do it just as the politicians and the writers will do it.[13]

In this statement, Williams expresses the optimistic sense of immanent social change that was bringing writers, artists, and activists together in the late 1960s, and he does so in the language of vision, of changing "the real seeing of the world." His defense of non-figuration in conjunction with his celebration of Amerindian or "primitive" art recalls Edna Manley's circuiting of modernist European primitivism through the Afro-Caribbean cultures of Jamaica and then back into the galleries of London in the 1920s and 1930s. Just as her work signified on primitivism, giving it new meaning, Williams, too, lends new significance to the Amerindian art he celebrates as "primitive," for it is not exotic to him, but a source of serious philosophy and aesthetics from ancient peoples who were among his own ancestors. Williams's faith in non-figuration as naturally comprehensible to the people of the Caribbean, perhaps especially those who are uneducated, supports Harris in his experimental prose, which deliberately breaks with representational realism. Williams's celebration, in later essays, of pre-Columbian pottery and the Mayan *cenote* joins with Harris's invocation of similar motifs in his writing. For example, Williams discusses the significance of the Mayan *cenote* in terms that help to explicate the image of the "Rock-Face of the Well" in *Tumatumari*: "From out of the amalgam of our pre-Columbian past, our slave past, our quick political growth and social-awakening – these blended with our cataclysmic position in our technology-ridden world – from this Cenote must come the visual identity of Modern Caribbean Man today."[14] Only a year later, Harris refigures this image of Caribbean identity, transforming the gender of its creative agent from male to female in the character of Prudence who reinscribes the past on the painted "rock face" lid of the well, or *cenote*.

The 1967 meeting took place in Williams's studio and included Kamau Brathwaite, John La Rose, and Andrew Salkey. While debates regarding the use of "dialect" in Caribbean poetry continued in CAM meetings, exchanges such as this one between the visual artists and writers of CAM generated ongoing conversations about the importance of the visual and of seeing, including the significance of visual abstraction in portraying landscape and myth. The relationship between Harris and Williams continued to grow in importance for both. As early as 1966, C. L. R. James had commented on their shared sensibilities,[15] and in 1970, Harris gave a lecture in Guyana on Williams's work. Both Harris and Williams were active in CAM throughout the late 1960s, and they exerted an influence on its primary founder, Kamau Brathwaite, who gave the opening speech at Williams's first one-man show in Jamaica in 1970. In this talk, titled "Timehri," Brathwaite expands his previous analysis of creolization to include the indigenous presence in the Caribbean represented in Williams's and Harris's work. In his appreciation for Williams's paintings and their Amerindian inspirations, Brathwaite pulls together many of the visual influences that have converged in the language of Caribbean literature and that he sees in Williams's work. Of the influence of the Warrau, he wrote:

Living with them placed [Williams] in a significant continuum with [the ancient art]; for high up on the rocks at Tumatumari, at Imbaimadai, people, who were perhaps of Maya origin – the ancestors of the Warrau and others in the area – had made marks or *timehri*: rock signs, paintings, petroglyphs; glimpses of a language, glitters of a vision of a world, scattered utterals of a remote *gestalt*; but still there, near, potentially communicative … But hints only; gateways to intuitions; abstract signals of hieroglyphic art.[16]

In language reminiscent of Harris's cross-cultural and synaesthetic prose, Brathwaite tropes on the act of painting, recalling also Lamming and James in his invocation of vodun ceremonies, and incorporating his own passion for jazz:

His paint brush is the door, the *porte cabesse* or central pole down which the gods often descend into the *tonnelle* during *vodun* worship. Like jazz musicians, still tunneling the ancient African tone scales and rhythms on European instruments … For others of us, the central force of our life of awareness is African … But Williams's choice of the Amerindian motif does not exclude the African … What is important is the primordial nature of the two cultures and the potent spiritual and artistic connections between them and the present. (84)

As Anne Walmsley remarks, " 'Timehri' triumphantly validates the three-year long association in CAM of major, innovative novelist, painter and poet; it shows how the exposure of their work to each other made possible real movement in creative understanding and exposition."[17] It also confirms the synaesthesia of word, image, and sound to which the turn to indigenous visual art was taking Caribbean artists: Williams's paintings, already perceived as highly "rhythmic" by Harris, were inspired in the early 1980s by Russian symphonic music; Harris's writing increasingly invoked the radical emergence of a new sensory body; and Brathwaite's highly rhythmic, jazz- and blues-inflected poetry later developed into a "video-graphics."

Most immediately, Harris began writing novels in which painting figured prominently as a trope for creativity, vision, and recovery of obscured peoples and histories of the past. The novels of the 1970s, *Companions of the Day and Night* (1975) and *Da Silva da Silva's Cultivated Wilderness* (1977) compare in their emphasis on paintings and painters with Walcott's first long poem, published in 1973, the ekphrastic autobiography titled *Another Life*. While Harris, Williams, and Brathwaite were debating in London a contemporary Caribbean aesthetics in dialogue with visual traditions of the past, Derek Walcott was working mostly in Trinidad, creating plays for and staging productions with the Trinidad Theatre Workshop and publishing several volumes of poetry. Walcott's plays and poetry, like Harris's novels, developed around images inspired by paintings.

Beginning his work as a playwright in the 1940s, Walcott took up where Una Marson and C. L. R. James had left off in the 1930s. As Marson did in *Pocomania*, though through different themes and techniques, Walcott attempted to bridge the gaps between middle-class and folk culture; like James, he was attracted to the Haitian Revolution as a theme and focused one of his plays on the character of Henri Christophe. Walcott's work in the theatre, however, won greater recognition than either Marson or James received for their plays. In 1959, he founded the Trinidad Theatre Workshop and concentrated on making plays that would represent the experience of the Caribbean and shape its cultural identity in keeping with the regional folk myths in a multiracial and multicultural region. His early plays drew heavily on the English dramatic canon, but increasingly, he incorporated non-European elements such as call and response, carnival motifs, and folk songs and dances. However, from the beginning, his dramatic productions took shape, as do many of his poems, from the visual images of European paintings recalled from his school days. In preparing to write the 1958 epic pageant *Drums and Colours*, commissioned for the opening of the West Indian Federation, Walcott began by remembering paintings he had seen in books. He wrote that he wanted "active tableaux, such as the paintings of Columbus and Raleigh and the boy Gilbert to remind the imagination of the audience."[18] Bruce King has described

Walcott at this time as "already seeing his plays as scenes in paintings, a characteristic of his drama and of how he directs productions" (20).

His highly successful play *Dream on Monkey Mountain* (1970) then took as its central theme the problem of competing cultural sources and racial allegiances in the Caribbean and in the Caribbean artist's work. The play mocks both imitation of European standards and the notion of a return to Africa and indicates instead the need for a fresh New World aesthetic.[19] This theme accords with the ideas expressed in essays Walcott published in the early 1970s and helps to explain his continued residence in the Caribbean. He was interested in a local, regional experience, re-created and universalized through art. In his essay "What the Twilight Says," published in the same year, 1970, as Brathwaite's "Timehri," Walcott articulates his concerns as a playwright and his position on what he perceives as competing cultural influences in Caribbean literature. He positions himself against state-sponsored folk culture, which he sees as commercializing the Middle Passage legacies such as limbo that become rich images in Harris's and Brathwaite's writing of the time. He also states, "we were all strangers here,"[20] excluding with the pronoun the indigenous peoples of the Caribbean and defending the value of a Euro-creole culture in "mongrel" mixture with cultures of Africa. In this mix of models for language he finds the potential for "the forging of a language that went beyond mimicry" and reflects on his own attempts in the past twenty years to create such an art. He sees the revolutionary politics of the time as misguided, insufficiently "sunk into our own landscape" (18). Finally, Walcott asserts as "the true vision" that of twenty years before when he and his generation had begun their efforts in "our own painful, strenuous looking, the learning of looking" (9), and his tone is one of disillusioned but continued commitment.

If Walcott's plays and essays reflect on the cultural tensions through which his art developed, his poetry expresses more personal themes. Most critics see autobiographical elements in all of his poetry, but in discussing *Another Life*, they most often place it alongside Wordsworth's *The Prelude* as a long autobiographical poem and Joyce's *Portrait of the Artist as a Young Man* as the story of the growth and development of an artist. Other influences shape the poem, such as Dante's *Vita Nuova*;[21] however, the most important works guiding the poem are not literary but visual. And in this respect, its poetic sources lie not so much in autobiographical models but in the tradition of ekphrasis.

Written over a period of seven years, during the Black Power movement, which had a tremendous impact on Trinidadian politics and art, and also during a time of professional conflicts for Walcott with the Trinidad Theatre Workshop,[22] *Another Life* asserts Walcott's overwhelming dedication to art. The poem begins with an epigraph from Malraux that signals the poem's genre and theme: "What makes the artist is the circumstance that in his youth he was more deeply moved by the sight of works of art than by that of the things which they portray."[23] The epigraph makes clear that, though in the *Künstlerroman* tradition, the poem is not primarily about the relationship between art and life; rather, it concerns the relationship between art and art. Pursuing this concern, it explores the master/apprentice relationship; the problem of imitation for the apprentice, a problem which extends in the context of the Caribbean to that of colonial imitation; and the relationship between the visual and the verbal arts. "Another life" is the life of art – life enhanced, elevated, and sacred. The repeated device of ekphrasis creates a mirage of "natural signs," where seeing becomes simultaneously a heroic and mystical act. However, in *Another Life*, art is often reproduced art; what the poet sees are images from a book of reproductions of European art. In this way, Walcott turns the device of ekphrasis to a new occupation: describing reproductions of works of art, he then claims them as a way of seeing his own world. He sees life as exalted when it approaches what is already a copy. As the distinction between original experience and representation is explored, crossed, and questioned, the distinctions among art, reproduction, and life also blur. For example, when he views a dead child at her funeral, he asks: "But was it her? / Or Thomas Alva Lawrence's dead child, / another Pinkie, in her rose gown floating?" (151). He continually claims images from European art as a way of illuminating his surroundings, seeing them differently: "Those bowls, / in whose bossed brass the stewards were repeated / and multiplied, as in an insect's eye, / some jeweled insect in a corner of Crivelli, / were often ours ..." (165). If his arguments in "What the Twilight Says" are any guide, we can read the value placed on this blurring of original experience, representation, and reproduction as a productive site for the poet, where the potential for a language "beyond mimicry" lies. However, the lens for seeing is always already a copy, and the tensions between visual and verbal art shape an enclosed space in which even the changes that move the poem are taught by the master, and the beauty sought lies in that of a preserved, reproduced past.

A view of the world through the pages of a book of reproductions launches the poem and provides the trope it explores throughout its narrative of a young artist who turns from paint to poetry: "Verandahs, where the pages of the sea / are a book left open by an absent master / in the middle of another life – / I begin here again, . . ." (145). The "absent master" develops several identities as the poem unfolds – most obviously, his teacher, for whom the poem becomes an elegy; also the poet's father, who died while the poet was very young and left "Craven's book" with its copies of paintings by Verochio, Leonardo, Vermeer, and Crivelli as a legacy to his son; and, as suggested by a later and repeated reference to "the light of the world," a divine, spiritual teacher. The image of an absent master in the Caribbean must also recall the early period of plantation slavery when the plantation owners left the running of their estates to managers and resided as absent landlords with their families in Europe and England. Indicating a multiple, composite master, both secular and divine, the poem's opening passages also put into play a multifaceted visual sense of being: the poet's vision of his island world as "a cinquecento fragment in gilt frame"(146), his sense of failure ("In its dimension the drawing could not trace / the sociological contours of the promontory") (148), and his sense that he, too, is being drawn by larger forces of history and nature: "The dream of reason had produced its monster: / a prodigy of the wrong age and colour" (145); "The moon came to the window and stayed there. / He was her subject . . ." (148).[24] The agent of creativity fragments in this interplay of vision, a multiplicity drawn together and resolved, not by the poet / painter but by his master who, at the end of the first section of the poem "with slow strokes . . . changed the sketch" (147).

This line presents a paradox at the heart of apprenticeship and imitation. For, as the master changes the sketch, change itself comes through the master's hand. Any change undertaken by the painter / poet will take him further on his artistic path yet will continue to imitate this act. The problem is compounded by the legacy of his father, who had left a "small blue library / of reproductions" which included "volumes of *The English Topographical Draughtsmen,* / Peter de Wint, Paul Sandby, Cotman, and in another / sky-blue book / the shepherdesses of Boucher and Fragonard" (202). He sees "as through the glass of some provincial gallery / the hieratic objects which my father loved" (183). Discovering his paternal legacy involves discovering the colonial legacy of English art and literature, inserted into the homes, schools, and churches of his village, and it means discovering them as reproductions, a doubling of the imitative relationship between colony and metropole.

The apprentice painter turns from painting to poetry precisely because he is such an excellent apprentice. His discipline, humility, and ability to copy "the visible world that I saw / exactly" hinders him: "my hand was crabbed by that style, / this epoch, that school / or the next"; he perceives his "sidewise crawling, this classic / condition of servitude" (201). In contrast, his friend Gregorias "abandoned apprenticeship / to the errors of his own soul" and through his paintings, alters their way of seeing: "Now, every landscape we entered / was already signed with his name" (201).

The poet decides that "I lived in a different gift, / its element metaphor" (201). The events that precede this change mark his coming-of-age: one involving a sense of overwhelming compassion, the other of falling in love. Soon, however, the poet translates both experiences into questions of aesthetics. Describing a transformative, near mystical moment of sudden compassion, the poet states that he "lost [himself] somewhere above a valley" and "dissolved into a trance" (184) in which he "wept for nothing and everything" and perceived "in that ship of night, locked in together, / through which, like chains, a little light might leak, / something still fastens us forever to the poor" (185). This allusion to the Middle Passage as source of a deep historical and empathic connection with the poor of the island then turns to a question concerning the light: "But which was the true light? / Blare noon or twilight, 'the lonely light that Samuel Palmer engraved,' / or the cold/iron entering the soul, as the soul sank / out of belief" (185). Already, the spiritual experience comes filtered to him through a phrase quoted from a description of an engraving, and it is through a litany of Romantic and Renaissance painters and paintings that he then describes his dual experiences of falling "in love with art" and with "[a] school girl in blue and white uniform, / her golden plaits a simple coronet / out of Angelico . . ." (187).

The turn to poetry appears to take him into the world of words, but this is the world of history and epic, one in which ekphrasis and, there-fore, visual art, returns to shape his gift, and the question of vision continues to propel the poem. Recalling the island's namesake, "Santa Lucia, / patroness of Naples," he describes a miraculous restoration of vision, after "they had put out her eyes" (218). "[S]aint of the blind," she is also the icon of renewed sight and of his own continued quest through poetry for renewed vision. This vision comes especially in his love for Anna, the school girl, who becomes "all Annas, enduring all goodbyes" but whom he betrays even before they part: "The hand she held already had betrayed / them by its longing for describing her" (236). He recog-nizes that in his attempts to describe her, he freezes her in epic devices: "My Anna, my Beatrice, / I enclose in this circle of hell" (269). The hero of the poem remains his painter friend Gregorias who has learned how to see: " 'I see, I see,' is what Gregorias cried, / living within that moment where he died" (273).

The death that grants Gregorias his vision is his own near-suicide. It is followed by an actual death, that of their teacher, Harry, who kills himself and who, for the poet, becomes "the fervour and intelligence / of a whole country" (277). The language of epic enters the poem here, as if in dialogue with the poet's earlier reference to "pseudo-epics." Now litanies of names of the peoples who have migrated to and created the cultures of the island appear in the poem, as the sound a child hears in a shell put to his ear:

> . . . everything
> that the historian cannot hear, the howls
> of all the races that crossed the water,
> the howls of grandfathers drowned
> in that intricately swiveled Babel,
> hears the fellaheen, the Madrasi, the Mandingo, the Ashanti,
> yes, and hears also the echoing green fissures of Canton,
> and thousands without longing for this other shore
> by the mud tablets of the Indian provinces,   (285)

Addressing his teacher, as his muse, the poet exclaims,

> You want to see my medals? Ask the stars.
> You want to hear my history? Ask the sea.
> And you, master and friend,
> forgive me!
> Forgive me, if this sketch should ever thrive,
> or profit from your gentle, generous spirit.
> When I began this work, you were alive,
> and with one stroke, you have completed it!   (282)

Previously, metaphors have transformed epic tropes into those of art – Gregorias has shouldered his easel, for example, like a rifle and, by truly seeing, become the poem's hero. Now the poet projects onto the stars and the sea the historical battles that propel the conventional epic and invokes the master of painting as his muse. This invocation, however, takes him back to the poem's beginning, where his master "changed the sketch"; now, the master, with his death, completes, "with one stroke," the poem. The poet remains his teacher's apprentice, even in the medium of poetry, and again, at the poem's end, he looks once more "from old verandahs at / verandahs, sails, the eternal summer sea / like a book left open by an absent master" (292). The final verse celebrates his poem's hero and their past, returning to the models of Renaissance art through and with which he had earlier fallen in love:

> Gregorias, listen, lit,
> we were the light of the world!

We were blest with a virginal, unpainted world
with Adam's task of giving things their names,
with the smooth white walls of clouds and villages
where you devised your inexhaustible, impossible Renaissance,
brown cherubs of Giotto and Masaccio.   (294)

Gregorias's art has revitalized the Renaissance masters in "our first primitive frescoes"; and the poem that celebrates his vision has altered the conventions of both the long autobiographical poem, the *Künstlerroman*, and the epic. He claims for their past a divine light and the Adamic power of original naming. However, the poem is still driven by the dilemma of apprenticeship and imitation, intersecting with the dynamic tension between the verbal and the visual arts. The trope of ekphrasis allows Walcott to create the illusion, as Murray Krieger would put it, of the "natural sign," the visual sign perceived as closer to the "Real" of life outside representation and to the sacred, the cosmic world of epic creation. At the same time, it allows the art of words to overtake, by incorporating it, the realm of visual art it celebrates. This conquest of the visual by the verbal, however, is countered by the trope of reproduction – for what is conquered is already a copy – and by the final power of his master's hand, all of which frame the poem and give it a sense of having preserved the past, as if "locked in amber."[25]

In the same year that *Another Life* appeared in print, Walcott delivered a talk at the University of Miami American Assembly's four-day conference on "The United States and the Caribbean."[26] Later published as "The Caribbean: Culture or Mimicry?" this essay offers a reflection in prose on the dilemma of imitation explored in *Another Life*. It also makes clear the crucial difference between his poetics and those of Wilson Harris in Walcott's statements regarding Amerindian culture in the Caribbean. In this talk, Walcott refutes V. S. Naipaul's notorious statement in *The Middle Passage* that "nothing has ever been created in the West Indies, and nothing will ever be created" by arguing that, historically, there can be no original act. Refuting also the derogatory accusation of the colonial as a "mimic man," also from Naipaul, Walcott claims that "Mimicry is an act of imagination, and, in some animals and insects, endemic cunning."[27] He celebrates craftsmanship, work, and hope as the means by which the Caribbean person creates and, turning Naipaul's words around, states that "Nothing will always be created in the West Indies, for quite a long time, because what will come out of there is like nothing one has ever seen before" (54).

As compelling as his argument may be, it is constructed on the basis of another notion, one with which Naipaul would likely have agreed: that genocide has destroyed the "original" of the Americas, "the Aztec, and

American Indian, and the Caribbean Indian." He adds, "All right, let us say what these had was not a culture, not a civilization, but a way of life, then . . . The point is that they broke" (56). Though we might "praise them for not imitating," Walcott argues, "even imitation has decimated them or has humiliated them . . . What have we been offered here as an alternative but suicide" (56). Discounting the continued Amerindian presence in the Americas as well as their past, and diminishing their cultures to "not a culture, not a civilization," Walcott clears the ground for his celebration of imitation and mimicry as the source of creativity. In effect, he commits, discursively, an epistemological genocide that allows him to become the Adamic poet of the New World.

Making this move, Walcott opposes his poetics to that of Harris for whom the ancient art of the Amerindian tribes was becoming a primary source of inspiration. By 1973, when Walcott asserted suicide as the only option offered by indigenous peoples, Harris had given at least seven public lectures, almost all of them appearing soon after in print, that focused on the significance of the Amerindian presence in the Caribbean for the creative arts. In one of them, "History, Fable, and Myth in the Caribbean and Guianas" (1981 [1970]), he begins with an extensive meditation on Haitian vodun, as if following up on Lamming's invocations of the Ceremony of Souls in *The Pleasures of Exile* and *Season of Adventure*. Harris's discussion of vodun ritual emphasizes the dance of possession as one that, like the limbo dance, born of the Middle Passage, dislocates and reshapes the spatial environment and makes possible an inner reassembly of lost parts of the past. He quotes an earlier essay in which he had compared the effect of the vodun rite with painting: "For what emerges are the relics of a primordial fiction where the images of space are seen as in an abstract painting."[28] He then stresses that these Afro-Caribbean spiritual practices share a "rapport with Amerindian omen" (27). Harris's language and argument in this essay echo the cross-cultural connections Brathwaite was making that same year in his essay "Timehri." Both Brathwaite and Harris were taking an approach completely different from that of Walcott in 1970, building on, rather than dismissing, Afro-Caribbean folk cultural practices such as the limbo and carnival and putting them into dialogue with the Amerindian cultures evoked in Aubrey Williams's paintings and Harris's fiction. Harris's major point in this essay is not to assert an origin for Caribbean culture but to stress the necessity of opening obscured connections between civilizations:

And furthermore in the Americas as a whole, it would seem to me that the apparent void of history which haunts the black man may never be compensated until an act of the imagination opens gateways between civilizations, between technological and spiritual apprehensions, between racial possessions and dispossessions in the way the *Aeneid* may stand symbolically as one of the first epics of migration and re-settlement beyond the pale of an ancient world. *Limbo* and *vodun* are variables of an underworld imagination – variables of phantom *limb* and *void* and a nucleus of stratagems in which *limb* is a legitimate pun on *limbo*, *void* on *vodun*. (35)

The metaphor of space and the reshaping of inner experience as a method of revising static histories of conquest takes Harris to the Amerindian carvings called *zemi*, in which he finds a rapport with the arts of Haitian vodun and contemporary painting. Mentioning painters as diverse as Turner, Van Gogh, Pollock, and Nolan, Harris writes of color and light as "poetic and liberating device[s]," and he stresses the synaesthesia of "*colours* within the vowel structure of a poem" and the "musical intimation" of Aubrey William's use of color, also a "character of metamorphosis." Through this interartistic vocabulary, Harris portrays Williams as a "painter of renascence who has been affected in an original way by an Amerindian 'resurrection' as Edward Brathwaite, for example, has been affected in an original way by an African 'resurrection'" (37).

Williams's paintings open for Harris what he calls the "gateway" between civilizations and between the arts; in the passage, the Arawak *zemi* are resurrected as icons of ancestral and natural spirits. Harris describes them as "signifying *hidden perspectives*":

We are involved therefore – if we can imaginatively grasp it – in iconic or plastic thresholds – in an architecture of consciousness or re-constitution of spaces in the West Indian psyche running through Negro *limbo* and *vodun* into sculptures or spaces equivalent to rooms of an Arawak cosmos (rooms of turtle, bird, lizard). (39)

Ironically, given Walcott's dismissal of Amerindian cultures, Harris interprets Walcott's poem "A Tropical Bestiary" as "a zemi-studded poem" and links it to Edward Brathwaite's long poem *Masks*, where he finds "areas of overlap or gateway drama between Africa and the West Indies – *between sound and sight*," and asserts that "*Masks* also subsists upon a dialogue with the zemi" (39–40). Through the icons of Amerindia, Harris opens gateways between writers from the Caribbean often perceived, especially in the 1970s, as opposed to one another: Walcott more oriented toward the English and European cultural influences in the Caribbean and Brathwaite toward the African.[29] He also stresses explicitly the notion of a "gateway" between senses, calling attention to a re-creation of the sensory body which he claims as part of the project of Caribbean literature.

In his first novel, *Palace of the Peacock* (1960), Harris had represented *zemi* "rooms of an Arawak cosmos" in the rock face of the waterfall climbed by the central character, Donne. These appear as mystical openings in the cliff wall through· which dynamic, living images of a Christ figure, a Madonna, birds, and animals appear, and they recall the ancient rock paintings of Guyana as well as the Arawak *zemi*. Following the representation of Amerindian art in *Palace of the Peacock* and the rock paintings in *Tumatumari*, Harris's novels of the 1970s, especially *Companions of the Day and Night*, *Da Silva da Silva's Cultivated Wilderness*, and *Tree of the Sun*, align Amerindian arts, such as the *timehri*, *cenotes*, and *zemi*, with the twentieth-century art of the mural, as practiced by Mexican artists such as Diego Rivera and, beginning in the 1950s, in the Amerindian renaissance art of Aubrey Williams.

In *Da Silva da Silva's Cultivated Wilderness*, da Silva, a painter of large canvases, living in the Holland Park area of London, prepares for an exhibition. The novel takes place in one day, but through the descriptions of the paintings, moves backwards and forwards through centuries and across the globe. Most remarkable about this narrative is the way in which da Silva seems to be painting, as it proceeds, the narrative that describes his painting. This larger mural of the novel's narrative action includes depictions of da Silva's exhibition paintings and also other works of visual and dramatic art, such as a reproduced print titled *Sex and the Portuguese in Brazil*, a portrait of the deceased wife of the Earl of Holland, a pornographic photograph, and a theatre performance in the midst of Holland Park. At one point the narrative describes da Silva's painting of the exhibition site itself, in which he re-envisions the Commonwealth Institute, located near his studio in Holland Park, and includes an actual sketch with notes, inserted on the page, of this newly imagined venue for his paintings. The concerns of reproduction, imitation and originality, paternal legacies, cross-cultural connections, and the ekphrastic representation of visual art as a means to a new understanding of vision that shape Walcott's *Another Life* also guide this novel by Harris, published four years after Walcott's long poem. However, Harris's approach to these problems leads to a completely different kind of narrative, one infused by tropes of openness, expansion, and revelatory sight rather than the metaphors of framing, enclosure, and preservation that prevail in Walcott's poem.

This approach is based on Harris's philosophical faith in the significance of Amerindian cultures to an understanding of the Caribbean and its diasporic legacies. It is not simply a matter of artifacts, such as the *zemi* and bone flute, or evidence of ritual practices, such as the *cenotes*, that provide metaphors for the narrative; equally, if not more important, is the sense of partially present cultures, perceived through their absence as much as their presence. The history of genocidal violence against the native tribes of the Americas leads most Caribbean writers to dismiss their significance and to erase even further their continuing actual presence as a means of nativizing creole cultures. In this way, Walcott, for example, can claim the position of an Adamic poet. This is not to say that Walcott ignores such Amerindian artifacts as the *timehri*. In *Another Life* and *Omeros*, they do appear in his poetry, and in *Omeros*, he includes sections that link the indigenous peoples of the Caribbean and their losses to the Sioux Indians and the Ghost Dance in North America. However, for Walcott, these are emblems and events of loss; pushed aside into the "shadow of History"[30] and no longer available as creative sources. For Harris, in contrast, that partial or "absent presence" becomes a trope for the hidden or obscured interconnections and unwritten histories of the past, through which he seeks a renewal of vision. In *Da Silva da Silva's Cultivated Wilderness*, da Silva's paintings become the site for this ongoing recovery and re-creation of the past in the present.

Through a metaphorical chain of association, da Silva's painting becomes a "Madonna Pool," linked to the lakes of Peru, home of his wife's ancestors, and also to the Mayan *cenote*, in its "near meanings," as Aubrey Williams put it, of "Total or Everything of Us . . . the amalgam of our pre-Columbian past, our slave past, our quick political growth and social-awakening . . . blended with our cataclysmic position in our technology-ridden world."[31] As da Silva paints it, this "Everything of Us" is always partial, always in process, always yielding new insight and new ways of seeing. The narrative prose, like much of Harris's writing, seems difficult to follow at times, though this novel, like others written in the 1970s, is perhaps more firmly anchored to characters and plot. A striking characteristic of the prose is the tendency towards phrases such as "half-economic, half-miraculous" or "half-human, half-god."[32] (68) which indicate a state of being only half present and joined to another partial presence, in a condition, then, of metamorphosis. The join of entities with their negation, such as "tone" and "non-tone," throughout the narrative also indicates, though differently, the lack of discrete identity in any thing; its partiality and condition of being both what it is and what it isn't. Again, Harris's regard for what he sees as the partially present Amerindian legacy in the Caribbean shapes what is for some readers a confusing prose style; it is a literature that Walcott predicted when he described what would come out of the West Indies as "[n]othing ... like nothing one has ever seen before."[33] Harris's prose performs the interconnections, erupting through the surface of conventional and coherent narrative realism, navigating between suppressed cultures, people, and events.

Da Silva encounters at his door a black man who announces his name as Legba Cuffey, reminding da Silva that he had advertised for a model:

Ah yes, I remember. *Black model wanted by painter. Legba (god of the netted crossroads) and Cuffey (eighteenth-century black rebel).* Legba is a crucial vacancy in the Brazilian panel in the mural I'm doing. A Haitian/ West Indian god as well. Uses a crutch for a bat according to legend. Assumes the aged limping form of a god with the face of a youth or a child, perennial child saddled by his own cradle. (9)

He remembers also his aesthetic problem: "How to join the fact of broken power long long ago into the crossroads of God, into netted Legba, as threshold to the game of universal divinity, cross-cultural divinity" (10). This problem of a broken past, lost god, and the composite, layered identity of the man who appears at his door echoes in the mystery and fragmented memories of da Silva's own life. He "was born in Brazil of Spanish and Portuguese parents, invisible black antecedents as well, seminal shadows they seemed in the madonna pool extending up into the Andes where fire was snow" (6). In the reference to the Andes comes an allusion to da Silva's wife, Jen, whose ancestors come from Peru, and the sense that, in their marriage, new and ancient cultures of many regions of the world are joined though they remain "seminal shadows ... in the madonna pool" of his painting. Da Silva was orphaned at a young age and raised by a British ambassador in whose large library he played and read as a child. Jen claims a "distant cousinship to Paul Gauguin, master banker, master painter," and the name Paul recurs in a young boy, child of a woman who has previously modeled for da Silva, and of a man met in a bar run by a West Indian named Cuffey. "Paul" signals the importance of vision, not only in the reference to Gauguin but in several allusions to Damascus and the revelatory blinding light followed by divine sight.

Facing Legba Cuffey in his doorway, da Silva paints them both, connecting them to the figure of Ferdinand Magellan, both "solid and non-solid": "Da Silva painted Legba face to face with Cuffey as inner antagonists, painted Legba Cuffey face to face with da Silva Magellan as outer antagonists, painted 'Magellan of glorious memory' as a quotable footnote springing up from the soil of history into life-size Cuffey" (11). In this disassembling and reassembling of identities, da Silva begins to discover what he refers to as "the reality of change, the origins of change" (10). He describes his methods as follows:

I am a deep-seated painter. Each ancient frame becomes a vacancy to sustain many canvases, many incarnations, new densities, old illuminations, new illuminations, unpredictable densities, that appear and disappear to reappear in order to immerse one in a new and just dialogue between what is apparently strong and what is apparently weak. (10)

Da Silva and Legba Cuffey confront one another in "new and just dialogue"; then with "[a] rich splash from da Silva's brush" (13), they dive into the pool of the painting. Da Silva thus paints his way in the novel so that, through the device of ekphrasis, extended to narrative excess, the novel itself becomes the *cenote*/canvas or pool into which everything is submerged, surfacing, swimming together or apart.

The problem of imitation, of a master who provides the model for change, which appears in Walcott's poem does not pertain in the same way in Harris's novel. Though Gauguin appears as a "master painter," he appears also as the child, Paul, in need of rescue, just as the child da Silva was rescued after his father's death, and as the apostle, Paul, blinded by a light and then granted new vision. The presence of absence, of "[e]ach ancient frame [as] a vacancy" opens previously unseen, unpainted, and unnarrated possibilities.

The problems of origin and originality take Harris to the moment of European/native contact, and here the trope of reproduction, which permeated Walcott's *Another Life*, becomes an opening through which to unsettle previous notions of that encounter. As da Silva paints himself walking through his neighborhood streets, he peers into a window to see a print on the wall, titled *Sex and the Portuguese in Brazil*, of which "he had his own copy, the identical print he saw there, on a black board in his studio, and in addition . . . a fashionable version of it (called Paradise) from an art shop near Christ Church in Oxford" (14–15). This often repeated image of a romanticized encounter between "Arawak beauties" and "Portuguese courtiers" appears to him through the watery glass of windows that reflect "bright lakes of the sky"; his paintbrush becomes a ship's masthead as he sees "across a calendrical lake or wilderness" and paints the scene, which is also the scene in which he moves:

Da Silva painted the lake, he painted the buried rivers that flowed beneath the London streets, he painted a canal in ancient Tenochtitlan on which Montezuma sailed and it was as if they all moved together and were one principle of advancing, complex, shadow or light within the mystery of a tidal body that vanished to reappear again where one least suspected it. (15)

In these passages, narrative action and what ought to suspend it – a description of a visual work of art – converge, and the effect is to alter relations between space and time. Da Silva moves across "a calendrical lake or wilderness" repeatedly as these hyper- and meta-ekphrastic scenes recover lost antecedents and suppressed cross-cultural connections in his and his wife, Jen's, past.

Harris's previous novels, including *Palace of the Peacock* (1960), *Tumatumari* (1968), and *Companions of the Day and Night* (1975), address the violence against women that the image reproduced in *Sex and the Portuguese in Brazil* masks. In each case, the narrative works through visual art – the *zemi* and *timehri* evoked in the moving tableau viewed by Donne as he climbs the cliff of the waterfall, the "sleeping rocks" of *Tumatumari*, and elusive paintings and sculptures sought by the protagonist, named Idiot Nameless, in *Companions of the Day and Night*. In *Companions of the Day and Night*, the question of origins shapes the novel's structure as a quest for its own continually elusive source in primary texts that, in their ekphrastic turn, refer to "a number of paintings and sculptures." We are uncertain whether these are actual works of art and, furthermore, they remain "incomplete" and allude to "absent" artist's models and "dead" ritual actresses. Clive Goodrich, the editor of the documents, writes in the Introduction that "the paintings and sculptures to which the writings related were doorways through which Idiot Nameless moved" (13).

Turning works of visual art, and hence the ekphrastic passages that describe them, into metaphorical "doorways" is especially apt for the crossing of sign systems and the illusion of divinity they offer. Incorporated into a narrative of quest for an elusive woman – the Arawak guide in *Palace*, for example, or the absent models in *Companions* and *Da Silva* – they bring ekphrasis to bear on the historiographical problem of what is absent from the reproduced images of colonial history. On the one hand, by invoking metaphors such as doorways or thresholds to stand in the place of absent or fleeing women, Harris's ekphrastic narratives replicate the construction of masculine identity as a questing agent, moving through spaces coded as feminine.[34] Read in this way, his novels risk reproducing the foundational sex/gender dynamics of conquest as inscribed in the epic voyages of discovery in which explorers and conquistadores construct themselves as masculine and heroic against descriptions of the land they claimed as virginal, still having, as Raleigh famously wrote of Guyana, its "maydenhead," and awaiting penetration and possession.[35] On the other hand, we recognize that what is truly absent is not simply the women, but their active agency and any representation of their subjectivities. In his narratives of the late 1960s and 1970s, Harris illuminates this absence through the "gateways" of Amerindian art and sculpture; in some of them, especially *Tumatumari* and *The Tree of the Sun*, the hyper-ekphrasis he employs allows him to disturb the sex/gender opposition that threatens to enclose his narratives within reproductions of, for example, *Sex and the Portuguese in Brazil*.

In *Tumatumari*, Prudence literally enters the earth, repeating with a crucial difference the colonialist trope of sexual possession, and simultaneously she is "possessed" by her husband's mistress Rakka, whose name alludes to the sleeping, painted rocks. In this and other scenes, Prudence becomes both the active questing figure in the narrative and the spatialized site of the land, previously figured as feminine and object of the quest. As she undoes these sex/gender oppositions, she sees through the fixed narratives of history to obscured events and cross-cultural links within the past of her family and country. *The Tree of the Sun* (1978) recasts Jen and da Silva of *Da Silva da Silva's Cultivated Wilderness* as simultaneously themselves and another couple, Francis and Julia Cortez, and eventually the doubles multiply into an entire troupe of theatrical players. Towards the end of the novel, Julia becomes the questing figure, who "descends" into her past, seeking the source of creation in "a mythical family" and community. Her quest, however, culminates in her rape during the carnival procession on the island of Zemi. Her voice disappears ("Did she or was it they who screamed . . .?") while she is fixed, "raped but wholly painted." The phrase "raped but wholly painted" reflects on the trope of ekphrasis as one through which women, through their portraits, are claimed and possessed by men. It expresses in 1968 a connection between sexual violence and representation that feminist critics such as Teresa de Lauretis explored theoretically in the 1980s. However, the conjunction "but" ("raped but wholly painted") suggests a disjunction and a possibility in the act of representation that exceeds or even counters the violence of rape. The rape is thus also portrayed as "her first substitute carnival gateway" (71). This phrase resembles the language that transforms the rape of Beatrice in *Companions of the Day and Night* from "the force of terror" into "nothing but a bridge," as the words "forced to conceive" gain more than one meaning: "Forced me to conceive . . . as if for the first time, the very earth in which I lie, into which I run" (50). When Harris's narratives position the women characters as both the questing actors and the feminized lands to be found and possessed, he recovers their lost agency and gives readers a glimpse of suppressed subjectivities. By confronting and repeating the tropes of conquest such as "penetrating Paradise" within the wider perspective evoked by the Amerindian art of the *zemi, cenote,* and *timehri,* and by thus activating the living presence of past lives, events, and cultures that have been historically perceived as absent, Harris's novels also present the possibility of what he calls an "original epic."

Asserting this possibility, Harris distinguishes his poetics from those of Walcott, who has resisted acknowledging his long poem *Omeros* as an epic. For Harris, however, the possibility comes from his deep engagement with the continuing Amerindian legacy of the Guyanas, especially indigenous visual art, as a crucial catalyst for more inclusive and dynamic visions of the past and more profound understanding of Caribbean subjectivities. As his novels of this period suggest, this larger, multilayered, constantly in-process re-imagining of the past requires, not the capture of female voices and consciousnesses through representation or reproduction, but their self-creation through active quest and self-possession. It requires their encounter with the mythical moment of first contact between Europeans and Amerindians and, with it, the act of their own suppression and even annihilation in history. The trick of revisionary ekphrasis, then, is to gesture towards that which cannot be represented. In novels by women writers of the 1980s and 1990s, tropes of visual art go further to figure this "elsewhere," outside of representation.

JEAN RHYS, JAMAICA KINCAID, AND MICHELLE CLIFF: REFIGURING "ELSEWHERE"

Early colonialist discourse of the Caribbean mapped it as somewhere else, neither the Indies nor Africa, and explicitly misnamed it as a variant on what it was not, "West" Indies. Troped as feminine, awaiting entry, penetration, and possession, the lands and islands of the Caribbean recede into the fog of representation that is, at its inception, mis-representation. Because ekphrasis appears to represent representation itself, it allows, as we have seen, for critical commentary on its own politics. A rhetorical device often employed to display or comment on the relation of women to men as one of property, ekphrasis becomes all the more significant for women writers who resist the conventions constituting narrative agency as masculine and who attempt to reclaim from colonialist textual discourses the colonized female body and to present a suppressed female consciousness emanating from the Caribbean.

Following on a novel by Jean Rhys and possibly other earlier influences, such as Edna Manley's and Ronald Moody's sculptural portraits of seeing "elsewhere," Jamaica Kincaid and Michelle Cliff have addressed distinct visual cultures – painting, photography, and film – in order to open possibilities for women as creative agents in the process of visual decolonization. Rhys's novel, *After Leaving Mr. Mackenzie*, published in 1930, exposes the representational effect of European primitivist painting as both icon for and suppression of the subjectivity of a migrant woman of uncertain cultural background. Kincaid, too, addresses the colonial and gender dynamics of primitivism and extends her critique to include the domestic culture of family photographs; Michelle Cliff expands ekphrastic narrative to include the description of commercial filmmaking and its neocolonial economy. Both Kincaid and Cliff turn ekphrasis to the project of suggesting that which cannot be represented, the subjectivity that, in Rhys's novel, continually eludes her protagonist.

In *After Leaving Mr. Mackenzie*, a primitivist portrait that appears to come to life and speak to Julia Martin is triply framed in a complex narrative quest for the "elsewhere" of a disappearing identity. Of vaguely Brazilian and English background, Julia attempts to tell the story of her life to a sympathetic young man whom she has met in a Parisian café just following World War I. Framing the story within another story in which she also tells the story of her life, some years ago, to a woman painter for whom she sat as a model, Julia describes the reproduction of a painting by Modigliani hanging on the wall of the painter's studio. The portrait depicts, in Julia's words, "a sort of proud body, like an utterly lovely proud animal. And a face like a mask, a long, dark face, and very big eyes."[36] In Julia's story, the painted woman speaks to Julia, laughing and claiming, "I am more real than you. But at the same time I *am* you. I am all that matters of you" (53). Framed within the narrative, then mocked by another literally framed woman, Julia describes "all my life and all myself ... floating away from me like smoke" (53).

In Rhys's novel, as in Walcott's *Tiepolo's Hound*, the "speaking out" that Françoise Meltzer identifies as an effect of ekphrastic portraits occurs literally, emphasizing all the more the story spoken by the painting. As with Walcott's use of this trope, it also emphasizes formally the powers of representational devices while stressing the social and historical failures of representation, the unfairness, as Walcott's poetic persona puts it, of remaining lost to representation. In Rhys's novel, however, the (reproduced) portrait's claim to be all that matters of Julia and more real than she indicates that it *has* represented her, and this is the occasion for unfairness. Julia must see herself in this copy of a visual discourse that denies her self-representation.

As men's mistresses and painters' models, Julia and the woman in the portrait are truly painted ladies. Unlike Achilles, encased, consolidated, and protected through ekphrasis, they have been framed socially and dispossessed of subjectivity. More like Campaspe, represented as object of exchange between Apelles and Alexander, then appropriated visually by Tiepolo and framed again, ekphrastically, by Walcott, they recognize themselves as reproduced commodities, exoticized, sexualized, and passed around. Excessive repetition of the ekphrastic convention brings the framing, as well as the picture, into view. In Julia's case, what W. J. T. Mitchell calls the "black hole of ekphrasis" – the visual language represented in the narrative – threatens to blot her out while it simultaneously depicts the threatening forces. Yet this black hole is precisely where, in Mitchell's analysis, we might find what lies "beyond" representation, the "real." Hence the portrait speaks, claiming to be, ekphrastically, "more real" than Julia. The "real," in this case, is the story which the dominant narrative cannot tell: Julia's denied subjectivity. The showing of the frames, the blurring of self and other make impossible a narrative progression which would result in the increasing consolidation of character. Julia becomes a ghost of her "self" and the novel a haunted narrative, circling mechanically around itself, shadowed by possibilities for a story continually blocked.

The speaking portrait discloses more than Julia's life story as a woman literally and figuratively painted over. As if in reference to the bequeathal of Achilles' shield to him by his mother, the woman in the portrait also comes to represent Julia's Brazilian mother who is ill and dying in England. Julia views her mother in terms which recall her description of the woman in the Modigliani painting. To Julia, the woman in the painting had exhibited "a sort of proud body, like an utterly lovely proud animal. And a face like a mask, a long, dark face, and very big eyes" (52). She perceives her mother's face as framed "against the white-frilled pillow. Dark-skinned, with high cheekbones and an aquiline nose ... she was still beautiful, as an animal would be in old age" (97). Her face, too, appears "like a mask" (124).

The primitivist style of the Modigliani portrait prompts verbal imagery associating women with the "primitive" in Julia's perceptions of her dying mother. The imagery reproduces the visual discourse made perhaps most famous in Picasso's *Les Demoiselles d'Avignon*, the painting completed in 1907 which depicts the women of a French brothel in styles which simultaneously allude to and distort European conventions of feminine beauty and the African tribal art which Picasso had viewed in Paris collections. As a number of critics have pointed out, early twentieth-century European concepts of evil and corruption as simultaneously dark, sexual, feminine, bestial, and hidden within the European masculine self are associated in primitivist painting with tribal people or, at least, with their art.[37] The association is an ambivalent one – attracting while repelling – and creates a site for reflection on and re-creation of masculine European identity in the context of empire building and decline. Identifying European women with aestheticized objects perceived as representing colonized tribal people, the imagery of primitivism circulates and recirculates in Julia's attempts to tell her life story, that is, to find a language through which to represent herself.

The imagery of masks, bestial bodies, and dark skins recurring in Julia's perceptions of her dying mother link the bodies of three women – those of Julia's mother, the woman represented in the painting, and Julia – as bodies repeatedly framed by the visual discourse of modernist primitivism.[38] As much as she wishes to discover "many deep things that she had only guessed at before" in this encounter with her mother, Julia cannot find a way out of the language that frames her. The image of Modigliani's portrait has entered Julia and possessed her to the point of speaking in her place; it inhabits the body of Julia's mother so that whatever knowledge Julia sought from her mother is blocked and whatever narrative might have developed from that knowledge does not develop.

In Rhys's novel, the device of ekphrasis works to critique ekphrasis as it is conventionally deployed. "Speaking out" about the dispossession of women, the portrait exposes its own visual discourse and suggests both metaphorical and material links between the colonialist history of primitivist art and the dispossession, in the urban centers of Europe, of women of unnarratable backgrounds. By impeding both the main narrative of romance and any possible counter-narrative of rediscovered matrilineal knowledge, the ekphrastic passages work also to expose narrative assumptions requiring the increasing consolidation of character. Such consolidation is conventionally achieved by overcoming obstacles of Otherness in order to find romance and self-knowledge. In this haunted narrative, Otherness overtakes the character's life and self. The illusion exposed, only a gaping "black hole" of ekphrastic absence remains to make us wonder as to what has not been represented.

Jamaica Kincaid's novel *Lucy*, published sixty years after Rhys's novel, echoes many of its textual and social concerns, especially the recurrence of ekphrastic passages as a means of exploring the various meanings of "possession." In Kincaid's more recent novel, however, we can see the shift that Gikandi states as a utopian possibility within the discourse of aesthetics: the possibility within artistic representation, even if its aesthetics are founded on the institutions of slavery and patriarchal commodification of women, to create a space in which the objects of representation may become the subjects of artistic agency and self-representation. *Lucy* portrays a young Caribbean woman working in a position similar to that of the 1920s painter's model, as an au pair for an upper-middle-class woman of Scandinavian descent in the United States. Through photographic portraits Lucy learns a truth that parallels the truth spoken to Julia by the portrait of Modigliani's mistress, and it emerges similarly in two faltering romance narratives and a blocked mother–daughter relationship. If a modernist culture of primitivist paintings dispossesses Julia Martin of her subjectivity, a more contemporary visual culture of family photographs threatens to dispossess Lucy. Unlike Julia Martin, however, Lucy reframes in her own visual terms the social relationships of heterosexual romance and the nuclear family.

In what seems an allusion to Julia Martin's struggle with the visual language of European primitivism and also to Walcott's and Harris's references to a "master painter," Lucy encounters a primitivized image of herself in a photograph taken by her boyfriend, Paul. The narrative introduces "Paul" following Lucy's description of her emotional identification with the painter Paul Gauguin and her realization that her rebellious departure from home has led her to a social position altogether different from that enjoyed by Gauguin: she is a woman and a servant. Her boyfriend's photograph imitates one of Gauguin's paintings of his thirteen-year-old Tahitian mistress, positioning Lucy not as the artist but as his exoticized model. In this photo, Lucy is "standing over a boiling pot of food . . . naked from the waist up; a piece of cloth, wrapped around [her] cover[s] [her] from the waist down."[39] In contrast to Julia's entrapment in a similar visual language, Lucy finds in it a revelation that frees her: "That was the moment he got the idea he possessed me in a certain way, and that was the moment I grew tired of him" (155). She then proceeds with her own photographic projects. Here, Kincaid's narrative recognizes the social power reproduced through early twentieth-century primitivism and, further, sees its continuation in more contemporary relations of representation.

These contemporary relationships include those reproduced in the family photos displayed all over her employer's house. In these pictures a visual culture of the happy nuclear family threatens Lucy by recreating the colonial metaphor of the family and attempting to incorporate her within it. She, however, exposes it – literally – through her own photographs of family members which reveal a false domestic happiness on which the colonial metaphor depends.

In the first days of Lucy's employment, Lewis and Mariah complain that she behaves "as if they weren't like a family" to her. The desire implicit in their complaint recalls the nineteenth-century colonialist discourse of the family in which the "mother country" governed her "children" who were supposedly not mature enough for self-governance and who, in the meantime, labored for the "mother's" well-being.[40] The metaphor depends upon and reinforces assumptions of the mother country's superiority and of its domestic happiness, illusions insistently maintained by Mariah and Lewis about themselves and their family.

In contrast to the family portraits exhibited by Mariah and Lewis in which, "they smiled out at the world, giving the impression that they found everything in it unbearably wonderful" (12), Lucy's first picture of the family shows Mariah's face reddened from tears and Lewis's from anger. Later, just before Mariah tells Lucy that she and Lewis are divorcing, Lucy surveys all the photographs she has taken: "All around me on the walls of my room were photographs I had taken, in black-and-white, of the children with Mariah, of Mariah all by herself . . . I had no photographs of Lewis and no photographs of myself" (120). Lucy's pictures speak out more truthfully than the smiling family portraits, and they also prophesy the future. For Lewis will indeed be absent from Mariah's life and eventually so will Lucy who leaves her employer for another job at the novel's end. The prophecy exposes as false the happy family image that threatened to dispossess Lucy at the beginning of her employment.

Lucy's resistance to the visual discourses of heterosexual romance and the family appears in another scene as a dream vision which she recounts to Lewis and Mariah:

Lewis was chasing me around the house. I wasn't wearing any clothes. The ground on which I was running was yellow, as if it had been paved with cornmeal. Lewis was chasing me around and around the house, and though he came close he could never catch up with me. Mariah stood at the open windows saying, Catch her Lewis, catch her. Eventually I fell down a hole at the bottom of which were some silver and blue snakes. (14)

Lewis and Mariah's response to her description of the dream makes clear the epistemological limitations of their interpretive imaginations and their simultaneous presumption of superior knowledge: "Mariah said, Dr. Freud for Visitor, and I wondered why she said that, for I did not know who Dr. Freud was. Then they laughed in a soft, kind way" (15). As other critics have pointed out, we might alternatively read the dream as a story of pursuit and escape that represents in condensed form the history of slavery and its legacies in employer–servant relationships like this one. While Helen Tiffin sees the cornmeal in the dream as conjuring "slave provisions and slavery,"[41] I would argue that, in keeping with the tradition already established in Caribbean literature by writers such as James, Marson, and Lamming, the yellow ground as if "paved with cornmeal" and the escape through a hole lined with snakes invoke the spiritual resistance of enslaved Africans through New World vodun ceremonies. At the beginning of vodun rituals, the houngon draws in cornmeal designs called vèvè, which invite the gods' presence. As Lucy runs in her dream, she tracks designs in the cornmeal, inviting a spiritual possession. The silver and blue snakes awaiting Lucy upon her escape suggest that the gods have indeed aided the runaway. It is not Dr. Freud who is "for her" but, in a refiguring of the divine inspiration given Achilles by Hephaestus, it is the rainbow serpent god Damballah.[42] The superiority assumed by Mariah and Lewis and the cultural gap between interpretations of these visual images reveal to Lucy at the very beginning of her employment the impossibility of her ever becoming a so-called family member. Instead, she creates photographic images, many of mothers and daughters, in which she is absent. From this absence of self-representation, Lucy gains a new understanding: "I understood that I was inventing myself, and that I was doing this more in the way of a painter than in the way of a scientist" (134). Unlike Julia Martin, who loses herself in a portrait, Lucy makes the move made possible by, in Gikandi's argument, the ideological notion of art as separate from material conditions of economic, social, and political relations. She invents herself as a creator of images rather than a prisoner of them. Rather than occupying an illusory autonomous realm of art, however, her images remain bound within a field of social relations in dynamic flux, exposed as contradictory and changing. As a character, she does not consolidate, nor does she float away; rather, she improvises a self within an ongoing series of contradictions and ambivalences.

I find in this postcolonial text an enactment of representation as W. J. T. Mitchel describes it – a discursive improvisation and dialectic with what can be figured and what lies outside that figuring. Mitchell develops for this model of representation the metaphor of a quilt, "assembled over time out of fragments . . . torn, folded, wrinkled, covered with accidental stains, traces of the bodies it has enfolded" (419). He also writes that "[w]hat lies 'beyond' representation would thus be found 'within' it (as the 'black hole' of the image is found within the ekphrastic text) or along its margins" (419). For Mitchell, however, this model makes representation "materially visible." Furthermore, he considers what he describes as a "postmodern pictorial turn" as responsible for our abilities to now see representation in these terms; he does not mention processes of decolonization. He offers his model as a universal one, independent of a historically understood colonial imagination, while Kincaid's representation of visual culture gains meaning as a historically situated story of the decolonization of vision and specific visual cultures. Like Rhys's novel, Kincaid's narrative renders visible in historical context the social power of visuality through ekphrastic passages. Moreover, Kincaid's narrative suggests that to "see" representation in visual terms, as Mitchell does, is to remain within the epistemological limitations of discursive practices formed in an historical period governed by colonialism. It is to remain within the purview of the "imperial eye" and under the illusion of the visual as offering a "natural sign."

The contradictions or folds of the representational model performed by this text emerge most powerfully at the novel's conclusion when Lucy picks up a blank book given her by Mariah – to begin, we sense, writing the story of her life free of Mariah – and writes her name at the top of the first page. The scene is steeped in an ambivalence typical of Kincaid's writing. For in a fit of weeping Lucy blurs with tears the first sentence she writes, and the novel ends.

The scene returns to the site of writing. Then, as Helen Tiffin has pointed out, the body itself, as tears, overtakes the resulting script. However, what the body leaves is a blurred image. The novel has crossed from verbal narrative to the language of visual art and its countersign in Lucy's photographs back to the scene of writing and through it, again, to the visual image – a blur. We could read this non-representational image, produced by the body, in the manner of an ekphrastic self-portrait, that is, as speaking out a story absent in the narrative and its other visual images, the absent representation of Lucy in the photographs she takes. As such, it speaks a full bodily and sensory experience of suffering – the dampness of tears, the sound of crying, the movements of head and shoulders as Lucy weeps. Thus the text remains open to the unrepresented, its blurs inviting us to relinquish the gaze as our predominant and dominating means of access to knowledge. Kincaid's narrative gestures, through the description of a blurred visual image, towards an extra-visual experience and toward the "real" beyond representation. In this "black hole" resides a subjectivity associated with the "elsewhere" of the Caribbean, previously unrepresented, and requiring an alternately sensed imagination. Michelle Cliff's novel *No Telephone to Heaven* takes on a similar project, blurring the boundaries between verbal narrative, filmic action, and performance art to create a sensory "elsewhere" through an expanded ekphrastic text.

The novel's title, *No Telephone to Heaven*, suggests active negation of the transcendence which has been traditionally the power of ekphrasis, as mirage and miracle, to grant. It also suggests radical disillusionment in a postcolonial novel with epic features, especially that of a widely ranging quest for national and cultural identity. Cliff's novel works *with* disillusionment, building on absence and negation to create the sense of an "elsewhere" by signaling the absent description of a work of visual art.

Published in 1987, *No Telephone to Heaven* concerns the political and social upheavals of Jamaica in the 1970s and early 1980s; it also represents the quests, in epic terms, for community and identity of two characters, one divided by internalized sex/gender difference (Harry/Harriet, a transvestite, also a nurse and revolutionary), the other divided by internal class and racial differences (Clare Savage, described as "a light-skinned woman, daughter of landowners, native-born, slaves, emigrés, Carib, Ashanti, English").[43] In portraying the struggles of these two characters to counter the neocolonialist violence and cultural imperialism imposed upon Jamaica by England and the United States, the narrative makes many references to visual art. These references range from descriptions of pictures and statues to the novel's numerous allusions to movies – *Gone with the Wind*, *The Incredible Shrinking Man*, *The Comedians*, *The Harder They Come*, *Viva Zapata!*, *Burn*, *Dr. No*. Some of these Hollywood films, *Gone with the Wind*, in particular, play annually in Jamaican theaters; others were made in the Caribbean, a situation that prompts Harry/Harriet's comment, "Our homeland is turned to stage set too much" (121).

At the novel's conclusion, Harry / Harriet, Clare, and their comrades in a resistance group revitalize the revolutionary legends of their Maroon ancestors in a plan to sabotage the shooting of a commercial film which pretends to be about the rebel Maroon leaders Cudjoe and Maroon Nanny but which grotesquely commercializes these heroes and their history. However, like other attempts at resistance throughout the novel, this one backfires – this time, literally. In a paradoxical and painful twist, army helicopters target the resistance group, shooting, in another sense of the word, so that a surreal scene unfolds in which fictional film reality mixes with fictional historical reality.

The representation of a film within fictional narrative does not technically count as an example of ekphrasis. Unlike the description of a painting or sculpture, the description of a film does not offer a stilled image to create the illusion of suspended narrative action. Obviously, it offers just the opposite, a motion picture. However, if we consider Françoise Meltzer's emphasis on ekphrasis as a "version of the intercalated story or 'frame story,' " we can see the film-within-the-novel as an intercalated story which suspends the action of the larger story in order to "concentrate on the 'telling in full' of a different tale."[44] In the relationship between the larger story of *No Telephone to Heaven* and the intercalated or framed film story, the "telling in full" takes an ironic turn. Rather than producing a full, multiple, and interleaved narrative, the frame collapses, and the difference between the two narratives is lost, creating a sense of a larger story suddenly aborted. In *No Telephone to Heaven*, these two lines of narrative action – that of the novel's characters' rebellion and that of the film within the novel – blend so confusingly that many readers find it difficult to distinguish between narrative descriptions of the film scene and those of the "real" attack. Here the text blurs narrative sequence – the main action – and what ought to appear as its suspension – a description of the "art" of the film scene.

When a similar dissolution of boundaries between visual and verbal action takes place in Harris's novel, *Da Silva da Silva's Cultivated Wilderness*, the effect is to expand the possibilities of creativity and to re-envision the past in emancipatory terms. Harris's narrative "paints" historically opposing forces into one another, seeking eclipsed interconnections between them. Cliff's novel, on the other hand, pits those forces against one another in contemporary versions of rebels and colonizing army. Within the rebel group, identities are hybridized in gender and racial mixings, but in the battle, they must shield themselves in the tradition of Achilles and preserve their rebel identities. A verbal description of the film *as film* would empower the rebels by distinguishing false images of the Maroons (the movie) from the relatively more authentic historical legends upon which the rebels model themselves, consolidating and naturalizing their identities and arming them for battle. Indeed, it works in this way briefly. But when the film, with its false images, can no longer be separated from the "real" narrative action, the rebels' power diminishes, and their reconceptualized identities and newly imagined community are lost.

On a formal level, what Mitchell refers to as "ekphrastic fear" – the fear of the collapse of difference – takes over, and readers lose sight of the distinction between film action and narrative action. Within the overall narrative, the filmed version of Jamaican history has so overwritten attempts to enact a new scene in its "real" history by Clare and Harry/ Harriet that the armed forces of the state co-extend with the power of Hollywood image making. The identities consolidated by the shields of army helicopters win the battle, while the hybridized rebel identities self-reflexively divided, joined in alliance with one another, and camouflaged in khaki are burned into the Jamaican earth. Multinational capitalist images become materially and concretely counter-revolutionary in this scene, their deadly violence more than "just a movie." At the end of this epic quest, then, we find a postcolonial ekphrasis which fails to create a new mirage and miracle: no telephone to heaven.

However, in a literally visual – typographical – space in the text, an alternative to the failed ekphrasis appears. We learn that shots find the bitterbush where Clare is crouched, hiding, and that Clare "remembered language. Then [space] it was gone" (208). The space within the sentence represents typographically the "language remembered" and gone. By signifying loss, the typographic space suggests, further, another absence that structures these concluding scenes and invites an alternate or parallel interpretation. It is the absent description of a work of visual art. In the essay which serves as an afterword to the novel, Michelle Cliff has stated that the earthworks of the Cuban-born sculptor Ana Mendieta greatly influenced her writing of the novel's conclusion,[45] and I would argue that this space, representing language remembered and gone, alludes simultaneously to the language of visual art and, more precisely, works of visual art never mentioned in the novel but, as Cliff claims, influencing its outcome. Only through an absent ekphrasis can a window open in the text to a language beyond the neocolonial film languages which Clare and Harry/ Harriet have found so inescapable.

As performance works, Mendieta's earth sculptures resist the assumptions which empower ekphrasis. They deliberately negate the notion of art as spatially fixed, objectifiable, or reproducible, and they depend upon their own erosion, transformation, and loss. The narrative sequence in Cliff's text which would frame a verbal representation of Mendieta's art, were it present, is one of loss: "language remembered. Then [space] gone." Such verbal representation is also gone; or rather, it exists somewhere else. The elsewhere of this subjectivity is specifically trans-gendered as Mendieta's performance art enacts, as self-representation, the "penetration of paradise" trope explored and overturned in Harris's novel, *Tumatumari*. Like Prudence in Harris's novel, Mendieta physically enters the earth and thus supplants with her creative agency the foundational discursive act of colonial conquest. The burning and erosion of that site then allows it eventually to disappear, commemorated, transformed, but also released.[46]

In this absent echo of the narrative, a parallel interpretation of the quest's ending opens up. The shots and explosions that join Clare and Harry/Harriet to their Maroon ancestors take on ritualistic meaning in Mendieta's recreations of the explosions of gunpowder in Santeria healing

13. Ana Mendieta, *Untitled (from the Silueta Series*, 1978), © The Estate of Ana Mendieta Collection, courtesy Galerie Lelong, New York.

rituals. As in Wilson Harris's novels of the late 1960s and 1970s, the meaning of "possession" – of a native woman or of a sovereign identity – transforms into the spiritual meaning of possession found in African New World religions: the gods absent in the New World are recalled, the languages lost through slavery remembered, the bodies and spirits of kin lost in the Middle Passage rejoined, and the absent histories of fractured communities recreated. The rituals of Santeria become an art of memory, echoing the story of Simonides, who, in Cicero's *De Oratore*, was able to remember the locations and identities of dismembered bodies following the collapse of a banquet hall during his brief absence. As an orator, Simonides remembered his arguments by locating their points within an architectural image, visualizing the speech he would give through images of place.[47] In Cliff's narrative, the emphasis on place as site of memory for lost language requires an ekphrasis that eludes the existing systems of representation. The sovereign masculine identity of epic conquest created through traditional ekphrasis thus overturns even as it seems to reconsolidate in the victory of the armed forces of the state. Through a space in the text, a window opens in the narrative, making possible an epistemological *marronage* to a location somewhere between the verbal text and the constantly changing site of performance art. The gesture takes us beyond verbal language and beyond also the privileging of the sense of sight. The unexpected space between printed words suspends the narrative by giving us literally nothing to see while it signifies an absent trope through which the objectifying gaze has previously prevailed. The words which follow signify a dismantled English prose, a cut-and-mix of sound:

> cutacoo, cutacoo, cutacoo
> coo, cu, cu, doo
> coo, cu, cu, coo
> piju, piju, piju
> cuk, cuk, cuk, cuk
> eee-kah, ee-kah, eee-kah
> krrr
> krrr
> krrr-re-ek
> cawak, cawak, cawak
> hoo hoo hoo hoo hoo hoo hoo hoo hoo hoo hoo
> be be be be be be be be be be be be be be be
> kut ktu ktu kut ktu ktu
> cwa cwa cwa   cwaah cwaah cwaah   (208)

Absent representation in the shape of a woman's body and smoking black hole recalls Lucy's absent figure in the photos she takes and the "life and self" which Rhys's character perceived as "floating away like smoke." It also recalls Mitchell's defining figure for representation in the "black hole of the image in ekphrasis." Though the representation does not appear verbally or visually in the text, the visual space signifying the presence elsewhere of Mendieta's re-creation of the Santeria healing ritual becomes, in Wilson Harris's words, "a stepping-stone into other dimensions." It takes us to the threshold of sight, calling upon other senses through which we can discern sounds of the earth, spoken language, music, and ritual movement. The illusion-making properties of ekphrasis are countered in these passages by extending their "mirage" and "miracle" into other dimensions, re-imagining the "elsewhere" of a Caribbean subjectivity outside of, or rather, in between, acts of representation.

WILSON HARRIS: THE RESURRECTED SENSORY BODY

In addition to ekphrastic fear, W. J. T. Mitchell also describes what he calls ekphrastic hope. Hope results from the promise ekphrasis makes to achieve the impossible: to render the visual image through words and, in doing so, to still narrative flow in a spatialized moment. Mitchell writes that, "Once the desire to overcome the 'impossibility' of ekphrasis is put into play, the possibilities and the hopes for verbal representation of visual representation become practically endless" (154). These hopes include overcoming the "estrangement of the image/text division" and the many other divisions that spin around that one, such as the separation of the senses into discrete modes of perception, or the divisions that underlie that of text/image, such as that of self/other and subject/object. Following the experience of ekphrastic hope, argues Mitchell, ekphrastic fear comes into play in a resistance to the imminent collapse of difference. Thus, we can read ekphrastic fear in Cliff's *No Telephone to Heaven* in the chaos generated by the collapse of narrative distinctions between film action and dominant narrative action. This anxiety takes on a moral as well as aesthetic aspect in its fear of mixing and the breaking of taboos. Mitchell comments on the fear of loss underlying this resistance as castration anxiety, but we might also read it as a fear of miscegenation, of the loss of a perceived purity and individuation. As a poetic device, ekphrasis activates both this hope and this fear and operates in the tension between them. We can see Walcott's poetics as highlighting this tension by, first, creating hope of overcoming the distinction between art and life, supplanting it with the relationship between art and art, and second, recognizing the fear of losing the identities framed by those distinctions. Hence, through an ekphrastic self-portrait, he blurs his own identity, fracturing it in the image of a painter and that of the African being painted, yet highlighting the framing devices that keep them (and the word/image) separate. In another way, Walcott calms ekphrastic fear by emphasizing that the art that threatens to overtake life is, in the Caribbean, already a reproduction.

In Wilson Harris's writing, other devices come into play that emphasize ekphrastic hope and allow the ekphrastic narratives of his novels continually to address the fear they produce. By insisting on the real, though partial, and imagined Amerindian presence in the Caribbean and by returning to the scene of European encounter with indigenous peoples, Harris revisits the foundational moment for the construction of discourses about the Caribbean. From this symbolic moment, the myths of European history and the distinctions between self and other necessary to conquest and colonization arise. Also from this moment develops the apparent divide between a pre-Columbian past and the written history of the Americas, a division that Harris's ekphrastic narratives hope to overcome and by doing so, transgress the divisions between colonized and colonizer, victim and victimizer. The result is a tremendous and often chaotic mixing of cultures, myths, subjectivities, and syntactical constructions within his prose that can cause readers delight and anxiety.

The notion of a partial or absent indigenous presence within the Caribbean as crucial to an emancipatory future raises both problems and risks. First is the problem of memory, alluded to earlier in the discussion of Harris's deployment of classical arts of memory and Renaissance notions of a memory theatre. Through these arts of memory, joined with Afro-Caribbean spiritual practices, and the indigenous ritual practices associated with the *timehri, cenote,* and *zemi,* Harris's fiction creates a New World mnemonics, directed toward the re-imagining of alternate histories. From a strictly historical standpoint, this creates the problem of documentation; how can such an alternate past be verified and incorporated within existing history? From the standpoint of actual indigenous peoples, it risks imaginative distortion of their past and makes them into necessary symbols in the development of a larger philosophical and aesthetic project.

Just as it seems impossible to render the actual experience of the visual in words, so does it seem impossible to remember in a verifiable way a past long denied to history. Finding a prose to breach this impossibility and to address the fears such a transgression produces becomes Harris's project. While it does require a symbolic use of indigenous cultures, it also requires symbolic use of the Christian resurrection, a trope of present absence that, to some degree, deflects the representational burden away from Amerindian peoples while amplifying the dimension of hope within the dynamics of ekphrasis. Indirectly entering the theological debates concerning the resurrection of Christ, Harris works with another configuration of oppositions related to those of ekphrasis: those between empirical sight and inner vision, the material and the "spiritual body." Addressing the intense desire to see the resurrected body which drives the controversies surrounding Gnostic inner vision, Harris also employs the language of mysticism, in particular the device of *apophasis* or, as Michael Sells translates it, "the language of unsaying."[48] Through apophatic language, his fiction becomes performative, no longer limited to representational devices such as ekphrasis, but actually presenting, by performing, the acts of vision the text describes.

In essays and interviews, Harris has noted an experience of "inner gnosis," confirmed his "allegiance to the gnostic heresy,"[49] and described himself as a "Christian Gnostic."[50] By allying himself with the traditions of gnosticism, Harris claims a multiform, diverse version of Christianity, one to which its early orthodox Christian critics referred as a "mixed Christianity."[51] This is a version of Christianity long denounced as heresy for its claims to original spiritual discoveries and characterized by its celebration of inner vision as the ultimate spiritual authority. In *The Gnostic Gospels*, Elaine Pagels comments that religious language for the Christian gnostic writers necessarily involved symbols and was a "language of internal transformation" (134). This observation seems to fit Harris's writing, but in Harris's essays and fiction, the language of transformation exceeds the project of description. More than representing or describing spiritual experiences of internal transformation, Harris's writing performs them through the poetics of apophasis. In the apophatic tradition, mystic writers convey their visions through the paradoxical claim that the experience cannot be expressed in language.

For example, in one of the gnostic texts discovered at Nag Hammadi, a teacher recounts to his student an experience of ecstasy in the following words:

I see! I see indescribable depths. How shall I tell you, O my son? . . . How [shall I describe] the universe? . . . I [am mind and] I see another mind, the one that [moves] the soul! I see the one that moves me from pure forgetfulness . . . I have said, O my son, that I am Mind. I have seen! Language is not able to reveal this.[52]

In an interview with Alan Riach, Harris speaks about his belief in a Creator with a similar rhetorical gesture, adding, however, a qualification that contradicts it:

But I believe that the Creator may be able to gather everything together and transform it. To see the Creator like that is to be aware of the dimensionality of the Creator as almost unimaginable. You can't grasp such dimensionality. A creator that can bring all conditions together so that nothing is wasted – and yet, change it into the inimitable trauma of joy – that is almost unimaginable. And yet one can still present it.[53]

Harris describes the Creator only to state that such a Creator is "almost unimaginable." The "almost" is important, allowing him to assert then that "one can still present" such a Creator. In this conversation, Harris acknowledges the rhetorical paradox of mysticism by qualifying and contradicting it so that he can address the possibilities open to the artist or writer. How does one present an ungraspable, "almost unimaginable" Creator? How does a writer present his or her experiences of inner gnosis, the insight through which knowledge of the Creator is received or revealed? In the interview Harris suggests that artists can do this through their "essentially creative" acts of "making links and connections." He states that these connections lend "a mystery to our lives, a kind of strange mystery that allows absence itself to inform our being as a vital ingredient in our presence" (57). In claiming for artists "a mystery to our lives," Harris dissolves the distinction between the mystic and the artist and makes a mystical state of being coextensive with the practice of creative expression and communication.[54]

In another example, Harris has described a daily religious "reckoning" in the following terms:

Each day is a reckoning with veils or densities that lie between us and a God with whom we have at times a sensation of inner rapport, or of whom we may have some inner gnosis or knowledge, but who remains unfathomable and beyond description; who seems to imply at times our orphaned predicament.[55]

Here, Harris engages the apophatic tradition when he describes a God who "remains unfathomable and beyond description." In apophatic writing, the definition (in language) of deity as beyond language unsays that description of it and opens a new discourse which continually turns back on itself or, to use one of Harris's phrases, "consumes its own biases." The discourse appears in Greek, Christian, Jewish, Buddhist, and Islamic traditions and, in Sells's analysis, performs itself semantically and grammatically in radical transformations that undo self–other, before–after, and here–there distinctions. Sells's emphasis on the performance enacted by apophatic language allows us to see that even writing by gnostic dualists, for whom matter and spirit, evil and good, are opposed, unsays its dualistic content in its rhetorical performance. "The result is an open-ended dynamic that strains against its own reifications and ontologies – a language of *dis*ontology."[56]

Sells describes apophasis in terms that echo Harris's description of the "mystery" in the life of the artist:

A key component of mysticism in apophatic writings is the location of "mystery." Mystery is neither a set of abstruse doctrines to be taken on faith nor a secret prize for the initiated. Mystery is a referential openness onto the depths of a particular tradition, and into conversation with other traditions. (8)

Sells states that the experience of mystery in a written text is elusive, yet there for all who read. "The decision to write takes the discourse out of the immediate control of the author and opens it to readers beyond any particular group or school" (8). Sells's description of apophatic writing not only includes a conversation within and among traditions, fitting to Harris's writing, but also supports Harris's crossing of the boundary between the mystic and the artist. Like Harris, he sees writing, not as an impossible effort for the mystic, but as an act of generosity that makes the mystical experience possible, engaging the writer and the reader in its performance.

A characteristic of apophasis found throughout Harris's fiction is what Sells calls the dialectic of transcendence and immanence whereby the transcendent is known through the immanent. Hena Maes-Jelinek has noted this effect of Harris's writing, describing the "descent into the self" as "a mysticism in reverse towards inner transcendence, a 'transcendence within immanence,' as opposed to a transcendence external to man and beyond his normal experience."[57] In this dynamic, "the extraordinary, the transcendent, the unimaginable, reveals itself as the common."[58] To put it another way, that which is sought is always there. It undoes any hierarchy of being that would elevate the transcendent and dissolves distinctions between the human and the divine, self and other. When we reach the final sentence of Harris's most well-known novel, *Palace of the Peacock*, we are immersed in this dialectic: "Each of us now held at last in his arms what he had been forever seeking and what he had eternally possessed" (152). The sense of fulfillment and transcendence is powerful. Yet the referent for "what" ("what he had been forever seeking and what he had eternally possessed") remains elusive and mysterious, described, yet not, unsaid by the very words that describe it. The sentence seems at once conclusive in an ultimate sense and at the same time it takes us back to the first page of the novel and also out beyond the novel in an intentional performance of open referentiality. The sentence states the dialectic of transcendence through immanence and also performs it in a "meaning event" of language. When Harris claims that "one can still present" an almost unimaginable Creator, he is not claiming the power of language to re-present but, rather, to "present" as if for the first time. The scene of language becomes a site for the act of an original experience.

Harris's writing thus enacts, on the scale of the sentence and, we might argue, of his entire body of writing, the language of unsaying associated with several traditions of mystical writing. His novels become "meaning events" which "present" or perform rather than represent the experiences they describe. Harris writes, however, for purposes that exceed those of many of the mystics that Sells or Pagels discuss. Though apophatic writing performs a dynamic interaction between transcendence and immanence, mystics in the Christian traditions, especially, tend to deny the material body and elevate the soul in a dualism that raises the spiritual realm above the material world. The gnostics in particular value inner vision or insight so much that, to them, the empirical gaze is blind, the material body corrupt, and the visible world a false one. Harris's writing certainly presents inner visions, music, and voices. However, even the "dead material eye" of Donne in *Palace of the Peacock* is crucial to the performance of mystical ecstasy as is the material body and all of its senses. In this respect, Harris's writing is heresy to the heretics. His writing about and of the body affirms even further the apophatic dynamic of transcendence within immanence. It links his writing to that of theologians such as Martin Buber for whom "the conversation with God" is an earthly and everyday matter,[59] phenomenologists such as Merleau-Ponty who celebrates vision and "the flesh of the world," and perhaps more significantly for the originality of Harris's epic prose, it draws on the spirituality of New World African and Amerindian performative traditions in the re-creation of social communities. The languages of transformation in Harris's writing are many and involve the metamorphosis of the material body, as its senses extend from one to another and its life is renewed physically and spiritually in connection with others. The transformation begins in his first novel, *Palace of the Peacock*, with the eye.

In Book IV of *Palace of the Peacock*, Donne, whose name suggests, among other possibilities, the metaphysical poet, Elizabethan voyager, and religious figure John Donne, ascends the cliff wall alongside an enormous South American waterfall. He is swept by a longing "to see the indestructible nucleus and redemption of creation ... he longed to see, *he longed to see* the atom, the very nail of moment in the universe."[60] Donne's powerful desire to see, emphasized by repetition and italization, stems from his past career as agent of conquest and cruel ruler of the savannahs. It also projects him forward into what soon becomes a blindness that allows him to "see his own nothingness and imagination constructed beyond his reach" (141). His past way of seeing is described in the opening pages of *Palace* as "his dead seeing material eye." Harris's depiction of the colonialist gaze in *Palace* and subsequent novels predates discussions of the "imperial eye" and "commanding gaze" of recent postcolonial criticism. Harris has long been interested in the politics of visuality, in representing the visual arts of drawing, painting, film, and sculpture and the visual technologies of surveying instruments, eye glasses, telescopes, and cameras. Like critics in postcolonial studies, he also describes the failures of the colonialist eye to truly see the lands and peoples commanded by its gaze. However, unlike these critics and unlike the dualistic gnostics, he is most interested in the failures of empirical vision as openings to transformations of the senses. In his fiction, these transformations enact change within the very structure of the imagination and have profound implications for our abilities to counter what Harris calls "death-dealing regimes." As Canaima, a legendary figure in *The Four Banks of the River of Space*, tells its protagonist Anselm, "Extending our senses, Anselm. We cannot solve the world's terrifying problems otherwise."[61]

In *Palace*, Harris's writing dwells in the dynamics of seeing, in the visual and the visionary, taking his twinned character of Donne and the Dreamer/narrator on a journey in which his dead material eye becomes blind and his inner vision is reborn. Partway on the journey, at the beginning of his ascent and in response to his longing, Donne "sees" through windows on the cliff wall into rooms in which moving tableaux appear to him – of the young carpenter, who seems to be creating himself as a sculpture carved of wood, and then of a woman, whose hair makes up the tapestry she is, and her child. He sees pictures framed and hanging on the walls of the rooms. More than representations, the pictures *are* the creatures they depict; one is a flying swallow, another a bounding and wounded animal. The room itself becomes a "dancing hieroglyph." The language of vision – images, visual art, the act of looking and looking closer – predominates in these passages yet continually reaches a threshold of sight. The figures of visual art seem alive and "real," involved in the dynamics of divine self-creation, which Donne sees until he becomes "truly blind." Similarly, in *Jonestown* (1996), as Francisco Bone seeks the truth that will free him from the burden of mass destruction, he learns through "Aboriginal paintings" and film to look further. His teacher urges him, " 'Look, Francisco! Look into the womb of my Virgin Camera' " until he recognizes that he "would need to see *through* his blindness."[62]

These passages revel in crossing the boundaries of life and art and of empirical vision and true vision, and the narrative does not attempt to calm the dizziness of ekphrastic fear. In fact, we might read them as generating even further anxiety by exceeding conventional dualities of mysticism in their presentation of spiritual insight as an experience of the material world. The pictures that appear to Donne on the face of the cliff above the waterfalls appear as Real in a spiritual sense, moving and alive, transforming themselves and Donne as his vision is undone. Yet, they simultaneously unsay the dualism that would elevate and confine them to a spiritual realm. For the pictures are also real in a material sense, alluding to the Guyanese landscape and prefiguring the *timehri* petroglyphs that appear in Harris's subsequent novels. In Harris's writing, these rock paintings operate between several conventionally discrete realms. They belong simultaneously to the realms of human and divine creation. They are visual signs, yet they also script the verbal narratives of the novels in which they appear. They offer occasions for explorations of the sense of sight; yet they also act as rhythmic forces of sound and music within the waterways of the Caribbean landscape.[63] Readers of Harris's oeuvre have "seen" them on the rock face of the cliff in *Palace of the Peacock*; they appear there and elsewhere as visions that guide the narratives. In all of his novels, vision is transported through the material or immanent world to insight and a transcendence that, we find, "it had eternally possessed." The eye journeys across the apparent opposites of empirical sight and spiritual vision, connecting them in a resurrection of its own capacities. This resurrection of a "dead living material eye" bridges the material and spiritual worlds and becomes a trope for other crossings.

In an interview with Charles Rowell, Harris has explored the question of resurrection from theological, political, and artistic perspectives. He is simultaneously critical of the Christian concept of resurrection and engaged in revising it:

Christian ideology invests, as you know, in the resurrection as the conquest of death. And I would suggest that to do so is to forfeit a re-visionary momentum within resources of language. The resurrection may imply *not conquest at all* but a transition from one dimension or universe of sensibility to another. This releases a capacity in which conventional "plot," conventional "structure," conventional "character" changes.[64]

Redefining the concept of resurrection as "a transition from one dimension or universe of sensibility to another," Harris brings questions of the body and its senses to bear on a religious problem.[65] Indirectly, he once more locates himself within theological conflicts that motivated the early Christian gnostics. Questioning the doctrine of the body's literal resurrection in Christ, the gnostics emphasized the "spiritual body" of a self that is also God and that, in some versions, creates God (itself). The gnostic departure from an orthodox Christianity that then suppressed gnostic practices had much to do with notions of the body and depended on a contested sense of sight. Elaine Pagels analyzes the conflict as motivated by issues of authority and power. She argues that the orthodox church had to denounce the gnostic celebration of inner vision as heretical in order to maintain the doctrine of apostolic transmission of authority. This doctrine, based on the literal resurrection of the actual body of Christ, gave divine authority in order of descent from Jesus Christ to the apostle Peter, who claimed to have seen Christ's actual resurrected body, and then down through the hierarchy of bishops, deacons, and priests. The hierarchy was an exclusively male order and explicitly denied the vision of Mary Magdalene who, the gnostics believed, was the first to "see" Christ following his crucifixion. The gnostic beliefs in insight or inner vision and in the symbolic meanings of resurrection potentially gave religious authority to anyone who could truly see and receive divine insight through the powers of their own minds. As Pagels points out, gnosticism then devalued the material body while the orthodox church acknowledged a sacred dimension to the human body and its activities of eating, sex, and procreation.

When we consider this history of distinctions between empirical sight and inner vision, the material and the "spiritual body," they appear as oppositions in part because of the politics motivating them and demanding that they be taken up as opposing positions. Harris's writing, emerging from a cross-cultural and postcolonial context, can explore the possibilities that might have developed had gnosticism remained in dialogue with orthodox Christianity. He can also place that imagined dialogue in conversation with the questions of decolonization that drive the revision of history and the reformation of language in his epic novels. These questions include the recovery of "eclipsed realities," the activation of memory in the resurrection of apparently lost people, knowledge, and traditions. By redefining resurrection as the transition from one realm to another, "from one dimension or universe of sensibility to another," Harris undoes the oppositions of the material and the spiritual, empirical and inner sight, exploring instead the dynamics of sensory transference.[66] In his prose, the act or journey of transference resonates in synaesthetic language, for example, which crosses from one sense, such as the eye, to another, such as the ear. When the character named Mageye in *Jonestown* exclaims "Synaesthesia!" and Francisco Bone replies that he "cried with sudden tears in my eyes" (34), we can parse "tears in my eyes" as (t)ears in my eyes or, on the other hand, understand it as suggesting that the eyes have suddenly torn. In this comment on a poetic device, Harris extends synaesthesia through the syntax of the body's organs, gesturing towards somatic alteration and re-creation.

In *Palace of the Peacock*, a poetics of transference is figured through an invisible cord binding the Dreamer and Donne which then becomes a "chord . . . within the density of the window" through which Donne views the living tableaux in the rock face of the cliff he climbs. The passage from eye to ear through "*the window that becomes a medium of transitive density*" extends their senses and circuits their bodies through one another. Synaesthetic transference becomes simultaneously a poetics, a spiritual discourse, and a method for recovering the past in language released from limiting oppositions.

Language is implicated in the conflict between gnostic and orthodox Christianity, for if one can empirically see an actual resurrected body, one can represent that experience based on the evidence of the senses. In this case, religious language gains legitimacy because it can claim to represent material reality. If, as the Gnostics claim, the experience of resurrected life comes not through material sensory evidence but through insight and transcendence of the body, what is it that language represents? And how? Harris restates this question through the performative aspect of his writing. Having acknowledged that "one can nevertheless present" an "almost unimaginable" and "unfathomable Creator," Harris has also turned the question of resurrection from an issue of re-presentation to one of pre-sentation: "How do you present the resurrected figure? It's not just a matter of saying he was resurrected. How do you present him? Here is a solid figure who comes through the wall. How is that going to happen?"[67] The language Harris chooses in posing this question emphasizes the problem facing the mystic / artist of writing beyond description, beyond "saying he was resurrected" to creating that event, making it "happen."

In the essay titled "Ways to Enjoy Literature," Harris makes clear the social and political implications of his concern with the resurrected body. In this essay he takes the meaning of "body" beyond that of the individual body and its sense organs. Writing about the re-composition "of the body of civilization," he describes it as a transcultural dynamic crucial to countering the violent political conflicts of our time. Harris describes this body as composed of various cultural organs: "One re-composes the body of civilization through organs drawn from the ancient Greek, from the Carib, from the ancient Maya" (205). In Harris's writing, then, the mystery of resurrection, the "transition from one dimension or universe of sensibility to another," and the task of the mystic/writer in making it "happen" on the page conjoin with the urgent political project of reconstituting "the body of our civilization." In *Jonestown*, they occur simultaneously in Bone's rewriting of history in his Dream-book.

In the passage from *Jonestown* in which Mr. Mageye exclaims, "Synaesthesia!" Mageye goes on to define synaesthesia for Bone in terms that merge the revision of history with the resurrection of the body: "The spontaneous linkage that you make between organs of the past and the present (your long-dead great-great-grandmother and your poor mother today) is a kind of synaesthesia or stimulation of different moral ages and visions" (34). The body, in this passage, is that of time, "the past and the present," and its organs are transferred into one another spontaneously as Bone writes his Dream-book of revisionary history. Both the voyage of historical revision, "between the organs of the past and the present," and the journey of resurrection, "from one dimension or universe of sensibility to another," move through "transitive densities" that carry the body through and outside of itself, a figured absence, into ecstasy.

The condition of being outside of oneself, ec-static, is activated by the transcultural mythologies of Harris's writing and again, moves beyond description to its own performance. Expanding on the image of the transitive chord that "fires, so to speak," Harris explains the notion further through the symbol of the tree: "The transitive chord within the window, within a body of density, fires – as I said before – and thus, coincident with the music, appears the lightning bark of a tree."[68] The lightning bark of the tree, associated with the "gods who write in fire," recalls the recurring symbol of the tree in many of Harris's novels – the "great tree of flesh and blood" that appears to the Dreamer in *Palace of the Peacock*, the tree felled by the Macusi woodman in *The Four Banks of the River of Space*, and the "Phallic tree" of "sacrificial sculpture" witnessed by Francisco Bone in *Jonestown*, to give a few examples. Each of these trees appears in a state of metamorphosis, as it shifts into the cross on which Christ was crucified, and simultaneously a peacock or bird, a ship, an ancient carving, or feathered mask of an ancestor. Here the "organs drawn from the ancient Greek, from the Carib, from the ancient Maya" and other civilizations draw together in Harris's re-composition of the body of civilization. In Harris's writing, the tree, "fired" by the chord of "transitive density" and circuit for the sensory transference of metamorphosis, becomes a site for the crossing of myths and spiritual traditions. Through the figure of the tree, we can see how that crossing is animated by the mystery of absence. In an essay on Jean Rhys's *Wide Sargasso Sea*, Harris has recounted the Arawak legend of the flaming tree: "The tree is fired by the Caribs at a time of war when the Arawaks seek refuge in its branches. The fire rages and drives the Arawaks up into space until they are themselves burnt and converted into sparks which continue to rise into the sky to become the Pleiades."[69] The flaming tree recalls cultural legacies of ancient Amerindian tribes that remain etched as "living absences" in the landscape and heard in the tidal waters of the rivers of Guyana. By locating absence within presence and the past within the present, the lightning bark of the Amerindian flaming tree evokes also the cross of crucifixion and the absent body/living presence of the resurrected Christ. These crossings join with the crossing or "limbo gateway" of the Middle Passage and the absent presence of the "phantom limb" in New World African spiritual practices.[70]

Harris presents the crossings of resurrection, makes them "happen," through ekphrastic and apophatic language. They are figured on the crafts, vessels, or ships of the *timehri* in *Resurrection at Sorrow Hill* and linger in the absent body of the legendary Chief Kaie of ancient Guyana, whose sacrificial leap took him home to the god Makonaima in the rocks below the Kaieteur Falls. Francisco Bone resurrects Kaie's leap as he falls over the edge of the cliff at the conclusion of *Jonestown*, "into the net of music," "closer and closer – however far removed – to the unfathomable body of the Creator" (234). The aporias or unsolvable dilemmas of this apparently concluding line resemble those of the last line in *Palace*. In *Palace*, the "what" in the sentence, "Each of us now held at last in his arms what he had been forever seeking and what he had eternally possessed," is unsaid by the words that describe it. The line that appears conclusive therefore actually opens the text to its own beginning and beyond, performing the idea it expresses. Similarly, in the concluding lines to *Jonestown*, the body of Bone falls "closer and closer" though "far removed" from a Creator's body described as "unfathomable." Yet in this description of Bone's body plunging into space, resurrecting the divinity of Chief Kaie's fall, the unfathomable is nevertheless fathomed as an intercorporeality of the human and the divine. The line presents the resurrected body by performing the spiritual leap described within it, unsaying itself, opening the ending to the beginning and this more recent novel to Harris's first. Thus, Harris attempts to affect the "reading eye," which he has described as "fixed, tend[ing] to force everything into linearities that enforce a static fate"[71] by opening his narratives away from patterns of linear progression through the "mystical language of unsaying."

In his philosophical exploration of vision, Maurice Merleau-Ponty has stressed an alternative to that of empirical sight. In this countervision, the visible folds back onto the invisible, and the body is constituted by the space in between bodies. He asks, "Where are we to put the limit between the body and the world, since the world is flesh? Where in the body are we to put the seer, since evidently there is in the body only 'shadows stuffed with organs,' that is, more of the visible?"[72] Readers of Harris's novels may recognize a similar "intertwining"[73] through what Harris calls "*The Body's Waking Instrument*": "The arousal of the body to itself as the sculpture by a creator one abuses. The body wakes to itself as inimitable art, inimitable multi-faceted, living fossil extending into all organs, objects, spaces, stars and the ripple of light."[74] In Harris's writing, however, such experiences and the language through which they are described and performed are grounded in the material traces of history and the act of recovering realities eclipsed by conquest, slavery, and colonialism. Thus the body "[w]akes also to self-confessional blindness, blindness to self-destruction and the destruction of others. The body wakes to the instrumentality of breath – 'sharpest extension of breath in sculpted body-senses'"[75] This is the body that Harris has described as created through New World African vodun rituals, refigured by the "phantom limb" that extends through space and across the "limbo gateway" of the Middle Passage. The possessed, entranced body, "one leg . . . drawn up into the womb of space," resculpts space and carries the past into the present through the presence of its absent limb.[76] Harris has described the Haitian vodun dancer as standing "like a rising pole upheld by earth and sky or like a tree which walks in its shadow or like a one-legged bird which joins itself to its sleeping reflection in a pool." He argues that this "intense drama of images in space" "has indeed a close bearing on the language of fiction."[77] Its many cultural crossings map the dynamics of creativity: "the phantom limb – the re-assembly of dismembered man or god – possesses archetypal resonances that embrace Egyptian Osiris, the resurrected Christ and the many-armed Goddess of India, Kali, who throws a psychical bridge with her many arms from destruction to creation."[78]

For Harris, the task of the writer is to resculpt in the space of language the lost and dispersed "organs" of past and present civilizations, countering through their own shadowed or sleeping resources the "conquest-driven imperatives" that have shaped them in the past. He finds in the material and spiritual arts of the Caribbean a model for a performative art of language that undoes hierarchical distinctions of spirit/body, self/other, and absence/presence in the resurrection of lost bodies of civilization. The collapse of difference threatened by ekphrasis transforms to a passage from one realm to another, avoiding loss and, instead, enabling the discovery of "what" one has always eternally possessed. Through such apophatic language, performance joins with representation as a textual dynamic of hope.

Conclusion

Bringing the fiery image of Turner's slave ship into the present yet also more deeply into the past,[1] Wilson Harris has written recently of "Immigrants who had arrived from the burning Ship," and he inquires into "arts of the drowned." Harris's burning ship is called the *Ulysses* and brings Chinese laborers to a fictional Harbourtown in South America, yet as its name suggests, it is kin to the ship carrying Homer's Ulysses, and the Chinese immigrants appear as did Ulysses on his arrival home, as beggars in disguise. They have survived a drowning, burning ship, and Harris's narrator raises questions raised also of the Middle Passage, "*Who were the drowned?*"[2]

The question activates a journey for the multiple narrators of Harris's novel, *The Mask of the Beggar* (2003), into the act and art of seeing. Written as a dialogue between an artist's creation and the artist, the novel performs a method of seeing deeply, with "holed eyes," and then questions that performance, seeking its own potential implication in an impulse for global mastery. In this way, Harris reflects on his lifelong project as a writer, and he portrays that project as one of a visual artist. Describing words as "thresholds into a universal medium of which we know so little," Harris's artist works on a vast, multi-figured self-portrait that crosses time, space, and cultures in its attempts to break with "frames" of violence that result from a one-dimensional vision.

In a passage early in the book, the narrator who is the artist's mother yet is also figured as the Mother of Space, a sculpture created by the artist, looks through the "holed eyes of [her] mind." These eyes compose a "Visionary Eye shared by sculptor and sculpted, painter and painted, writer and written, and extending into many nameless others who create and are created" (39). Through this Eye, the mother/Mother of Space travels with Homer's disguised beggar around the world to pre-Columbian South

America until he arrives "in the gravity of art" "in a twentieth-century extension of himself," a beggar encountered by her child on the streets of Harbourtown (40). As soon as she indicates to her son the beggar's identity, it decomposes: "The mask of the Beggar was crumbling into ancient fragments one of which lay on the ground at my feet and I was able to read what had been written there by a god it seemed: 'SEATED PRE-COLUMBIAN SAGE WITH A CUP'"(40). In this passage, historical figures join identities in a work of art, the pre-Columbian mask. It immediately fragments into shards bearing inscriptions which describe works of art, one of which is the seated pre-Columbian sage with a cup. The passage thus portrays an ongoing metamorphosis of present-into-past-into-present through transcultural links created by an act of seeing that is both an art in itself and an act of seeing art. As a verbal description of a work of visual art, this passage breaks out of its own ekphrastic frame through the breaking of the mask. Citing words written on the crumbled fragments of the mask, the passage extends into another ekphrastic description of another work of art. Visual and verbal art reside within one another and break out of one another, though ultimately, as a verbal narrative, the novel sustains an extended ekphrastic inscription of their relationship.

Through these ongoing transmutations of verbal-into-visual-into-verbal art, the novel portrays a vision of a humanity linked, through contradiction and often violence, across seas and cultures, and it portrays the method of seeing which yields this cross-temporal, cross-spatial, and cross-cultural vision. In one view, the sage's cup, reminiscent of an "oriental sage" with a gambler's cup of dice, becomes a pre-Columbian bowl, on which appears a child's face; the child later appears in the artist's studio as a "Child-like man," pointing a gun. In another view, a pregnant woman, imprisoned in Harbourtown, reminds the narrator of the reclining female figure of a pre-Columbian sculpture, and the shape of both women echoes that of the bowl, overturned, and the child's face on its curved sides. This way of seeing requires the "holed eyes" of the Mother of Space who, through her visionary journey, becomes the beggar's mask. In that phrase, we might hear "hold eyes" as if the vision came from the hold of the burning ship, and we might hear "wholed eyes," as if it were able to see the fragment whole, yet riddled, as it were, with "hole[s]." The phrase recalls, as well, the "black hole of the image" described by W. J. T. Mitchell as the representational effect of ekphrastic poetics. The vision is, thus, deeply historical in sensing a past not recorded or made visible, coming from the hold of the drowned immigrant ships. It is also more whole, encompassing the multiple antecedents that compose historical identities and link them to others in contradictory "mutualities," rather than oppositions. As the vision crosses time, space, and cultures, it also casts the powerful illusion of crossing sign systems, from the verbal into the visual. But as always in Harris's writing, the resulting wholeness is partial and requires, in fact, a rupture, weakness, or vulnerability which becomes a window into another pattern of connection.

As I have argued in this book, writers from the Caribbean throughout the twentieth century have engaged in various forms of seeing through "holed eyes." Beginning with their contributions to a transatlantic modernism in the century's early decades, they have also reflected on the act of vision itself as both an institutionalized form of violence and a potential gateway into an alternate sensory body. Borrowing Harris's poetic figure, we might read each of the texts discussed in the chapters of this study as fragments of a larger project or "mask," one whose many personae have emerged through dialogue among the writers and artists and through aesthetic, historical and, as Harris might claim, intuitive interconnections discoverable in the works of art themselves. Following the figure of the Beggar's mask further, the fragments of this larger project could easily land beyond the scope of this study; we could identify other writers from the Caribbean and writers from other regions of the Anglophone postcolonial world within their fall. Though I have limited this study to the Anglophone Caribbean, other texts come to mind as participants in a more broadly postcolonial "art of seeing." Invoking the category "postcolonial" recalls a number of controversies over the usefulness and limits of the term. One objection cautions against the centering of imperial history as the basis for categorizing literary texts, and another, related, critique questions the linear and progressive notion of time conveyed by the prefix "post-." Yet, it may be worthwhile to indicate some other possible "fragments," relying on the partiality the image insists upon for a critique of "postcolonial."

One fragment might bear the works of Salman Rushdie alongside those of Harris, C. L. R. James, and V. S. Naipaul. On it, we could read the words of Rushdie's character and narrator in *The Moor's Last Sigh*, Moraes Zogoiby or "Moor," the son of an artist mother, whose descriptions of her paintings signal the development of the narrative:

The so-called "Moor paintings" of Aurora Zogoiby can be divided into three distinct periods: The "early" pictures, made between 1957 and 1977, that is to say between the year of my birth and that of the election that swept Mrs. G. from power, and of Ina's death; the "great" or "high" years, 1977–81, during which she created the glowing, profound works with which her name is most often associated; and the so-called "dark Moors," those pictures of exile and terror which she painted after my departure, and which include her last, unfinished, unsigned masterpiece, *The Moor's Last Sigh* (170 × 247 cms., oil on canvas, 1987), in which she turned, at last, to the one subject she had never directly addressed – facing up, in that stark depiction of the moment of Boabdil's expulsion from Granada, to her own treatment of her only son.[3]

Following the narrative structure and describing, as well, the historical palimpsest of the novel, this passage performs an exhibit of paintings that portray its narrator and map the novel itself. It recalls the exhibit of paintings in Harris's *Da Silva da Silva's Cultivated Wilderness* (1977), one of which is a mural that appears to "paint" the novel's larger narrative.

Not only does Rushdie's narrative follow the ekphrastic form employed so extensively by writers such as Harris, Cliff, and Walcott, in several instances, *The Moor's Last Sigh* alludes to preceding works by Caribbean writers, as if nodding to a shared project. For example, with a brief reference to C. L. R. James's title *Beyond a Boundary*, Rushdie creates a Hindu nationalist cricketer and political philosopher who forms a new violent, right-wing political movement and brings about the separation of son from mother. Arguing for "the Indian game's origins in inter-community rivalry," this villainous character claims that the Hindu teams, collectively, are stronger than those of the Parsis and Muslims and states, "By-the-same-token we must make changes beyond the boundary" (231).

As critics have noted, Rushdie caricaturizes right-wing Hindu nation-alist leaders in this fictional character.[4] Through him, however, glimpses of James's writing and life appear, inverted, like the shapes of a negative image. While celebrating cricket and analyzing its history as part of a nationalist movement, Rushdie's character names his movement after a Hindu goddess, invoking religion in ways that would have been anathema to James, and he organizes his movement into neo-Stalinist cadres, a politics abhorrent to James who was a Trotskyist and internationalist. Furthermore, this comic yet devilish character secures a Faustian pact through his attack on visual art, the cultural form on which James modeled his aesthetics of cricket. While Rushdie's character offers this oddly inverted, negative homage to James, the real tribute appears in the ekphras-tic aesthetics of the novel in which history and visual art mutually shape one another, a dynamic that engaged James throughout his life.

V. S. Naipaul also appears in *The Moor's Last Sigh*, by name and with a back-handed tribute to *The Enigma of Arrival*. Clearly contrasting his narrator with Naipaul, Rushdie describes the destruction of the mosque at Ayodhya as "history-obliterating work," while noting ironically that "Sir V. Naipaul has approvingly called [the destruction] their 'awakening to history'" (363). More indirectly Rushdie refers to Naipaul through allusion to *The Enigma of Arrival* which, as discussed in Chapter 3 of this study, works with the image and title of Georgio de Chirico's painting of a palace in a city by a sea, haunted by two distant human figures. In *The Moor's Last Sigh*, a commercial painter and exile from Goa named Vasco Miranda creates a "lair" or "folly" modeled on Aurora Zogoiby's paintings and recalling Chirico's image:

A palace set by a mirage of the sea; part-Arab, part-Mughal, owing something to Chirico, it was that very place which Aurora once described to me as one "where worlds collide, flow in and out of one another, and washofy away. Place where an air-man can drown in water, or else grow gills; where a water-creature can get drunk, but also chokeofy, on air." Even in its present state of slight dilapidation and horticultural decay, I had truly found Mooristan. (408)

In spite of these crossings of cultures, species, and arts, the palace reveals itself as "not a miracle, after all ... but an ugly pretentious house" (409). The illusion and its flaws result from the commercial artist's obsessive attempts "to appropriate [Aurora's] vision for himself" (409). The ugly house with its stolen art soon imprisons the son with the false imitations of his mother's creations, and the narrative thus raises complex questions concerning postcolonial subjectivity, nationalist iconography, the ethics of imitation, and the potential for a more truly transcultural creativity.

Whatever we make of these allusions to Naipaul, the literary engagement with his work lies in the adoption of the extended ekphrastic form that shapes *The Enigma of Arrival* and that Jean Rhys, Wilson Harris, Derek Walcott, and Michelle Cliff have also developed through much of their writing. Like the mural in Harris's *Da Silva da Silva's Cultivated Wilderness*, Aurora's paintings and the Chinese tiles of the Cranganore synagogue in *The Moor's Last Sigh* perform many roles: they prophesy in detail the future; they represent the past; and they portray the present as encounters between historically opposed figures that reveal the Other within the Self and, thus, the potential for an alternate, more accurate, alive, tolerant and creative history.

Most important, Rushdie's ekphrastic narrative engages with the work of these Caribbean writers to re-envision the postcolonial epic (in this case, Mother India) as one dependent on the politics of vision. Invoking the interdependence of nationalist movements and visual art, *The Moor's Last Sigh* promotes visual art as a language through which the violence of conquest, colonialism, and exile and the abuses of nationalism may be re-imagined. Like the writing of Walcott and Harris, Rushdie's novel portrays works of art as the visual scripts for the narratives in which they appear, opening windows within those narratives for alternate stories, multiple in direction and possibility, even taking on lives of their own, yet remaining within, while creating, the larger narrative.

Postcolonial theorists have long argued for the importance of what Homi Bhabha calls a *time-lag* within modernity, modernity conceptualized as a construction dependent on that which it excludes from its forward movement. In modernity's construction of itself, colonized subjects and regions of the world become, then, "belated," educated in the ideals of liberty and progress, yearning for them, yet necessarily positioned as the sign of the past, the primitive, the not-modern. To explain his notion of this time-lag, Bhabha begins one of his essays with the often-quoted epithet from Frantz Fanon's "The Fact of Blackness": " 'Dirty nigger!' Or simply, 'Look, a Negro!' "[5] In Bhabha's reading of this line and of Fanon's essay, he stresses the exclusion of the black man from the "temporality of modernity within which the figure of the 'human' comes to be authorized" (193). Though Bhabha does not explore the connection, his stress on temporalization coincides with Fanon's emphasis on the capacity for sight attributed to the universalized subject of modernity who, by seeing ("Look . . .!"), judges the "Negro" as "dirty" or a "nigger." This social act of seeing constitutes yet again the relationship wherein the one who looks attains the status of the modern subject, and the "Black man" or colonized person occupies once more the position of object seen and judged. The man who sees constructs the time of modernity to which he accedes as the universal Subject, and Bhabha along with others such as Anne McClintock have argued for recognition of "the time-lag of cultural difference," which interrupts and fragments the "progressive, future drive" of modernity (214). It is not surprising that Bhabha cites a number of writers from the Caribbean such as Walcott, James, and Harris as performing, through their writing, this necessary distortion of modernity's time, claiming "*Time-lag keeps alive the making of the past*" (215).

If *The Moor's Last Sigh* follows Harris's earlier work, Harris's *The Mask of the Beggar* carries forward their intertextual ekphrastic dialogue, especially in the central figures of mother and son and the focus on dynamics of history intertwined with relationships of creativity. Modernity's time-lag ruptures both narratives in sudden appearances of the past through devices offered by visual art and the act of seeing. Into the rooms of the artist's studio in *The Mask of the Beggar* throng the crowds of carnival who are simultaneously figures from the artist's work and real celebrants who create a riot of books, papers, paintings, and sculpture. The "Child-like man," created by the artist's imagination yet shut out of his art, turns up as a "real man" and hurls a "Stone of Time" through the windows of the studio. He then appears inside the studio, aiming, or at least seeming to aim, a gun at the artist. In this confrontation, the artist realizes his responsibilities for what he has created and what, in turn, creates him. The realization takes place as he sees the Beggar's mask – "a rag-and-bones body sliced into eyes" – through the beautiful cloth of the Child-like man's suit and discovers that "[h]e was broken" (165). The pronoun's reference becomes ambiguous, referring simultaneously to the Child-like man and to the artist, as the bullet strikes the artist's "self-portrait – with its many faces – on the wall" (168), and the artist asks whether "each break signif[ied] an unscripted, creative gateway into an infinity of compassion, an infinity of love?" (171). Rushdie concludes *The Moor's Last Sigh* with a similar confrontation: a bullet strikes the breast of the portrait of the artist, the narrator's mother, opening a hole through which pours the blood of another woman who has fled behind it. In both novels, a vision remains that in Rushdie's words, affirms "the most profound of our needs, . . . our need for flowing together, for putting an end to frontiers, for the dropping of the boundaries of the self" (433) and for Harris's narrator, "would require future Imaginations beyond me."

As a fragment of a postcolonial art of seeing, reading *The Moor's Last Sigh* alongside writings by Harris, James, and Naipaul suggests a dialogue beyond the frames of "South Asian," "postmodern," "Caribbean," or "postcolonial." In that dialogue a scene emerges in counterpoint to what Ian Baucom has called the foundational scene of drowning bodies in the Middle Passage. The new scene confronts and transforms the old as the figure excluded from the realm of art encounters the artist/writer, and they interpenetrate one another. The bullet shot by one through the portrait of the other opens a hole through which to see deeply to another body, another time, layered behind and before the present. This act exposes the subject-who-sees as his own self-portrait. It opens that self-constructed image of universal humanity into the masks of the historically colonized, exiled person at whose expense the modern subject paints himself; it reveals how interlayered they always were. "*Who was that masked man?*" quips Rushdie's narrator on introducing the man who would fire the bullet. In *The Mask of the Beggar*, the artist describes making the mask with "fissures and subtle cavities"; these wounds open "*a curious, creative possibility of bringing together cultures that are separate into an unseizable wholeness*" (77). Practicing this art of seeing brings forth a new body, no longer imprisoned in a single identity, its wholeness newly and dynamically diversified and thus "unseizable." Seeing the Beggar, worn by his travels into "an eye of

Space," the artist reports: "But as he looks deep into the past and ever deeper, he sees Life, the Journey of Life. And he feels *a new brain, a new bloodstream* run through him. An immense cross-culturality – in the midst of terror and risk – he has never experienced before" (74).

* * *

I have argued that, throughout the twentieth century, writers from the Caribbean participated in a project of transfiguring the sense of sight. To appreciate the arts of the black Atlantic and Caribbean diaspora as predominantly sound cultures risks reproducing the hierarchical sensory divisions of eighteenth-century aesthetics. Developed at the height of the slave trade, these categories denied Africans and indigenous peoples the capacity for contemplative sight that defined the free man of reason. This construction of modernity's Subject created a double bind for colonized artists in which they were required to enter the realm of art in order to attain the status of the fully human, yet dismissed as merely imitative when they did. Lingering well into the twentieth century, this politics of vision has met a sustained response on the part of writers and visual artists from the Caribbean. Rather than avoiding or denying their simultaneous exclusion from the realm of art and modernity, they have contributed to critiques of visuality through their sculpture, drama, essays, fiction, and poetry by directly confronting the social and aesthetic dynamics of sight. Their confrontations with the visual epistemology and ontology of modernity invite new readings of other postcolonial writers, such as Rushdie, and dialogues among them come into relief, raising questions and inviting critical analysis beyond the limits of this study. We might ask, for example, how *The Bone People*, a novel by New Zealand writer Keri Hulme participates in this larger transformation of the visual dynamics of modernity. In Hulme's novel the work of a sculptor models also a creative intervention into colonialist legacies of violence. How might we read her emphasis on visual art alongside Rushdie's *The Moor's Last Sigh* and Harris's *The Mask of the Beggar*? Working with Rushdie's "Moor" again, how might we read him alongside Walcott's reading of "the Moor silent with privilege" in Tiepolo's painting of *Apelles Painting Campaspe before Alexander*? Or, to give another example, what patterns in this larger politics of vision would emerge if we read in this same company the Irish writer John Banville's novel *Ghosts*, in which the characters and events of the narrative resemble those of a painting depicted within it? Such postcolonial revisions of ekphrasis, a poetic device long associated with the epic, indicate a shared project that reflects on this poetic tradition, on the cycles of conquest, nation building, and state violence associated with it, and the epistemology of the visual on which it depends.

More than critical reflection, however, the countervisual arts of the Anglophone Caribbean and its diaspora have offered inspired alternatives to the temporal reason of a modernity constituted through their exclusion. By directly confronting vision as a social act, a discourse and institution of aesthetics, and a trope for spiritual transformation, they have transfigured the oppositions of self and other across time and space, asking us to reconceptualize the temporal chronologies implicit in the "*post*colonial." Through "holed eyes," in all senses of the phrase, an alternate sensory body has emerged in these arts of seeing, shot through with its other, alive with the making of the past, and projecting beyond our current imaginations.

Notes

1 TRANSFIGURATIONS

1. Stuart Hall, "C. L. R. James: A Portrait," *C. L. R. James's Caribbean*, ed. Paget Henry and Paul Buhle (Durham: Duke University Press, 1992), p. 15.
2. For a review of problems involved in the term *diaspora*, see Brent Hayes Edwards, *The Practice of Diaspora: Literature, Translation, and the Rise of Black Internationalism* (Cambridge, MA, and London: Harvard University Press, 2003), pp. 12–13.
3. George Lamming, *The Pleasures of Exile*, "Foreward" by Sandra Pouchet Paquet (Ann Arbor: University of Michigan Press, 1992 [1960]), p. 107.
4. Derek Walcott, "What the Twilight Says," *What the Twilight Says, Essays by Derek Walcott* (New York: Farrar, Straus, and Giroux, 1998), p. 9.
5. Derek Walcott, *Tiepolo's Hound* (New York: Farrar, Straus, and Giroux, 2000), p. 7.
6. Some of these writers do not focus exclusively on sound as evidenced in Brathwaite's "videographics" and Gilroy's essays on contemporary black British art. However, the predominant critical trend stresses black Atlantic music, sound, and orality. In US literary studies, a similar emphasis prevails as in Patricia McKee's recent argument that "whiteness" is produced through visual media, while a "black response" emerges through representation of oral and aural culture. *Producing American Races: Henry James, William Faulkner, Toni Morrison* (Durham and London: Duke University Press, 1999).
7. Joseph Roach uses the term "circum-Atlantic" to designate "the insufficiently acknowledged cocreations of an oceanic interculture ... [which] shares in the contributions of many peoples along the Atlantic rim – for example, Bambara, Iroquois, Spanish, English, Aztec, Yoruba, and French." *Cities of the Dead: Circum-Atlantic Performance* (New York: Columbia University Press, 1996), p. 5.
8. David Dabydeen, *A Harlot's Progress* (London: Jonathan Cape, 1999), p. 207.
9. Sean Shesgreen describes the paintings as depicting "Jonah outside Nineveh" and "David dancing before the Ark while Uzzah, attempting to touch it, is knifed in the back." The portraits are of "two contemporaries held to be atheists, Samuel Clarke and Thomas Woolaston." *Engravings by Hogarth: 101 Prints*, ed. Sean Shesgreen (New York: Dover Publications, 1973), No. 19, Plate II.

10. According to George Dickie, Kant did not demonstrate but assumed that judgments of taste were disinterested and, thus, universal. *The Century of Taste: The Philosophical Odyssey of Taste in the Eighteenth Century* (New York and Oxford: Oxford University Press, 1996), pp. 107–109. Moreover, the subject experiences himself as personally and socially free in making aesthetic judgments: "taste in the beautiful may be said to be the one and only disinterested and *free* delight." *The Critique of Judgement*, trans. James Creed Meredith (Oxford and London: Clarendon Press, 1952), p. 49.

    Though countering Kant's emphasis on the subject in the aesthetic relation, Schiller, too, stresses the aesthetic as the realm in which freedom develops: "it is the aesthetic mode of the psyche which first gives rise to freedom." *On the Aesthetic Education of Man in a Series of Letters*, ed. and trans. with intro. and glossary by Elizabeth M. Wilkinson and L. A. Willoughby (Oxford and London: Clarendon Press, 1967), "Twenty-Sixth Letter," p. 191.

11. Dabydeen states that English painting depicted black people as servants, often posed alongside or as a mirror image to an adoring dog. Prints, on the other hand, depicted the black person among the lower classes. *Hogarth's Blacks: Images of Blacks in Eighteenth-Century English Art* (Kingston upon Thames: Dangaroo Press, 1985), pp. 21–26.

12. In most cases throughout this book, the first citation of a source appears in a note and, when the source is thus clear, subsequent references appear as page numbers within the text.

13. Dabydeen describes, for example, Hogarth's atypical comments on the painterly beauty of black people (*Hogarth's Blacks*, pp. 46–47). See essays by James Grantham Turner, David Bindman, Lubaina Himid, and Bernadette Fort in *The Other Hogarth: Aesthetics of Difference*, ed. Bernadette Fort and Angela Rosenthal (Princeton and Oxford: Princeton University Press, 2001), for additional and sometimes conflicting views of Hogarth's racial and visual politics.

14. Quoted in Simon Gikandi, "Aesthetic Reflection and the Colonial Event: The Work of Art in the Age of Slavery," *Journal of the International Institute*, University of Michigan http://www.umich.edu-iinet/journal/vol4no3/gikandi.html (Summer 1997). Gikandi quotes from the 1753 reprint of the 1748 essay, as does Peter Fryer in his discussion of the eighteenth century in *Staying Power: The History of Black People in Britain* (London: Pluto Press, 1984), pp. 150–65. In the 1748 edition, the sentence reads, "I am apt to suspect the Negroes to be naturally inferior to the Whites," omitting "and other species of men" and concentrating, thus, on people of Africa and African descent. *The Philosophical Works of David Hume*, Vol. III (Edinburgh and London: Adam Black and William Tait, and Charles Tait, 1826), p. 236n.

15. Hume, "National Characters," *Philosophical Works*, Vol. III, 236n. Gilroy makes a similar point concerning Hegel's *The Philosophy of History*, in which Hegel's notion of universality places black people "outside of the realm of authentic aesthetic sensibility." "Art of Darkness: Black Art and the Problem of Belonging to England," *Third Text*, 10 (1990), 45–59.

16. Gikandi, "Aesthetic Reflection," p. 1.

17. Hume, "Standard of Taste," *Philosophical Works*, Vol. III, p. 10.
18. Ibid., p. 13.
19. Hume, "National Characters," p. 229.
20. Ibid., p. 231.
21. Ibid., p. 236.
22. Ibid.
23. Ibid., p. 14.
24. Dickie writes that Kant's first *Critique* was meant "to respond to David Hume's skeptical views that we know objects external to our perception." *Century of Taste*, p. 88.
25. Thus, as David Lloyd stresses, a narrative of the organization of the senses proceeds in parallel with a narrative of the development of the human race. "Race under Representation," *Oxford Literary Review: Neocolonialism*, ed. Robert Young, 13: 1–2 (1991), 62–94.
26. Schiller, *Aesthetic Education*, p. 195.
27. Ibid. The translators and editors of the Oxford (1967) edition note that Schiller's depiction of the "higher senses" refers predominantly to the eye (p. 285).
28. Kant positions the Carib and Iroquois at the beginning of the stages of development. *Critique of Judgment*, p. 78.
29. Lloyd, "Race under Representation," p. 74.
30. Gikandi, "Aesthetic Reflection," p. 2.
31. Ibid., p. 3 and p. 4.
32. Ibid., p. 7.
33. Mario Relich, "Pope, Thackeray and Africana in Non-Standard English Playing Cards of the Restoration and Eighteenth Century," *Kunapipi*, 12: 1 (1990), 21.
34. By the 1760s, in London alone, this figure may have been as high as 15,000–20,000. Gretchen Gerzina, *Black London: Life before Emancipation* (New Brunswick, NJ: Rutgers University Press, 1995), p. 5 and Fryer, *Staying Power*, p. 68.
35. Fryer, *Staying Power*, p. 31.
36. Gerzina, *Black London*, p. 22 and pp. 22–23.
37. Simon Gikandi, "Race and the Idea of the Aesthetic" *Michigan Quarterly Review* (Spring 2001), 1–14.
38. Sander Gilman, "The Figure of the Black in German Aesthetic Theory," *Eighteenth-Century Studies*, 8: 4 (Summer 1975), 377. Glenn W. Most stresses also that the concept of the sublime, in the eighteenth century, identified increasingly with the subject experiencing it. "After the Sublime: Stations in the Career of an Emotion," *Yale Review*, 90: 2 (April 2002), 112–13.
39. Gilman, "Figure of the Black," p. 391.
40. For example, Sander Gilman, "Black Bodies, White Bodies: Toward an Iconography of Female Sexuality in Late Nineteenth-Century Medicine and Literature," *"Race," Writing and Difference*, ed. Henry Louis Gates, Jr. (Chicago and London: University of Chicago Press, 1986), pp. 223–61.
41. Lloyd, "Race under Representation," p. 68.

42. Robert Farris Thompson, *Flash of the Spirit: African and Afro-American Art and Philosophy* (New York: Random House, 1983), p. 5.
43. Gikandi offers a complex analysis of Frobenius's work and its implications for modernism in "Africa and the Epiphany of Modernism," *Geomodernisms: Race, Modernism, Modernity*, ed. Laura Doyle and Laura Winkiel (Bloomington and Indianapolis: Indiana University Press, 2005), pp. 31–50.
44. Roger Fry, "Negro Sculpture," *Vision and Design*, ed. J. B. Bullen (London and New York: Oxford University Press, 1990), p. 73 (essay originally published 1920).
45. We might read this double-bind of visuality as an example of what Aldon Nielsen has recently called the *mise en abyme* of modernity and diasporic blackness. "The Future of an Allusion: The Color of Modernity," *Geomodernisms*, ed. Doyle and Winkiel, pp. 17–30.
46. Shesgreen, *Engravings by Hogarth*, No. 19, Plate II.
47. Gikandi, "Race and the Idea of the Aesthetic."
48. Debates regarding the term *modernism* and its relationship as a movement in the arts to the larger historical span of *modernity* have been ongoing since, at least, the 1970s. The following citations highlight a few of the continuing turns in this discussion and indicate influences on modernist studies of Marxist, postcolonial, feminist, and cultural studies: Marshall Berman, *All That Is Solid Melts into Air* (London: Verso, 1983) and Perry Anderson's response in "Modernity and Revolution," *New Left Review* 144 (March–April 1984), 96–113; Frederic Jameson, "Modernism and Imperialism," *Nationalism, Colonialism, and Literature*, intro. Seamus Deane (Minneapolis: University of Minnesota Press, 1990), pp. 43–66; Alison Light, *Forever England: Femininity, Literature and Conservatism between the Wars* (London and New York: Routledge, 1991); Paul Gilroy, *The Black Atlantic: Modernity and Double Consciousness* (Cambridge, MA: Harvard University Press, 1993); Edward Said, *Culture and Imperialism* (New York: Knopf, 1994); Rita Felski, *The Gender of Modernity* (Cambridge, MA: Harvard University Press, 1995); Deborah Ryan, "The *Daily Mail* Ideal Homes Exhibition and Suburban Modernity, 1908–1951," Ph.D. thesis, University of East London, 1995; Elleke Boehmer *Colonial and Postcolonial Literature* (Oxford: Oxford University Press, 1995) and *Empire, the National, and the Postcolonial, 1890–1920* (Oxford University Press, 2002); and *Geomodernisms*, ed. Doyle and Winkiel, 2005.
49. See W. J. T. Mitchell, "The Pictorial Turn," in *Picture Theory* (Chicago and London: University of Chicago Press, 1994), and Martin Jay, "Introduction," *Vision in Context*, ed. Teresa Brennan and Martin Jay (New York and London: Routledge, 1996).
50. Mary Louise Pratt, *Imperial Eyes: Travel Writing and Transculturation* (London and New York: Routledge, 1992); Gilman, "Black Bodies, White Bodies"; David Spurr, *The Rhetoric of Empire: Colonial Discourse in Journalism, Travel Writing, and Imperial Administration* (Durham and London: Duke University Press, 1993).

51. Houston Baker, *Modernism and the Harlem Renaissance* (Chicago: University of Chicago Press, 1987), p. xvi and 8.
52. A number of critics have objected to Gilroy's influential book, *The Black Atlantic* for reasons ranging from Gilroy's privileging of African America at the expense of Africa and the Caribbean to his emphasis on male journeys. See, for example, several articles in *Research in African Literatures*, 27: 4 (Winter 1996), including those by Ntongela Masilea, Natasha Barnes, and Joan Dayan. Others include Laura Chrisman, "Journeying to Death: A Critique of Paul Gilroy's *The Black Atlantic*," *Black British Culture and Society: A Text Reader*, ed. and intro. Kwesi Owusu (London: Routledge, 2000), pp. 453–64; Charles Piot, "Atlantic Aporias: Africa and Gilroy's Black Atlantic," *South Atlantic Quarterly*, 100: 1 (2001), 155–70; Shalini Puri, *The Caribbean Postcolonial: Social Equality, Post-Nationalism, and Cultural Hybridity* (New York: Palgrave Macmillan, 2004), pp. 28–29; and Alison Donnell, *Twentieth-Century Caribbean Literature: Critical Moments in Anglophone Literary History* (London and New York: Routledge, 2006), pp. 77–80.
53. Fryer gives a detailed account of the incident and the legal proceedings in *Staying Power*, pp. 127–30.
54. Gilroy, *Black Atlantic*, pp. 13–14 and "Art of Darkness."
55. Tobias Döring, *Caribbean-English Passages: Intertextuality in a Postcolonial Tradition* (London and New York: Routledge, 2002), pp. 147–48. Taking another approach, in *The Art of Exclusion: Representing Blacks in the Nineteenth Century* (Washington: Smithsonian Institution Press, 1990), Albert Boime does not accept the status accorded the painting as art or as a powerful statement about slavery (p. 70). Marcus Wood, on the other hand, offers an extensive defense of Turner, the painting, and Ruskin's description of it. *Blind Memory: Visual Representations of Slavery in England and America 1780–1865* (London and New York: Routledge, 2000).
56. Gilroy, *Black Atlantic*, p. 16.
57. Ian Baucom, "Specters of the Atlantic," *South Atlantic Quarterly*, 100 (Winter 2001), 69.
58. Lee Jenkins discusses Philip's poems in *The Language of Caribbean Poetry* (Gainesville, FL: University of Florida Press, 2004), pp. 171–74. Lubaina Himid's series of paintings, titled *Revenge: A Masque in Five Tableaux*, are discussed by Alan Rice in *Radical Narratives of the Black Atlantic* (London and New York: Continuum, 2003), pp. 72–77.
59. Michelle Cliff, *Free Enterprise* (New York: Dutton, 1993), p. 105.
60. Orlando Patterson, *Freedom*, Vol. I: *Freedom in the Making of Western Culture* (New York: Basic Books, 1991).
61. Toni Morrison, *Playing in the Dark: Whiteness and the Literary Imagination* (Cambridge, MA: Harvard University Press, 1992), p. 38.
62. Susan Buck-Morss, "Hegel and Haiti," *Critical Inquiry*, 26: 4 (Summer 2000), 821. Recently, Laura Doyle has argued for the English Revolution of the 1640s as the "crucial first scene" of Western modernity when the rhetoric of race and freedom first began to merge. "Liberty, Race, and Larsen in Atlantic

Modernity: A New World Geneaology," *Geomodernisms*, ed. Doyle and Winkiel, pp. 51–76.

63. Thompson, *Flash of the Spirit*, p. 109.

64. David Dabydeen, *Turner* (London: Jonathan Cape, 1994), p. ix.

65. The cry "Nigger!" echoes, but in the past, the cry famously quoted by Frantz Fanon in the chapter titled "The Fact of Blackness," in *Black Skin, White Masks*, trans. Charles Lam Markmann (New York: Grove Weidenfeld, 1967), p. 109.

66. Evidence for such a character appears in Thomas Clarkson's *History of the Rise, Progress, and Accomplishment of the Abolition of the African Slave Trade*, published in a new edition in 1839. Boime cites Clarkson's book as making available to Turner an account of the *Zong* incident, evidently first told to Granville Sharp on March 19, 1783, by "an African who escaped the *Zong*" (*Art of Exclusion*, p. 67).

67. Fred D'Aguiar, *Feeding the Ghosts* (London: Chatto and Windus, 1997), p. 165.

68. Thompson, *Flash of the Spirit*, p. 28.

69. Araba Ekó, quoted in Thompson, *Flash of the Spirit*, p. 9.

70. Thompson, *Flash of the Spirit*, p. 21.

71. Sally and Richard Price, *Maroon Arts: Cultural Vitality in the African Diaspora* (Boston: Beacon Press, 1999), p. 285.

2 EXHIBITIONS/MODERNISMS 1900–1939

1. Dionne Brand, *Bread out of Stone: Recollections, Sex, Recognitions, Race, Dreaming, Politics* (Toronto: Coach House Press, 1994), p. 171.

2. V. S. Naipaul, *The Enigma of Arrival* (New York: Knopf, 1987), p. 7.

3. Colin Holmes, *John Bull's Island: Immigration and British Society, 1871–1971* (Basingstoke, Hampshire: Macmillan, 1988), p. 112.

4. Kwame Anthony Appiah, "Race," *Critical Terms for Literary Study*, ed. Frank Lentricchia and Thomas McLaughlin (Chicago and London: University of Chicago Press, 1990), pp. 274–87; Ian Baucom, *Out of Place: Englishness Empire, and the Locations of Identity* (Princeton, NJ: Princeton University Press, 1999); Gilroy, *Black Atlantic*.

5. Holmes, *John Bull's Island*, pp. 113–14.

6. Ibid.

7. Marcus Garvey, quoted in P. Olisanwuche Esedebe, *Pan-Africanism: The Idea and Movement*, 1776–1991, 2nd edition (Washington DC: Howard University Press, 1994), p. 81.

8. See David Killingray, " 'To do something for the race': Harold Moody and the League of Coloured Peoples," *West Indian Intellectuals in Britain*, ed. Bill Schwarz (Manchester: Manchester University Press, 2003), pp. 51–70.

9. David A. Vaughan, *Negro Victory: The Life Story of Dr. Harold Moody* (London: Independent Press, Ltd, 1950), p. 21.

10. Simon Gikandi, *Maps of Englishness: Writing Identity in the Culture of Colonialism* (New York: Columbia University Press, 1996), p. xiii.

11. Belinda Edmondson, *Making Men: Gender, Literary Authority, and Women's Writing in Caribbean Narrative* (Durham and London: Duke University Press, 1999), p. 36.

12. Gikandi, *Maps of Englishness*, p. xviii.

13. Baucom, *Out of Place*, p. 12.

14. Michael Dash and Chris Bongie also discuss the colonialist positioning of the Caribbean as "elsewhere." See Dash, *The Other America: Caribbean Literature in a New World Context* (Charlottesville and London: University Press of Virginia, 1998), p. 35. However, Carol Boyce Davies writes of "elsewhere" as a positive creation, indicating the extent to which writers, artists, and intellectuals from the Caribbean have transformed the significance of this imagined location. *Black Women, Writing and Identity: Migrations of the Subject* (London and New York: Routledge, 1994), p. 13.

15. Writing about Caribbean intellectuals in the USA, Michelle Ann Stephens makes a similar point, arguing for the "Red Summer" of 1919 as a "pivotal year." *Black Empire: The Masculine Global Imaginary of Caribbean Intellectuals in the United States, 1914–1962* (Durham and London: Duke University Press, 2005), p. 28.

16. Holmes, *John Bull's Island*, p. 108, and from a confidential police report cited by Fryer, *Staying Power*, p. 301.

17. *African Telegraph* (July–August 1919) 253. British Newspaper Library.

18. In *Art of Exclusion*, Boime documents the visual tradition of associating black people with animals, and in *Hogarth's Blacks*, Dabydeen gives many examples of the association with dogs made by English artists.

19. *African Telegraph* (December 1919) 302. British Newspaper Library.

20. Fryer, *Staying Power*, p. 318. See also Winston James, "A Race Outcast from an Outcast Class: Claude McKay's Experience and Analysis of Britain," *West Indian Intellectuals*, ed. Schwarz, pp. 71–92.

21. Quoted in J. A. Mangan, " 'The Grit of our Forefathers': Invented Traditions, Propaganda and Imperialism," *Imperialism and Popular Culture*, ed. John M. Mackenzie (Manchester: Manchester University Press, 1986), p. 130.

22. Mangan, "Grit," p. 132.

23. Ibid., p. 133.

24. Jeffrey Richards, "Boy's Own Empire: Feature Films and Imperialism in the 1930s," *Imperialism and Popular Culture*, ed. Mackenzie, p. 147.

25. "Foreword," *British Empire Exhibition 1924 Official Guide* (London: Fleetway Press, 1924). British Library. In this chapter, I am working with two versions of the guide. One was edited by G. C. Lawrence; the other is anonymously authored and contains the "Foreword" from which I quote here and the map reproduced in this chapter.

26. Jeffrey Green, *Black Edwardians: Black People in Britain, 1901–1914* (London and Portland, OR: Frank Cass, 1998), p. 3.

27. John M. Mackenzie, *Propaganda and Empire: The Manipulation of British Public Opinion, 1880–1960* (Manchester: Manchester University Press, 1984), p. 114.

28. Homi K. Bhabha, "Of Mimicry and Man: The Ambivalence of Colonial Discourse," *The Location of Culture* (London and New York: Routledge, 1994), pp. 85–92.
29. "Foreword," *British Empire Exhibition 1924 Official Guide.*
30. Krista A. Thompson discusses "Sunny Jamaica" as visually emblematic of "the market woman icon" that represented Jamaica from the 1890s through the 1920s. "'Black Skin, Blue Eyes': Visualizing Blackness in Jamaican Art, 1922–1944," *Small Axe*, 16 (September 2004), 7–8.
31. In *A History of Wembley* (UK: Brent Library Service, 1979), p. 188, Geoffrey Hewlett describes the Wembley exhibit as a (failed) "tonic for the empire." In *Propaganda and Empire*, p. 98, MacKenzie argues instead for the successful propagandistic power of the exhibition.
32. Roger Fry, "The Art of Florence," *Vision and Design* (Oxford: Oxford University Press, 1990), p. 124 (essay first published 1919).
33. Lawrence, *Official Guide to the British Empire Exhibition*, p. 57. British Library.
34. Ibid.
35. See the essays by Clive Bell in *Art* (New York: Frederick A. Stokes Company, 1913), especially "The Aesthetic Hypothesis," pp. 3–37, and by Roger Fry in *Vision and Design*, especially "An Essay in Aesthetics," pp. 12–27.
36. Bell, "Aesthetic Hypothesis," *Art*, p. 16.
37. Peter Stansky, *On or about December 1910: Early Bloomsbury and its Intimate World* (Cambridge, MA: Harvard University Press, 1996).
38. Fry, "The French Post-Impressionists," *Vision and Design*, p. 167 (essay first published 1912).
39. For a more detailed development of this argument, see Mary Lou Emery, "Woolf Re-Visits Wembley: Pre-War Bloomsbury Aesthetics and Interwar British Empire," in the on-line journal *Virginia Woolf: Across the Generations/ Selected Papers from the Twelfth Annual Conference on Virginia Woolf*, An Electronic Publication (Spring 2003), 29–40.
40. Virginia Woolf, *To the Lighthouse* (New York and London: Harcourt, Brace, Jovanovich, 1927), p. 53.
41. Hewlett, *History of Wembley*, p. 176.
42. For an extended analysis of this matrilineage and its simultaneous inclusion and exploitation of the working-class women in the novel, see Mary Lou Emery, "'Robbed of Meaning': The Work at the Center of *To the Lighthouse*," *Modern Fiction Studies*, 38: 1 (Spring 1992), 217–34 and repr. in *Twentieth-Century Literary Criticism*, Vol. 101 (Detroit: Gale Research Co., 2000), pp. 307–18.
43. Lawrence, *Official Guide*, pp. 44–45.
44. Mackenzie, *Propaganda and Empire*, p. 110.
45. Fryer, *Staying Power*, p. 324.
46. Imanuel Geiss, quoted in Fryer, *Staying Power*, p. 325.
47. Fryer, *Staying Power*, p. 325.
48. Jan Morris, *Farewell the Trumpets: An Imperial Retreat* (New York: Harcourt, Brace Jovanovich, 1978), p. 302.

49. Virginia Woolf, "Thunder at Wembley," *Collected Essays*, Vol. IV (New York: Harcourt, Brace and World, 1967), p. 185.

50. See Duncan Wilson, *Leonard Woolf: A Political Biography* (New York: St. Martin's Press, 1978) for discussion of Leonard Woolf's anti-imperialist writings and activities.

51. This reading of the Pan-African congresses as countervisions to Wembley supports Michelle Ann Stephens's argument in *Black Empire* for black inter- nationalism as a vision of global community or even, in Garvey's case, a counter-empire (pp. 4–5, 6, and 76).

52. Fryer, *Staying Power*, pp. 322–23.

53. Quoted in Esedebe, *Pan-Africanism*, p. 71.

54. Quoted in ibid., p. 74; Fryer, *Staying Power*, p. 324.

55. Quoted in David Boxer, *Edna Manley, Sculptor* (Kingston: National Gallery of Jamaica and Edna Manley Foundation, 1990), p. 10.

56. Marlene Nourbese Philip, "Social Barbarism and the Spoils of Modernism," *Frontiers: Essays and Writings on Racism and Culture, 1984–1992* (Stratford, Ontario: Mercury Press, 1992), p. 97. See also Mariana Torgovnick, *Gone Primitive: Savage Intellects, Modern Lives* (Chicago: University of Chicago Press, 1990); Hal Foster, "The 'Primitive' Unconscious of Modern Art, or White Skin Black Masks," *Recodings: Art, Spectacle, Cultural Politics* (Port Townsend, Washington: Bay Press, 1985), pp. 181–208; and James Clifford, "Histories of the Tribal and the Modern," *The Predicament of Culture: Twentieth-Century Ethnography, Literature, and Art* (Cambridge, MA: Harvard University Press, 1988), pp. 189–214.

57. Sieglinde Lemke, *Primitivist Modernism: Black Culture and the Origins of Transatlantic Modernism* (Oxford and New York: Oxford University Press, 1998).

58. Simon Gikandi, "Picasso, Africa, and the Schemata of Difference," *Modernism/Modernity*, 10: 3 (September 2003), 471. Aldon Nielsen has recently reminded us of arguments made by black intellectuals as early as the 1920s concerning the dependency of modernist visual, literary, and musi- cal arts on Africa and its diaspora. "The Future of an Allusion: The Color of Modernity," *Geomodernisms*, ed. Doyle and Winkiel, pp. 17–30.

59. Wayne Brown, *Edna Manley: The Private Years, 1900–1938* (London: Deutsch, 1975), p. 167.

60. Quoted in ibid., p. 183.

61. Quoted in ibid., p. 183 and p. 184.

62. This fuller sense of movement, represented in a female figure created by a woman artist, makes this sculpture an exception to Michelle Stephens's argument that the emphasis on movement in black internationalism is an exclusively masculine image of freedom and mobility. See *Black Empire*, pp. 8, 19, and 20. Stephens omits any mention of Manley or Una Marson, or from an earlier period, Mary Seacole, all Jamaican women whose identities were largely shaped through geographical, cultural, and political movement.

63. Quoted in Brown, *Edna Manley*, p. 226.

64. Quoted in Boxer, *Edna Manley*, p. 25.

65. *Edna Manley: The Diaries*, ed. Rachel Manley (Kingston, Jamaica: Heinemann Publishers, Caribbean, 1989), p. 203.
66. Nadine Althea Scott, "Fine Art as an Expression of Religion in the Jamaican Culture: Implications for Art Education," Ph.D. thesis, Ohio State University, 1991.
67. Annie Paul, "Uninstalling the Nation: The Dilemma of Contemporary Jamaican Art," *Small Axe*, 6 (September 1999), 57–78.
68. Robert Farris Thompson, *Face of the God: Art and Altars of Africa and the African Americas* (New York : Museum for African Art, 1993).
69. Veerle Poupeye, *Caribbean Art* (London: Thames and Hudson, 1998), p. 75.
70. Paul, "Uninstalling the Nation," p. 61.
71. David Boxer, "Introducing Fifteen Intuitives," *Fifteen Intuitives, Exhibition Catalogue, National Gallery of Jamaica, July 12–October 31, 1987*, p. 2.
72. Interview conducted by Emery with Poupeye at the National Gallery, Kingston, Jamaica, July 8, 2002.
73. Andrea N. Douglas makes a similar point from a different angle when she states in a subsequent issue of *Small Axe* that "At stake in both Boxer's and Poupeye's narrative and Paul's criticism of Jamaica's art institution is the idea of authenticity." "Facing the Nation: Art History and Art Criticism in the Jamaican Context," *Small Axe*, 16 (September 2004), 56.
74. David Boxer, "The Life of Edna Manley (1900–1987)," *Fifty Years – Fifty Artists: 1950–2000, The School of Visual Arts*, ed. Petrine Archer-Straw (Kingston, Jamaica: Ian Randle Publishers, 2000), p. 13; Archer-Straw, "Vision and Design: Where Nationalism Meets Arts and Crafts," *Fifty Years – Fifty Artists*, pp. 17–27.
75. Poupeye, *Caribbean Art*, p. 74.
76. Joseph Clarke, "Caribbean Modernism and the Postcolonial Social Contract in Voyage in the Dark," *Journal of Caribbean Literatures*, 3: 3 (Summer 2003), 1–16.
77. Other critics have faulted the masculinity of these icons of the nation, a critique addressed by Krista A. Thompson, who recognizes that Manley "had to negotiate both colonial icons of Jamaica and colonial hierarchies of art," and that, in celebrating the black male worker, Manley's sculptures turned away completely from earlier tourist images of market women. " 'Black Skin, Blue Eyes,' " 28–30.
78. Thomas C. Holt, *The Problem of Freedom: Race, Labor, and Politics in Jamaica and Britain, 1832–1938* (Baltimore: Johns Hopkins University Press, 1992).
79. Cynthia Moody, "Ronald Moody (1900–1984)," Unpublished Manuscript, April 1995, Tate Gallery Archive, p. 1.
80. Sadler was also the publisher who, in 1934, published Jean Rhys's *Voyage in the Dark*, but only after insisting that she rewrite the ending "to give the girl a chance" and keep the novel from being too depressing. Nancy Hemond Brown, "Jean Rhys and *Voyage in the Dark*," *London Magazine* 25, 1 and 2 (April/May 1985), 40–59.
81. Michael Sadler, "Preface," *"Negro Art" Exhibition Catalogue, Adams Gallery, January 19–February 16, 1935*. Tate Gallery Library.

82. For example, William Rubin, *"Primitivism" in Twentieth-Century Art: Affinity of the Tribal and the Modern* (New York: Museum of Modern Art, 1984).

83. Brown, *Edna Manley*, pp. 187–88.

84. "Ronald Moody Talks . . . Sculpting," National Gallery Archives, Kingston, Jamaica.

85. Tate Collections June 7, 2000 http://www.tatenet.tate/servlet/.

86. Rasheed Araeen, "In the Citadel of Modernism," *The Other Story: Afro-Asian Artists in Post-War Britain* (London: Hayward Gallery, South Bank Centre, 1989), p. 16.

87. Ronald Moody, "The 'Wheel' Within," Ronald Moody Papers, Tate Gallery Archive.

88. On a list written in 1973 of works to be included in an exhibit, Moody lists *Johanaan* and then notes "Idea: The Spiritual Man." Ronald Moody Papers, Tate Gallery Archive.

89. Boxer, *Edna Manley*, pp. 24–25.

90. Manley's sculptures exceed the categories used by Hazel Carby to describe the appropriation of black male bodies in service to "modernist strategies of inwardness and the satisfaction of individual desire." *Race Men* (Cambridge, MA: Harvard University Press, 1998), p. 74. Instead, they represent simultaneously an inward awakening and the anticipation of collective action.

91. Denys J. Wilcox, *The London Group 1913–1939: The Artists and their Works* (Aldershot, England: Scolar Press; Brookfield, VT: Ashgate Publishing Co., 1995), p. 112.

92. Claude McKay, *Banjo: A Story without a Plot* (London, New York, and San Diego: Harvest/HBJ, 1929), p. 130.

93. In "Caribbean Models for Modernism in the Work of Claude McKay and Jean Rhys," *Modernism/Modernity*, 11: 2 (April 2004), 219–38, Leah Rosenberg also addresses "the scene of posing" in these novels (p. 222).

94. Jean Rhys, *After Leaving Mr. Mackenzie* (New York: Random House, Vintage Books, 1974 [orig. 1931]), p. 52.

95. Williams, quoted in Gikandi, "Picasso, Africa," p. 455.

96. Duncan Grant, Letter to Vanessa Bell, February 11, 1930, The Charleston Papers, Special Collections, University of Sussex Library. On February 5, 1930, Vanessa had written the following to Duncan: "This is more or less my new composition [sketch of three female nudes]. The middle figure is going to be a negress and I hope Brinkworth will pose for her" (350). Regina Marler, the editor of Bell's letters, identifies Brinkworth as "another model." *Selected Letters of Vanessa Bell*, ed. Regina Marler (New York: Pantheon Books, 1993), p. 349.

97. Virginia Woolf, *A Room of One's Own* (London: Penguin, 1928), p. 52.

98. Frances Spalding, *British Art Since 1900* (London: Thames and Hudson, 1986), p. 63.

99. Charles Harrison, *English Art and Modernism, 1900–1939* (London: Allen Lane; Bloomington, IN: Indiana University Press, 1981).

100. Wilcox, *London Group*, pp. 112–113.

101. Dennis Farr and Alan Bowness, "Historical Note," *London Group 1914–64 Jubilee Exhibition, Fifty Years of British Art Exhibition Catalogue, Tate Gallery, July 15–August 16, 1964*, Tate Gallery Library.
102. As a small exception to these striking omissions, Wilcox's *London Group* does include Manley's name in the list of artists showing their work in the Selfridges exhibit and includes a brief biography. Though omitting mention of her success in this period, Wilcox at least represents the record accurately.
103. As recently as 1996, in an essay written for the Tate Gallery exhibition, "Picturing Blackness in British Art, 1700s–1990s," Paul Gilroy omits Edna Manley's work, though he includes that of Ronald Moody. On the other hand, Edna Manley (but not Ronald Moody) is included in Richard J. Powell's *Black Art and Culture in the Twentieth Century* (New York: Thames and Hudson, 1997).
104. Fry, "Negro Sculpture," *Vision and Design*, p. 73.
105. Fry, "Negro Art," *Last Lectures by Roger Fry*, intro. Kenneth Clark (Boston: Beacon Press, 1934), pp. 75–84.
106. See Wilcox, *London Group*, pp. 14–24, for a discussion of Fry and the "Bloomsbury domination" of the London Group during the 1920s and early 1930s.
107. In *Caribbean Art*, Poupeye includes both Manley and Moody in a diasporic approach to the Caribbean. Though differentiating Moody from Manley by his lack of a "nationalist agenda," she notes the stylistic similarity of Moody's work to carvings by Manley (79).

3 EXILE/CARIBBEAN EYES 1928–1963

1. Homi K. Bhabha, "Introduction," *The Location of Culture* (London and New York: Routledge, 1994), p. 6.
2. For biographies of James and Marson, see Anna Grimshaw, "Introduction: C. L. R. James: A Revolutionary Vision for the Twentieth Century," *C. L. R. James Reader*, ed. Anna Grimshaw (Oxford and Cambridge, MA.: Blackwell, 1992); Kent Worcester, *C. L. R. James: A Political Biography* (Albany, NY: State University of New York Press, 1996); Delia Jarrett-Macauley, *The Life of Una Marson, 1905–65* (Manchester and New York: Manchester University Press, 1998).
3. Reinhard Sander, *The Trinidad Awakening: West Indian Literature of the Nineteen-Thirties* (New York: Greenwood Press, 1988), p. 25.
4. Hazel Carby, "Proletarian or Revolutionary Literature? C. L. R. James and the Politics of the Trinidadian Renaissance," *Cultures in Babylon: Black Britain and African America* (London: Verso, 1999), pp. 135–45.
5. For more on links between James's work and writers of the Harlem Renaissance, see Cynthia Hamilton, "A Way of Seeing: Culture as Political Expression in the Works of C. L. R. James," pp. 429–43, and Helen Pyne-Timothy, "Identity, Society, and Meaning: A Study of the Early Short Stories

of C. L. R. James," pp. 51–60, in *C. L. R. James, His Intellectual Legacies*, ed. Selwyn R. Cudjoe and William E. Cain (Amherst: University of Massachusetts Press, 1995).

6. Paget Henry, *Caliban's Reason: Introducing Afro-Caribbean Philosophy* (New York: Routledge, 2000), p. 53.

7. C. L. R. James, "La Divina Pastora," *James Reader*, ed. Grimshaw, pp. 25–28.

8. For example, Aldon Lynn Neilsen, *C. L. R. James: A Critical Introduction* (Jackson, MS: University Press of Mississippi, 1997), p. 12 and p. 18.

9. C. L. R. James, "Triumph," *James Reader*, ed. Grimshaw, pp. 29–40.

10. Eric Keenaghan, " 'His Eyes Almost Fell through the Crease': Using Voyeurism and Sexuality to Ascertain the Modernist Attributes of C. L. R. James's *Minty Alley*," *Schuykill* 2:1 (1998), 3.

11. C. L. R. James, *Minty Alley* (London: New Beacon Books, 1971 and Mississippi: University Press of Mississippi, 1997), p. 24.

12. H. Adlai Murdoch, "James's Literary Dialectic: Colonialism and Cultural Space in *Minty Alley*," *C. L. R. James*, ed. Cudjoe and Cain, p. 67.

13. For a discussion of *Minty Alley* as an experiment with the *bildüngsroman* form, see Nicole King, *C. L. R. James and Creolization: Circles of Influence* (Jackson, MS: University Press of Mississippi, 2001).

14. Bhabha, "Of Mimicry and Man: The Ambivalence of Colonial Discourse," *Location*, p. 88.

15. Paul Buhle describes this passage as a "sidelight" on the "rise of the Black middle class." *C. L. R. James: The Artist as Revolutionary* (London and New York: Verso, 1988), pp. 32–33.

16. Alison Donnell discusses fully the period of 1900–1945 in Jamaican poetry and argues for a reassessment of its importance to the study of Caribbean literature. *Twentieth-Century Caribbean Literature*, Chapter 1.

17. Giovanna Covi has recently stressed the broad yet rooted cosmopolitanism of Marson's work and life ("Refiguring Diasporic Agency: Una Marson, Afro-Jamaican New Woman," Paper presented at the Seventh Annual Modernist Studies Association Conference, Loyola University, November 2005).

18. Jarrett-Macauley, *Una Marson*, p. 41.

19. Alison Donnell, "Contradictory (W)omens?: Gender Consciousness in the Poetry of Una Marson," *The Routledge Reader in Caribbean Literature*, ed. Alison Donnell and Sarah Lawson Welsh (London and New York: Routledge, 1996), p. 189. In a more recent discussion of Marson's poetry, Donnell refers to her strategies as a "double-agency." *Twentieth-Century Caribbean Literature*, pp. 156–62. Denise deCaires Narain questions the tendency to find subversion in Marson's poems, finding some of them awkwardly imitative, but concludes that, overall, the poems present a complex array of voices and forms including those of resistance and subversion. *Contemporary Caribbean Women's Poetry: Making Style* (London and New York: Routledge, 2002), pp. 1–29.

20. J. E. Clare McFarlane, "The Value of Right Reading," *Cosmopolitan*, 1: 4 (August 1928), 100, Una Marson Papers, National Library of Jamaica.

21. Bhabha, "Of Mimicry and Man," *Location*, p. 86.

22. Una Marson, "In Vain," *Routledge Reader*, ed. Donnell and Welsh, p. 128.

23. J. E. Clare McFarlane, "The Fleet of the Empire," *Routledge Reader*, ed. Donnell and Welsh, p. 49.

24. Erika S. Smilowitz " 'Weary of Life and All My Heart's Dull Pain': The Poetry of Una Marson," *Critical Issues in West Indian Literature*, ed. Erika S. Smilowitz and Roberta Q. Knowles (Parkersburg, IA: Caribbean Books, 1984), pp. 19–32.

25. Una Marson, "Summer Days," *Tropic Reveries: Poems by Una Marson* (Kingston, Jamaica: Published by the Author, 1930), p. 13. British Library.

26. Hope's poem was set to music by the English composer Amy Woodforde-Finden and appeared in sheet music as one of "Four Indian Love Lyrics from 'The Garden of Kama' by Laurence Hope" (London; New York: Boosey and Co., 1903).

27. Artistic, "Kismet – A Review," *Cosmopolitan* (June–July 1930), 53, Una Marson Papers.

28. Mary Lago, *Rabindranath Tagore: Perspectives in Time* (Houndmills, Basingstoke: Macmillan, 1989), p. 24.

29. Ibid.

30. Rabindranath Tagore, *Gitanjali*, intro. W. B. Yeats (New York: Scribner, 1913), Song 45, p. 61.

31. Elleke Boehmer, *Empire, the National, and the Postcolonial, 1890–1920: Resistance in Interaction* (Oxford and New York: Oxford University Press, 2002).

32. Rev. J. Leslie Webb, "On Being a Cosmopolitan," *Cosmopolitan*, 1: 6 (October 1928), 165, Una Marson Papers.

33. Quoted in Boehmer, *Empire*, p. 23.

34. Una Marson, "Renunciation," *Routledge Reader*, ed. Donnell and Welsh, p. 128.

35. Philip M. Sherlock, "Introduction," *The Moth and the Star* by Una Marson (Kingston, Jamaica: published by the author, 1937), pp. x–xix. The British Library.

36. Frantz Fanon, *Black Skin, White Masks* (New York: Grove Press, 1967), p. 109.

37. deCaires Narain, *Contemporary Caribbean Women's Poetry*, p. 24.

38. C. L. R. James also addressed the cinema and its degrading effects on body image in a short story titled "The Star that Would Not Shine." It first appeared in the *Beacon* in 1931 and was reprinted in *At the Rendezvous of Victory* (London: Allison and Busby, 1984), pp. 9–12.

39. James changed the spelling of L'Ouverture for the title, omitting the apostrophe to signal that Toussaint was deliberately "naming himself rather than accept[ing] a name given to him by the French." Selwyn Cudjoe, "C. L. R. James Misbound," *Transition under Review*, 58 (n.d.), 124–36.

40. For example, the introduction to the *Cambridge Guide to African and Caribbean Theatre* neglects Marson in favor of James, claiming that "[n]ew ground was broken" with the production of *Toussaint Louverture* in London. Oddly, in a specific entry on Marson, the *Guide* then describes her as "the most significant playwright of the 1930s." Martin Banham, Errol Hill, and

George Woodyard, eds., *Cambridge Guide to African and Caribbean Theatre* (Cambridge: Cambridge University Press, 1994), p. 142 and p. 200.

41. Kole Omotoso, *The Theatrical into Theatre: A Study of the Drama and Theatre of the English-Speaking Caribbean* (London and Port of Spain: New Beacon Books, 1982), p. 62.

42. Una Marson, *At What a Price: A Jamaican Play in Four Acts* (in collaboration with Horace D. Vaz), III.1. British Library Manuscript Collection. Subsequent play citations will appear in parentheses in the text, indicating the act and scene in which the line appears and, where possible, the manuscript page number.

43. The cast is listed by name and nationality in a review published in the *Keys* 1: 3 (January 1934), p. 50, The Schomburg Center for Research in Black Culture Library, New York. Marson played the lead female character, and Harold Moody played the father.

44. Reviews of *At What a Price* in the *Keys* mention positive reviews in the *Manchester Guardian* and *West Africa*. I have not been able to locate any other reviews or references to them. James's play, on the other hand, was reviewed in the major and many of the minor English papers, as well as some from Glasgow and Malta.

45. *Daily Mail*, London (March 17, 1936) #2048, C. L. R. James Institute, New York.

46. *Time and Tide* (March 21, 1936), C. L. R. James Institute.

47. *Observer* (March 22, 1936), C. L. R. James Institute.

48. Simon Callow, "Voodoo Macbeth," *Rhapsodies in Black: Art of the Harlem Renaissance*, exhibition devised by Richard A. Powell and David A. Bailey; catalog ed. Joanna skipworth (Berkeley, Los Angeles, and London: Hayward Gallery, Institute of International Visual Arts, South Bank Centre, 1997), p. 41.

49. Gertrude Stein's opera, *Four Saints in Three Acts*, was produced in 1934 in New York, also with an all-black cast. According to Simon Callow, the cast was chosen by Virgil Thomson "for no other reason than that Thomson thought them more aesthetically pleasing." Ibid., p. 36.

50. Jarrett-Macauley, *Una Marson*, p. 70 and p. 129.

51. Ibid., p. 73.

52. For a discussion of the West Indian market woman as icon for the Jamaican tourist and fruit industries, see Thompson, " 'Black Skin, Blue Eyes,' " pp. 1–31.

53. Una Marson, *London Calling*, unpublished manuscript, Una Marson Papers, MS 1944B, p. 3 of Act I, Scene 1.

54. Richard D. E. Burton describes a number of slave uprisings as "originally timed to coincide with Christmas" and especially stresses the revolt organized by Samuel Sharpe in Christmas of 1831, along with earlier uprisings in 1816 and 1823. *Afro-Creole: Power, Opposition, and Play in the Caribbean* (Ithaca and London: Cornell University Press, 1997), p. 85. The political role of carnival in the Caribbean has long been debated. For recent comments on these debates in the context of theatre, see Tejumola Olaniyan, *Scars of Conquest/Masks of Resistance: The Invention of Cultural Identities in African, African-American, and Caribbean Drama* (New York and Oxford: Oxford University Press, 1995),

pp. 25–28, and Shalini Puri, *The Caribbean Postcolonial.* Puri analyzes Derek Walcott's play *Pantomine* as a "transposition of Carnival into theater" (p. 115), a phrase that might also describe the improvised performance in Marson's much earlier play.

55. Burton, *Afro-Creole*, p. 76.

56. See ibid., pp. 66–67, for a full discussion of *Jonkonnu*.

57. Burton notes one of these plays, described by Erroll Hill, as starring Henri IV of France and also notes modified and "rude representations" of Richard III. Ibid., p. 78n.

58. *Keys*, 2: 3 (January–March 1935), 83. Schomburg Library.

59. Boxer, *Edna Manley*, p. 57.

60. Leah Rosenberg, "Una Marson's *Pocomania* (1938): Class, Gender, and the Pitfalls of Cultural Nationalism," *Essays in Theatre*, 20: 1 (November 2001), 38.

61. Una Marson, *Pocomania*, unpublished manuscript 1944B, II.1, p. 18, Una Marson Papers. As Rosenberg notes, the play manuscript appears in one complete draft plus several fragments. "Una Marson's *Pocomania*," p. 39, n. 1. The playbill for the performance shows a different order for the scenes in Act III than appears in the complete draft, indicating that the actual performance script is not available. However, we can assume that the complete draft comes very close, and the differences in scene order in Act III would not be likely to affect the staging devices that are central to my analysis. Unless otherwise indicated, I follow and cite the complete draft. An excerpt from *Pocomania*, Act I, Scene 1, has been published in *The Whistling Bird: Women Writers of the Caribbean*, ed. Elaine Campbell and Pierette Frickey (Boulder, CO, and London: Lynne Rienner, 1998; and Kingston, Jamaica: Ian Randle, 1998), pp. 131–38.

62. Grimshaw, "Introduction," *James Reader*, p. 6.

63. Anna Grimshaw's decision to publish the 1967, revised version in the *C. L. R. James Reader* in the section devoted to Britain in the 1930s met with some controversy. Selwyn Cudjoe published a review ("C. L. R. James Misbound"), in which he states that Dexter Lindersay revised the play, rather than James, and he criticizes the selection as "highly unrepresentative of James's intellectual position and his power as a dramatist in 1936" (134). In an email correspondence dated November 28, 2002, the late Jim Murray, who was then director of the C. L. R. James Institute, stated that James "authorized" the 1967 play with his signature. The 1967 version, first produced at the University of Ibadan, Nigeria, was staged again in 1982 in Kingston, Jamaica, by the Graduate Theatre Company of the Jamaica School of Drama, and then in 1986 by Yvonne Brewster of the Talawa Theatre Company at the Riverside Studios, London.

I am working in this chapter with three versions of the 1936 play and with the playbill. Two play versions are full-length typescripts, and the third is Act II, Scene 1, which James published in the Spring 1936 issue of *Life and Letters*. In James's "Author's Note" on the playbill, he states that "The play was conceived four years ago and was completely finished by the autumn of 1934."

The two typescripts, then, may have been composed anytime between 1932 and 1934. They are similar to one another, yet contain some differences which allow me to speculate that the one labeled "Original Typescript" and contained in the Special Collections Library at the University of the West Indies in St. Augustine, Trinidad, is a slightly later version of the other, held among the Richard Wright Papers in the Beinecke Library at Yale University. The St. Augustine script is very similar to the Beinecke script but has added handwritten corrections and minor revisions and also, in at least one place, added stage directions. The list of scenes and characters on the playbill indicates that some of the scenes contained in these typescripts were omitted for the performance. The scene published in *Life and Letters* appears in both typescripts and on the playbill; however, it has been revised and differs somewhat from both typescripts. I believe that the *Life and Letters* scene must be the closest to the actual performance script since it appeared in print during the season of the play performance. Therefore, when referring to or quoting from this scene, I cite the *Life and Letters* publication (as LL within the text). Otherwise, I quote from the St. Augustine manuscript, which I believe is a slightly revised version of the typescript in the Wright Papers.

64. In the playscript held in the Richard Wright Papers at the Beinecke Library, Boukman's gesture of ripping off the cross hanging around his neck is absent in the stage directions for this scene. Since I believe that this version predates the playscript held in the West Indies Collection at the University of the West Indies, St. Augustine, Trinidad, I am assuming it was added to the revised version for the performance.

65. One of the songs offered to Legba, guardian of the gateways in Haitian vodun, repeats the phrase, "ouvri barié pou moin," meaning "open the gate for me." Michel S. Laguerre, *Voodoo Heritage* (London and Beverly Hills: Sage Publications, 1980), p. 48.

66. Carolyn Cooper, "'Something Ancestral Recaptured': Spirit Possession as Trope in Selected Feminist Fictions of the African Diaspora," *Motherlands: Black Women's Writing from Africa, the Caribbean and South Asia*, ed. Susheila Nasta (London: Women's Press Ltd, 1991), p. 66.

67. Leah Rosenberg points out the significance of Marson's attempt to make this bridge in the year when members of the Jamaican middle and professional classes, such as Norman Manley and Alexander Bustamante, were attempting to speak for the workers and gain positions as national leaders. "Una Marson's *Pocomania*," p. 29.

68. The *Cosmopolitan* was billed as "A Monthly Magazine for the Business Youth of Jamaica" and "the Official Organ of the Stenographers' Association."

69. "Interview with George Lamming," *Kas-Kas*, ed. Ian Munro and Reinhard Sander (Austin, TX: African and Afro-American Research Institute, 1972), p. 16.

70. Fryer documents the post-World War II emigration from the Caribbean to Britain in *Staying Power*, Chapters 10 and 11.

71. George Lamming, *The Pleasures of Exile* (Ann Arbor: University of Michigan Press, 1992 [1960]), p. 214.

72. Anne Walmsley, *The Caribbean Artists Movement, 1966–1972: A Literary and Cultural History* (London: New Beacon Books, 1992), p. 6. See also Glyne Griffith, " 'This Is London Calling the West Indies': The BBC's *Caribbean Voices,*" *West Indian Intellectuals in Britain*, ed. Bill Schwarz (Manchester and New York: Manchester University Press, 2003), pp. 196–208.

73. Lamming, "The Sovereignty of the Imagination: An Interview with George Lamming" by David Scott, *Small Axe*, 6: 2 (2002), 86.

74. Jarrett-Macauley, *Una Marson*, p. 159.

75. David Ellis, " 'The Produce of More Than One Country': Race, Identity, and Discourse in Post-Windrush Britain," *Journal of Narrative Theory* 31: 2 (Summer 2001), 220.

76. Gordon Rohlehr, "The Problem of the Problem of Form," *The Shape of that Hurt and Other Essays* (Port of Spain, Trinidad: Longman Trinidad Limited, 1992 [1983]), p. 8.

77. Quoted in Simon Gikandi, *Writing in Limbo: Modernism and Caribbean Literature* (Ithaca, NY: Cornell University Press, 1992), p. 5.

78. Mervyn Morris, "The Poet as Novelist," *The Islands in Between: Essays on West Indian Literature*, ed. Louis James (London and Ibadan: Oxford University Press, 1968), p. 77.

79. Peter Hulme, "Reading from Elsewhere: George Lamming and the Paradox of Exile," *The Tempest and Its Travels*, ed. Peter Hulme and William Sherman (Philadelphia: University of Pennsylvania Press, 2000), p. 132.

80. Gikandi, *Writing in Limbo*, p. 5.

81. Janet Butler, "The Existentialism of George Lamming: The Early Development of a Writer," *Caribbean Review* 11 (Fall 1982), 15 and 38–39.

82. Lamming, "Interview," Scott, p. 87.

83. Mary Chamberlain stresses the importance of this conference to Lamming's development in "George Lamming," *West Indian Intellectuals*, ed. Schwarz, pp. 180–82.

84. Lamming, "Interview," Scott, p. 87.

85. For descriptions of vodun rituals, see Zora Neale Hurston, *Tell My Horse* (Philadelphia and New York: J. B. Lippincott, 1938) and Thompson, *Flash of the Spirit*.

86. George Lamming, *Season of Adventure* (London: Michael Joseph, 1960), p. 25.

87. George Lamming, *In the Castle of My Skin* (New York, Toronto, and London: McGraw-Hill, 1953), p. 69.

88. Sartre's *Being and Nothingness* was published in its entirety in English in 1953, a year before *The Emigrants* appeared. In the chapter titled "The Look," Sartre explains that through the look of the Other, the Self simultaneously recognizes the subjectivity of the Other and discovers itself. *Being and Nothingness*, trans. and intro. Hazel Barnes (New York: Washington Square Press, 1953), pp. 340–400.

89. James D. Herbert, *Paris 1937: Worlds on Exhibition* (Ithaca and London: Cornell University Press, 1998), figure 7.

90. George Lamming, *The Emigrants* (London and New York: Allison and Busby, 1980 [1954]), p. 14.

91. Jean Rhys, *Voyage in the Dark* (New York: Popular Library, n.d. [1934]), p. 160.
92. Quoted in Patrick Taylor, *The Narrative of Liberation: Perspectives on Afro-Caribbean Literature, Popular Culture, and Politics* (Ithaca and London: Cornell University Press, 1989), p. 196.
93. For discussions of the violence against women in Lamming's fiction, see Supriya Nair, *Caliban's Curse: George Lamming and the Revisioning of History* (Ann Arbor: University of Michigan Press, 1996); A. J. Simoes da Silva, *The Luxury of Nationalist Despair: George Lamming's Fiction as Decolonizing Project* (Amsterdam and Atlanta, GA: Rodopi, 2000); and Taylor, *The Narrative of Liberation*.
94. The shifts from narrative prose to dramatic dialogue in *The Emigrants* and *In the Castle of My Skin* indicate the influence of poetic theatre, including the verse plays of T. S. Eliot, which had a major impact on Lamming during the 1950s ("Interview," Scott, p. 107). In this influence from a major high modernist in a decade following those associated with high modernism, we see the blurring of boundaries between various modernisms rather than a distinct division between, for example, Anglo-European modernism and Caribbean modernism.
95. Lamming, *Emigrants*, p. 67.
96. Janet Butler ("Existentialism of George Lamming") has discussed the pervasive influence of Sartre's *Nausea* and *Being and Nothingness* on Lamming's first novel *In the Castle of My Skin*, focusing on notions of bad faith, responsibility, and personal freedom. These influences are also everywhere in *The Emigrants* and *Season of Adventure*, especially in their portrayals of the alienating effects of sight.
97. Quoted by Martin Jay in his discussion of *Nausea* in the context of theories of visuality. "Sartre, Merleau-Ponty, and the Search for a New Ontology of Sight," *Modernity and the Hegemony of Vision*, ed. David Michael Levin, (Berkeley, Los Angeles, and London: University of California Press, 1993), p. 153.
98. Sartre, *Being and Nothingness*, pp. 347–65 and elsewhere.
99. Ibid., p. 365.
100. Sander Gilman, *Difference and Pathology: Stereotypes of Sexuality, Race and Madness* (Ithaca: Cornell University Press, 1985); Anne McClintock, *Imperial Leather: Race, Gender and Sexuality in the Colonial Contest* (New York and London: Routledge, 1995).
101. Lévi-Strauss quoted in Simone de Beauvoir, *The Second Sex*. trans. and ed. H. M. Parshley (New York: Vintage Books, 1974) [orig English pub. 1952], p. 80.
102. Lamming, *Pleasures of Exile*, p. 10.
103. Supriya Nair emphasizes the importance of the vodun rituals in *Season of Adventure* and as a trope for reinventing history in *The Pleasures of Exile*. In discussing the vèvè, she describes them as a resistant "code language" rather than as visual art (*Caliban's Curse*, p. 120).
104. Lamming accurately quotes the passage in which Miranda states that she has taught Caliban to speak. However, Lamming prefaces the quote by stating

that, though spoken by Miranda, the words are "obviously the thought and vocabulary of her father" (109).

105. See Nadi Edwards, "George Lamming's Literary Nationalism: Language between *The Tempest* and the Tonelle," for an overview of the importance of language in Lamming's work to the constitution and dismantling of colonial relationships. *Small Axe*, 6: 1 (2002), 59–76.

106. See Helen Tiffin for Lamming's use of the Ceremony of Souls as model for experiments with language and form. "The Novels of George Lamming: Finding a Language for Post-Colonial Fiction," *Essays on Contemporary Post-Colonial Fiction*, ed. Hedwig Bock and Albert Wertheim (Munich: Max Hueber, 1986), pp. 253–74.

107. Lamming, *Season of Adventure*, p. 25.

108. In the interview with Scott, Lamming reaffirms his allegiance to a Hegelian notion of negation and describes this process in Fola: "There are many stages of a journey that Fola makes to becoming at the end the Fola that she wants to be; and then of course this seed of negation all the time" (p. 156).

109. Gordon Rohlehr analyzes the character of Fola as one who undergoes, through the Ceremony of Souls, an archetypal interior descent into the unconscious that is, simultaneously, a state of possession by Legba, the Caribbean god of the crossroads. "Possession as Metaphor: Lamming's *Season of Adventure*," *The Shape of that Hurt*, pp. 66–96.

110. Lamming has said that the love affair between Chiki and Fola "gets broken" because "they may in fact be family" and notes that "what that does too is to break the possibility of any sentimentality clinching the relationship" ("Interview," Scott, p. 156).

111. The rape, commited by Chiki's friend, Powell, echoes the rape of Agnes by the black man who may be Chiki's brother. Thus, the male characters double one another, Powell acting as a kind of "secret sharer" to both Chiki's character and the persona of the "author" who, in a note inserted into the narrative, claims Powell as his half-brother.

112. Lamming, "Interview," Scott, p. 157.

113. Hall, "C. L. R. James: A Portrait," *C. L. R. James's Caribbean*, ed. Henry and Buhle, p. 15.

114. Hazel Carby has written that *Beyond a Boundary* is "one of the most outstanding works of cultural studies ever produced" (quoted by Neil Lazarus, p. 342). Lazarus, "Cricket and National Culture in the Writings of C. L. R. James," *Liberation Cricket: West Indies Cricket Culture* ed. Hilary McD. Beckles and Brian Stoddart (Manchester and New York: Manchester University Press), pp. 342–55.

115. C. L. R. James, *Beyond a Boundary* (Durham: Duke University Press, 1993), p. 3.

116. C. L. R. James, "What Is Art?" *Beyond a Boundary*, p. 199.

117. In his stress on movement and real-world action as art, James joins other colonial critics of Western modernist aesthetics such as Mulk Raj Anand, who proposes an aesthetics of "kinetic rhythm" to counter Clive Bell's notion of "significant form." *Conversations with Bloomsbury* (Delhi: Oxford University Press, 1995), p. 116.

118. See Kenneth Surin, "C. L. R. James's Material Aesthetic of Cricket," *Liberation Cricket*, ed. McD. Beckles and Stoddart, pp. 370–83, for a discussion of James's view of cricket as "anti-work."
119. C. L. R. James, "Garfield Sobers," *James Reader*, pp. 383–84.
120. See Surin for a fuller discussion of James's adoption of an Hegelian notion of art.
121. Hilary McD. Beckles, "A Purely Natural Extension: Women's Cricket in West Indies Cricket Culture," *Liberation Cricket*, ed. McD. Beckles and Stoddart, pp. 222–38.
122. In his analysis of cricket as national passion in India, Arjun Appadurai has made similar points, commenting on the role of cricket in both decolonization and the assertion of a masculine claim to nationhood and modernity. *Modernity at Large: Cultural Dimensions of Globalization* (Minneapolis and London: University of Minnesota Press, 1996), pp. 110–13.
123. Hilary McD. Beckles and Harclyde Walcott, "Redemption Sounds: Music, Literature, and the Popular Ideology of West Indian Cricket Crowds," *Liberation Cricket*, ed. McD. Beckles and Stoddart, pp. 370–83.
124. See Mary Lou Emery, "C. L. R. James: *Beyond a Boundary* and Out of Sight," *Journal of Commonwealth and Postcolonial Studies*, 6: 1 (Spring 1999), 66–81, for a fuller discussion of James's response to *Guernica* and further analysis of the gender dynamics in his writings about cricket.

4 EKPHRASIS/DIASPORIC CARIBBEAN IMAGINATIONS 1960–2000

1. Derek Walcott, *Tiepolo's Hound* (New York: Farrar, Straus and Giroux, 2000), p. 129.
2. In *Picture Theory: Essays on Verbal and Visual Representation* (Chicago and London: University of Chicago Press, 1994), W. J. T. Mitchell refers to ekphrasis as the defining figure for representation (419).
3. Most theorists of ekphrasis comment on its role in affirming or denying social power. See, e.g., Page Dubois, *History, Rhetorical Description, and the Epic: From Homer to Spenser* (Cambridge: D. S. Brewer, 1982).
4. Mitchell, *Picture Theory*, p. 181.
5. See Françoise Meltzer, *Salome and the Dance of Writing: Portraits of Mimesis in Literature* (Chicago and London: University of Chicago Press, 1987).
6. Michael Levey suggests that the painter's eyes widen in viewing the breasts revealed to him by the model but unavailable to the eyes of the painting's viewer (*Giambattista Tiepolo: His Life and Art* [New Haven and London: Yale University Press, 1986], p. 18). However, Campaspe's eyes, as represented in the painting, are also wide and resemble those of the painter. Furthermore, the line of sight from Apelles's eyes appears uplifted, away from Campaspe's breasts and more toward her eyes, establishing the connection between the two figures as one of vision and thus twinning them, as much as opposing them.
7. Gikandi, "Race and the Idea of the Aesthetic," p. 10.

8. Döring, *Caribbean-English Passages*, p. 173.

9. See Anne Walmsley's *The Caribbean Artists Movement, 1966–1972: A Literary and Cultural History* (London: New Beacon Books, 1992) for an extensive documentary history of this movement. For a more personal account, see Louis James, "The Caribbean Artists Movement," *West Indian Intellectuals*, ed. Schwarz, pp. 209–27.

10. Wilson Harris, *Tumatumari* (London: Faber and Faber, 1968), p. 88.

11. Quoted in Walmsley, *Caribbean Artists Movement*, p. 174.

12. Shalini Puri finds in Harris's metaphor of the Carib bone flute an alternative to Walcott's poetics and also to the trope of cannibalism as put forward by the Brazilian modernist Oswald de Andrade. *The Caribbean Postcolonial*, pp. 73–75. Jodi Byrd appreciates Harris's acknowledgment of Amerindian cultures as crucial to Caribbean identities but also criticizes what she sees as his denial of their contemporary, living presence. "Colonialism's Cacophony: Natives and Arrivants at the Limits of Postcolonial Theory," Ph.D. dissertation, University of Iowa, 2000.

13. Aubrey Williams, "The Predicament of the Artist in the Caribbean," *Guyana Dreaming*, compiled by Anne Walmsley (Sydney, Australia, and Mundelstrup, Denmark: Dangaroo Press, 1990), p. 19.

14. Aubrey Williams, "Caribbean Visual Art: A Framework for Further Inquiry," ibid., p. 28.

15. C. L. R. James, "Search for the Guyanese Reality," ibid., p. 80.

16. Edward Kamau Brathwaite, "Timehri," ibid., p. 83.

17. Walmsley, *Caribbean Artists Movement*, p. 222.

18. Quoted in Bruce King, *Derek Walcott and West Indian Drama* (Oxford: Clarendon Press, 1995), p. 20.

19. See John Thieme, *Derek Walcott* (Manchester and New York: Manchester University Press: 1999), p. 74, for an analysis of the play along these lines; also, King, *Derek Walcott and West Indian Drama*, p. 136 and p. 143.

20. Derek Walcott, "What the Twilight Says," *What the Twilight Says: Essays/ Derek Walcott* (New York: Farrar, Straus, and Giroux, 1998), p. 10.

21. Maria Cristina Fumagali has written about the influence of Dante on Walcott's poetry in *The Flight of the Vernacular: Seamus Heaney, Derek Walcott and the Impress of Dante* (Amsterdam and New York: Rodopi, 2001).

22. For more details on these years, see King, *Derek Walcott and West Indian Drama*, Chapter 7.

23. Derek Walcott, "Another Life," *Derek Walcott: Collected Poems, 1948–1984* (New York: Noonday Press, 1986), p. 144.

24. Paul Breslin notes the allusion in "monster: / a prodigy of the wrong age and colour" to Goya's *El sueno de la razón produce monstruuos* and concludes that "Walcott depicts himself as the feared, repressed other of European civilization." *Nobody's Nation: Reading Derek Walcott* (Chicago and London: University of Chicago Press, 2001), p. 163.

25. Edward Baugh has commented on the images of enclosure, containment, and fixed preservation that permeate the poem. "Painters and Painting in *Another*

Life," Critical Perspectives on Derek Walcott, ed. Robert D. Hamner (Washington DC: Three Continents Press, 1993), pp. 239–50.

26. See King, *Derek Walcott and West Indian Drama,* p. 183.
27. Derek Walcott, "The Caribbean: Culture or Mimicry?" *Critical Perspectives on Derek Walcott,* ed. Hamner, p. 55.
28. Wilson Harris, "History, Fable, and Myth in the Caribbean and Guianas," *Explorations,* ed. and intro. Hena Maes-Jelinek (Mundelstrup, Denmark: Dangaroo Press, 1981 [essay orig. pub. 1970]), p. 33.
29. For accounts of that opposition and attempts to resolve it, see Patricia Ismond, "Walcott Versus Brathwaite," *Critical Perspectives on Derek Walcott,* ed. Hamner, pp. 220–36 and, more recently, Charles Pollard, *New World Modernisms: T. S. Eliot, Derek Walcott, and Kamau Brathwaite* (Charlottesville: University of Virginia Press, 2004).
30. Derek Walcott, *Omeros* (New York: Farrar, Straus, and Giroux, 1990), p. 164.
31. Williams, "Caribbean Visual Art: A Framework for Further Inquiry," *Guyana Dreaming,* comp. Walmsley, p. 28.
32. Wilson Harris, *Da Silva da Silva's Cultivated Wilderness* (London: Faber and Faber, 1977), p. 68.
33. Walcott, "The Caribbean: Culture or Mimicry?" *Critical Perspectives,* ed. Hamner, p. 54.
34. Teresa de Lauretis has argued that the questing hero is constructed as masculine through the feminization of space, which he must encounter, pass through, or overcome as an obstacle. "The Violence of Rhetoric: Considerations on Representation and Gender," *Technologies of Gender: Essays on Theory, Film, and Fiction* (Bloomington: Indiana University Press, 1987), pp. 31–50.
35. For a fuller analysis of this discourse and its implications for understanding the language of Harris's fiction, see Mary Lou Emery, "Limbo Rock: Wilson Harris and the Arts of Memory," *Callaloo,* special issue on Wilson Harris, ed. Nathaniel Mackey, 18: 1 (Winter 1995), 110–24, and "Reading 'W. H.': Draft of an Incomplete Conversation," *Wilson Harris and the Uncompromising Imagination,* ed. Hena Maes-Jelinek (Mundelstrup, Denmark: Dangaroo Press, 1991), pp. 170–83.
36. Jean Rhys, *After Leaving Mr. Mackenzie* (New York: Vintage, 1931), p. 52.
37. See William Rubin, *"Primitivism" in Twentieth-Century Art: Affinity of the Tribal and the Modern* (New York: Museum of Modern Art, 1984) and Torgovnick, *Gone Primitive.*
38. For a fuller analysis of the narrative linking of these three women's bodies, see Mary Lou Emery, "Refiguring the Postcolonial Imagination: Tropes of Visuality in Writing by Rhys, Kincaid, and Cliff," *Tulsa Studies in Women's Literature,* 16: 2 (Fall 1997), 259–80.
39. Jamaica Kincaid, *Lucy* (New York: Plume, 1990), p. 155. The Plume edition reproduces Gauguin's painting, 'Young Girl with Fan,' on its cover.
40. Judith Raiskin ("Jean Rhys: Creole Writing and Strategies of Reading," *ARIEL: A Review of International English Literature,* 22: 4 [October 1991],

51–97) discusses the colonial metaphor of the family as addressed by Rhys in her short stories. See also Kathleen Renk, *Caribbean Shadows and Victorian Ghosts* (Charlottesville: University Press of Virginia, 1999), for a discussion of the metaphor as addressed by a number of women writers from the Caribbean.

41. Helen Tiffin, "Cold Hearts and (Foreign) Tongues: Recitation and the Reclamation of the Female Body in the Works of Erna Brodber and Jamaica Kincaid," *Callaloo*, 16: 4 (Fall 1993), 909–21.

42. Mitchell notes that for Gotthold Lessing, "arbitrary visual signs (emblems, hieroglyphs, pictographs) such as, for instance, serpents that signify divinity, are well on their way to being a form of writing." *Picture Theory*, p. 155, n. 13. If we were to read Lucy's dream snakes along these lines, they would prophesy her attempts at writing in the novel's concluding scene.

43. Michelle Cliff, *No Telephone to Heaven* (New York: Vintage International, 1987), p. 5.

44. Meltzer, *Salome and the Dance of Writing*, pp. 22–23.

45. Michelle Cliff, "Clare Savage as a Crossroads Character," *Caribbean Women Writers: Essays from the First International Conference*, ed. Selwyn R. Cudjoe (Wellesley, MA: Calaloux Publications, 1990), pp. 263–68.

46. Mitchell makes a similar statement concerning the phrase "a story not to pass on" in Tony Morrison's *Beloved. Picture Theory*, pp. 203–207.

47. See Frances Yates, *The Art of Memory* (Chicago: University of Chicago Press, 1966), Chapter 1, and Mitchell's comment about the relevance of this story to the role performed by slave narratives. *Picture Theory*, pp. 195–96.

48. Michael A. Sells, *Mystical Languages of Unsaying* (Chicago and London: University of Chicago Press, 1994).

49. Wilson Harris, "Quetzalcoatl and the Smoking Mirror (Reflections on Originality and Tradition)," *Review of Contemporary Fiction* 17: 2 (Summer 1997), 22, and "Ways to Enjoy Literature," *Union in Partition: Essays in Honour of Jeanne Delbaere*, ed. Gilbert Debusscher and Marc Maufort (Liège: L3 – Liège Language and Literature, 1997), p. 207.

50. Wilson Harris, "Wilson Harris Interviewed by Alan Riach," *The Radical Imagination: Lectures and Talks by Wilson Harris*, ed. Alan Riach and Mark Williams (Liège, Belgium: Liège Language and Literature, 1992), p. 57.

51. Elaine Pagels, *The Gnostic Gospels* (New York: Vintage Books, 1979), p. 14. A number of studies of the gnostics describe the heterogeneous traditions which have syncretically comprised gnosticism or in various periods characterized it. These include Platonism, medieval mystery cults, and the hermetic arts and philosophies. Many scholars also see gnosticism expressed in the works of modern writers such as Blake and Yeats. See Tobias Churton, *The Gnostics* (London: George Weidenfeld and Nicolson Ltd, 1987), and more recently, Roelof van den Broek and Wouter J. Hanegraaf, eds., *Gnosis and Hermeticism from Antiquity to Modern Times* (Albany, NY: State University of New York Press, 1998). For a structuralist or "morphodynamic" analysis of gnosticism, see Ioan P. Couliano, *The Tree of Gnosis: Gnostic*

Mythology from Early Christianity to Modern Nihilism (San Francisco: Harper, 1990).

52. Quoted in Pagels, *Gnostic Gospels*, p. 137.

53. Harris, "Wilson Harris Interviewed by Alan Riach," p. 57.

54. An influential historian of religion, Evelyn Underhill, has argued the opposite. In her book, *Mysticism*, first published in 1911 and reprinted in numerous subsequent editions, Underhill distinguishes the mystic from the artist, arguing that the artist receives only glimpses of mystical union and cares much more than the true mystic about communicating these glimpses to others. Because Underhill elevates the mystic above the artist, she misses the performative aspect of mystical language. *Mysticism: A Study in the Nature and Development of Man's Spiritual Consciousness* (New York: Meridian Books, 1960).

55. Harris, "Quetzalcoatl," pp. 21–22.

56. Sells, *Mystical Languages*, p. 7. Apophasis is often considered a "negative" discourse (see, e.g., Shira Wolosky, *Language Mysticism: The Negative Way of Language in Eliot, Beckett, and Celan* [Stanford, CA: Stanford University Press, 1995]). It may be contrasted to the affirmations of *kataphasis* ("affirmation, saying, speaking-with") (Sells, *Mystical Languages*, 2–3). Sells makes the point that the negative moment of apophasis is part of a dialogical tension; it assumes a "saying" to be unsaid and becomes itself a statement inviting an "unsaying."

57. Hena Maes-Jelinek, "Another Future for Post-Colonial Studies? Wilson Harris's Post-Colonial Philosophy and the 'Savage Mind,' " *Wasafiri*, 24 (Autumn 1996), 5–6.

58. Sells, *Mystical Languages*, p. 7.

59. Martin Buber, *I and Thou*, trans., prologue and notes Walter Kaufmann (New York: Simon and Schuster, 1970), p. 182. Harris has acknowledged the influence of Martin Buber in "Wilson Harris Interviewed by Alan Riach," p. 62.

60. Wilson Harris, *Palace of the Peacock* (London: Faber and Faber, 1960), p. 130.

61. Wilson Harris, *The Four Banks of the River of Space* (London: Faber and Faber, 1990), p. 9. Here Harris puts into dialogue a figure from Guyanese folk culture, often portrayed as an evil spirit, and a character whose name alludes to the eleventh-century Archbishop of Canterbury, Saint Anselm, known for his ecclesiastical reforms and scholasticism.

62. Wilson Harris, *Jonestown* (London: Faber and Faber, 1996), p. 200 and p. 233.

63. In an interview conducted by Kerry Johnson, Harris has described his discovery as a hydrographic surveyor of "the way the rocks were shaped, the rhythm of the rocks in the rapids." "Interview with Wilson Harris," *Journal of Caribbean Literatures* 1: 1 (Spring 1997), 84.

64. Wilson Harris, "An Interview with Wilson Harris," by Charles H. Rowell, *Callaloo* 18: 1 (Winter 1995), p. 194.

65. Hena Maes-Jelinek has commented extensively on the multiple aspects of Harris's concept of resurrection as expressed in *Resurrection at Sorrow Hill* in her essay "Chartering the Uncapturable in Wilson Harris's Writing," *Review of Contemporary Fiction* 17: 2 (Summer 1997), 94–96.

66. Glyne Griffith has criticized Harris's prose as a nihilistic exclusion of difference in its undoing of dualities. *Deconstruction, Imperialism, and the West Indian Novel* (Kingston, Jamaica: University Press of the West Indies, 1996), Chapter 3. However, I see Harris emphasizing instead the dynamic of the transition between and among differences, rather than production of an inclusive, undifferentiated whole.

67. Harris, "Wilson Harris Interviewed by Alan Riach," p. 55.

68. Harris, "Questzalcoatl," p. 14.

69. Wilson Harris, "Carnival of the Psyche: *Wide Sargasso Sea*," *Kunapipi*, 2: 2 (1980), 143–44.

70. Harris, "History, Fable and Myth," *Explorations*. ed. Maes-Jelinek, pp. 20–42.

71. Wilson Harris, "Aubrey Williams," *Journal of Caribbean Literatures*, 2: 1–3 (Spring 2000), 28.

72. Maurice Merleau-Ponty "The Intertwining – The Chiasm," *The Visible and the Invisible* (Evanston, IL: Northeastern University Press, 1968), pp. 137–38.

73. "Intertwining" is Merleau-Ponty's word for the complex folding over of perception into phenomena that he proposes as a model for epistemology. He states, for example, "It is a marvel too little noticed that every movement of my eyes – even more, every displacement of my body – has its place in the same visible universe that I itemize and explore with them, as, conversely, every vision takes place somewhere in tactile space." "The Intertwining – The Chiasm," *The Visible and the Invisible*, p. 134.

74. Wilson Harris, "Introduction" to *The Carnival Trilogy* (London and Boston: Faber and Faber, 1993), p. xix.

75. Ibid.

76. Harris, "History, Fable and Myth," *Explorations*, ed. Maes-Jelinek, pp. 20–42.

77. Ibid., pp. 32–33.

78. Ibid., p. 27.

CONCLUSION

1. Though Turner's *Slave Ship* does not portray an actually burning ship, a number of viewers have described it in such terms. Thackeray, for instance, described it as setting "the corner of the room in which it hangs into a flame," and Ruskin wrote about "the fire of the sunset" (quoted in Wood, *Blind Memory*, p. 43 and p. 62).

2. Wilson Harris, *The Mask of the Beggar* (London: Faber and Faber, 2003), p. 21.

3. Salman Rushdie, *The Moor's Last Sigh* (New York: Vintage, 1995), p. 218.

4. In "Postcolonial Lack and Aesthetic Promise in *The Moor's Last Sigh*," Alexandra W. Schultheis identifies Bal Thackeray as the nationalist leader Rushdie's character satirizes. *Twentieth Century Literature*, 47: 4 (Winter 2001), 5.

5. Homi K. Bhabha, "Conclusion: 'Race,' Time and the Revision of Modernity," *Location*, p. 193.

Bibliography

UNPUBLISHED AND ARCHIVAL SOURCES

The African Telegraph (July–August 1919 and December 1919), British Newspaper Library.

Artistic, "Kismet, – A Review," *Cosmopolitan* (June–July 1930), 53, Una Marson Papers, National Library of Jamaica.

Boxer, David, "Introducing Fifteen Intuitives," *Fifteen Intuitives, Exhibition Catalogue, National Gallery of Jamaica, July 12–October 31, 1987*, National Gallery of Jamaica.

British Empire Exhibition 1924 Official Guide, London: Fleetway Press Ltd, 1924, British Library.

Byrd, Jodi, "Colonialism's Cacophony: Natives and Arrivants at the Limits of Postcolonial Theory," Ph.D. dissertation, University of Iowa, 2000.

Covi, Giovanna, "Refiguring Diasporic Agency: Una Marson, Afro-Jamaican New Woman," paper presented at the Seventh Annual Modernist Studies Association Conference, Loyola University, November 2005.

Farr, Dennis, and Alan Bowness, "Historical Note," *London Group 1914–64 Jubilee Exhibition, Fifty Years of British Art, Exhibition Catalogue, Tate Gallery, July 15–August 16, 1964*, Tate Gallery Library.

Gilroy, Paul, "Picturing Blackness in British Art," *Picturing Blackness in British Art 1700s–1990s, Exhibition Catalogue, November 28, 1995–March 10, 1996, Tate Gallery*, Tate Gallery Library.

Grant, Duncan, Letter to Vanessa Bell, February 11, 1930, Charleston Papers, Special Collections, University of Sussex.

James, C. L. R., *Toussaint Louverture*, "Original Typescript," Special Collections Library, University of the West Indies, St. Augustine, Trinidad.

Playbill, *Toussaint Louverture: A Play in Three Acts*, The Incorporated Stage Society, Westminster Theatre, Sunday 15th March 1936 at 8.30 and Monday 16th March at 2.30, Special Collections, University of the West Indies, St. Augustine, Trinidad.

Toussaint Louverture, Richard Wright Papers, Beinecke Library, Yale University.

The Keys: The Official Organ of The League of Coloured Peoples, intro. Roderick J. Macdonald, Schomburg Center for Research in Black Culture Library, New York.

Lawrence, G. C., *Official Guide to the British Empire Exhibition*, British Library.

Marson, Una, *London Calling*, MS 1944B, Una Marson Papers, National Library of Jamaica.

   Pocomania, MS 1944B and unmarked alternate version, Una Marson Papers, National Library of Jamaica.

   "Summer Days," *Tropic Reveries: Poems by Una Marson*, Kingston, Jamaica: published by the author, 1930, p. 13, British Library.

McFarlane, J. E. Clare, "The Value of Right Reading," *Cosmopolitan*, 1: 4 (August 1928), 100, Una Marson Papers, National Library of Jamaica.

Moody, Cynthia, "Ronald Moody (1900–1984)," April 1995, Ronald Moody Papers, Tate Gallery Archive.

Moody, Ronald, "The 'Wheel' Within," Ronald Moody Papers.

Reviews (cited) of *Toussaint Louverture* (1936 London Performance)

   Brown, Ivor, " 'Toussaint L'Ouverture' by C. L. R. James," *Observer* (March 22, 1936), C. L. R. James Institute.

   Disher, M. Wilson, "Mr. Paul Robeson's Thrilling Part, Toussaint L'Ouverture," *Daily Mail*, London (March 17, 1936), C. L. R. James Institute.

   Time and Tide (March 21, 1936), C. L. R. James Institute.

"Ronald Moody Talks . . . Sculpting, A Way of Life," National Gallery Archives, Kingston, Jamaica.

Ryan, Deborah, "The *Daily Mail* Ideal Homes Exhibition and Suburban Modernity, 1908–1951," Ph.D. thesis, University of East London, 1995.

Sadler, Michael, "Preface," *Negro Art, Exhibition Catalogue, Adams Gallery, January 19–February 16, 1935*, Tate Gallery Library.

Scott, Nadine Althea, "Fine Art as an Expression of Religion in the Jamaican Culture: Implications for Art Education," Ph.D. thesis, Ohio State University, 1991.

Sherlock, Philip M., "Introduction," *The Moth and the Star* by Una Marson, Kingston, Jamaica: published by the author, 1937, pp. x–xix, British Library.

Webb, Rev. J. Leslie, "On Being a Cosmopolitan," *Cosmopolitan*, 1: 6 (October 1928), 165, Una Marson Papers.

PUBLISHED SOURCES

Anand, Mulk Raj, *Conversations with Bloomsbury*, Delhi: Oxford University Press, 1995.

Anderson, Perry, "Modernity and Revolution," *New Left Review*, 144 (March–April 1984), 96–113.

Appadurai, Arjun, *Modernity at Large: Cultural Dimensions of Globalization*, Minneapolis and London: University of Minnesota Press, 1996.

Appiah, Kwame Anthony, "Race," *Critical Terms for Literary Study*, ed. Frank Lentricchia and Thomas McLaughlin, Chicago and London: University of Chicago Press, 1990, pp. 274–87.

Araeen, Rasheed, "In the Citadel of Modernism," *The Other Story: Afro-Asian Artists in Post-War Britain*, London: Hayward Gallery, South Bank Centre, 1989, pp. 16–49.

Archer-Straw, Petrine, "Vision and Design: Where Nationalism Meets Arts and Crafts," *Fifty Years-Fifty Artists*, ed. Archer-Straw, pp. 17–27.

ed., *Fifty Years-Fifty Artists: 1950–2000 The School of Visual Arts*, Kingston, Jamaica: Ian Randle Publishers, 2000.

Baker, Houston, *Modernism and the Harlem Renaissance*, Chicago: University of Chicago Press, 1987.

"Scene . . . Not Heard," *Reading Rodney King: Reading Urban Uprising*, ed. and intro. Robert Gooding Williams, New York: Routledge, 1993, pp. 38–48.

Banham, Martin, Errol Hill, and George Woodyard, eds., *Cambridge Guide to African and Caribbean Theatre*, Cambridge: Cambridge University Press, 1994.

Barnes, Natasha, "Black Atlantic – Black America," *Research in African Literatures*, 27: 4 (Winter 1996), 106–107.

Baucom, Ian, *Out of Place: Englishness, Empire, and the Locations of Identity*, Princeton, NJ: Princeton University Press, 1999.

"Specters of the Atlantic," *South Atlantic Quarterly*, 100 (Winter 2001), 61–82.

Baugh, Edward, "Painters and Painting in 'Another Life'," *Critical Perspectives on Derek Walcott*, ed. Robert D. Hamner, Washington DC: Three Continents Press, 1993, pp. 239–50.

Beauvoir, Simone de, *The Second Sex*, trans. and ed. H. M. Parshley, New York: Vintage Books, 1974 (first English pub., 1952).

Bell, Clive, *Art*, New York: Frederick A. Stokes Company, 1913.

Bell, Vanessa, *Selected Letters of Vanessa Bell*, ed. Regina Marler, New York: Pantheon Books, 1993.

Berman, Marshall, *All that Is Solid Melts into Air*, London: Verso, 1983.

Bhabha, Homi K., *The Location of Culture*, London and New York: Routledge, 1994.

Boehmer, Elleke, *Colonialism and Postcolonial Literature*, Oxford: Oxford University Press, 1995.

Empire, the National, and the Postcolonial, 1890–1920, Oxford: Oxford University Press, 2002.

Boime, Albert, *The Art of Exclusion: Representing Blacks in the Nineteenth Century*, Washington: Smithsonian Institution Press, 1990.

Boxer, David, *Edna Manley, Sculptor*, Kingston: National Gallery of Jamaica and Edna Manley Foundation, 1990.

"The Life of Edna Manley (1900–1987)," *Fifty Years – Fifty Artists*, ed. Archer-Straw, pp. 13–15.

Brand, Dionne, *Bread out of Stone: Recollections, Sex, Recognitions, Race, Dreaming, Politics*, Toronto: Coach House Press, 1994.

Brathwaite, Kamau, *History of the Voice: The Development of Nation Language in Anglophone Caribbean Poetry*, London: New Beacon Books, 1984.

"Timehri," *Guyana Dreaming*, comp. Walmsley, pp. 82–85.

Brennan, Teresa, " 'The Contexts of Vision' from a Specific Standpoint," *Vision in Context*, ed. Brennan and Jay, pp. 217–230.

Brennan, Teresa, and Martin Jay, eds., *Vision in Context*, New York and London: Routledge, 1996.

Breslin, Paul, *Nobody's Nation: Reading Derek Walcott*, Chicago and London: University of Chicago Press, 2001.

Broek, Roelof van den, and Wouter J. Hanegraaf, eds., *Gnosis and Hermeticism from Antiquity to Modern Times*, Albany, NY: State University of New York Press, 1998.

Brown, Nancy Hemond, "Jean Rhys and *Voyage in the Dark*," *London Magazine*, 25: 1 and 2 (April/May 1985), 40–59.

Brown, Wayne, *Edna Manley: The Private Years, 1900–1938*, London: Deutsch, 1975.

Buber, Martin, *I and Thou*, trans., prologue, and notes Walter Kaufmann, New York: Simon and Schuster, 1970.

Buck-Morss, Susan, "Hegel and Haiti," *Critical Inquiry*, 26: 4 (Summer 2000), 821–65.

Buhle, Paul, *C. L. R. James: The Artist as Revolutionary*, London and New York: Verso, 1988.

Burnham, Douglas, *An Introduction to Kant's* Critique of Judgement, Edinburgh: Edinburgh University Press, 2000.

Burton, Richard D. E., *Afro-Creole: Power, Opposition, and Play in the Caribbean*, Ithaca and London: Cornell University Press, 1997.

Butler, Janet, "The Existentialism of George Lamming: The Early Development of a Writer," *Caribbean Review* 11: 4 (Fall 1982), 15, 38–39.

Callow, Simon, "Voodoo Macbeth," *Rhapsodies in Black*, ed. Powell et al., pp. 34–43.

Campbell, Elaine, and Pierette Frickey, eds., *The Whistling Bird: Women Writers of the Caribbean*, Boulder, CO, and London: Lynne Rienner, 1998; Kingston, Jamaica: Ian Randle, 1998.

Carby, Hazel, *Cultures in Babylon: Black Britain and African America*, London and New York: Verso, 1999.

  Race Men, Cambridge, MA: Harvard University Press, 1998.

Chamberlain, Mary, "George Lamming," *West Indian Intellectuals*, ed. Schwarz, pp. 175–95.

Chrisman, Laura, "Journeying to Death: A Critique of Paul Gilroy's *The Black Atlantic*," *Black British Culture and Society: A Text Reader*, ed. Kwesi Owusu, London: Routledge, 2000, pp. 453–64.

Churton, Tobias, *The Gnostics*, London: George Weidenfeld and Nicolson Ltd, 1987.

Clarke, Joseph, "Caribbean Modernism and the Postcolonial Social Contract in *Voyage in the Dark*," *Journal of Caribbean Literatures*, guest ed. Mary Lou Emery, 3: 3 (Summer 2003), 1–16.

Cliff, Michelle, *No Telephone to Heaven*, New York: Vintage International, 1987.

  "Clare Savage as a Crossroads Character," *Caribbean Women Writers: Essays from the First International Conference*, ed. Selwyn R. Cudjoe, Wellesley, MA: Calaloux Publications, 1990, pp. 263–68.

  Free Enterprise, New York: Dutton, 1993.

Clifford, James, "Histories of the Tribal and Modern," *The Predicament of Culture: Twentieth-Century Ethnography, Literature, and Art*, Cambridge, MA and London: Harvard University Press, 1988, pp. 189–214.

Cooper, Carolyn, " 'Something Ancestral Recaptured': Spirit Possession as Trope in Selected Feminist Fictions of the African Diaspora," *Motherlands: Black Women's Writing from Africa, the Caribbean and South Asia*, ed. Susheila Nasta, London: Women's Press, Ltd., 1991, pp. 64–87.

Noises in the Blood: Orality, Gender, and the "Vulgar" Body of Jamaican Popular Culture, Durham: Duke University Press, 1993.

Couliano, Ioan P., *The Tree of Gnosis: Gnostic Mythology from Early Christianity to Modern Nihilism*, San Francisco: Harper, 1990.

Cudjoe, Selwyn R., "C. L. R. James Misbound," *Transition under Review*, 58 (n.d.), 124–36.

Cudjoe, Selwyn R., and William E. Cain, eds., *C.L.R. James: His Intellectual Legacies*, Amherst: University of Massachusetts Press, 1995.

Dabydeen, David, *Hogarth's Blacks: Images of Blacks in Eighteenth-Century English Art*, Kingston upon Thames: Dangaroo Press, 1985.

Turner: New and Selected Poems, London: Jonathan Cape, 1994.

A Harlot's Progress, London: Jonathan Cape, 1999.

D'Aguiar, Fred, *Feeding the Ghosts*, London: Chatto and Windus, 1997.

Dash, Michael, *The Other America: Caribbean Literature in a New World Context*, Charlottesville and London: University Press of Virginia, 1998.

Davies, Carol Boyce, *Black Women, Writing and Identity: Migrations of the Subject*, London and New York: Routledge, 1994.

Dayan, Joan, "Paul Gilroy's Slaves, Ships, and Routes: The Middle Passage as Metaphor," *Research in African Literatures*, 27: 4 (Winter 1996), 7–14.

deCaires Narain, Denise, *Contemporary Caribbean Women's Poetry: Making Style*, London and New York: Routledge, 2002.

Dickie, George, *The Century of Taste: The Philosophical Odyssey of Taste in the Eighteenth Century*, New York and Oxford: Oxford University Press, 1966.

Donnell, Alison, "Contradictory (W)omens?: Gender Consciousness in the Poetry of Una Marson," *Routledge Reader*, ed. Donnell and Welsh, pp. 187–93.

Donnell, Alison, and Sarah Lawson Welsh, eds., *The Routledge Reader in Caribbean Literature*, London and New York: Routledge, 1996.

Twentieth-Century Caribbean Literature: Critical Moments in Anglophone Literary History, London and New York: Routledge, 2006.

Döring, Tobias, *Caribbean-English Passages: Intertextuality in a Postcolonial Tradition*, London and New York: Routledge, 2002.

Douglas, Andrea N., "Facing the Nation: Art History and Art Criticism in the Jamaican Context," *Small Axe*, 16 (September 2004), 49–60.

Doyle, Laura, and Laura Winkiel, eds., *Geomodernisms: Race, Modernism, Modernity*, Bloomington and Indianapolis: Indiana University Press, 2005.

"Liberty, Race and Larsen in Atlantic Modernity: A New World Geneaology," *Geomodernisms*, ed. Doyle and Winkiel, pp. 51–76.

Dubois, Page, *History, Rhetorical Description, and the Epic: From Homer to Spenser*, Cambridge: D. S. Brewer, 1982.

Edmondson, Belinda, *Making Men: Gender, Literary Authority, and Women's Writing in Caribbean Narrative*, Durham and London: Duke University Press, 1999.

Edwards, Brent Hayes, *The Practice of Diaspora: Literature, Translation, and the Rise of Black Internationalism*, Cambridge, MA, and London: Harvard University Press, 2003.

Edwards, Nadi, "George Lamming's Literary Nationalism: Language between *The Tempest* and the Tonelle," *Small Axe*, 6: 1 (2002), 59–76.

Ellis, David, " 'The Produce of More than One Country': Race, Identity, and Discourse in Post-Windrush Britain," *Journal of Narrative Theory* 31: 2 (Summer 2001), 214–32.

Emery, Mary Lou, *Jean Rhys at "World's End": Novels of Colonial and Sexual Exile*, Austin, TX: University of Texas Press, 1990.

"Reading 'W. H.': Draft of an Incomplete Conversation," *Wilson Harris and the Uncompromising Imagination*, ed. Hena Maes-Jelinek, Mundelstrup, Denmark: Dangaroo Press, 1991, pp. 170–83.

"Limbo Rock: Wilson Harris and the Arts of Memory," *Callaloo*, 18: 1 (Winter 1995), 110–24.

"Refiguring the Postcolonial Imagination: Tropes of Visuality in Writing by Rhys, Kincaid, and Cliff," *Tulsa Studies in Women's Literature*, 16: 2 (Fall 1997), 259–80.

"C. L. R. James: *Beyond a Boundary* and Out of Sight," *Journal of Commonwealth and Postcolonial Studies*, 6: 1 (Spring 1999), 66–81.

" 'Robbed of Meaning': The Work at the Center of *To the Lighthouse*," *Modern Fiction Studies*, 38: 1 (Spring 1992), 217–34; repr. in *Twentieth-Century Literary Criticism*, 101, Detroit: Gale Research Co., 2000, pp. 307–18.

"Woolf Re-Visits Wembley: Pre-War Bloomsbury Aesthetics and Interwar British Empire," *Virginia Woolf: Across the Generations/Selected Papers from the Twelfth Annual Conference on Virginia Woolf*, An Electronic Publication (Spring 2003), pp. 29–40, http://www.csub.edu/woolf_center/.

Esedebe, P. Olisanwuche, *Pan-Africanism: The Idea and Movement, 1776–1991*, 2nd edition, Washington DC: Howard University Press, 1994.

Fanon, Frantz, *Black Skin, White Masks*, trans. Charles Lam Markmann, New York: Grove Wedenfeld, 1967.

Felski, Rita, *The Gender of Modernity*, Cambridge, MA: Harvard University Press, 1995.

Fort, Bernadette, and Angela Rosenthal, *The Other Hogarth: Aesthetics of Difference*, Princeton and Oxford: Princeton University Press, 2001.

Foster, Hal, "The 'Primitive' Unconscious of Modern Art, or White Skin Black Masks," *Recodings: Art, Spectacle, Cultural Politics*, Port Townsend, Washington: Bay Press, 1985, pp. 181–208.

Fry, Roger, *Last Lectures by Roger Fry*, intro. Kenneth Clark, Boston: Beacon Press, 1934.

Vision and Design, ed. J. B. Bullen, London and New York: Oxford University Press, 1990 (orig. pub. 1920).

Fryer, Peter, *Staying Power: The History of Black People in Britain*, London: Pluto Press, 1984.

Fumagali, Maria Cristina, *The Flight of the Vernacular: Seamus Heaney, Derek Walcott and the Impress of Dante*, Amsterdam and New York: Rodopi, 2001.

Gerzina, Gretchen, *Black London: Life before Emancipation*, New Brunswick, NJ: Rutgers University Press, 1995.

Gikandi, Simon, *Writing in Limbo: Modernism and Caribbean Literature*, Ithaca, NY: Cornell University Press, 1992.

  Maps of Englishness: Writing Identity in the Culture of Colonialism, New York: Columbia University Press, 1996.

  "Aesthetic Reflection and the Colonial Event: The Work of Art in the Age of Slavery," *Journal of the International Institute*, University of Michigan (Summer 1997), http://www.umich.edu~iinet/journal/vol4no3/gikandi.html (accessed 16 September 2003).

  "Race and the Idea of the Aesthetic," *Michigan Quarterly Review* (Spring 2001), 1–14.

  "Picasso, Africa, and the Schemata of Difference," *Modernism/Modernity*, 10: 3 (September 2003), 455–80.

  "Africa and the Epiphany of Modernism," *Geomodernisms*, eds. Doyle and Winkiel, pp. 17–30.

Gilman, Sander, "The Figure of the Black in German Aesthetic Theory," *Eighteenth-Century Studies*, 8: 4 (Summer 1975), 373–91.

  Difference and Pathology: Stereotypes of Sexuality, Race and Madness, Ithaca: Cornell University Press, 1985.

  "Black Bodies, White Bodies: Toward an Iconography of Female Sexuality in Late Nineteenth-Century Medicine and Literature," *"Race," Writing, and Difference*, ed. Henry Louis Gates, Jr., Chicago and London: University of Chicago Press, 1986, pp. 223–61.

Gilroy, Paul, "Art of Darkness: Black Art and the Problem of Belonging to England," *Third Text*, 10 (1990), 45–59.

  The Black Atlantic: Modernity and Double Consciousness, Cambridge, MA: Harvard University Press, 1993.

Green, Jeffrey, *Black Edwardians: Black People in Britain, 1901–1914*, London and Portland, OR: Frank Cass, 1998.

Griffith, Glyne, *Deconstruction, Imperialism, and the West Indian Novel*, Kingston, Jamaica: University Press of the West Indies, 1996.

  "'This Is London Calling the West Indies': The BBC's *Caribbean Voices*," *West Indian Intellectuals*, ed. Schwarz, pp. 196–208.

Grimshaw, Anna, ed., *The C. L. R. James Reader*, Oxford and Cambridge, MA: Blackwell, 1992.

  "Introduction: C. L. R. James: A Revolutionary Vision for the Twentieth Century," *C. L. R. James Reader*, ed. Grimshaw, pp. 1–22.

Hall, Stuart, "C. L. R. James: A Portrait," *C. L. R. James's Caribbean*, ed. Henry and Buhle, pp. 3–16.

Hamilton, Cynthia, "A Way of Seeing: Culture as Political Expression in the Works of C. L. R. James," *C. L. R. James*, ed. Cudjoe and Cain, pp. 429–43.

Harris, Wilson, *Palace of the Peacock*, London: Faber and Faber, 1960.

Tumatumari, London: Faber and Faber, 1968.

Companions of the Day and Night, London: Faber and Faber, 1975.

Da Silva da Silva's Cultivated Wilderness, London: Faber and Faber, 1977.

"Carnival of the Psyche: *Wide Sargasso Sea*," *Kunapipi* 2: 2 (1980), 142–50.

"History, Fable, and Myth in the Caribbean and Guianas," *Explorations*, ed. and intro. Hena Maes-Jelinek, Mundelstrup, Denmark: Dangaroo Press, 1981 (essay orig. pub. 1970), pp. 20–42.

The Four Banks of the River of Space, London: Faber and Faber, 1990.

"Wilson Harris Interviewed by Alan Riach," *The Radical Imagination: Lectures and Talks by Wilson Harris*, ed. Alan Riach and Mark Williams, Liège, Belgium: Liège Language and Literature, 1992, pp. 33–65.

"Introduction," *Carnival Trilogy*, London and Boston: Faber and Faber, 1993, pp. vii–xix.

"An Interview with Wilson Harris," by Charles H. Rowell, *Callaloo*, 18: 1 (Winter 1995), 194.

Jonestown, London: Faber and Faber, 1996.

"Interview with Wilson Harris," by Kerry Johnson, *Journal of Caribbean Literatures* 1: 1 (Spring 1997), 83–95.

"Quetzalcoatl and the Smoking Mirror (Reflections on Originality and Tradition)," *Review of Contemporary Fiction* 17: 2 (Summer 1997), 12–23.

"Ways to Enjoy Literature," *Union in Partition: Essays in Honour of Jeanne Delbaere*, ed. Gilbert Debussher and Marc Maufort, Liège: L3 – Liège Language and Literature, 1997, pp. 201–208.

"Aubrey Williams," *Journal of Caribbean Literatures*, 2: 1–3 (Spring 2000), 26–30.

The Mask of the Beggar, London: Faber and Faber, 2003.

Harrison, Charles, *English Art and Modernism, 1900–1939*, London: Allen Lane; Bloomington, IN: Indiana University Press, 1981.

Hebdige, Dick, *Cut'n' Mix: Culture, Identity, and Caribbean Music*, London and New York: Methuen, 1987.

Henry, Paget, *Caliban's Reason: Introducing Afro-Caribbean Philosophy*, New York: Routledge, 2000.

Henry, Paget, and Paul Buhle, eds., *C. L. R. James's Caribbean*, Durham: Duke University Press, 1992.

Herbert, James D., *Paris 1937: Worlds on Exhibition*, Ithaca and London: Cornell University Press, 1998.

Hewlett, Geoffrey, *A History of Wembley*, UK: Brent Library Service, 1979.

Himid, Lubaina, *Revenge: A Masque in Five Tableaux*, Lancashire, England: Rochdale Art Gallery, 1992.

Holmes, Colin, *John Bull's Island: Immigration and British Society, 1871–1971*, Basingstoke, Hampshire: Macmillan, 1988.

Holt, Thomas C., *The Problem of Freedom: Race, Labor, and Politics in Jamaica and Britain, 1832–1938*, Baltimore: Johns Hopkins University Press, 1992.

Hulme, Peter, "Reading from Elsewhere: George Lamming and the Paradox of Exile," *The Tempest and Its Travels*, ed. Peter Hulme and William Sherman, Philadelphia: University of Pennsylvania Press, 2000, pp. 220–35.

Hume, David, *The Philosophical Works of David Hume*, Vol. III, Edinburgh and London: Adam Black and William Tait, and Charles Tait, 1826.

Hurston, Zora Neale, *Tell My Horse*, Philadelphia and New York: J. B. Lippincott, 1938.

Jacobs, Karen, *The Eye's Mind: Literary Modernism and Visual Culture*, Ithaca and London: Cornell University Press, 2001.

James, C. L. R., *Toussaint Louverture* (Act II, Scene I), *Life and Letters*, 14: 1 (Spring 1936), 7–18.

"The Star that Would Not Shine," *At the Rendezvous of Victory*, London: Allison and Busby, 1984, pp. 9–12.

"Search for the Guyanese Reality," *Guyana Dreaming*, comp. Walmsley, pp. 79–80.

"La Divina Pastora," *C. L. R. James Reader*, ed. Grimshaw, pp. 25–28.

"Garfield Sobers," *C. L. R. James Reader*, ed. Grimshaw, pp. 383–84.

Beyond a Boundary, Durham: Duke University Press, 1993 (orig. 1963).

"Triumph," *C. L. R. James Reader*, ed. Grimshaw, pp. 29–40.

Minty Alley, London: New Beacon Books, 1971; Jackson, MS: University Press of Mississippi, 1997.

James, Louis, "The Caribbean Artists Movement," *West Indian Intellectuals*, ed. Schwarz, pp. 209–27.

James, Winston, "A Race Outcast from an Outcast Class: Claude McKay's Experience and Analysis of Britain," *West Indian Intellectuals*, ed. Schwarz, pp. 71–92.

Jameson, Fredric, "Modernism and Imperialism," *Nationalism, Colonialism, and Literature*, Minneapolis: University of Minnesota Press, 1990, pp. 43–66.

Jarrett-Macauley, Delia, *The Life of Una Marson, 1905–65*, Manchester and New York: Manchester University Press, 1998.

Jay, Martin, "Sartre, Merleau-Ponty, and the Search for a New Ontology of Sight," *Modernity and the Hegemony of Vision*, ed. Levin, pp. 143–85.

"Vision in Context: Reflections and Refractions," *Vision in Context*, ed. Brennan and Jay, pp. 1–12.

Jenkins, Lee, *The Language of Caribbean Poetry*, Gainesville, FL: University Press of Florida, 2004.

Kant, Immanuel, *The Critique of Judgement*, trans. James Creed Meredith, Oxford and London: Oxford University Press, Clarendon Press, 1952.

Keenaghan, Eric, " 'His Eyes Almost Fell through the Crease': Using Voyeurism and Sexuality to Ascertain the Modernist Attributes of C. L. R. James's *Minty Alley*," *Schuykill*, 1 (October 1998), 29–41.

Killingray, David, " 'To Do Something for the Race': Harold Moody and the League of Coloured Peoples, *West Indian Intellectuals*, ed. Schwarz, pp. 51–70.

Kincaid, Jamaica, *Lucy*, New York: Plume, 1990.

King, Bruce, *Derek Walcott and West Indian Drama*, Oxford: Clarendon Press, 1995.
Derek Walcott: A Caribbean Life, Oxford: Oxford University Press, 2000.

King, Nicole, *C. L. R. James and Creolization: Circles of Influence*, Jackson, MS: University Press of Mississippi, 2001.

Krieger, Murray, *Ekphrasis: The Illusion of the Natural Sign*, Baltimore, MD: Johns Hopkins University Press, 1992.

Lago, Mary, *Rabindranath Tagore: Perspectives in Time*, Houndmills, Basingstoke: Macmillan, 1989.

Laguerre, Michael S., *Voodoo Heritage*, London and Beverly Hills: Sage Publications, 1980.

Lamming, George, *In the Castle of My Skin*, New York, Toronto, and London McGraw-Hill, 1953.
Season of Adventure, London: Michael Joseph, 1960.
"Interview with George Lamming," *Kas-Kas*, ed. Ian Munro and Reinhard Sander, Austin, TX: African and Afro-American Research Institute, 1972, pp. 5–21.
The Emigrants, London and New York: Allison and Busby, 1980 (orig. pub. 1954).
The Pleasures of Exile, "Foreword" Sandra Pouchet Paquet, Ann Arbor: University of Michigan Press, 1992 (orig. pub. 1960).
"The Sovereignty of the Imagination: An Interview with George Lamming," David Scott, *Small Axe*, 6: 2 (2002), 72–200.

Lauretis, Teresa de, "The Violence of Rhetoric: Considerations on Representation and Gender," *Technologies of Gender: Essays on Theory, Film, and Fiction*, Bloomington: Indiana University Press, 1987, pp. 31–50.

Lazarus, Neil, "Cricket and National Culture in the Writings of C. L. R. James," *Liberation Cricket*, ed. McD. Beckles and Stoddart, pp. 342–55.

Lemke, Sieglinde, *Primitivist Modernism: Black Culture and the Origins of Transatlantic Modernism*, Oxford and New York: Oxford University Press, 1998.

Levey, Michael, *Giambattista Tiepolo: His Life and Art*, New Haven and London: Yale University Press, 1986.

Levin, David Michael, ed., *Modernity and the Hegemony of Vision*, Berkeley, Los Angeles, and London: University of California Press, 1993.

Light, Alison, *Forever England: Femininity, Literature and Conservatism between the Wars*, London and New York: Routledge, 1991.

Lloyd, David, "Race Under Representation," *Oxford Literary Review: Neocolonialism*, ed. Robert Young, 13: 1–2 (1991), 62–94.

McClintock, Anne, *Imperial Leather: Race, Gender and Sexuality in the Colonial Contest*, New York and London: Routledge, 1995.

McD. Beckles, Hilary, and Brian Stoddart, eds., *Liberation Cricket: West Indies Cricket Culture*, Manchester and New York: Manchester University Press, 1995.
"A Purely Natural Extension: Women's Cricket in West Indies Cricket Culture," *Liberation Cricket*, ed. McD. Beckles and Stoddart, pp. 222–36.

McD. Beckles, Hilary, and Harclyde Walcott, "Redemption Sounds: Music, Literature and the Popular Ideology of West Indian Cricket Crowds," *Liberation Cricket*, ed. McD. Beckles and Stoddart, pp. 370–83.

MacFarlane, J. E. Clare, "The Fleet of the Empire," *Routledge Reader*, ed. Donnell and Welsh, p. 49.

McKay, Claude, *Banjo: A Story without a Plot*, London, New York, and San Diego: Harvest/HBJ, 1929.

Banana Bottom, New York and London: Harper, 1933.

McKee, Patricia, *Producing American Races: Henry James, William Faulkner, Toni Morrison*, Durham and London: Duke University Press, 1999.

Mackenzie, John M. *Propaganda and Empire: The Manipulation of British Public Opinion, 1880–1960*, Manchester: Manchester University Press, 1984.

ed., *Imperialism and Popular Culture*, Manchester: Manchester University Press, 1986.

Maes-Jelinek, Hena, "Another Future for Post-Colonial Studies? Wilson Harris's Post-Colonial Philosophy and the 'Savage Mind,'" *Wasafiri*, 24 (Autumn 1996), 3–8.

"Charting the Uncapturable in Wilson Harris's Writing," *Review of Contemporary Fiction* 17: 2 (Summer 1997), 90–97.

Mangan, J. A., "'The Grit of our Forefathers': Invented Traditions, Propaganda and Imperialism," *Imperialism and Popular Culture*, ed. Mackenzie, pp. 127–35.

Manley, Edna, *Edna Manley: The Diaries*, ed. Rachel Manley, Kingston, Jamaica: Heinemann Publishers (Caribbean), 1989.

Marson, Una, "Renunciation," *Routledge Reader*, ed. Donnell and Welsh, p. 128.

Masilea, Ntongela, "The 'Black Atlantic' and African Modernity in South Africa," *Research in African Literatures*, 27: 4 (Winter 1996), 88–96.

Meltzer, Françoise, *Salome and the Dance of Writing: Portraits of Mimesis in Literature*, Chicago and London: University of Chicago Press, 1987.

Merleau-Ponty, Maurice, "The Intertwining – The Chiasm," *The Visible and the Invisible*, Evanston, IL: Northwestern University Press, 1968, pp. 130–55.

Mitchell, W. J. T., *Picture Theory*, Chicago and London: University of Chicago Press, 1994.

Morris, Jan, *Farewell the Trumpets: An Imperial Retreat*, New York: Harcourt, Brace Jovanovich, 1978.

Morris, Mervyn, "The Poet as Novelist," *The Islands in Between: Essays on West Indian Literature*, ed. Louis James, London and Ibadan: Oxford University Press, 1968, pp. 73–85.

Morrison, Toni, *Playing in the Dark: Whiteness and the Literary Imagination*, Cambridge, MA: Harvard University Press, 1992.

Most, Glenn, "After the Sublime: Stations in the Career of an Emotion," *Yale Review*, 90: 2 (April 2002), 101–21.

Murdoch, Adlai H., "James's Literary Dialectic: Colonialism and Cultural Space in *Minty Alley*," *C. L. R. James*, ed. Cudjoe and Cain, pp. 61–71.

Naipaul, V. S., *The Enigma of Arrival*, New York: Knopf, 1987.

Nair, Supriya, *Caliban's Curse: George Lamming and the Revisioning of History*, Ann Arbor: University of Michigan Press, 1996.

Nielsen, Aldon, *C. L. R. James: A Critical Introduction*, Jackson, MS: University Press of Mississippi, 1997.

Bibliography

"The Future of an Allusion: The Color of Modernity," *Geomodernisms*, ed. Doyle and Winkiel, pp. 17–30.

Olaniyan, Tejumola, *Scars of Conquest/Masks of Resistance: The Invention of Cultural Identities in African, African-American, and Caribbean Drama*, New York and Oxford: Oxford University Press, 1995.

Omotoso, Kole, *The Theatrical into Theatre: A Study of the Drama and Theatre of the English-Speaking Caribbean*, London and Port of Spain: New Beacon Books, 1982.

Pagels, Elaine, *The Gnostic Gospels*, New York: Vintage Books, 1979.

Parkes, Kineton, *The Art of Carred Sculpture*, New York: Scribner, 1931.

Patterson, Orlando, *Freedom*, Vol. I: *Freedom in the Making of Western Culture*, New York: Basic Books, 1991.

Paul, Annie, "Uninstalling the Nation: The Dilemma of Contemporary Jamaican Art," *Small Axe*, 6 (September 1999), 57–78.

Philip, Marlene Nourbese, "Social Barbarism and the Spoils of Modernism," *Frontiers: Essays and Writings on Racism and Culture, 1984–1992*, Stratford, Ontario: Mercury Press, 1992, pp. 93–102.

Piot, Charles, "Atlantic Aporias: Africa and Gilroy's *Black Atlantic*," *South Atlantic Quarterly*, 100: 1 (2001), 155–70.

Pollard, Charles, *New World Modernisms: T. S. Eliot, Derek Walcott, and Kamau Brathwaite*, Charlottesville: University of Virginia Press, 2004.

Poupeye, Veerle, *Caribbean Art*, London: Thames and Hudson, 1998.

Powell, Richard J., *Black Art and Culture in the Twentieth Century*, New York: Thames and Hudson, 1997.

Powell, Richard J. et al., *Rhapsodies in Black: Art of the Harlem Renaissance*, exhibition devised and selected by Powell and David A. Bailey; catalog ed., Joanna Skipworth, Berkeley, Los Angeles, and London: University of California Press; and London: Hayward Gallery, Institute of International Visual Arts, South Bank Centre, 1997.

Pratt, Mary Louise, *Imperial Eyes: Travel Writing and Transculturation*, New York: Routledge, 1992.

Price, Sally, and Richard Price, *Maroon Arts: Cultural Vitality in the African Diaspora*, Boston: Beacon Press, 1999.

Puri, Shalini, *The Caribbean Postcolonial: Social Equality, Post-Nationalism, and Cultural Hybridity*, New York: Palgrave Macmillan, 2004.

Pyne-Timothy, Helen, "Identity, Society, and Meaning: A Study of the Early Short Stories of C. L. R. James," *C. L. R. James*, ed. Cudjoe and Cain, pp. 51–60.

Raiskin, Judith, "Jean Rhys: Creole Writing and Strategies of Reading," *ARIEL: A Review of International English Literature*, 22: 4 (October 1991), 51–97.

Relich, Mario, "Pope, Thackeray and Africana in Non-Standard English Playing Cards of the Restoration and Eighteenth Century, *Kunapipi*, 12: 1 (1990), 1–31.

Renk, Kathleen, *Caribbean Shadows and Victorian Ghosts*, Charlottesville: University Press of Virginia, 1999.

Rhys, Jean, *Voyage in the Dark*, New York: Popular Library, n.d. (orig. pub. 1934). *Good Morning, Midnight*, London: Constable, 1939.
 After Leaving Mr. Mackenzie, New York: Random House, Vintage Books, 1974 (orig. pub. 1931).

Rice, Alan, *Radical Narratives of the Black Atlantic*, London and New York: Continuum, 2003.

Richards, Jeffrey, "Boys Own Empire: Feature Films and Imperialism in the 1930s," *Imperialism and Popular Culture*, ed. Mackenzie, pp. 140–64.

Roach, Joseph, *Cities of the Dead: Circum-Atlantic Performance*, New York: Columbia University Press, 1996.

Rohlehr, Gordon, *The Shape of that Hurt and Other Essays*, Port of Spain, Trinidad: Longman Trinidad Ltd, 1992 (orig. pub. 1983).

Rosenberg, Leah, "Una Marson's *Pocomania* (1938): Class, Gender, and the Pitfalls of Cultural Nationalism," *Essays in Theatre*, 20: 1 (November 2001), 27–42.

 "Caribbean Models for Modernism in the Work of Claude McKay and Jean Rhys," *Modernism/Modernity*, 11: 2 (April 2004), 219–38.

Rubin, William, *"Primitivism" in Twentieth-Century Art: Affinity of the Tribal and the Modern*, New York: Museum of Modern Art, 1984.

Rushdie, Salman, *The Moor's Last Sigh*, New York: Vintage, 1995.

Said, Edward, *Culture and Imperialism*, New York: Knopf, 1994.

Sander, Reinhard, *The Trinidad Awakening: West Indian Literature of the Nineteen-Thirties*, New York: Greenwood Press, 1988.

Sartre, Jean-Paul, *Being and Nothingness*, trans. and intro. Hazel Barnes, New York: Washington Square Press, 1953.

Schiller, Friedrich, *On the Aesthetic Education of Man in a Series of Letters*, ed. and trans with intro. and glossary by Elizabeth M. Wilkinson and L. A. Willoughby, Oxford and London: Clarendon Press, 1967.

Schultheis, Alexandra W., "Postcolonial Lack and Aesthetic Promise in *The Moor's Last Sigh*," *Twentieth Century Literature*, 47: 4 (Winter 2001), 569–96.

Schwarz, Bill, ed., *West Indian Intellectuals in Britain*, Manchester and New York: Manchester University Press, 2003.

Sells, Michael A., *Mystical Languages of Unsaying*, Chicago and London: University of Chicago Press, 1994.

Shesgreen, Sean, ed., *Engravings by Hogarth: 101 Prints*, New York: Dover Publications, 1973.

Simoes da Silva, A. J., *The Luxury of Nationalist Despair: George Lamming's Fiction as Decolonizing Project*, Amsterdam and Atlanta, GA: Rodopi, 2000.

Smilowitz, Erika S., " 'Weary of Life and All My Heart's Dull Pain': The Poetry of Una Marson," *Critical Issues in West Indian Literature*, ed. Erika S. Smilowitz and Roberta Q. Knowles, Parkersburg, IA: Caribbean Books, 1984, pp. 19–32.

Spalding, Frances, *British Art since 1900*, London: Thames and Hudson, 1986.

Spurr, David, *The Rhetoric of Empire: Colonial Discourse in Journalism, Travel Writing, and Imperial Administration*, Durham and London: Duke University Press, 1993.

Stansky, Peter, *On or about December 1910: Early Bloomsbury and its Intimate World*, Cambridge, MA: Harvard University Press, 1996.

Stephens, Michelle Ann, *Black Empire: The Masculine Global Imaginary of Caribbean Intellectuals in the United States, 1914–1962*, Durham and London: Duke University Press, 2005.

Suleri, Sara, *The Rhetoric of English India*, Chicago and London: University of Chicago Press, 1992.

Surin, Kenneth, "C. L. R. James's Material Aesthetic of Cricket," *Liberation Cricket*, ed. McD. Beckles and Stoddart, pp. 370–82.

Tagore, Rabindranath, *Gitanjali*, intro. W. B. Yeats, New York: Scribner, 1913.

Taylor, Patrick, *The Narrative of Liberation: Perspectives on Afro-Caribbean Literature, Popular Culture, and Politics*, Ithaca and London: Cornell University Press, 1989.

Thieme, John, *Derek Walcott*, Manchester and New York: Manchester University Press, 1999.

Thompson, Krista A., " 'Black Skin, Blue Eyes': Visualizing Blackness in Jamaican Art, 1922–1944," *Small Axe*, 16 (September 2004), 1–31.

Thompson, Robert Farris, *Flash of the Spirit: African and Afro-American Art and Philosophy*, New York: Random House, 1983.

Face of God: Art and Altars of Africa and the African Americas, New York: Museum for African Art; Munich: Prestel, 1993.

Tiffin, Helen, "The Novels of George Lamming: Finding a Language for Post-Colonial Fiction," *Essays on Contemporary Post-Colonial Fiction*, ed. Hedwig Bock and Albert Wertheim, Munich: Max Hueber, 1986, pp. 253–74.

"Cold Hearts and (Foreign) Tongues: Recitation and the Reclamation of the Female Body in the Works of Erna Brodber and Jamaica Kincaid," *Callaloo*, 16: 4 (Fall 1993), 909–921.

"Cricket, Literature and the Politics of De-Colonisation: The Case of C. L. R. James," *Liberation Cricket*, ed. McD. Beckles and Stoddart, pp. 356–69.

Torgovnick, Mariana, *Gone Primitive: Savage Intellects, Modern Lives*, Chicago: University of Chicago Press, 1990.

Underhill, Evelyn, *Mysticism: A Study in the Nature and Development of Man's Spiritual Consciousness*, New York: Meridian Books, 1960 (orig. pub. 1911).

Vaughan, David, *Negro Victory: The Life Story of Dr. Harold Moody*, London: Independent Press, 1950.

Walcott, Derek, *Dream on Monkey Mountain and Other Plays*, New York: Farrar, Straus, and Giroux, 1970.

"Another Life," *Derek Walcott: Collected Poems, 1948–1984*, New York: Noonday Press, 1986, pp. 141–294.

Omeros, New York: Farrar, Strauss, and Giroux, 1990.

"The Caribbean: Culture or Mimicry?" *Critical Perspectives on Derek Walcott*, ed. Robert D. Hamner, Washington DC: Three Continents Press, 1993, pp. 51–57.

"What the Twilight Says," *What the Twilight Says: Essays/Derek Walcott*, New York: Farrar, Strauss, and Giroux, 1998, pp. 3–35.

Tiepolo's Hound, New York: Farrar, Strauss, and Giroux, 2000.

Walmsley, Anne, *The Caribbean Artists Movement, 1966–1972: A Literary and Cultural History*, London: New Beacon Books, 1992.

(compiler), *Guyana Dreaming: The Art of Aubrey Williams*, Sydney, Australia, and Mundelstrup, Denmark: Dangaroo Press, 1990.

Wilcox, Denys J., *The London Group 1913–1939: The Artists and their Works*, Aldershot, England: Scolar Press; Brookfield, VT: Ashgate, 1995.

Williams, Aubrey, "Caribbean Visual Art: A Framework for Further Inquiry," *Guyana Dreaming*, comp. Walmsley, pp. 21–28.

"The Predicament of the Artist in the Caribbean," *Guyana Dreaming*, comp. Walmsley, pp. 15–20.

Wilson, Duncan, *Leonard Woolf: A Political Biography*, New York: St. Martin's Press, 1978.

Wolosky, Shira, *Language Mysticism: The Negative Way of Language in Eliot, Beckett, and Celan*, Stanford, CA: Stanford University Press, 1995.

Wood, Marcus, *Blind Memory: Visual Representations of Slavery in England and America 1780–1865*, London and New York: Routledge, 2000.

Woolf, Virginia, *To the Lighthouse*, New York and London: Harcourt Brace Jovanovich, 1927.

A Room of One's Own, London: Penguin, 1928.

"Thunder at Wembley," *Collected Essays*, Vol. IV, New York: Harcourt, Brace and World, 1967, pp. 184–87.

Worcester, Kent, *C. L. R. James: A Political Biography*, Albany, NY: State University of New York Press, 1996.

Yates, Frances, *The Art of Memory*, Chicago: University of Chicago Press, 1966.

Index